TAINTED SAINT

The Autobiography of *D-Rock SOUL-Jah*

TAINTED SAINT

The Autobiography of
D-Rock SOUL-Jah

AL BEY
Owner of
Tribal Metal Spear-it Publishing, LLC

IN LOVING MEMORY OF MENTORING SOULS WHO PASSED ON BEFORE ME ...

HISTORICAL LEGENDS

Zumbi de Palmares, William Wallace, Noble Drew Ali, Marcus Garvey, Honorable Elijah Muhammad, Booker T. Washington, W.E.B. DuBois, Malcolm X, Martin Luther King Jr., Huey Newton, Jimi Hendrix, Oskar Schindler, Tupac Shakur, Osiris, Isis, and many more noteworthy achievers.

PERSONAL COHORTS

Richard "Pop Pop" Bell, Reverend Uncle Charles Wyatt, Todd Ramos, Chris Williams, Johnny David, Keisha Simpson, Rosa & Bernie Balmuth, Barbara Beebe, Myrna "Peach" Crenshaw, Prince Ramisis Bey, Ebon Dooley, AL Johnson my physical Father, and Eternal Princess in the Heavens of the Sea – Amira Asuñé Lacey Bey. Axé Axé.

THIS BOOK IS ALSO DEDICATED TO INSPIRATIONAL ARTISTS STILL DWELLING ON THIS PLANE WHO I'VE MET IN SOME WAY ...

KRS-1 & Boogie Down Productions, Chuck D & Public Enemy, Black Rock Coalition, AfroPunk Crew, Rock SOUL-U-TION Core alumni, OutKast, David Ryan Harris, Saul Williams, Jada Pinkett-Smith, Amel Larrieux, Mad Max Cavalera & the SOULFLY Tribe, Benji Webbe, ATL Musicians, and several more noteworthy artists.

PROFESSIONAL ACKNOWLEDGEMENTS

Rita Martin State Farm Insurance, Philip Whitmarsh, Self-publishing.com, Frank Humphreys of Hamby & Aloisio, Lynch Law Group, Cyrano Hardy, Maggie Suttle, Portrait Innovations, Amen-Ra Tehuti, Larry Eaglin of Common Cause Productions & Anger Management Music Services, Alex Auto, West End Tattoo, Friends & Colleagues from WRFG Atlanta 89.3FM, and all professionals who have been and/or continue to be positive associations.

Contents

Foreword

It's been said by wise ones that experience is the best teacher. However, I know as well, that you can learn a lot from the experiences of others, as with this book. I've learned that a lot of individuals in this world have been through some experiences that can really alter their consciousness. From there, these mind-altering experiences can also determine their basis as to how they will see, feel and act in their lives. Some may not believe and/or know that from the time you are conceived, we are receiving all types of messages from all that is within our environment. This also includes the interaction of our friends, other relatives and especially our parents! Our parents provide the basis for how young men and women will eventually and potentially interact with those of the same and opposite sex. Simplistically explained, it's like this: if you come up in a world/environment of genuine affection, communication, unconditional love, and acceptance, the child will reflect that through his/her thoughts, feelings, and actions. If the home life is the complete opposite of the example of above, the child will reflect that environment also. You see, our past, what we retain in our minds, and how we act upon what we've retained will determine our future lives. Our beginning will determine whether we create Heaven or Hell during and towards the end of our lives!

This autobiography by my best friend, Al (D-Rock SOUL-Jah), provides some great examples of how our beginnings can affect our present and future. It also gives examples of how our emotions can allow us to make unwise decisions and actions. In other words, our emotions can allow us to do some off-the-wall shit that others may interpret as crazy and dangerous! This book also shows how deep love and affection for others may not be returned to us in the ways we wish and how it can distort our view of the reality of so-called good and bad. I've witnessed a major portion of his life from the time we met up to now. And I must say that if it wasn't for the genuine friendship from me, and all involved, who knows how his life would've turned out. Friendship, you will learn in the book, can aid in saving lives and allowing us to better ourselves in the process thereof.

With so-called bad things, or in the case of this book, bad experiences, there comes a time in our lives where we will get tired of going through all the drama and bullshit of life. Unfortunately one may choose to go downward possibly to "The Land/Mindset of No Return." This will eventually bring forth in our realities, thoughts and feelings that we are somehow justified to direct our pains on everyone else. With some of Al's experiences detailed in this book, some may think that he may have become a pimp or some type of exploiter of women, or even a murderer! As you will read about Al — from his childhood struggles, to his troubles entering manhood, towards his emergence as D-Rock SOUL-Jah, and his eventual fade into retirement — you will learn that he was not just a "Tainted Saint" who became Atlanta's Unofficial Urban Rock Minister for six years, but he was/is most importantly a Survivor and continues to be a Progressively Evolving Spirit.

Through the strength of his willpower, he didn't allow himself to fall into mind states that would allow him to direct his anger back at those in his past and those who came along in his future. He accepted that things/people in this world are not what he personally wishes them to be. Things are what all individuals on this plane wish to be! He learns that individuals are going to do whatever they wish to do. The only thing he and others have in their power to do is to accept all the way it is whether we love it or not. We can only decide how we deal with reality, period! Most importantly, Al learns that what appears great and wonderful in the long run may be your "Worst Nightmare!"

I recommend for those who read this book to not look at it as someone attempting to get rich off their bad experiences like others out there in the world have. Look at it as a manual that gives some examples of the pitfalls of life and the methods to survive them. For those who read this book and find that your life has been very similar in experiences, know that you aren't the only one. You can take those examples and map out how to get out of those situations and how to prevent them from happening in the first place. For those of you reading this book and haven't been through things of the sort, learn from these stories how to aid and support those who do live it similarly. You can learn how to not be like some of the individuals he's contacted in his life that reflected and aided in his torment.

And most importantly, let's allow ourselves to clean up our acts just by our thoughts and actions alone in order to aid in creating a better world for our descendants. This way they won't repeat the negligence of our negative cycles. Otherwise, enjoy and learn from Al's experiences. I say to you all in the ancient Kemetic tongue which means Unified Peace, Hotep!!!

Amen-Ra Tehuti Herukhuti Heru

EARLY CHILDHOOD BLURS

On July 30, 1973, Mary gave birth to seven-pound, three-ounce Albert Johnson at Holy Cross Hospital in Silver Spring, Maryland. He was the first and only son of Al and Mary who had already pro-created three older daughters. No more kids were necessary in the Johnson household since a boy was finally brought to life. That boy is me, and this book details my life experiences.

Before I explain more on my personal life, I must give background info on my parents and sisters. My father was born in Jackson, Tennessee (seventy-five miles outside of Memphis) in the segregated Jim Crow-era South. In 1963, he dropped out of Tennessee State University (same alma mater as Oprah Winfrey) and took a summer intern job at NBC News in New York. From there, he went on to become one of the first African-American correspondents of a major television network. Al Johnson stayed in the St. Albans area of Queens, New York with his Uncle James. Right next door, he met seventeen-year-old Mary.

Mary's father, Richard Bell, was hired as one of the first African-American members of the Drug Enforcement Agency (DEA). Mary, however, did not have an obvious appearance of a Black female. She is a pale-skinned mulatto birthed from a white Jewish mother who abandoned her and Richard when she was just a few months old. Richard was only eighteen years old at the time and had no idea how to raise a baby, let alone one who was white-looking and racially mixed. So he let his mother, Nana, raise Mary while he proceeded to start a family with his newlywed wife, Philamena.

Mary was a beautiful and bright young lady with college aspirations, and Al was an upstart broadcaster headed for professional success. Mary had a high school boyfriend, but Al out-charmed and out-witted him to capture her heart. Eventually, Al and Mary wedded in 1964, and shortly after, Mary graduated from high school. Even though Mary had college offers, she mostly desired a "normal" family to call her own. So immediately, she became pregnant with Katey, who was born prematurely in 1965 and died weeks later. Al and Mary still had a strong desire for offspring, which led to the conception of Stephanie, who was born in 1966.

Al's broadcasting career continued to flourish, and he landed a reporting job in Washington, D.C. From there, he and Mary procreated June (born in 1971) and ended their conceptions with me.

Around 1976-1977, Father was promoted to anchorman of the Chicago NBC station. So we moved to a nice brick house in Evanston, Illinois. Even though I was only a toddler, I have fond memories of that time. I seemed to get along with most of the kids in my class. I remember going to birthday parties, including those held for me. I acted out-of-control as one would expect of a tiny kid. I don't remember exactly what I said, but I managed to scare girls my age with horrific threats. There were times I recall girls crying in the car when we rode home with Mother from school. They would run into their houses crying to their mothers. Mother's sister, Aunt Jane, said I was a little hell raiser. She recanted a story of me pouring syrup on Stephanie's hair while eating breakfast at McDonald's. She also told of me threatening to chop up my cousin Kenya into little pieces. Perhaps I did have slight behavioral problems at this early stage in my life, but I don't recall many bad feelings from this period. I even remember being good friends with a girl named Jenny. She was sad when I moved.

My ill behavior wasn't a major concern until my family moved back to New York in 1979 where Father was now a head correspondent for the primary NBC affiliate.

I was first enrolled in a public elementary school located in Jamaica, a suburban neighborhood of Queens, New York. Apparently I had trouble paying attention in class so my first grade teacher recommended for my parents to transfer me to a "special" school. In other words, I was a student at a school for kids with behavioral problems. At this institution, I often saw kids get into fights. I was in a small class of about ten students most of who were inner-city males in the third, fourth, and fifth grades. I was peaceful most of the time but eventually ended up in my own fights after repeatedly being picked on and punched. At this school, I learned how to say the word, "motherfucker." I first heard it when I saw a tall girl beat up a boy.

Overall, my memories of New York were mostly negative. I recall several times when I cried out of resentment. Mother often told me that I was acting stubborn. Father, on the other hand, occasionally threw my defensive moods back in my face. One time I poked a toy doctor's needle in his arm, and he poked me back. Another time, he put a pocket-knife in my face after I was wielding the object around the kitchen. I remember trying to expose a blanket on a grill and let it ignite on fire in order to get Father's attention. Of course he was pissed. My sisters frequently told me I had a big mouth and needed to shut up. I hated eggs and hamburgers that were served to me, except for the small White Castle bites, so Father made me eat a whole hamburger at McDonalds. He told me we weren't leaving until

I finished the sandwich. He reiterated that I must eat beef to be a man.

New York presented a nasty pressure-packed attitude towards my family, and when Father was laid off from NBC in 1980, the whole family needed a new environment.

From here, we ended up in a place that we never knew was on the map. This place was Pocatello, Idaho. The only famous thing I heard about Idaho was their potatoes.

My older sister June and I were enrolled at Edahow Elementary School. I was a seven-year old second-grader, and that's all I knew until I got called a nigger by a swarthy complexioned Mexican kid. Up until this point, I had no idea what racism was. For most of my young life, I was in classrooms with kids of all colors. But now, I saw clearly that June and I were the only "black" kids in our school. My oldest sister Stephanie was one out of maybe ten black kids in her high school. She often complained that the yearbook pictures of blacks were "overexposed."

It seems ironic that a Hispanic kid, one of color himself, would be the one to harshly introduce me to the word "nigger." As I look back, it seemed he was just trying too hard to impress his white friends. He was a couple of shades darker than me but had straight hair. He repeatedly called me the N-word, but since I didn't know the definition I wasn't offended.

Reality hit me harder when one of my white classmates said I was a nigger because I'm black. I was also one of the few kids in my class with brown eyes, so I felt even more isolated. Even though I was the "nigger boy" of my school, kids thought I was adopted when they saw my mother. Since she is "white-looking," they had a hard time understanding how she could be the mother of a black kid. I didn't fully understand this either. So I laughed along at the jokes saying I was like the black kids on the TV series *Different Strokes*.

I'm not sure whether my tendency toward disobedient behavior was the result of an attention disorder, environmental deprivation, or a combination of both. Regardless, my deviant acts continued in Idaho as I stole approximately forty dollars from my parents' piggybank. This was the first time I felt overwhelming shame and guilt. My parents forgave me and said they wouldn't send me to jail unless I did it again. I also felt guilt-ridden when I copied off a test from a girl named Barbie. Overall, I hardly fit in with the class. I remember my teacher making an example out of one my worksheets calling it "unneat." I colored some people yellow on an art project and was mocked by my peers. Every day I became more aware of kids' cruelness when mean jokes were bullied on me. A few kids would often steal my backpack and throw it in the girls' bathroom. As I retrieved it, I got laughed at by a bunch of other students. I also got punched by a blonde-haired bully once for no apparent reason.

Perhaps all these bitter situations of rudeness on me were karma from my semi-psychotic behavior in other cities. Or maybe it was a combination of my being black and dressing like a vampire one Halloween. My mother put lipstick on me and since then I've always felt disgusted around makeup.

I survived second grade and made it to the third grade at Edahow. With all my young despair, I did have some good memories. I had a nice friend in my class and neighborhood named Carrie. She was a sweet brown-eyed girl who was born on an Air Force base in Berlin, Germany. I picked worms with her on my house's front lawn and showed her pictures of my family after she recovered from a broken leg. I was sad when she moved away. I was also good friends with a "white" boy whose family had relocated from Saudi Arabia.

The most fun I had in Pocatello came when I participated in a downtown parade even though people laughed at me for wearing an angel costume. Not only did it appear feminine to most, but it was weird for residents to see a "black" angel. I didn't want to come across as being evil after the vampire costume, but I was still perceived strangely.

As I entered the 3rd grade, there was more promise for multicultural communication. One of my classmates was a proud Mexican-American girl. My teacher taught us how to sit and chat "Indian style" with our legs crossed, and I eventually learned the history of Abraham Lincoln "freeing" black slaves. My spirit was finally accustomed to Pocatello, but I got rattled again when Father was fired from his job as a news director.

From this point on, we ended up moving to a "real" multicultural city, Las Vegas, NV. Originally, I didn't know why this move happened, but I got a clue when Uncle Chuck and his family visited us in Idaho.

LAS VEGAS SETTLEMENT

At or near November of 1981, my family and I moved into a small two-bedroom apartment in Las Vegas, Nevada. This was a drastic change for everyone, especially me. I wasn't comfortable living in a tiny space and whined about how good things used to be in the old house. I was just being a spoiled brat. Still though, my living condition was good compared to the rest of the family. I had my own room with a mini-TV because I was the only boy. Stephanie and June shared a small room with bunk beds and my parents slept on the living room sofa. My parents wanted a bigger place, but the apartment was all that was both available and affordable at the time. I continued, like a jackass, to complain about how poor we were.

I guess I was too young at the time to understand how badly the environment change impacted the family. June often told me to stop complaining because it would result in Father yelling at everyone. Father appeared more stressed than I ever knew because he was making less money as a reporter for Channel 3 News (NBC affiliate) in Vegas.

Since money was tight, Mother decided to stop being a housewife and found a job at J.C. Penney. Father didn't adjust well to Mother's new role. He feared several things: 1) That Mother was having an affair; 2) That she was befriending whores in her cosmetics apartment; 3)That she was stealing money from the family bank account; and 4) She wasn't cooking and cleaning enough at home.

In the midst of the holiday season of 1981, the mood was very stressful. Father's paranoia of Mother's job success made him disturbingly angry. On a Saturday night in December, a couple weeks shy of Christmas, Father picked Mother up from work. He was very upset about something. Apparently, Mother didn't do something properly with a check for a utility bill. I don't remember exactly what the argument was about, but it definitely was about money, and Father was screaming louder than I ever heard him in my early life. As the yelling forged, I heard a smacking sound. Father somehow had hit Mother. I was concerned but perceived this as being a normal male out-burst. Yet, there were five more smacking sounds and Mother repeatedly yelling "Ow." I became more frightened. I was brief-ly relieved when Father called Uncle Chuck and told him that Mother and the kids needed to spend the night at his place. Stephanie was already hanging out with friends so June and I got our coats and nightclothes prepared. As we came into the living room, we saw Father repeatedly kick Mother in her left ribs while she was trying to back off against the kitchen wall. June and I sighed with frightening sobs. Mother started to cry, and I felt intensely scared, witnessing her tears for the first time.

My recollection of this moment is hazy. All I remember next is that Father was driving June and I in the Ford Pinto. Mother was running down the street in her raincoat trying to get to a payphone. Father stopped the car. He got out, grabbed Moth-er, and kicked her directly in her ass about three times before throwing her back in the Pinto. He drove all of us to Uncle Chuck's place, dropped us off, and left the parking lot cussing and fussing. Aunt Minda immediately gave Mother an ice pack and I saw her crying again. June and I dressed up in our night-clothes and watched cable TV in the living room. Stephanie was picked up by cousin Florence. Sobs dripped from Stephanie's face as she yelled at Mother. She also continually screamed at

Cousin John, "I hate you." Mother settled into night clothes and spoke with Aunt Minda. She was calmer, but I could still hear her cry. The whole night was exceedingly painful and sad.

Mother took June and I to the mall to go X-mas shopping the next night and told us that Father didn't mean to hurt her. We all ended up as a whole family again back at the apartment but the tension-filled drama of that Saturday night would taint the SOUL of me and my family forever!

MUSIC proved to be the background noise (sounds) used as healing nourishment for a wounded SOUL!

Most of my memories through the rest of the third grade life are vague. However, I was becoming more aware of societal stereotypes. Once I was interviewed over my elementary school's TV system. A girl asked me what I wanted for Christmas. I said "SOUL Music." This answer resulted from what I viewed on pop culture TV shows like *American Bandstand*. I perceived that black people did SOUL Music and white folks performed Rock'n'Pop. Since I was a black kid, I denied liking "Pop" music even though I really did. June would often tease me after some friends of hers caught me singing pop tunes like "Tainted Love." She tickled and teased me while tape-recording me saying "I like Pop Music!" in a joking manner.

Watching TV and listening to the radio was my escape from the drama of my household. Father's temper died down somewhat but was still frightening enough to make everyone duck and hide. I remember him destroying the whole inside of the refrigerator because he couldn't find any milk to make eggs. I covered my ears during this tumultuous display while my sisters nearly died laughing. After angry outbursts like this, I would use the TV and radio as my emotional refuge. I guess this is a big part of the reason why I had trouble making friends in my neighborhood and at school. Kids picked on me and called me a retard. The kids who seemed nice to me ended up being shunned by me out a fear that every person usually ends up mean (like Father). For example, a Swiss girl said hi to me, and I told her to shut up.

My trust in people became even more narrow after an incident where my softball was stolen.

During a sunny Sunday, I was playing catch with a couple of neighborhood boys. We threw and rolled my softball around for much of the afternoon. Suddenly, they ran off with the ball and I couldn't find them. Father was walking from the pool after taking a swim. I told him that a couple of boys who I played with took my ball before we ran into the apartment's security guard and his dog.

We looked around at the other complexes but couldn't find them. Father thanked the security guard and then said that he had to talk to me. This became one of the most frightening moments of my life. Father shoved me a couple of times while screaming "They took your ball." I cried heavily feeling like a fool-hearted wimp. Father kept shoving and suddenly I tripped over something on the sidewalk, fell, and scraped my forehead and right cheekbone against the ground. I cried so loudly out of fear from Father's temper that I didn't notice how badly I was bleeding. I ran back into the apartment boo-hooing with much horror. My sisters screamed in fright seeing me bloodied while they were preparing for a swim. June thought some kids beat me up, but I sobbed, "Daddy did this to me." Father said that I just fell. He took me in the bathroom and forcefully placed alcohol-infused pads on my face which only made me scream and cry more. All this pain started to numb as I rested in my bed for the rest of the afternoon. I felt guilty because Father said that I needed to be punished. Mother came home early that evening and asked me what happened to my face. I said, "Daddy beat me up." Father said I just fell after crying over the boys taking my ball. I asked Mother if she agreed on me being punished and she responded, "No. I don't agree."

It was difficult going to school for the next couple of weeks with bandages covering nearly half my face. Parents and teachers alike asked me what happened to my face. I told them I just fell. Overall, I did make a big fall. I fell out of trust with practically everyone around me. Even though I was still just a little boy, I lost hope that I could ever make true friends. This incident put another dent in a young soul that was already tainted.

By the fourth grade, I was too ashamed to socialize with anyone. I was being picked on quite often. Classmates often called me retarded. This cruel label seemed justified as I struggled in reading. I was placed in a special library program to help me with this skill. Father threatened to hold me back one grade if my reading didn't improve. This terrified me and led me further into depression even though I was only nine years old.

My reading did improve after Father encouraged me to read the stats on the sports pages of the local newspaper. Since I liked sports on television, this helped. I was still mocked by my classmates during sports and every other activity I participated in, and was usually one of the last guys picked for teams. Some boys said that I played like a girl and started calling me "gay." I was called gay so much that I eventually agreed with them and started believing it. This freaked them out, so they stopped messing with me for a short while.

Matters weren't made much better because kids in my neighborhood still picked on me. Some of them harassed me and June during our thirty minute walk home. Father was so irate from this story that he gave me a soft push-kick to the face while spewing, "If you don't fight back and beat someone up, I'll beat you up. I will not have my son growing up to be a sissy."

My parents were holding steady on their jobs while not letting their arguments become too explosive. They moved the family to a slightly bigger two-bedroom townhouse where there was more room for my family to function. Times though were still difficult and I became more depressed.

Towards the latter part of my fourth grade year, I faced another emotional challenge.

During a recess break of a nice sunny day, I was in line to play tetherball. It was my turn to play, but some kids cut in front of me. I whined, but froze with fear when a taller, skinny black girl called me a son-of-a-bitch and told me to stay in line. A bunch of kids laughed at me, and I felt embarrassed and low. I felt so worthless that I started to act on thoughts and words I repeated to Mother on drives home, "I wish I were dead." Lo and behold, I grabbed my neck real hard and started squeezing it. Literally, I tried to strangle myself. A classmate looked at me alarmingly as if I was choking and told my teacher. She walked me to the principal's office while I cried out my reasons for wanting to kill myself. The principal sent me back to class before school ended and my teacher spoke with the class and encouraged them to treat each other better. Some kids stated that I was a cool kid to get along with.

Later that night, my parents spoke with me privately in my room. Father asked me who my favorite ball player was. I said "Dr. J (Julius Erving of the Philadelphia 76ers)." Father then asked me if Dr. J. would choke himself like I did when Celtic fans booed him. I said no, so he encouraged me to be strong like Dr. J.

I was inspired to hang tough after this conversation, but my parents were still very worried. They enrolled me into sessions at the Children's Behavioral Center (CBC). I vaguely remember what the counselors spoke to me about. However, I recall doing fun stuff with kids who had similar problems and receiving meditation tapes as homework. One counselor asked me what the most important thing in my life was, but I hardly remember my response. Overall, the CBC helped me recover from pre-teen suicidal tendencies and the absolute worst times of my school-days. Yet, I developed a habit of being more of a passive social-ite than an adventurously wild kid.

OREO LABEL

It was fall of 1983. I was a ten-year old fifth grader. My teacher initially viewed me as a troublemaker. I don't remember doing bad things, but the peers I kept company around certainly gave Ms. Rozier the impression that I caused disturbances. For example, all I did with friends was yell out in the boys' bathroom how much some poop stank and she yelled at me for making too much noise during a recess break.

By this time, I made friends with a white boy who I initially thought was a girl. Jonas had long "girly" blond hair when I first met him pissing in the boys' bathroom. After he told me he was a boy, we hung out on the playground. A girl named Joe Lee from my old apartment neighborhood mocked us by asking me who my girlfriend was. Jonas frowned and said he was cutting his hair the next day. And so he did.

Jonas often wore Led Zeppelin T-shirts. He told me they were the greatest band of all time. I had no knowledge of Led Zeppelin or any rock band until I started watching MTV after my parents finally ordered cable. During this time, I explored MTV and all the movie channels.

With MTV and KOMP 92.3FM, I learned a lot about popular music artists. Yet, I still had a close-minded black-white music mindset. I didn't allow myself to like "white boy" rock bands until the latter part of my fifth grade year. With constant exposure to heavy metal from Jonas and another stoner friend named Seth. I eventually admitted my admiration for rock'n'roll. With parental allowance, I bought a plethora of heavy metal tapes including Ratt *(Under the Cellar)*, Ronnie James Dio *(Last in Line)*, Ozzy Osbourne *(Diary of a Madman)*, Twisted Sister *(Were Not Gonna Take It* – single), Quiet Riot *(Critical Condition)*, and a Judas Priest T-shirt.

I was now a black metal-head and found a niche for releasing my emotional trauma. Father was okay with my newfound musical tastes as long as I didn't behave like a perceived satanic rock fans. Little did I know how my music interests would reap painful consequences.

One afternoon, Jonas and I were talking on the phone. June yelled out some cruel joke poking fun at Jonas. Jonas took this as a challenge and used me as a mediator to exchange warring words with June. It was funny at first, but then Jonas told me to tell June that she was a nigger. June got so upset that she grabbed the phone and cussed him out. I continued to laugh because I thought Jonas won the words battle and was happy for him as my friend. Yet June complained to the rest of the family about my prejudiced white friend. Stephanie told me that "nigger" was the worst word someone could call a black person. Mother suggested I talk to him on the phone and ask him if he hates black people. Jonas said that he was only prejudiced against June.

Stephanie and June didn't buy it and continually mocked my fanatical worship of stoner "white boy" metal bands. They said most of them were untalented and probably listened to Frank Sinatra as their real music interests. Then they called me an "oreo – black on the outside, white on the inside." This insult was very painful because I honestly couldn't disagree. I often dreamed of myself as a Czech white boy with long straight black hair playing in a cool heavy metal band. I had no knowledge of rock bands with black members at that time. Stephanie and Father also told me that white folks had stolen rock'n'roll from black blues and doo-wop artists like Little Richard and B.B. King.

Even though these historical revelations were disturbing, I continued to listen to heavy metal with much joy. I was so engulfed in hard rock sounds that I asked Father to buy tickets to the Quiet Riot October '84 concert at UNLV's Thomas & Mack Center. Father agreed to go but couldn't because he was busy with his new job as Manager of black/urban radio station, KCEP 88.1FM, so Stephanie accepted the responsibility of taking me.

My sisters were not completely prejudiced against white artists. They liked Culture Club and Hall & Oates, and even attended their shows. But they still had a passionate angst against racist whites who they felt were dominant in the hard rock genre. Before Stephanie took me to the show, she was laughed at by her black friends in college. Her friend Junta said that she and I would be like ink spots on a white sheet of paper at that concert. This made me feel very nervous about encountering racists. Stephanie and I attended the performance featuring Quiet Riot, Whitesnake, and Kick Axe, and only saw one other black person in a crowd of about 13,000 people. From this moment forward, my interest in heavy metal faded even though I still liked the sounds. Stephanie wrote a college paper on this concert describing it as a barbaric display of weed-smoking, drunkenness, and nudity. Quiet Riot even appeared to have homosexual tendencies by groping each other and flashing their spandex-laden behinds on stage. Various news reports of kids' hideous behavior made it seem that I was headed in the wrong direction.

I was still good friends with Jonas, but we became more distant as a result of his lies. He often lied about going to concerts and having a lot of money. He also lied by having me call a girl he liked. His obsessive pursuit of her annoyed her, causing her parents, who were lawyers, to complain to Ms. Rozier about disorderly phone calls. I was named as the prime suspect until I pointed out that Jonas initiated the phone calls.

Jonas's incessant behavior would often piss me off to the point where we almost came to blows a few times. However, I was empathetic towards his reasoning when I saw his parents arguing over custody. His parents were divorced, and I lost contact with Jonas for good when he moved into his mother's house and changed schools. I pray that Jonas is alive and well today.

From this moment forward, I was still associating well with non-black people. Yet my musical tastes became more biased and would remain this way for the rest of my proclaimed adolescence. Thus, my social interaction was diseased.

MOVING ON TO SIXTH AND SEVENTH GRADE YEARS.

I made a valiant attempt to become part of the social norm. I hung out with more kids in my neighborhood and played a lot of football and baseball in the condominium yards.

I enjoyed being active, except for an older boy's bullying tactics. Roy was the star jock on the block and he always threatened to beat up all of us who were smaller than if we didn't play with him. I don't hold a grudge against him today. Now I realize that he took his sports seriously while the rest of us just wanted to have fun. Plus, I was more interested in studying and playing music. As fate turned out, Roy would play the trumpet in my junior high school junior varsity band while I played the drums. He would go on to be the starting quarterback of Western High

School's football team for all of his senior year. I on the other hand stayed more dedicated to academics.

Roy and I became more distant friends when my parents bought a new 3-bedroom house on 1100 Hazard Avenue in April, 1985. They owned this house for ten years. Apparently, we were finally settled in a space convenient for the entire family. Mother was so comfortable that she bought us a cockapoo dog and named her Brandy because she looked like Brandon on the NBC sitcom *Punkie Brewster*.

In my new Vegas neighborhood, I hung out with more kids from my sixth grade class. The same kids who seemingly mocked me were now cool acquaintances. Perhaps it was because we were all reaching the end of our pre-teen days. My peers now talked a lot about dating each other instead of playing silly boy versus girl games. I even had a secret crush on a girl named Marie who I often poked fun at for being tall and skinny. I never admitted it to her but deep down she knew. She stopped hating me once we ended up in separate classes during the seventh grade.

As my social interaction changed, so did my musical tastes. During the latter part of my fifth grade year, breakdancing was the hot new style of dance. Even Jonas participated in breakin' and pop-lockin' dance groups. I always shied away because I felt I had no rhythm. Breakdancing was part of a new style of music which I never knew existed until I saw Run-DMC's "King of Rock" music video on UNLV's college video channel. As I found out later, rap music was the fresh new genre of music that appealed to the youth. Even though at least ninety-nine percent of the artists I knew about were black, their music incited movements amongst kids of every ethnicity. Stoner white boys would blast their boom boxes and banging their heads to Run-DMC, LL Cool J, and Whodini. They also mimicked the human beat-box sounds of the Fat Boys. I did too and always had a barrel of laughs watching their "Jailhouse Rap" video.

I was not surprised to see white rap act, Beastie Boys, get most of the attention. They had more of a punk-rock-infused rap sound on their first album *License to Ill*. And I learned white artists profited more from "black" music. Overall, I didn't like the Beastie Boys because of their annoying squeaky voices and frivolous party antics, and not because of their pale-skin tone.

Yet, my mind was vast becoming more one-sided when it came to music. Even though I heard about "black" rockers like Jimi Hendrix and Fishbone, they were still too far and few between in a mostly white man's game. Therefore, rap, hip-hop, and R&B were my only outlets of music from 1984-1997.

Meanwhile in the seventh grade, I asserted myself more academically despite forthcoming social challenges. My best friend was a short white boy named Don. We were classmates in an advanced math class and a few other average level classes. We received good grades but were often bullied by boys (mostly black and Latino) in average level and lower classes. We thought we would fit better in advanced classes, but most of those students were stuck-up whites and Asians. Adding to the disparities, Don was constantly referred by peers as a wimp. I began to agree with the peers and eventually distanced myself from him as well.

I never fully escaped the "oreo" label. I was a good black student who got along with most kids, but I still never knew where I belonged. Therefore, my sociopathic cycle continued on through high school.

SOCIAL RECLUSE

By the summer of 1986, I was so afraid of bullies that I became more socially reclusive. Instead of hanging with peers, I stayed at home and watched movies through cable and a VCR. I was tired of being picked on by everyone, including honors course students. Even though I earned straight A's twice in the previous spring semester, I didn't feel happy because I had few friends. I even sat alone during a luncheon honoring straight-A students.

My sister June claimed I was "anti-social." June pointed a finger at me in an argument saying she was going to persuade our parents to make me hang out with people outside of the house. I became mad and threw a punch at her. We ended up wrestling. I could have thrown more punches at June's face, but my intention was not to seriously injure her. She continued to swing and eventually pinned me to the ground. She won this brawl, but I was still in a whimpering fury.

I eventually got on top of her and put my hands on her neck. I said I was worthless so I might as well kill her. I started strangling her and she screamed. I let go feeling shocked that I was capable of murdering my own flesh and blood. Father woke up from a nap. Then he grabbed me and told me not to touch her. I went to my room and wept the rest of the day. I bruised myself with self-inflicted punches and tore my seventh grade yearbook to pieces.

As a result of this incident, Father forced me to go with

June and her friends to a teen dance club called That's Entertainment. I was uncomfortable because I had no confidence in dancing and talking with girls.

Overall, this summer set the tone for how I would socially interact for the bulk of my adolescence. I went back to school in the fall wearing loose-fit out-of-style corduroy pants (ironically now in-style for today's kids) instead of popular tight-fit Levi jeans. I had no desire to be part of any cliquish norm.

For the rest of my days at Gibson Junior High, I pretty much avoided a social life. I had virtually no friends and did not hang out with fellow students outside of the Bowling Club. I was the number one-positioned snare drum player in the varsity band, but I quit after the eighth grade citing more of a need to focus on academics. June got tired of band two years prior in her junior high school days, so I followed suit. My band teacher, Mr. Mulky, approached me during a lunch recess and tried to convince me to stay. He questioned how someone with my tempo could give up on music. I told him it was time to let it go. I would regret this decision years later. Stephanie told me I could've gone to college on a marching band scholarship, but I didn't foresee myself as a well-coordinated marcher. Therefore, I carried on as a bookworm.

In the eighth grade, I was assigned to advanced level three honors classes in almost every subject, but I never felt good enough to compete with mostly stuck up white kids. Plus my skills tests usually had lower scores in everything but math. So even though I maintained decent grades, I convinced my school counselor to place me in level two courses during my ninth grade year in every subject except math. For English class, I forged Mother's signature in order to get placed in an average class. My teacher, Mrs. Hull, was so shocked and upset that she called Mother urging her to rescind her signature. Mother did not remember signing such a document because she never did, but she still allowed me to feel sorry for myself and not burden myself with any more challenges. Mrs. Hull labeled me as an academic wimp. I didn't care because I had trouble identifying with assigned stories based on nothing but non-black culture.

In the ninth grade, I was labeled a weirdo. I didn't feel comfortable talking to anyone. I felt everyone would eventually just make fun of me regardless of how friendly I was. My physical education class was the primary example. Since other boys kept calling me a fuck-up player, I would sit out on various matches. Then, the boys would end up mad at me for not participating and leaving them short of players for their teams. Even with such inactivity, I could have earned A's in this class, but I would always wear plain clothes on frequent days to purposely cut enough points to earn only B-grades. I still avoided being an out-of-place straight-A student.

For the most part, students would stay clear of me out of fear. Just like my experiences in the fourth grade, I made peers believe I was wacko despite the fact I was only a shy kid. In my level two English class, I did a book report on witchcraft and serial killers. I was fascinated with occult figures and the reasons they were ousted from societies. I finally found some characters to identify with my personality. I also liked watching horror movies at home. Ironically, Father couldn't stand grotesque and gory movies. His phobias overshadowed the abusive reality he perpetuated on me and the entire family.

In the summer of 1987, my parents got involved in another scary argument. Again, I don't have an exact memory of what the argument was about. Yet, I remember waking up hearing Father screaming, cursing, and banging tables. I wanted no part of that day's actions, so I just retreated back to sleep and stayed in my room for the day's remainder. I figured that the smoke would clear by the evening. It only inflamed more. After I woke up in the afternoon from another nap, I heard Father scream and cuss louder. He warned Mother to back off. She left the house and he walked out the door yelling, "Go on. Get the fuck out of here!" I continued to stay quiet in my room, fearing Father would spread his anger to me. Then I heard the phone ring.

Father answered and told Mother he wanted a divorce. Listening to this brief conversation gave me brief but bittersweet relief as I thought, "It's about time." Then nighttime approached and my sisters phoned me giving me the scoop on the argument's details.

What resulted was that Father was drunk over frustration with his general manager position at KCEP. He purchased a gun to protect himself from scandalous underwriters in the urban community. During the argument, he was so upset that he pointed the gun at Mother. She retreated to the home of Aunt Minda and Uncle Chuck. Stephanie and June were already out with friends, so my cousins, John and Florence, picked them up and drove them back to Aunt Minda's.

Stephanie, while still driving her '78 Chevette, along with Mother and June, stopped by during nights, while Father was at work. They picked up extra belongings for overnight stays at Aunt Minda's. I stayed behind initially out of fear. However, Mother ordered me on another stop to tag along.

For about one week, I was a resident of Aunt Minda's place. Stephanie begged Mother not to go back to Father. However, Mother insistently called a family meeting. We went back to 1100 Hazard Avenue. Mother told us to speak freely. June yelled at Father by pointing out all his flaws. I blurted out that I always felt like shit and was never good enough for appreciation. Mother said I sounded just like Father. Stephanie was packing as she prepared to go to Washington, D.C. on a Senatorial internship. She was silent until she cried out how Father pushed her too hard in school and work. Stephanie later admitted to us all how she almost committed suicide one night as she was ready to swallow an overdose of sleeping pills.

At the end of this family meeting, Mother moved us back home and Father vowed to give away the gun and cut down his drinking and fussing. My sisters and I were still doubtful. I adopted an attitude that I would never get married. This sarcastic vow cursed my relationships with females.

Back at school, my interaction with girls came with resentment. When other boys proclaimed their machismo to have sex with every girl they knew, I became silent. I didn't think this was respectful to the female species, especially since I had two older sisters. Rumors flew around again like in the fourth grade that I was gay. First it started when a couple of classmates told me that a girl name Beatrice liked me. I responded saying, "That stuck up bitch doesn't like me. She's just toying with me. I can't get a date, even if it's with a guy." My low self-esteem had me more interested in cussing out girls rather than communicating with them.

The gay rumors were more invoked during my initial interaction with a girl named Celia. She was a cute dark-haired, brown-eyed, and pale-skinned Latina with a firm body. She had a birth mark on the left side of her forehead, but she still looked good to me. I frequently cracked jokes on her to purposely get her attention. Her friend asked if I liked her and I repeatedly denied it. Celia became so annoyed by my jokes that she snapped back at me with remarks such as, "It's Halloween and you don't need a mask." Her words were so harsh I didn't laugh. Then, she constantly turned her head back at me during a reading class telling me I stunk and I was ugly. Seemingly, she was joking but I was not in a happy mood that day. These disparaging comments coupled with my parents' arguments and mean classmates sent me into a near-murderous rage. As Celia left class laughing, I grabbed her throat and threatened to strangle her if she ever said anything mean to me again.

From this point, I was ready to kill her, but things changed. The next day, she started talking to me in a friendly tone. She asked me if I was dating anyone. I said no girl likes me. She told me that wasn't true because she knew two girls in the cafeteria who said they liked me. I said that was bullshit. Then, I said that having sex with a guy was fun. Most people at Gibson really became scared of me by this time. This was my way of rebelling against Father's homophobic attitude. I remember him screaming at me one time when I told him how I pushed away a boy in a pool who wanted me to grab his nuts. Father blew at me, "If you ever reveal being gay to me, I'll kill you."

Even though I didn't partake in homosexuality, my actions showed mostly bitterness towards people, especially females. I would continue to sit by myself during lunch and my physical education class. Celia, though, would constantly greet me with warm smiles. She repeatedly gave me good rapport for the rest of the time I knew her. She was my only wonderful social memory of the ninth grade.

During the last school day, I purposely retreated to sit by myself on a closed-off stairway in the gym. I knew this would attract her attention because she was the only person (let alone girl) who ever tried to talk to me during my anti-social escapes. She walked up the stairs and yelled "Ha" to me, and I acted like I awoke from a dead sleep. She asked me in a sobbing voice what was wrong. I said no one liked me. She said, "I like you. I'll be your friend." Finally, class ended and school was out for the summer. She repeated to me that she'll by me friend. I shook her hand and told her thanks.

Celia's warmth gave me a productive social dream for high school.

By fate, she was in my biology class during our sophomore

year. We were good friends at this point and often exchanged meaningful conversations.

One day, I finally decided to let my crush out of the closet. Normally, most kids at Western High School would eat at fast food places off campus. I told Celia that I needed to tell her something that would change my life, so we met at the AM/PM gas station/food mart. I said simply, "I like you." Celia responded, "I'm going with someone else. We can still be friends." I quickly walked out the store trotting fast back to school. My first revealed crush had crushed me. I felt so hurt that I spoke with Father. He was amused to hear me finally admit that I have infatuations for girls. After talking more, I agreed that it was time for me to get a social life so I started dressing in clothes that June recommended and hung out with her and her friends.

And I started chasing girls.

As for Celia, I remained a close friend to her before she embarked on a more traumatic social path. I often remember another biology student calling her "innocent." She didn't like this label, but I thought it was an appropriate description of the girl I was in love with. Celia was smart, but her grades dropped as she became more of a party animal. Sometimes she would show up to class crying out her desire to drop out of school. I often gave her my class notes since I was still attracted to her.

Celia had problems at home after finding out she had two brothers she never knew until her eighth grade year. She beat up one of her girlfriends and subsequently dropped out of school for a year. I lost touch with her mostly for good. I ran into her a couple of times and we said hi but by this time, we were in separate worlds. She often dressed like a sleek woman often seen in heavy metal band videos, while I started following messages of militant hip-hop artists. She admitted to being drunk and stoned too much. I guess this is what led to her school problems. Ironically, I smoked weed with a Latino stoner in an attempt to fit in more socially. Even though Celia was not my official high school sweetheart, she has a special place in my heart as a dear friend. After my relationship with her faded, I would continue to be involved with the wrong crowds. I pray that Celia is alive and well on this realm or the next.

Meanwhile, I continued to be an honor student even though most my classes were not on advanced levels. I maintained good grades and frequently tutored fellow students, especially fine-looking girls. I even helped a couple of hotties cheat on their tests. I remember helping a popular girl in my Spanish class cheat because I felt guilty about being a stingy student who wouldn't share pencils and paper during our previous ninth grade year. Despite all my blending actions, I still felt like an outcast because I didn't have a consistent ride to and from school.

Initially, my parents bought me a speedy low-seat bicycle. I was comfortable for a while, but during one fateful afternoon, I went to the bike rack and didn't find my ride. I looked all over until all I found was my combination lock. My bike was stolen as a result of my irresponsible locking habit. I reported it missing to school security, and Father picked me up from school. I felt so depressed for the rest of that day. Unless my parents or sisters were available to pick me up, I walked to school every day from that moment forward.

During most of my walks, I became discouraged seeing my sophomore peers earn their drivers' licenses and subsequently drive nice cars bought by their parents. I decided it was time for me to start driving. I persistently asked my parents to teach me how to drive. Mother said she couldn't because she wasn't an expert, especially since she had a freeway phobia. She recommended that Father teach me. With Father giving me instructions from the mini-truck passenger side, I practiced on weekends. Even though I felt tense from Father's criticism, the lessons were going well. I wanted so badly to be a flawless driver. Yet this pressure for safe-driving perfection almost led to an accident.

One Sunday afternoon, Father had me drive in a nearby neighborhood. Then he instructed me to make a left turn onto busy Rancho Boulevard. I was scared to death because I had to look to my left passing three lanes and then look to my right and make a left while still in a middle lane. I passed the first three lanes but quickly made a left passing the intersection lane without fully seeing what was on my right. Father quickly said, "Hey lookout for this car!" I kept driving and a car quickly hopped into the farthest right lane before it could hit the Isuzu mini-truck we drove in. Father screamed at me and had me park at a 7-Eleven store so he could purchase milk and cigarettes. First he told me with disappointment that I knew that street and shouldn't have gotten us in a life-threatening predicament. He proceeded to shout at me, concluding, "This is our (the family's) only means of transportation. We can't afford to have you fuck it up!" Then he snatched the keys from me and drove us home.

Suddenly, I was more depressed because I felt Father was right. Mother tried to negotiate me into driving school. Father was okay with this since he felt I didn't listen to him. This idea fell through the cracks because I would still not be able to drive the Isuzu much, even if I did pass the drivers' test. So I kept updating my learners' permit.

At age fifteen, I started working at Arby's Roast Beef to earn my own income to get a car. However, I stayed in the honor student mentality. I decided that saving my earnings was more important than trying to buy a car. I opened up a savings account and started building my own wealth.

The joy of my earnings was short-lived for several reasons. I had money but still practically no social life. There were nice girls who would occasionally give me rides to and from school, the bank, and even work. I liked them, but they already had boyfriends with cars. Peer pressure made me think that I needed a car to have a girlfriend.

Since my money was not being spent on recreational activities or girlfriends, my parents took note of this. Coincidentally, they asked to borrow a substantial amount of my savings. My parents were still recovering from bankruptcy proceedings and were trying to improve their credit rating. They were behind on their mortgage payments, so I loaned them two hundred dollars on one occasion and eight hundred dollars on another. I repeatedly asked for this money back, and Father always blurted, "We ain't got no money. We got bills to pay so we can stay in our house and off the streets." My family endured another period of tough financial times when Father quit KCEP radio before being rehired to their community center sponsor, Economic Opportunity Board, after a year. I never again asked for my money back and never received it. I felt I was being too greedy since my parents provided the daily basics of food, shelter, and clothing during the course of my whole life.

Back at school, I communicated with peers okay but had no access to popular parties without a car and friends with cars. I tried to hang out and be cool with my eleventh grade classmates with cars but was labeled "a damn nerd." I felt this was unfair since I was a hardworking honor student and Arby's employee. I was literally all work and no play. I was even more discouraged as I kept walking home from work and school watching sophomore underclassmen drive cars and work cooler jobs at the malls.

By the middle of my eleventh grade year, I was miserable and needed a change. A good friend of mine at Arby's named Brody quit and started to work at Vons supermarket as a courtesy clerk. I followed suit and was happier working at a less stressful job with a slightly higher minimum wage. While bagging groceries and pushing shopping carts, I found time to converse more with co-workers in my age range. From here, I started to hang out more with friends who had cars. I finally had friends on my own without June's help and officially made it to a full-fledged social life, yet I was unaware of the ill consequences.

VONS CROWD

"The friends you have in high school, you hardly remember. But the friends you ha*ve in college will stay with you for life."*

This quote from my twelfth grade Physics teacher turned out to be true in many ways. Today, I don't have contact with any of my high school friends, but I remember my experiences with them very well. These times shaped and defined how I would socialize for most of my life up until the present.

I worked at Vons supermarket from the latter part of my eleventh grade year until the summer before I entered college. I also worked there during the summer after my college freshman year as well.

Initially, Brody was the only person I knew at this store. Then, my upper-classmen friend Shorty from my Accounting class started working there. Shorty proceeded to spread the word to his neighborhood friends about a cool summer job. That's when Sal and Perry started working there too. A vocational tenth grader from my elementary school neighborhood named Ronnie and his schoolmate Shan also worked at Vons that summer.

As one can see, I had a lot of cohorts to converse with more than any previous period of my short life. My co-worker friends and I had such a blast with each other during work that we decided to kick it on a regular basis after hours.

First, Brody and Shorty were the only ones with cars. So we

rode with them while proceeding to several functions (dances, concerts, movies, basketball games, etc.). The "fellas" would always tease me for being a virgin. Of course, I felt uncomfortable by these remarks. I wasn't trying to have sex with every girl I met and profess to being a "master player." Perhaps I was not adamant about getting pussy because I never even masturbated in high school. I would however follow the ass-seeking advice of my peers.

I often hung out with Shorty at his older brother's apartment. Initially, we drank beer and rapped about girls. One night, Shorty invited over a couple of girls from our school. We chatted and drank. One of the girls, who was a slightly heavyset blonde-haired girl, got drunk, to say the least. Since she was sitting right next to me, Shorty persuaded us to kiss each other. I proceeded to caress her lips and tongue. This was my first kiss ever. Shorty further persuaded me to take her into a bedroom, but I stopped fondling her. I just didn't feel right trying to fuck a girl directly after my first kiss. Plus, I hardly knew her and didn't want to take advantage of her drunkenness. Her friend gave me some "dap" for not being a dog. Shorty, on the other hand, kept hollering, "You could've had dem draws!" The girls were taken home after puking from their intoxication. The girl I groped had a hangover and claimed she remembered nothing.

Shorty and I spent the rest of the night talking at the apartment. In the morning, a friend of Shorty's brother poked fun at me for using a proper English statement when I told him I didn't want the French toast because "It contains eggs." He repeated this sentence in mockery about ten times. Shorty joined in the laughter, and I thus became the butt of intellectual jokes amongst my "friendly" crew.

I was so much of an intellectual that I was labeled Preacher John. I talked about what I knew, and thus made no mention of pussy. Shorty and the fellas agreed that they had to get A-Bear laid. I hated being called A-Bear by anyone outside of Father.

However, a girl named Dana loved it. She was a sensuous new courtesy clerk at Vons. She looked like a voluptuous sandy brown haired white girl with blue eyes but she claimed to be Latina. Regardless of her official ethnicity, I was turned on.

Late one night, the fellas and I went to a teen summer dance at Cashman field. All of us wore the in-style polka-dot shirts and had high-top faded hair. I was never a confident dancer and felt uncomfortable at first. Then, we spotted Dana and her sister. Dana insisted on dancing with me so I followed her on to the floor. Never in my life had I grinded my hips so hard while my penis was erect. My homeboys even said, "Goddamn" from their observations of how we danced. Dana was hugging and kissing me virtually the whole night. I honestly didn't feel emotionally attached to her but was enjoying her passes toward me. Dana and her sister didn't have a ride home, so I persuaded Shorty to have them ride with us in an already over-stocked vehicle. Dana sat on my lap and locked lips with me virtually the entire way to her home. From the examples of my player friends, I acted cold-hearted and called out to a girl walking on the street who had a nice ass. Shorty was thoroughly irritated at the end of the drive but was happy I had a potential fuck. Dana gave me a long, tongue kiss goodnight, and my dick was swollen into the morning. The fellas gave me props for having a girl, but all I said was, "I'm not looking for a relationship. I just wanna bone her." They mocked me again from this statement because I still sounded too intellectual.

The next day at Vons, my co-worker friends were gossiping about the previous night. Dana approached us and told us, "Look. Whatever happened last night, let it drop." Dana was more content with being the ho-girlfriend of our co-worker who drove a glitzy Chevy truck. I really was not heart-broken since she came across as a ho from the moment I met her. I still fondled and kissed her on two other occasions during work breaks. Her so-called boyfriend was ready to fight me over these incidents until he realized how promiscuous she was. Dana eventually quit Vons, and for all I know she became a prostitute on the Vegas strip. I proceeded on more attempts to lose my virginity. Often, I look back at my moments with Dana as being some of the most enjoyable of my life.

By my twelfth grade year, my circle of friends changed. Shorty enrolled in the army. Brody found a girlfriend and was promoted to a different department at Vons. Ronnie and Shan quit Vons. Sal started driving with his own set of friends, and Perry encountered drug addiction. I was still cool with this circle but now needed friends to associate with consistently.

During fall, 1990, my twelfth grade classmate Dick was hired at Vons. We had cool conversations at work and I became a part of his "mob." Initially I had doubts about joining his clique because he stood me up on outings during my sophomore year. One time he promised to bring a fine-looking black girl who I spoke with to my house, but they never showed up. From that moment on, I labeled him, "Con Man." Eventually, I forgave him since I had nobody else to affiliate with.

The biggest change I faced with Dick's group was that I now hung out with mostly Italian and Irish Caucasian males as opposed to mostly black males in Shorty's group. However, I did not hide my black pride while hanging out with Dick and his friends—T.R., Shane, Daron, Jake, and others. During one of our first nights out on the town, we drank a few beers and I spoke freely after becoming slightly tipsy.

Vehemently, I spewed out comments of black anger against the white racist power structure. I repeatedly mentioned how black people were robbed and raped of their cultural identity and historical accomplishments. At first the mob was offended

48

but then found my chatter amusing. T.R., who was driving the car, said "This guy is just a passenger and he has the nerve to talk shit. "

T.R. started laughing even harder as my tone became more militant. Overall, I had no major racial intolerance from Dick's mob despite ignorant slurs that were frequently exchanged. For the most part, we were humored in our dialogue—Dick and T.R. threatening to smoke me with their Italian mob while I would counter with the F.O.I. (Fruit of Islam). HA! HAAAAH!

The only thing that remained the same in Dick's group was that I was intellectual Preacher John who got no pussy. Dick and company would mock me worse than the old Vons crowd. They often pulled rude childish pranks on me such as dog-piling on top of me, gang tackling, spits and punches, pulling my pants down, swindling me out of money during video game bets, and squeezing my nipples like they were homosexuals.

One time, they scared the hell out of me when they completely acted like gay men. During a drive home, they made obscene faces and said they were going to gang fuck me in the ass. I didn't take this seriously until they grabbed me inside Dick's house. As I pushed them away, I fell down. They were moaning and smirking like strip club customers as they grabbed my legs and pulled my pants off. I ran into the bathroom and locked the door. They continued laughing, "We're coming to get you." This was the only time in my life that I ever feared being raped. The guys stomped the door open and laughed hysterically saying, "Don't worry Al! We're not faggots!" I was not laughing and ran out of the house. T.R. threatened to beat my ass at first, but then gave me a football hug as he repeated that the mob was only joking.

I let this incident slide but soon lost tolerance for their crude pranks. I continued to get drunk and pursue pussy with them at parties before and after high school graduation. I was always at my stupid worst when I was drunk. Nobody could tolerate my company. I woke up a couple of times in the trunk of someone's car after feeling knocked out from hangovers. The guys smacked me around and mocked me more. I only put up with all their bullshit because I thought hanging out with them would get me laid.

As college approached for me, Dick and his mob acted more immature than ever. They told me stories of how they drove through various neighborhoods and threw eggs at people's cars. Then I mentioned how my parents saw broken eggs on Stephanie's Chevette. Dick questioned with denial, "So you think we did it?" I said I didn't know. I started to hang out with them less, and they sensed my distance. Father approached me one morning and said some young punks threw eggs at the house on the previous night. I told him I had friends who were egging people, and he told me not to hang around them anymore. I had no problem with this demand. Dick continued to call me and even showed up at the house offering to tag me along for pool parties with hot chicks. I turned him down and his mob said, "Good luck at college."

Since that moment, I ran into Dick one time while I was working at Vons after my freshman year in college. He smiled and yelled "A-Bear!" I only nodded. It was now clear that Dick's mob were not friends who I would ever associate with again.

I still pursued the mission of killing my virginity but would encounter even more danger.

Whenever Shorty's crew or Dick's mob were indisposed for cruising, I would hang out with a dark-skinned brother named Jerome. This cat and I had good conversations during class and on walks home from Western High School. He shared similar pro-Black intellectual concepts with me. Jerome was also a smart brother who finished high school a full semester ahead of schedule.

On the surface Jerome and I had a mature friendship, but I would soon learn the harsh reality of his cold and calm demeanor. Jerome was out to make money "by any means necessary." Initially, I perceived him as just a hard-working brother. He worked overnight stock shifts at Lucky's, a rival supermarket of Vons. Jerome also knew that I was struggling virgin, so he frequently scooped me up for journeys into his underworld.

On a sunny day off from school, Jerome drove us to the apartment of one of his girlfriends. She was a recovering crack-addicted white woman with two biracial kids. Jerome's plan was to have this woman's biracial friend babysit while he tapped her ass in her bedroom. While Jerome was getting busy, he intended for me to swoop in on the biracial female and get some pussy. I didn't feel comfortable with this setting, so all I did was strike a nice conversation with the lady and her neighbors while watching TV. Jerome was disappointed with my lack of play but was still gasping in the aftermath of his sexual performance. Then he proceeded to make some business calls.

This situation did not present evidence that Jerome was a drug dealer, so I proceeded to cruise with him. I eventually met his older brother Ray and his friends. They seemed cool but also carried the mentality to do whatever possible to make cash. Jerome used his car to help me on a double date one time, yet, it still resulted in no pussy. So he called on Ray and a cat named Bo-Bo to help me out.

Late one night, Jerome had some type of appointment. He dropped me off at Ray's place and told him to take me out. Ray and Bo-Bo first drove me to an apartment on 28th Street. I felt very nervous because 28th Street was a notorious area for Crips and Mexican gangs. Ray gave me a 40-ounce of Olde English (OE) and told me to drink it up so I could relax.

We arrived at the apartment and I drank half the bottle. A black woman who looked like she was at least in her mid-for-ties opened the door. Ray asked her if she would suck my dick. She angrily refused, pushed Ray away, and told us to leave. Ray said to her, "You may not suck dick now, but you've done it for me before."

Apparently, this woman was another crack-addict customer of his business. I was glad this "pussy attempt" failed because it made me feel dirty and cheap.

Bo-Bo and Ray were still determined to get me some, so they drove us to another project home on Donna Street in North Las Vegas. I finished the rest of the OE but was even more nervous since this location had a worse reputation for gang infestation and drug dealers. We entered this place, and I noticed a bunch of cigar and marijuana smoke along with black teenage boys with corn-rows playing dominoes. Ray, Bo-Bo, and I just sat down and settled here for the night. Two young men approached us and said, "You must be here to get your dick sucked." Bo-Bo told them that only I was there for that purpose. Bo-Bo also advised me on how I should spit game to one of the crack-addict hoes so she would eventually fuck me. I wasn't with this game, so I took a nap on the couch.

After awakening, I saw a group of five guys have a discussion over a piece of crack tinier than a penny. They seemingly found a product to sell. Then, I heard Ray speak with an older gentleman who looked at least fifty-five. The old man asked why Ray was picking up a product instead of Jerome. Ray gave him a false excuse. The elderly man directed us to leave the crack house, and Ray felt disappointed that he wasn't given a stash of weed to sell. Ray dropped me off back at my house. I said my thanks, and gave Bo-Bo a tic tac.

I was now fully convinced that Jerome's drug-dealing tasks were bad news for me. However, there was another night when we were supposed to hang out. Jerome arrived at my house at about one o'clock in the morning while I was asleep. I asked him why he was so late, and he told me that he had to help Bo-Bo out because he stabbed someone after a deal went sour. I told Jerome I was too tired to hang out. This was the last time we ever spoke to each other, but he did come by my house on the night before I flew off to college. I initially didn't know it was him until he drove off from the deck after knocking on the door. Nobody answered because we thought it was another one of my punk friends trying to cause trouble.

Overall, I have the best wishes possible for Jerome on this realm or the next. I don't have any bitterness from my time with him. I understand better why he was money hungry. He fathered a kid when he was only fifteen and wanted to provide better for the rest of his family back in Louisiana. But it was still best that I distanced myself from him and most of my high school friends.

The original Vons crowd stayed friends with me well into my college days before I lost touch with them.

Brody enlisted in the Marines after taking Fire Marshall courses at Clark County Community College. He was a good friend, but I allowed him to become distant from me as I engulfed on more militant pro-black philosophies in college. Brody angrily asked me in a heated discussion "Why are you going to a black college?" I told him I needed more exposure around black people to gain pride as a black man. This black pride made me view him in a racist light as a "white devil." I pray Brody is doing well today.

As for Shorty and Ronnie, I simply lost touch with them after college. I hung around with them often during semester breaks with further intentions of pussy pursuit.

Ronnie eventually married his high school sweetheart who also birthed his son, Ronnie, Jr. I hope his family is alive and happy today.

And as for my best friend from high school Shorty, I sincerely hope his life is not too overwhelming at this present time. He was the ladies' man of the initial crew. After he returned from army duty in the 1991 Persian Gulf War, he found himself in more drama with women. He fathered kids from at least three different females and divorced a woman on welfare who had five of her own kids. I tried to be a more positive influence to him by showing a video called "The African Origins of Civilization" by Ashra Kwesi. Shorty and his mother on the other hand only shunned me as an intellectual book worm that couldn't attract any females because he didn't know how to communicate with an angry father. This insulting reaction from them was upsetting but also true, so I proceeded to hang out with Shorty one last time in December, 1994.

Once again we hung out at his older brother's place. Shorty was drinking heavier than ever and would often recite rhymes while drunk. I drank a little myself but would always eat a lot of food beforehand so I wouldn't become drunk and stupid like I did during my high school days. Shorty invited over his current girlfriend along with one of her friends. While Shorty was getting busy, his brother smiled, "We've arranged it. You gonna get some ass tonight. I spoke with ole girl, and she likes you but didn't want to sound easy." I was very nervous. For some strange reason, my body was not in a horny mode even though this girl was laid out for me on the bathroom floor. I put on a condom and tried to penetrate her vagina but couldn't get it in. At first I thought I put the condom on wrong. So I put another one on upside down but still couldn't enter the pussy. The break of dawn arrived and I spoke with Shorty outside the house. I told him I couldn't enter the pussy and that it also stank. Shorty was very irate, so he gave me another condom, "My best friend ain't staying no virgin." I tried one last time to get laid. Again, I failed to go inside. I told the girl to get on top of me and suck my fingers. She did but still I was useless. I pre-maturely ejaculated and was immersed in shame.

Soon afterwards I had a conversation with Shorty's brother. Ironically, the same guy who literally dented his foot in my ass years back from one of my dumb drunk moments was now giving me pep talk. He counseled me, "Don't worry man. For some reason, God didn't want you to have sex. Honestly, I'd rather be in your position. Look at all the bitches and hoes Shorty and I fucked. One of us may have AIDS, while you have your whole life ahead of you..." Shorty's brother drove me home with more encouraging pep talk. I was still overwhelmed with humiliation. I asked him, "Was my dick too small to enter the pussy?" He said, "No. If anything it was too big. It's never too small." I found out later that my attempted sexual partner was on her menstrual cycle and was too tight for an inexperienced virgin like me to copulate. This girl had feelings for me, but I saw her as nothing more than another failed attempt at sex.

The next day, I spoke with Father about my sexual failure. He reassured me that it was nothing to be embarrassed about and went on to advise me on how to be responsible with condoms and women's feelings. He even demonstrated a condom's use with a banana. This was one of the few times in my life when I felt Father's communication with me was positively strong.

I last spoke with Shorty after Tupac Shakur was assassinated in Las Vegas. Shorty seemed to be more into God by this time. I, on the other hand, was more socially messed up than ever.

Overall, my intellectual personality resulted in less conversation with my high school friends. I hold no regrets about my time with them and hope to retrieve their contact information some day. Now I realize it was the divine plan set from the Universe for me to use my intellectual gift to embark on a more important soul search that would change my circle of friends for good.

LOVE CURSE

Before I entered college and distanced myself from the Vons crowd, I did manage to befriend two females.

On an early Saturday morning while working at Vons in 1990, Brody told me "This girl outside wants your phone number." I gave him the okay to pass it on.

A few days later, the girl called me and introduced herself as Keema. I asked her what she found interesting about me. She told me that she and her sister were selling candy bars outside the supermarket to raise money for the Upward Bound precollege program that they had membership in. Then she explained how she spotted me as a cute guy and told Brody to get my number. I was flattered by her attraction towards me, so I continued to have consistent phone conversations with her.

Keema didn't live very far from me, but she attended Valley High School on the outer side of town due to the busing regulations of integration for the mostly black Westside neighborhoods. Neither of us had cars initially, so we didn't meet each other until about two months after we first talked on the phone. I had no idea what she looked like but still projected a positive attitude toward our friendship.

We finally met in person when I persuaded Father to drop me off at her house one evening. Keema was shocked and amused at my unexpected arrival. My observation of her physique displayed her as a shy, dark-skinned, firm-bodied girl with black glasses. We chatted on her front porch and she said, "So now you see me. I'm dark." I said that looks didn't matter. I honestly didn't have a problem with her appearance, but I was not attracted to her romantically because it felt awkward for any girl to be deeply interested in me.

Consequently, Keema and I were only platonic. We often had extensive chats on the phone about our social lives. She relayed to me her sexual experiences, while I revealed my crush on a girl who worked at Dino's Pizza. One time Keema mentioned when a guy was ready to fuck her and how she held back because she thought about me. I didn't say a word while listening to this.

She continued to give me more signs that she loved me by sending me pictures of her with a note saying, "I hope you keep me in your dreams." I was still unmoved. I cared about her but not romantically.

Keema was finally given a car for her eighteenth birthday in October, 1990. Once she drove over to my house and brought her friend, Lita. As we all hung out in the living room, my cockapoo, Brandy, was running and hopping on the rug. Lita screamed and laughed in a goofy and frightening way. This marked my impression of her – a shy geeky girl who stimulated me sexually. She often wore mini-skirts that made me curious to explore what was between her thighs.

Another night, Keema drove us all to the movies. My dick was erect again over Lita wearing a mini-skirt in the winter. Sure Vegas can be warm during this season, but the wind-chill factor would usually make the city blistering cold. Regardless, I was horny and made advances to Lita while Keema sat in between us. After Keema dropped me off at home, I asked Lita for her phone number. She looked scared and shocked as her head bounced against the refrigerator. I sensed she was attracted to me, and I felt that I had too easy of an opportunity to get laid.

However, I still couldn't drive a car.

I wouldn't let my vehicular handicap hold me back, so I arranged a double date with my friend Jerome. My plan to snuggle up with Lita was executed well. Jerome cooled out with Keema and kissed her goodnight while I locked my tongue down Lita's throat and turned her out after we saw a movie. Lita called me the next day and in her shy, goofy tone asked, "What is in the air between us?" I just said something like, "Anything we want."

Lita and I hardly dated since both of us didn't drive, but we often ran into each other and smooched. She worked part-time at the West Las Vegas Library, and I often went there to read and check out black history books. When I spotted her, I persuaded her to kiss me even though she was uncomfortable doing that on the job. I put enough tongue caresses on her to leave her lurking for me.

June called me a dog for leading Lita on during one moment and then calling other girls afterwards. I couldn't disagree, but I was only acting out of influence from peers and family members who treated women as expendable playthings.

Despite my "dogging" affection towards Lita, I asked her to the senior prom. Initially, I asked my best female friend, Keema, but she told me to take Lita, so I continued planning this way.

Lita eventually called me frantically saying, "I've never felt this way before about anyone. I don't know what it is. It must be love." I laughed silently in my mind as I sensed I had further power to eventually fuck her. So I ended the phone conversation by telling her, "I love you." Of course this was a lie.

This lie led to rejecting fallout from peers and family when I told them I'm taking Lita to the prom. Father led the "Prom Filibuster" by whining, "How can you take an ugly girl to the prom? You're going to regret having pictures with her for the rest of your life." Father continued his disapproval by making obscure facial gestures mocking Lita's buck-toothed overbite.

June and Mother joined in the mockery by suggesting I should take a better looking girl to the prom.

My "Prom Filibuster" received more fire when Dick and his mob said they weren't going because they didn't feel it was worth the money. My best friends Shorty, Brody, and Jerome didn't go to their senior proms either. I started to see their points since I was rejected after I asked a girl to the homecoming dance. I thought, "I need to keep saving for college. There's no guarantee I'll get any pussy and it ain't worth three hundred dollars or more anyways." Therefore, I told Lita I couldn't afford the prom and sat it out. They went to their prom at Valley High School with their girlfriends instead. Father boasted, "At least I won't have to look at pictures of an ugly girl."

Even though I shamefully dissed Lita for the big dance, she still wanted to kick it with me. I arranged for Dick to pick her up from her house and hang out with us at the place of one of his girlfriends. I felt intimidated because Dick was making out with a girl who I liked. He already had a girlfriend but sat in a closer position to this girl on a previous night when we hung out. He snuggled up against her and had her interest for sex.

While Dick was playing touchy-feely games with his prospect, I rubbed up against Lita on the couch. I had condoms in my wallet and asked her if she wanted to go upstairs. She started to follow me, but the girlfriend of Dick's friend, T.R., interceded and said "No guys allowed in my parents' room." I was annoyed and humiliated. Dick added to this insulting moment by saying, "Look if you want to make out bad enough you can go to the bathroom or the car." By this time my horny mood was ruined. I wanted to fuck Lita badly but not bad enough to make my sexual experience into a pointless fling. We all just hung loose for the rest of the night. Dick drove Lita home and she kissed me goodnight. I didn't put any tongue into the exchange because I was hugely disappointed that I didn't score. Dick was mad that I had him drive into the Westside ghetto to pick up a goofy girl that I failed to fuck. He said, "She's as skinny as wires and dark as tires."

I guess it was poetic justice that I flunked this attempt at losing my virginity. Deep down, I still wanted my first time to be special. I give thanks that I didn't take advantage of Lita in a worse way. Yet she is still the only female I ever seriously mistreated. Treating one female badly is mistreating one too many.

So lo and behold, my deceitful demeanor towards Lita started a curse that would hinder my relationships with females permanently. It's often said in witchcraft that any spell you cast will come back on you three-fold. This wasn't further from the truth as I would end up falling in love with more than three women who didn't love me.

For all the pain I endured, which is revealed later in this book, I can now honestly say that I'm sorry for lying to Lita and hurting her the way I did. Lita seemed to forgive me when she wrote me a letter in college revealing her engagement to a wonderful man. I was happy for her.

I was also shocked to learn more disturbing news from Keema. She ended up pregnant and moved into the Gerson Park Housing Projects (located next to where Father was presently working). I visited her there during the summer after my freshman year in college. Keema was in good spirits and said she wasn't getting married even though her "babydaddy" asked her to. She also told me that Lita had an abortion right before she graduated from high school. If this was true, then perhaps Lita wasn't deeply infatuated with me like I had thought. Regardless, I ended up playing myself into a social rut with women. Perhaps if I had been a better friend to Keema, she wouldn't have become a single mother at a very young age. I pray that she and her family are doing well today, and I am still working on breaking the love curse from my phony relationship with Lita.

RAP UPRISING TO HISTORY— LOST, STOLEN, OR STRAYED

My initial research into racism and Black History would spawn my proudest high school memory.

At home, Father indulged in alcohol and expressed his frustrations about his general manager position at KCEP radio. He often ranted about how this black station was dictated by a redneck white woman trustee who only listened to country music. Father's outrage spread to me when he chewed me out for not knowing the historical struggles of black people. During one sunny afternoon, Father yelled out, "*Have you ever read up on your history? Do you know what Jackie Robinson went through? Fans poured beer on him…. called him a nigger…. and threatened to kill him. Do you know who Satchel Paige was? How could you not know? Satchel Paige was the greatest athlete ever. No one else comes close. You need to understand the struggles he went through before he was allowed to play in the major leagues. Do you know how our people have fought for our rights, been beaten, and even killed? Read up on your history!*"

At first, I didn't understand why Father stressed this on me. Now I recognize that the reason stemmed from his encounters with racism in the broadcasting industry. On frequent occasions, he was passed up for jobs because he was black. He resigned from Channel 3 News in 1984 with an out-of-court settlement after he threatened to sue them for racial discrimination.

This angry foray from out of the blue sparked my journey into Black History.

I started by reading *They Dared to Lead: America's Black Athletes* by Phyllis and Zander Hollander. This book provided insight on black athletes such as Jackie Robinson, Bill Russell, Pete Brown, Muhammad Ali, Althea Gibson, and many more. The book had sat unread in my bedroom for several years until Father's research plea.

I received more motivation to read Black History from the politically charged lyrics of several rap artists.

First I heard a song called "Why Is That?" by Boogie Down Productions (BDP) in which KRS-1 rapped about how major biblical characters (Noah, Shem, Ham, twelve tribes of Israel, Moses, and Jesus) were members of the black race. Weeks later, I purchased BDP's album called *The Blue Print of Hip-Hop* and was inspired by more of their knowledge-teaching songs and albums such as "You Must Learn" and *Edutainment.*

From this point forward, I listened to mostly socially conscious hardcore rap music.

I also purchased the audio cassette of Public Enemy's *Fear of a Black Planet.* On their song, "Welcome to the Terrordome," Chuck D rhymed, *"The shootin' of Huey Newton, from the hand of a nig that pulled the trig."* Out of curiosity, I asked Father, "Who was Huey P. Newton?" Father told me that Huey Newton was the co-founder of the Black Panther Party (BPP) along with a man named Bobby Seale. He also told me that Huey Newton was killed in an Oakland, California alley fight in 1989.

This info added to my curiosity. I was very disturbed that my eleventh grade history book contained only one sentence about the BPP as well as only one paragraph about Malcolm X and the Nation of Islam, and only a page about Martin Luther King and the Civil Rights Movement.

Since I felt the school system was too racist to teach me about blacks, I started checking out "black" books (fictional and historical) from the West Las Vegas Library. First I read several depictions about the BPP including *Soul on Ice* by Eldridge Cleaver and *Revolutionary Suicide* by Huey Newton. Next , I read books that included speeches by black leaders—W.E.B. DuBois, William Monroe Trotter, Ida B. Wells-Barnett, Frederick Douglass, Booker T. Washington, Angela Davis, H. Rap Brown (Imam Jamil Abdulla Al-Amin), Ralph Bunche, and others. Then I read several novels by black authors including *Native Son* by Richard Wright, *Giovanni's Room* by James Baldwin, and *Invisible Man* by Ralph Ellison. Finally, I read *The Autobiography of Malcolm X* by Alex Haley and felt a burning desire to dedicate myself to black causes and awareness.

My awareness heightened when I purchased Paris' album *The Devil Made Me Do It*. This cassette featured a series of songs and summaries praising the Black Power Movements of Malcolm X, the BPP, and the Nation of Islam while scorning racism in the White Power Structure of the U.S. Government. The raw fury of these songs as well as my observance of music videos by X-Clan filled me with angry glee as I was happy to hear militant stories with positives about black perseverance.

On the flipside, I became more upset about the negative stigmas of blacks in the media.

During July 1990, there was an incident that predated the controversial 1991 videotaped police beating of Rodney King. An unarmed black man named Charles Bush was strangled to death by three white Las Vegas police officers. These cops were working undercover and dressed in plain clothes during the incident. News outlets also reported that Charles Bush apparently thrusted at the cops in an attack mode because he didn't know who they were when they busted his apartment door open while he was asleep. In the end the three cops were acquitted of manslaughter charges due to a mistrial stemming from an 11-1 not guilty verdict handed down by an all-white jury. Vegas' black community was so outraged that they called on Minister Louis Farrakhan to speak at Cashman Field months later. I was very excited because Father gave Mother and me front-row tickets to attend this rally. Father also gave me an autographed signature of Min. Farrakhan wishing me "Peace, Love, and Success" after he interviewed him for the radio. I thoroughly enjoyed his poised militant tone as he recited a message of "Stop the Killings," encouraging an end to injustice against blacks and black-on-black crime.

I was further inspired by this black unity message while watching rappers collectively preach against black-on-black crime in the music videos "Self Destruction" and "We're All in the Same Gang."

Initially, I was confused by how some of these same rappers who bragged about their gangbanger lifestyles could then boast about "peace amongst brothers." While listening to Public Enemy and BDP, I also paid attention to the violent raunchiness of N.W.A. and the Geto Boys. Even though their songs glamorized criminal behavior, they still gave me a more "realistic" depiction of "urban" life than the mainstream media. N.W.A.'s "Fuck Tha Police" increased my awareness of racism and police brutality in black neighborhoods. And despite their psychotic rhyme overtones, the Geto Boys still stressed an importance for black-owned business in their song "No Sell Out."

I understood all these black messages far too clearly when gang violence reaped at school.

On the first day of my senior year in high school, a student was fatally shot at Eldorado High School. Even though this incident was outside my school, all Las Vegas high schools were being monitored more restrictively.

One week later, a fight broke out right outside my homeroom class. The end result was two guys stomping a heavy-set male. But later in the day, someone told me that a kid got stabbed in this same gang-related brawl. This was confirmed when I saw news cameras swarming the campus.

The fallout from this fight and the Eldorado shooting led to all varsity high school sporting events starting no later than 4:30pm with required entrances through security guards and metal detectors. Sure there was gang infestation at Western High, but I didn't think it affected me because I knew I wasn't a gangster. Some of my classmates however, bragged about their affiliation with the Crips. Lo and behold, I was searched one day by a school cop for looking "suspicious" in my blue L.A. Dodgers' jacket. Gang violence really hit home when the brothers of June's friends, named Todd Ramos and Chris Williams, were killed in drive-by shootings.

I tried to understand black violence better after observing school fights where scores of black guys would beat down outnumbered white guys. From my perspective, blacks were often angry and unfriendly because either they or their neighborhood friends were bused all over town to separate schools. Meanwhile, white kids, who these same blacks were forced to integrate with, were privileged to attend schools with their neighborhood friends.

I was also bothered by the fact that I was the only black male in Western High's Honor Society and Math Club.

So after two years of being just a master-of-ceremony standout in Western's Annual Black History Shows, I decided to recite a speech based on quotes from Public Enemy, Minister Farrakhan and the book *Black History: Lost, Stolen, or Strayed* by Otto Lindenmeyer. I spoke the following words:

Black History: Lost, Stolen, or Strayed was a book written by Otto Lindenmeyer to show people how significant parts of history have been hidden or distorted. An example of this is when you hear certain groups say something like, "Oh, you niggers have done nothing but bring this country down. You take our tax money for welfare. You sell drugs in our streets, and you're endangering society." Now when I hear this, I'm just as appalled as you are. But what upsets me (the most) is how untrue this statement is.

If black people have brought down and are still bringing down this country, then explain how we've poured our religion, our culture, our music, art, dance, poetry, and our blood, sweat, and tears into the United States of America. Doesn't black music reflect American culture? Was it not our music that started and helped to make America's sound? Was it not our dance as well as our poetry and art that helped build culture in this society? Was it not our blood that helped to build the economy, win wars, and keep this country as so-called "free?" What I'm really asking is, "Where's the credit?"

Black music helped to revolutionize rock'n'roll and music as we know it today. Where's the credit? Our art reflects American culture. For example, the clothes that a lot of you wear, the shoes on your feet, and various designs and paintings come from African culture. Jan Matzeliger invented the last machine responsible for the manufacturing of the shoes you wear today. Where's the credit? Our dance is responsible for the dancing of yesterday and today which show up in the Charleston, the Twist, tap music, disco, hip-hop, the Running Man, the Roger Rabbitt, and many other dances. Where's the credit? Our poetry with authors like Langston Hughes, Paul H. Robison, and W.E.B. Dubois reflects American literature. Where's the credit? Our ancestors slaved for hundreds of years to make this country into the economic power it is today. NOW, where's the credit? Our people fought and died with their blood, sweat, and tears in every war America has been involved in. And don't forget the Persian Gulf War going on right now where our brothers are over there suffering, will come home, and probably still say, "Where's the credit to the flag?" (The crowd stood up and applauded for a whole minute). Even today, we pour our tax money and our SOOOOOOUL into making this country as great as it is today. So, where is the credit? Where's the pay back? Not even a simple "40 acres and a mule, Jack? Where is it? Why you try to fool the Black?" Now listen to me closely as I (continue to) quote a very famous rap group (Public Enemy), "It wasn't you, but you pledge allegiance to the red, white, and blue. Suckers that stole the soul."

That's right! Blacks were robbed and raped of their native homeland, their religion, their culture, language, name (Akeemulan), identity, history, or you could just say that someone "stole the soul." (Of course) We were also robbed of our credit. Charles Drew built the blood bank system. Norbert Rillieux built the sugar evaporating pan. Matthew Henson was one of the five people who first made it to the North Pole. Danielle Hale Williams was the first to perform open heart surgery. Garret Morgan made the traffic lights, and with all of this, I ask again, "Where is the credit?" You see now that black history has been "lost, stolen, or strayed." It is so distorted that it even shows up in everyone's so called family name. My name isn't really Johnson. It was most likely a name given to me by some slave master. So very likely your name isn't Smith, or Brown, or White, or whatever name you have. My whole point is that you shouldn't lose touch with your African roots, which have also been distorted.

So, Black History helps us to never lose touch of our history or our past. Or else we'll never be able to make it through the future. Hopefully one day, history won't be a mystery and there won't be a need to try and learn one's past all in (just)

one week. So we need to keep searching for information hidden from us.
   THANK YOU!

When this speech was done, the audience roared to their feet clapping with shock and awe. Most people that knew me, even Father, couldn't believe that this shy intellectual kid came across like Malcolm X. There was even some controversy when I quoted Public Enemy from their song "Who Stole the Soul?" The teacher/advisor for that show told me not to mention the name of the rap group who I quoted because they had affiliation with L.A. Crips. I told this woman she mistook Public Enemy for N.W.A. . She still whined that gangs are spread out all over the country, so I couldn't mention their group name without the school administration shutting down the Black History Program on a permanent basis.

Despite their dumbfounded fears of gang violence, I only mentioned my quote from "a very famous rap group" during the speech. Yet, I still got scolded following my speech because the advisor said that "40 acres and a mule" is not accredited history. First I was amused that my speech was introduced with a school disclaimer, "*Lost, Stolen, or Strayed* does not represent the views of Western High School." HA HAAAH! In the end though, I was irate that my black advisors acted like "Aunt Jemima sell-outs."

This disturbance only fueled my fire further as I continued my radical pro-black tone by writing a research paper for my English Literature class called "Is America a Democracy for Blacks?" I included the following books as references: *Black Robes, White Justice* by Bruce Wright, *From Plantation to Ghetto* by August Meir and Elliot Radwick, and *Black Power* by Stokely Carmichael and Charles V. Hamilton. I was inspired to write this paper by a female who participated with me in the Black History Show. She used a copy of my speech to reference her research paper entitled "Should Blacks Separate from America?" With all this info compiled, I generally stated that America has been mostly an apartheid-type caste system for blacks and that perhaps blacks should form a separate nation until America displays consistent justice. I even quoted KRS-1 from one of BDP's songs where he called America "The Land of the Thief, Home of the Slave."

In addition to my growing prejudice of white capitalism, I rejected recruitment offers from the military. First, the U.S. National Guard offered me service pay along with college tuition money. This sounded good until the Marines came with a more aggressive offer. I was ready to sign up for their reserve program, but another recruiter told me that I needed to enlist full-time to get the gist of their program. Afterwards, I spoke with Father about this, and he was furious. He literally hated the Marine Corp and said that they were macho idiots who were the first in line to be killed in wars. Marine recruiters called Father, but he told them to fuck off. Father then explained to me that Mother would not stay with him if I was ever sent off to war. Despite my parents' rejection of my military contemplations, a Marine recruiter still called me at home. I told him I'd think about it but eventually ignored him as I developed the notion used by the character Furious Styles in the 1991 movie *Boyz N The Hood*, "*A Black Man has no place in Uncle Sam's army.*" My army buddy Shorty seconded this emotion after he returned from Saudi Arabia.

With this separatist attitude, I was committed to attending a black college. I felt that I needed to be surrounded with most, if not anything but black folks, if I were to prosper as a black man in the white man's world.

I received more endorsements to attend a black college when June and Stephanie pleaded for me to leave the house run by our drama-filled parents. Both of my sisters graduated from UNLV but said that I would be better off out of Vegas. Judging from my parents' behavior, they were right.

Father's temper tirades continued abruptly. He sank deeper into drunkenness, unemployment, and abusive behavior. One day he was so depressed over his job status that he grabbed and threw Mother from the truck after trying to make her stay home from work. Mother hit the ground hard and broke her arm. She missed work for several weeks. Father also threatened to commit suicide on at least three different occasions. He was so down on himself that he even called the police and paramedics to rescue him a few times. I least forget the time when he tackled me and spit in my face after June and I joked about killing him. Plus, I remember him chasing after Mother when he was drunk and wearing nothing but his underpants. June and I often covered up and lied about these stories to protect the household from negative press and bill collectors.

Clearly, I had enough drama from my household and peers in Vegas. Therefore, I sought refuge from abuse and racism at a black college. Little did I know that this experience would add to my already tainted cycle instead of providing relief.

BLACK COLLEGE

June's boyfriend, Dominic, accepted a full scholarship to attend a small and relatively unknown Historically Black College and University (HBCU) called Fayetteville State University (FSU). Initially, he told everyone he was going to Duke since it was a familiar North Carolina school. However, his uncle from Monroe, North Carolina informed him about the small college in Fayetteville, NC. Dominic attended the University and thus became an honor student there. He knew I was interested in attending an HBCU, so he sent me a registration package.

Originally, I wanted to attend Howard University (HU) because of their reputation as "the black Harvard." Plus, Stephanie's husband, Damon, worked as a security guard there. HU accepted me but offered no financial aid. I also applied to a small school outside of Los Angeles, California called Woodbury University. They offered me a half-paid scholarship. I vowed I wasn't going out-of-state unless all of my tuition was granted.

It appeared I was going to attend the University of Nevada, Las Vegas (UNLV) until I received a phone call from a man named Mr. Burlington. He told me my ACT score of 22 qualified me for a full scholarship. I jumped for joy and boasted, "I'm going to Fayetteville."

To confirm my acceptance, I had to sign their acceptance letter. My "full-ride" appeared intact until I read a clause stating that my FSU scholarship was full at an "in-state rate." This meant that I would have to pay the difference of out-of-state fees minus in-state tuition. Again, I thought for sure I was staying in Vegas. Yet Dominic and Mr. Burlington assured me that financial aid would cover the rest of my fees. Dominic told me, "Don't worry! Most of the scholarship recipients are white. They won't let a good black student like you go astray." Plus, June and Stephanie encouraged me more to get away. Therefore, I packed up and flew to the city nicknamed "Fayette-nam."

Fayette-nam was Fayetteville's moniker because this city is home to the two largest military bases in the world—Fort Bragg (U.S. Army Base) and Pope Air Force Base. Ain't it ironic how I passionately turned away offers from the military but still ended up going to college in a military town?

My first view of FSU was a run-down boys' dormitory called Vance Hall. Dominic stayed in this dorm situated for mostly jocks and upper-classmen. I stayed in Dominic's room through my first night at FSU.

I was subsequently assigned to the other male dorm called Bryant Hall. This complex was slightly cleaner than Vance Hall, but it still had living conditions similar to urban housing projects. Several bedroom windows were cracked and the bathrooms contained several unsanitary conditions including: leaky and rusty ceilings, grimy sinks and showers, bugs running rampant on the floors, no toilet paper, and frequently out-of-service payphones. Of course I was disgusted, but I allowed myself to adjust for the betterment of my "black" education.

As I settled into Bryant Hall, I met my roommate, Timothy Jessie. Tim was a model country boy scholar from Lumberton, NC. He was voted "most likely to succeed" by his senior class when he graduated as valedictorian. He frequently went home on weekends to help his mother and younger brother with house duties. As one can tell, he was an astutely responsible young man. With this trait explained, it's easy to say that Tim and I got along great. We rarely had arguments. When we did though, we resolved our differences like gentlemen. Tim and I ended up as roommates for all of our four years attending FSU. We also got involved as teammates in many of the same campus organizations.

Before I got involved with FSU's extracurricular activities, I was known as the kid from Vegas. I hated revealing my hometown to classmates because they always reacted with dumbfounded shock, "Vegas? Why did you come all the way out here? Why didn't you go to UNLV? What the hell are you doing on another side of the world? You're a long way from home!"

Indeed I was far from home. I became increasingly homesick during my freshman year as I discovered more about FSU's campus culture.

One of the first events I attended before class started was a Marcus Garvey tribute. It started off with little kids performing a dramatization of their plea for a white teacher to conduct lessons about Marcus Garvey. Then, there were lectures by an FSU professor, an Afro-Islam guru named Jakim, and an FSU alumnus named Val. I was disturbed when Val mentioned that FSU's campus appeared dead at the present moment compared to four or five years prior when the student population had "only a handful of white folks." This statement signaled that the black college I enrolled in wasn't so black after all. Dominic informed me that classes are usually populated with fifty percent whites, but blacks make up ninety-five percent of the on-campus residents. I became even more disturbed during the ceremony when an audience member said how white students use FSU like a community college before they enroll at larger mostly-white schools like UNC-Chapel Hill. Once the presentation ended, I felt more compelled to do more in helping FSU preserve its "blackness."

I thought my struggles with racism were over, but they were just beginning.

As I attended class and familiarized myself more with FSU, I also learned that this school used to have a bad academic reputation. Various classmates and teachers told me that people used to joke about how a person was only required to take a "mirror test" to be accepted to FSU. But according to my scholarship advisors, FSU's academic stance was vastly gaining respect under the leadership of Chancellor Lloyd V. Hackley, who started his tenure in the fall semester of 1988. Dr. Hackley was the most famous person at FSU as well as one of the most popular chancellors in the whole UNC college system. Sometimes, I thought he was famous because he was a close friend of U.S. President Bill Clinton. Clinton used to supervise Dr. Hackley when he was Arkansas' governor, while Dr. Hackley served as chancellor of the University of Arkansas-Pine Bluff. In actuality, Dr. Hackley was famous because he used statistician techniques to display FSU's yearly progress of improved grade point averages (GPAs), faculty and student retention, and scholarship recipients. From a multicultural perspective, this info was magnificent, but to young party-seeking pro-black students and Afrocentric teachers, this was an outrage. Dr. Hackley was often labeled an Uncle Tom for "making FSU more white while improving its academic reputation." I followed these sentiments from much of the student body and decided that it was time for me to be fully involved in preserving FSU's heritage.

Thus I became a staff writer on FSU's student newspaper, *Broncos' Voice*.

When I first entered the *Broncos' Voice* office at the student center, I met a jet ebony-toned woman who had a short afro, a slightly heavyset stomach, and a Bohemian dashiki-styled outfit. This woman introduced herself as Barbara Beebe. I quickly stated that I was interested in writing for the newspaper because I was concerned about FSU losing its grip on black culture. Barbara then asked me questions from an opposing viewpoint such as, "Do you know that there are black students who are also using FSU as a community college stepping stone?" I was speechless as she continued with her onslaught. She reiterated, "See! I'm going to challenge you to look at situations from all viewpoints."

Indeed Barbara posed challenging tasks to me. Myself, along with Tim and a militant English major named Will, wrote an abundance of articles dealing with racism and miseducation. Some of my articles were "Remembering the BPP (Black Panther Party)," "Tales from the Darkside of Movies, "Experiences with Miseductation," and "Review of PE (Public Enemy): The Enemy Strikes Black CD." Before these pieces were printed, Barbara frequently gave them edit overhauls and constantly chewed out my writing style. Often I was frustrated with her, but I grew to appreciate her demand for first class journalism.

Will had more of a burning desire to act with solutions to miseducation. He founded an organization with his roommate, Tom, called MASK (Males Achieving Success through Knowledge).

I was criticized by Will and Tom as well but proud enough to work under their vision. I was still offended when they told me, "You ain't black!" They said that I talked too much about Black History and not enough like a loose-fit social "nigga." I couldn't disagree as they emphasized, "Get a 4.0 (GPA), but don't be a 4.0.." Although this was inspirational, I still felt it was unfair to label me not black enough for not talking slang or for eating fried chicken with napkins. Nevertheless, I overcame my differences with them. Two years later, I helped them to tutor junior high school students from a local Baptist church.

By the end of my freshman year, I achieved a 4.0 GPA but was very disgruntled. Only part of my out-of-state tuition difference was paid by grants and work-study. The rest was paid by loans. I was more insulted when FSU's administration offered me a "Chancellor's Scholar of Distinction" award. I bluntly refused. I wrote about my bitter financial woes in an article titled "Full Scholarships (for in-state students only)." Several classmates asked if I planned to return to FSU. I told them I would even though I really wasn't sure. In addition to licking my chops over FSU's partial scholarship, I regretted turning down Woodbury University's half scholarship after they offered me grants to cover the other half of their tuition cost.

Before my sophomore year started, I sensed that I would somehow stay in Vegas. I didn't have desire to return to a school that treated a scholar like me as a secondary student. Plus, I knew several high school classmates who had bad experiences with Black Colleges and transferred back to UNLV. My fears were seemingly confirmed when I received my fall semester 1992 letter of Financial Aid. I was awarded some grants but no loans. Even though I received a scholarship from Mother's workplace, J.C. Penney, it still wouldn't be enough to cover the rest of the expenses. I was in shock that I was seemingly destined not to go back to FSU.

Father though looked at the finances and said, "You're going (back)!" I threw a temper tantrum stating that he couldn't afford it and I was tired of their bullshit anyways. Father kept stressing that I need to stay in school and not allow myself to be drawn out into a possible 5-8 year college student. The rest of my immediate family agreed. Before I adhered to their view, I locked myself in my bedroom and cried my eyes out. Father came in later scolding to me that FSU wasn't my problem before yelling, "It's your attitude (that's the problem). Sure the system sucks, but you're going to have to learn to deal with it ..." As I screamed in more rage, Father left my room encouraging me to "Let it out!" So I punched a hole in the wall and felt a humble relief. I grabbed Father by the back of his neck in a manly hug and told him, "You'd better be damn sure you can pay for this shit." He emotionally assured me he would. Father really didn't have the funds to pay for my education, but he repeatedly told me not to worry about the money. His confidence emerged as a self-fulfilling prophecy when a new Presidential Bill allowed college students from all economic backgrounds to apply for emergency PLUS loans. This funded the rest of my time at FSU. It's amazing how Father initially tried to talk me out of going to a black college but was now my staunchest supporter.

I still returned to FSU as a very angry student. Major portions of my grants were reduced since the J.C. Penney scholarship was an out-of-school scholarship. Plus, my classmates adopted similar negative attitudes about FSU's bureaucracy. I often heard rumors about FSU's black population filling transfer applications to other schools. I considered doing the same but decided instead to become fully involved in campus life.

I continued with the *Broncos' Voice* for a brief period before operations collapsed. Barbara graduated and left the paper in the hands of a white conservative student. Internal feuding amongst staff members and administrative bureaucracy left the paper in limbo my entire sophomore year, and so I moved on to other activities.

Since I majored in Accounting, I joined FSU's Accounting Society. I attended professional seminars and participated in their community food donation project called S.H.A.R.E.. My affiliation with fellow Accounting majors subsequently helped me obtain widespread interviews with major corporations and Big 6 Accounting firms during the October, 1994 convention of N.A.B.A. (National Association of Black Accountants). Eventually, one of these companies hired me two months after graduation out of their intrigue by my honorable resume.

Meanwhile back at school, I experimented deeper into campus life.

I thought about pledging a fraternity. It seemed to be the cool thing to do for college students. Plus, my sisters wanted me to join one badly because they felt it would toughen my social manly skills. I didn't consider pledging Omega Psi Phi because they had a reputation for acting like dogs. Kappa Alpha Psi came across as cane-juggling pretty boys. Then I attended a recruitment meeting by Alpha Phi Alpha. Seemingly, I was suppose to become one of them since their sister sorority was Alpha Kappa Alpha, of which both of my sisters belonged. Yet, I perceived them as arrogant intellectuals. So finally, I appeared ready to join Phi Beta Sigma. By destiny though, they decided not to have a recruitment line in the spring semester. They also interviewed me with questions about hazing. Their stance came across to me as college gangsters. Thus, I never went on line. Close friends of mine also told me that I was better off looking for an Afrocentric-based brotherhood rather than become a "pseudo black Greek." FSU also had social fellowships like Groove Phi Groove and Beta Phi Beta, but their branded skin made me think that they were worse than the Greeks.

Following my black Greek trial run, I moved on to the Student Government Association (SGA). My roommate, Tim, helped me with my campaign for SGA Business Manager by drawing catchy pictures of me posing as Malcolm X with a machine gun. I came up with a slogan saying it was time for FSU "to safeguard your assets by any means necessary." This attention grabber along with my opponent's dropout got me elected.

I felt confident going into this position since I served as treasurer of my ninth grade student body, and I was good at accounting. Plus, I was contracted for more than $150 per month that would be used as work study towards tuition. Little did I know what disasters I would face!

FSU had a troubled history of producing homecoming concerts. Black colleges were often placed in high regards by their students according to party success. With FSU being no different, setting up a concert was the SGA's initial goal. The officers and I negotiated with a couple of promoters, but we felt they were crooked. We decided to postpone concert planning until after Homecoming '93. While we were setting up other homecoming functions, I received a call from a promoter in South Carolina. He told me he could get FSU three or four acts for free. I was so excited that I set up a meeting between him, the SGA, and FSU's Vice Chancellor of Student Affairs, Dr. B. The promoter told me the meeting was a success and was certain the contract would be signed. Excited, I pre-announced a concert headlined by 2Pac over the student center intercom and was ready to announce it at FSU's homecoming comedy show.

Before the headliner comedian came on stage at Seabrook Auditorium, I ran up the stairs anxious to grab the microphone. I quickly asked Dr. B if the concert was set. He told me it wasn't but that it was close to being enacted. I didn't listen and proceeded to tell the student body that 2Pac was set to perform in November. I got booed by them because they were still pissed off about a concert not taking place during Homecoming.

Despite not having a concert, Homecoming '93 turned out okay.

Soon after, I received a nauseating phone call from the promoter. He told me that negotiations had broken down between him and Dr. B and that it was time for his company to move on. Suddenly, I felt like vomiting for telling FSU there was going to be a concert. This was the sickest moment of my life.

I didn't know how to publicly explain this to the whole student body. So I planned on telling the SGA Senate. Before I could speak, Dr. B showed up and broke down an explanation of the contract negotiations. The Senate reacted with shock by stating that they didn't know about the details of this offer. I tried to state my reasons for not initially approaching them but the SGA Secretary exploded into a temper tantrum and yelled at a Senator in my defense. By the end of this meeting, everyone agreed that FSU needed legal assistance before ever planning future shows. Even though I felt like a jackass, no one publicly prosecuted me. When 2Pac was arrested in Atlanta, Georgia for allegedly shooting two cops, FSU's student body officially knew no concert would occur.

I survived this fiasco, helped the SGA produce weekly spring parties, and was elected un-opposed as Business Manager of the newly created organization called the Student Activities Council (SAC). This group was formed to take entertainment pressure off the SGA. Once again, though, the primary focus of my job was to bring a concert to FSU.

I started calling various concert promoters during summer '94 and convinced my roommate Tim to design a t-shirt to model my Wu-Tang Clan-inspired slogan "FSU Ain't Nothin' to Buck Wit." The results of Homecoming '94 were—1) FSU's Administration got involved and signed a contract with the William Morris Agency three months prior to the concert to promote a show featuring Queen Latifah, Zhané, and Fu-Schnickens. 2) The concert flopped with an attendance of approximately two hundred people at a facility with a six thousand-seat capacity. 3) T-shirt sales were poorly organized and delegated by both SAC and FSU's Administration. And 4) FSU lost approximately $31,000 to homecoming expenses and was left with a scarce budget for student activities for the academic year of 1994-95.

I was staunchly depressed over my failures to bring FSU an uprise in school spirit. So I released my frustration by writing a truthful account of the Homecoming '94 disaster in a *Broncos' Voice* article titled "No Buck$ Left for the Broncos."

Realistically, I didn't fully redeem my spirit from these disappointments until years later. However, I still did a good job of marketing my success at and beyond FSU.

I was proud to convince the SGA to assist on a charitable bone marrow donor drive called African-Americans Uniting for Life.

My proudest moments at FSU occurred as an alternate teammate on the Honda Campus All-Star Challenge quiz bowl team. This was the only activity where I was able to put my stubborn racial pro-black mentality behind me. Dennis, the white guy on our team who was also a part-time starter, was my roommate at a Greensboro, North Carolina hotel. Ironically, I was a roaring fan of his when the tournament officials unfairly disqualified him from a match that nearly cost our team a chance at the finals.

Tim was team captain of FSU's quiz bowl team for three years. He persuaded me to get involved during my junior year. This was the year that FSU finished second at the Southeast Regional Tournament and qualified as one of the eight teams to compete for the championship in Hollywood, California. FSU lost in the first round but we were just happy to be in L.A.. We were catered to several fun activities hosted by famous black entertainers including Glynn Turman, Larenz Tate, Jada Pinkett, Dawnn Lewis, Terry McMilan, Tichina Arnold, Vanessa Bell Armstrong, and more. Ironically, commentary paragraphs written by Tim and me about the whole quiz bowl tournament were selected to be used as promotional clips for Black Entertainment Television (BET). This was the first time in my life where I felt like a Hollywood actor.

During my senior year, I qualified as a part-time starter on the quiz bowl team. This time, FSU finished one win shy of competing for a trip to the Quarterfinals. Despite this disappointing finale, I was proud of myself for putting my ego aside and participating with a successful team that was diverse in race and gender.

The icing of my success cake at FSU came when I graduated Magna Cum Laude with a 3.73 GPA in May, 1995.

Two days before the ceremony, the Registrar's office told me to see my academic advisor before I could be placed on the graduation list. I was fuming and ready to kill someone. By the time I found my advisor and returned to the office, they placed me on the list citing a mix-up with credits approved from a summer internship I participated in two years prior. Even though FSU didn't announce me as an honor student during the graduation ceremony, I was relieved just to be out of school. All I wanted at this point was to work in the "real world."

I wasn't prepared for the real world to hit me hard despite some warnings. My professor from a Critical Thinking course twice suggested that I major in something different because I seemed more passionate about writing for the newspaper than becoming an accountant. Eventually he proved to be right, but I didn't listen because I only wanted to be out of school in four years. I did almost every possible activity at college except find my true purpose in life. I tried too hard to be an all-good purposeful black male. I still didn't lose my virginity and was twenty-one years old when I first masturbated.

All my pent-up frustration would not be released until I became a DJ. Who would have thought that a clean-cut, high yellow, aspiring young accountant would later become *D-Rock SOUL-Jah.*

As for my college friends, most of them turned out fine.

I served as best man at Tim's wedding. He is now a doctor.

Will became Will X when he joined the Nation of Islam. Then, he was elected as the SGA President after I graduated. The last time I spoke with him he was teaching at a school and recording a rap CD.

Barbara Beebe founded a magazine called Real African World (R.A.W.) and served as a writer for Atlanta's musical network called Black Alternative Artist Movement (B.A.A.M.). She gave me much needed information when I became deeply involved in Atlanta's music scene. She subsequently passed away from a heart condition several years later. I pray her spirit is at peace.

I also attended funerals for good friends Johnny David, who passed in a motorcycle crash, and Keisha Simpson, who was murdered at an FSU dorm by a jealous boyfriend.

FSU was indeed a growing experience. I eventually learned that the quality of a school's education was more important than its racial make-up and party atmosphere. Through divine intervention, I dug deeper into understandings of racism before I found my true life purpose after attending a Black College.

WHITE DEVIL CONSPIRACIES

dvisor – This chapter is not intended to spur racial intolerance. However, it is necessary for this information and my experiences to be told. Complex problems can't be resolved unless its details are specifically explained.

When I was in the third grade, I remember my teacher Miss Kristol conducting lessons about Christopher Columbus. She said that Africans, Chinese, Phoenicians, Nordic Vikings, and several other nationalities all arrived in America before Columbus. Yet she proceeded to say, "They all arrived by accident. Columbus had actual intentions for this land we call our great country (USA)."

I actually believed this load of bull until my ninth grade World History teacher, Mr. Conley, revealed a more detailed explanation. He told my class that Columbus was actually commissioned to set sail for India and bring back spice. By "accident," he traveled the wrong way and ended up in the land we now call America. Columbus still thought America was India, and he mistakenly referred to the tribes as Indians. When Europeans finally revealed to Columbus that he never made it India and brought back some different crops, Columbus died a disgrace.

My curiosity over historical contradictions was heightened even further during my World History class. The introduction of the class book stated that the greatest civilizations on Earth prior to Europe's Industrial Age belonged to Africa, Asia, Mesopotamia, and the Ancient Americas. Despite this info, most of the book and class teachings were dedicated to European conquest. When Africa was studied, I along with several other black classmates felt depressed over the facts that Africa contained the most ravaged display of war, disease, poverty, and starvation on the planet. Naturally, us black students were left feeling inferior. When Mr. Conley repeatedly bragged about Germany's dominant accomplishments in world politics and sports, a black girl asked, "Are there any black Germans?" She was laughed at by everyone including me, even though I subconsciously felt ashamed of my blackness as well.

I held on to all this degradation until I started reading worldly Afrocentric books in the archives of FSU's library. I became even more suspicious as I wondered why a black college would place this information in an area where books couldn't be checked out.

I started my Afrocentric journey by reading *Stolen Legacy* by George G.M. James. This book along with Will X's influence and KRS-1's song "Black Man's in Effect" inspired me to recite a speech in my freshman Speech class called "Misconceptions in Greek History."

Next, I purchased a copy of *What They Never Told You in History Class* by Indus Khamit-Kush. This book generally says that the first humans in every geographic Earth region were black.

From this point forward, I skimmed through books and studies published by the following authors: Ivan Van Sertima, Asa G. Hilliard, Molefi K. Asante, Dr. Naim Akbar, Leonard Jeffries, Anthony T. Browder, Chancellor Williams, and J.A. Rogers, who wrote a book called *The 5 Negro Presidents*.

I felt an incredible sense of black pride from these readings, but it would soon evolve into a false sense of superiority.

During spring break in March '93, I visited relatives in Stone

Mountain and Atlanta, Georgia. I told them that I was frustrated with my black college experience yet still contemplated transferring to another school. I also explained that I wanted to stay at FSU, attempting to make positive changes. My Uncle Kevin heard my plea, so he invited me to watch a lecture video in his room.

After watching *The African Origins of Civilization Volume I* by Ashra Kwesi, who is also a protégé of Dr. Josef ben-Jochanan, I had a few questions about his cave man theory. I asked Uncle Kevin, "If white people were just caste-off cave folks in Europe, then where did they come from?" Uncle Kevin told me that they were grafted mutants. "You mean Elijah Muhammad's Yakub theory is correct?" I asked in awe. Uncle Kevin said emphatically, "Yes!"

My mind was blown away!!!

I listened and learned more while watching Volume 2 of Ashra Kwesi's lecture series along with his slide show of *The African Origins of Judeo-Christianity*. I thanked Uncle Kevin for the enlightening video footage, and he told me not to call him that. "Just call me Ka, short for Kadeem Allah. I'm a member of the Five Percent Nation....I'm no longer an active member of Omega Psi Phi (fraternity). I told them 'Fuck you, I'm God.' You might be on line for a fraternity, but be warned that they won't explain the concept behind 'crossing the burning sands.'"

My uncle's anti-Greek pro-black stance led me to explore further research about the Nation of Islam (NOI). Brothers from this group often recanted how Malcolm X repudiated his teacher. Initially, I dismissed this claim, but I eventually changed my mind after believing more of the info I read in Elijah Muhammad's *Message to the Blackman.*

Even though much of Muhammad's teachings were based on parabled myths, his mixed-race theories contained some truth. In *Message to the Blackman*, he states that Indians were the

Asiatic red brothers of the Blackman and that they were exiled out of India for rejecting Islam. This may be partly true despite genetic studies that prove that East Indians and Native Americans are mostly a mixture of African and Asian tribes. Muhammad's Islamic and white-devil theories concerning India made more sense to me since their current dominant religion, Hinduism, involves casting out darker-skinned people as destined poor peasants. This practice is a pre-dated trendsetter to South African apartheid.

Malcolm X eventually split from the Nation of Islam and moved away from white-devil race baiting. Yet, there were several different Islamic factions formed before and after Elijah Muhammad's 1975 death. Some denounced Malcolm X for his philosophical change while others supported. They included the Five Percenter Nation founded by Clarence 13X in 1964, the Lost & Found NOI founded by Silas Muhammad, and the revived NOI founded by Louis Farrakhan after Elijah's son Wallace Deen Muhammad converted the NOI into orthodox Sunni Muslim temples. Uncle Kevin professed that Malcolm X was talking a lot of shit for preaching brotherhood with white Muslims after his 1964 Mecca pilgrimage, despite Farrakhan's claim that Malcolm had first traveled to Saudi Arabia in 1959 and saw white Muslims.

I ended up siding with Elijah Muhammad's early viewpoint "the black Man is God and the white man is the devil." I fed more into this closet racist point-of-view when I heeded messages from Ice Cube and Da Lench Mob in their rap songs—"Cave Bitch," "Horny Lil' Devil," "I Wanna Kill Sam," and "(Fuck) You and Your Heroes." Originally, I didn't agree with these tones. It still felt good though to hear black men yell out racial epithets in the same way that white racists had used against black people for centuries.

My fascination with Islam and different variations of white

devil theories led to my involvement with brothers from an organization called Unity for Prosperity (UFP). I was already familiar with Brother Jakim, who often hung around the FSU campus selling books, incense, and oils. I became more acquainted with him after Brother Alim invited me to one of the UFP classes. Alim was one of the few FSU students I knew who studied deep into Afrocentricity and metaphysics. We became brother-like friends when I made a Five Percenter Nation-inspired statement telling him, "God is me and God is you!" He gave me a friendly slap on my hand and repeatedly to this day greets me, "What up Gawd?!"

From the moment I first attended a UFP class, my mind constantly became scrambled with conspiracy theories. Alim was usually the teacher. He had an advanced reading background of biblical texts, the Qur'an, and ancient Babylonian scriptures. Often, he pointed out discrepancies and contradictions contained in these books. Since I didn't practice any religion consistently, I didn't refute any of his findings.

Most of UFP's inspiration came from a religious organization called Ansaarallah Nation, which was founded by Imam Issa, who is now known by his legal name, Dr. Malachi Z. York. UFP used to be affiliated with them but broke away to the belief, "All religions are false." This concept left me very confused since I had barely grasped Islam and Christianity. However, I understood this better when Alim shouted at black leadership, "Will the real nigga Jesus please stand up?" Alim further explained that his exploration into black consciousness started when he learned about "Black Jesus" from the Bible's Revelations chapter 1, verses 14-15. He said, "This fucked me up."

We all felt more "fucked-up" as we learned that almost every major black American religious sect, including Yahweh ben Yahweh and the African Hebrew Israelites, had some Jesus-type leader.

Elijah Muhammad first started an anti-Christian savior trend with his story of God coming in the half-white, half-black man known as Master Fard (Farad) Muhammad. Subsequently, we learned from Dr. York that Farad was a white man[1] named Wallace Dodd Ford—a nephew of the Ford car company founder and a member of the Ford Foundation. He was convicted of fraud and drug trafficking and met Elijah Muhammad following his stint in prison.[2] So then I asked, "Why would Elijah Muhammad give black people a fake Jesus who just happened to be white?" Alim explained by saying that Muhammad probably thought black people would accept a white-looking Jesus better since they're used to having a white Jesus shoved down their throats. I also found out that Elijah Muhammad originally studied the teachings of Honorable Marcus Garvey and Noble Drew Ali. Muhammad joined the NOI founded by Farad after Garvey was deported and Ali mysteriously died.[3]

Today Louis Farrakhan is at the NOI helm as a so-called savior. Dr. York taught us that he was originally known as Louis Walcott before joining the NOI. Like most, I suspected that Farrakhan was involved in the assassination of Malcolm X. Farrakhan only admitted to "fostering the environment" that lead to his murder. Regardless of how involved he was, I came to the conclusion that the CIA and FBI were the main culprits of this murder as well as many other large-scale crimes against humanity.

Apparently, white devil conspiracy theories had ties deeper

1 He was actually Caucasian/Polynesian mixture according to Wikipedia.org.

2 Even though I never found official proof linking Wallace Dodd Ford to the Ford Foundation, some of Dr. York's members used this info to justify a conspiracy theory that the NOI is a product of the "white devil" controlled Illuminati.

3 According to a report from Rense.com – http://www.rense.com/general172/ free.htm, Farad assassinated Ali. This was never proven but still remains a controversial mystery along with most of Farad's identity.

into black leadership than I ever imagined. Even though I didn't know how to make much sense out of Black Jesus savior gossip, I still managed to comprehend "white devil" race origins very well.

I was so impressed by the mind-blowing classes at UFP's Hall of Knowledge that I eventually purchased a collective of conspiracy-oriented books from their store.

The first book I bought from the hall was *Behold a Pale Horse* by William Cooper, a former Naval Intelligence officer. Cooper revealed "classified" documents and information about secret societies, governmental conspiracies, New World Order plots, UFO/Alien technology, slave race cover-ups, CIA-financed drug wars, Global Warming, weather manipulation, population control, and more. The most shocking detail was on page 446, which displayed a Department of Defense strategy for the AIDS virus. It said that AIDS was developed in Frederick, Maryland in 1968, injected into Africans by way of the smallpox vaccine, and used on homosexuals in New York and San Francisco as test subjects.

Originally, I thought this type of scheme only existed in blaxploitation movies like *3 The Hard Way*, which was shown to me by Uncle Ka. There were even more frightening facts to be studied. Alim told me this info had to be true since it came from a "Paleman." Even today, ABC News reports how 600,000 people die every day in Africa from AIDS. Cooper also gives accounts of world leaders' involvement with satanic worship as well as Nazi ties amongst the family of former President George H.W. Bush. A book called *The Unseen Hand* by Ralph Emerson and an article by John Buchanan George in *The New Hampshire* also revealed the Bush family's links to financing Nazi Germany during World War II.

All this info made me a firm believer that all white people are devils, and the U.S.A. is the "United Snakes of America."

I became more infused with white race bashing when I studied origins behind Uncle Ka's assessment of "crossing the burning sands." Various students of Afrocentricity and Moorish Science often reveal that this Greek fraternity practice was formed after pale-skinned albinos were casted out of Africa for their polluted ways. A similar theory was revealed in Dr. Francis Cress Welsing's *The Isis Papers*. Welsing called the Adam & Eve story the beginning of white supremacy by saying that they were ran out of the Garden of Eden due to their pale naked shame. I further learned from genetic research that the woman was actually created before man, which makes all accounts of Adam & Eve false. In spite of Welsing's inaccuracies, her psychiatric medical experience gave her enough credence to warrant authenticity for her Color Confrontation Theory, which breaks down white supremacy symbols into all societal functions— sports, media, sex, government, etc.. The most baffling symbol Welsing conveys is the invention of the gun—made by Europeans to control people of color and prevent their anatomical "guns" from genetically wiping out the white race.

I also skimmed through Michael Bradley's *Iceman Inheritance* for heightened verification of caveman origins. Bradley himself is generally Caucasian but is also one-fourth Native American. He thoroughly says that Europeans are more aggressive than the rest of the world because of their roots from the Ice Age.

Almost every informational piece that excited me justified rising resentment of whites. The following articles further confirmed my belief that there was a conspiracy to destroy the whole black race: The "Germ Warfare" article by Mosalagge Ditshego in the November 16, 1984 edition of *Final Call*; a book called *Vaccines Are Dangerous;* an article in the *Atlanta-Journal Constitution* (AJC) on the similarities of the monkey SIV to the human HIV; and Jimmy Carter's National Security

Council (NSC) plan to keep U.S. blacks and black Africans divided (September 18, 1980 edition of *Sun Reporter*).

After all this reading, nobody's words could change my mind about white devils. The more I studied though, the more confused I became when I discovered even more variations of white devil philosophies.

The African Hebrew Israelites led by Ben Amin and a group called the Nation of Yahweh espoused a philosophy that black people are the original Jews and whites are "imposters and Euro-gentiles." This made sense to me due to my prior readings about how every type of human originates from blackness.

Dr. York professed a different variation by saying that Canaanites from the Caucus Mountains were the original caste-off Caucasians. The Bible, though, teaches that Canaan was a refuge land of milk and honey where Moses led the ex-Egyptian slaves to freedom. Alim constantly hinted to me that the Bible was not entirely factual because it contained several interpretations and contradictions. For many years I heard about biblical verses which justified labels of blacks as cursed devils. Now, I was presented with biblical verses saying how whites originated from "cursed" leprosy.

Regardless of how much I studied biblical inaccuracies, my "cursed" white race beliefs were justified more by science.

Cheik Anta Diop, a historical anthropologist, said Caucasians spawned from the Earth's Ice Age around 20,000 B.C., about the same period when Neanderthals emerged.

Standard elementary science teaches most kids that mankind evolved from apes, Neanderthals, and the Cro-Magnon species. Yet, this contradicts multiple anthropological claims that the first humans originated millions of years ago in the Lake Victoria area of southern Africa. From here, I concluded that a high degree of white racism had been coerced into science. While I assumed this as fact, I also found out about white scientists who defied racist ideologies.

Gregory Mendel formed a genetic theory stating dominant genes were with dark-haired and dark-skinned people and recessive genes were possessed by people with pale hues and light (blonde) hair *(BB-Black, Bb-Red, bB-Yellow, bb-White)*. Seemingly, all people have dominant and recessive genes in every physical category. Yet, I used Mendel's theory to justify a mindset of black superiority.

Dr. York and other Afrocentrics further taught how Caucasians also came from mutant experiments with apes, pigs, and other primordial beasts. The Qur'an has a chapter called "The Cave" detailing mankind's "filthy" mongrel actions with beasts. Even movies like *The Island of Dr. Moreau* and *Blade II's* depiction of the "Reaper Strain" give accounts of mankind's amalgamation with animals.

No matter how pale-skinned people originated— grafted mutation, genetic experimentation, environmental adaptation, and/or albinism—it was crystal clear to me, "White people are a sub-human freak of nature."

This notion was unchallenged until my white devil studies evolved deeper into alien research. According to various UFO accounts, there are seven-foot tall, pale-skinned aliens (sometimes referred to as Greys) who settled in the Nordic regions of Scandinavia. This particular account has correlations to the Norse mythology that is the basis for the comic book *Thor*. Dr. York gave accounts of a similar tribe that dwells in a different solar system, most commonly referenced as Pleiades. Adolf Hitler often referred to these huge godly looking beings as Aryans, despite language studies connecting actual Aryans closer to the Middle East. Other alien book accounts say they were actually reptilians who disguised themselves as pale-skinned humans (very similar to the NBC movie & series *V*). These so-called aliens would eventually help Europeans conquer the world and enslave humanity through the Industrial Age.

At this point, my mind was overloaded in an exploration for universal life origins. Several Greek myths told of beings called Centaurs—half-horse, half-human beings who were the final stage of animal interbreeding before gods made perfect erect two-legged humans. I finally stopped my studies asking "Who are the Gods?"

My intentions of studying white devil philosophies were not originally to become a hate monger. Yet, it was only natural to feel a high degree of distrust towards whites as I dug deeper into the core meanings of racism. I guess it's impossible for anyone to truly understand bigotry without being a bigot. I wouldn't learn this until later in my life.

While I comprehended white devil philosophies in classes, I also attended lectures and wrote papers on these subjects.

I became socially bored. Subsequently, Alim helped me by letting me rent videotaped lectures of Dr. Khalid Muhammad. Alim warned me, "Muhammad's tone could start a war." The first tape I watched was a lecture promoting a book called *The Secret Relationship Between Blacks and Jews*. I thoroughly enjoyed Dr. Muhammad's comical race roasting of whites and Jews. Then I rented *The Great Debate: Jesus Was a Black Man of African Descent*. Dr. Muhammad virtually ripped apart a Southern Baptist lawyer who said Jesus was not black. The lawyer admitted he wasn't qualified to debate on this topic. Dr. Muhammad's "cracker" baiting excited me so much that I convinced Alim to drive me to his lecture at North Carolina A&T State University (NCATSU) in Greensboro, North Carolina. Since I had associates at NCATSU from the North Carolina Black Student Governments Association, I was allowed to sit on stage with a panel of students while Dr. Muhammad spoke in front of us. Alim and I had a ball listening to Dr. Muhammad "pin the tail on the honky." My mother was irate enough at my black Muslim tendencies to send me an article detailing Dr. Muhammad's fancy lifestyle in an all-white suburban New Jersey neighborhood. This information contradicted Dr. Muhammad's anti-white stance, but I didn't care because I heeded his speeches as truth.

Alim and I also attended a couple of lectures by Steve Cokely, who often spoke about New World Order/Illuminati conspiracies against blacks.

I was too convinced about my conspiracy beliefs being true. Next, I wrote a class speech and research paper entitled "The Coming of the New World Order." I used sources from library magazines and store books. Most of my classmates reacted with mockery and disbelief. They laughed at my forecast of a black East Indian named Lord Maitreya emerging as an anti-Christ in 1996. One student asked, "What if I say to you 'I'm God?'" I told him, "I'll say you're God, but you're not the Almighty Creator."

This was only the beginning of a karmic series of intellectual attacks thrusted back at me.

Since Will X was out of school during my junior year, I helped revive Males Achieving Success through Knowledge (MASK) with video presentations by Ashra Kwesi. The auditorium became more packed during each program after I passed out hyped-up flyers saying "WARNING: This video will blow your brains out like no bullet ever could." Most black attendants were amused, and most white folks walked out. I received a heap of backlash from MASK members. The organizational president, Tom, called these videos "biased" and said MASK would not support Kwesi. Most other members said, "We don't want to be pro-black." Shamefully, MASK was also perceived as a group of sell-outs for letting Chancellor Hackley sponsor us.

This attitude was also prevalent in the Student Government Association. I tried to convince the Senate to allocate funds towards bringing Kwesi to FSU. They flatly rejected. I tried too hard to convince them it was necessary, but they already approved of an Ivan Van Sertima appearance with co-sponsorship by a Sunni Muslim group.

I didn't think Dr. Van Sertima's tone was hardcore enough, so I pleaded with MASK one last time. Tom said I was too caught up in idol worship of Ashra Kwesi to listen to different perspectives of black culture. When he said that blacks were catching present-day hell as karma for kicking albinos out of Africa, I was silent. I finally compromised with MASK and the Sunnis to co-sponsor a presentation by Wekesa Madzimoyo, which eventually received praise from both blacks and whites.

My stance on white devil beliefs was slowly deteriorating. However, it would forever affect how I functioned with society, especially my family.

My sisters called me a Scrooge for refusing to celebrate Thanksgiving and Christmas. I responded by telling them how most holidays had pagan roots.

My parents feared that I was involved with a cult. I told them I was a Muslim by nature, and I would never again eat pork. They feared that I would eventually sign papers with the Nation of Islam, allowing them to take 20 percent of my income after taxes. Coincidentally, my white devil studies would lead me towards deeper research into the occult.

Meanwhile, Mother tried to quell me by repeatedly phrasing, "You ain't got that much black in you." I constantly responded, "Once you're mixed with color you never go back. The white in me is obsolete." I may never be viewed as white in this lifetime. Yet, the whiteness of my family was revealed in spring '94.

Mother received a letter from a woman in North Hollywood named Rita. Rita turned out to be my long lost white Jewish grandmother. Mother was so happy and quick to forgive. My sisters initially had no interest in meeting Rita, but they proceeded to do so for Mother's love. I was the last to meet her because I labeled her "an imposter Jew." Mother was hurt by my pro-black stance, and Father was furious. He shouted to me over the phone, "You're a stupid fucking idiot!"

After a barrage of heated exchanges with my family, I mellowed out and conversed with them more. Father told me about his grandmother, who was full-blooded Apache Indian and hated the white man. He feared that I inherited too much of her hatred. Eventually, I met Grandma Rita, Aunt Shirah, Uncle Jim, and Cousin Nikita at June's masters' degree commencement ceremony. My angry pro-black mentality made it difficult for me to accept whites as my immediate family. Ironically, Alim was the one who first convinced me to make peace with Grandma Rita. Even though he generally doesn't like whites, he professes "tolerance" of them. He also told me, "All blacks have white relatives from slavery."

My anger clouded me so much during this period that I never brought myself to read a book called *Not Out of Africa* and a journal called "Fallacies of Afrocentricity" by Grover Furr. My mind wasn't open enough back then to listen to perspectives calling Afrocentricity a movement of racist crap. This "movement" indeed provided positive inspirations for blacks, and I still think blacks are the original humans that have created great civilizations and inventions since the beginning of time. Afrocentricity, though, also lacked enough spirituality to present black history as more than "feel-good history."

For example, black and brown-skinned people from North Africa called the Moors occupied Spain and various other parts of Europe for a period of more than seven hundred years. By 1482, the Moors were officially exiled from Spain and thus left behind a disease called the Black Plague. After Europe recovered from this onslaught, they caught enough fresh breath to travel and imperialize the whole world. Subsequently, Europeans imported all the world's materials, including slaves as labor for their new world colonies. Apparently, Africa's tribal wars were major signs of this continent's decline as the world's trend-setting civilization. The possibly hundreds of millions of people that died in the middle passage slave ship routes, along with four hundred plus years of induced labor appeared to be karmic punishment on dark-skinned Africans for casting out and dominating pale-skinned Europeans. In no way does Africa's civil decline justify the macabre horrors of European imperialism, but on the same token, Africa and all her descendants around the world must bear responsibility for her mistakes in order to repair human relations.

One more disturbing fact I learned was the Arabs' role in the enslavement of black Africans. Lighter skinned "Caucasian" Arabs as well as other hybridized Muslims have traded blacks as slaves for more than 1,000 years.[4] Muslims had a significant role in enslaving blacks during the Trans-Atlantic Slave Route Passages. Plus, the Indian Ocean Slave Trade—which involved Arabs, Hindus, and several other Asian tribes as captors—has been traced by some scholars as far back as third century B.C.E.[5]. Almost every major religion on Earth has a flawed history of oppressing all types of people, especially when it comes to enslaving blacks. At the same time, all the world's major religions have black African roots. Granted, Almighty Creation is probably too big for one type of worship. Yet, any flaw in religious and/or cultural worship leads to slavery and the ultimate worst—death.

My anger towards oppression of blacks would not be quelled

---

4 This information is according to http://www.wikipedia.org.

5 This information is according to http://www.historycooperative.org/journals/jwh/14.2/vink.html.

until years later. I still feel that blacks need reparations beyond empty governmental apologies.

I believe that most people would like to act in accordance to a multi-colored rainbow philosophy, in which the only perfection is the human race. However, absolute perfection is mostly a myth. No two sources of energy are exactly the same and nobody's version of the truth is one hundred percent accurate. I would still not learn the following lesson until years later: the quantity of melanin one person possesses doesn't matter. What matters most is the quality of how one person uses whatever amount of melanin they possess to preserve life.

After absorbing all these studies and vibes, I was still overloaded with a warped hope for the perfect lifestyle, thus leading to more cycles of abuse. Indeed white devils exist and continuously play a major part in all life's destruction. Eventually, though, black devils in and out of my own spirit would hinder me most.

EGYPTIAN QUEEN

Before I developed a view of black women as Nubian queens, I fell in love with an underclass gal at FSU.

Arnethia introduced herself as Niecy for short when I first met her at the student center. Initially, she seemed like a down-to-Earth tomboy. She enrolled at FSU in fall '92 after graduating from high school in Rocky Mount, North Carolina. I next saw her at a January dance with her tongue down the throat of a sharp-dressed high-yellow man. This moment didn't seem important to me since I barely knew her, but her boyfriend's story proved to be of utmost significance after I encountered her again at the student center.

As I walked down the stairs to the basement to play ping pong, Niecy was at the midpoint of the stairwell standing with a look of relaxed bewilderment. A nice brief conversation ensued. I was ready to finish my walk downstairs when suddenly, her conversation topic took a surprising turn. She appeared bothered. I asked her what was wrong. She said, "You look like someone I can tell this to."

Niecy told me how she was raped in high school. I just stood silent and listened. Her revealed accounts of trauma emerged from fear that her boyfriend would get killed while helping his drug-addict cousins in Louisiana. We sat down on the steps and talk more. I encouraged her to smile.

Many students passed by us that day, and rumors started to circulate that Niecy was my girl. I brushed them off saying she was just a friend. Yet, I was emotionally frazzled how a female just told me something intimate without hardly knowing me.

Niecy seemed fine when I saw her again. All she said was, "He's gone." She was also in a laughing mood when we watched the Super Bowl on a big screen TV in a lounge area. One of the staff asked me, "Is that your girlfriend?" Again, I brushed off those rumors even though my feelings for her were growing stronger.

Valentine's Day arrived. I felt slight loneliness without an official girlfriend. I sensed this was going to be a hard day for some people. I didn't mope in misery. Instead I just chilled out and watched TV at the student center. Everything felt calm until Niecy walked inside with a glum look on her face. I asked, "What's wrong?" She nodded silently while blowing a huge breath out of her lips. Then I asked, "Do you wanna talk about it outside?"

We strolled into a corridor pavement area. Both our heads were leaning over a brick wall staring at the parking lot and forest trees. It was a cloudy and damp afternoon.

Again, Niecy was feeling depressed about her boyfriend's departure. As she moaned, I placed my arms around her while standing behind her. She then sobbed, "I don't know why bad things keep happening to me!" She cried profusely with her makeup smearing on the arm of my yellow-hooded jeans coat. I just held her with comfort while listening to her release her sorrows. I walked her back to New Residence Hall, and then I gave her a hug. Rumors now swirled more than ever that she was my girl. This time though, I really felt deep attraction for her.

Days later we met again at the student center, and I told her how I felt. She responded with a laugh, "I'm speechless." She elaborated that she wasn't ready for another relationship right away. So we remained platonic friends.

There was hardly anything I would not do for Niecy. I took

her to a play, bought her food, wrote her poems, helped pack her bags for summer break, and even had my roommate Tim drive her to and from a doctor's office.

We talked a lot over the phone. On a nonstop basis, I pursued involvement with her. Still, she just wasn't ready. I wrote her seven letters over summer '93. She only wrote back once.

During fall semester of my junior year, I tried one last gasp effort to win her heart. The result proved near tragic. I brought over food from the Bryant Hall X-mas party. I was still reeling over the SGA's rejection of my proposal to sponsor a video presentation by Ashra Kwesi. I firmly put my hands on Niecy's shoulders, pleading for her to embrace me without fighting her feelings. She pulled my arms off her three times and said, "Don't be so pushy." I stated, "You know we both want each other." Niecy gave me a frantic look as I reached for her one last time before she abruptly walked back to her room. I sat in the living room irate while chewing down on spicy fried chicken. Niecy came back with slight disgust saying, "You're taking out your problems on me. 'No' means 'no!'" I kept chewing away while offering her some food. She took some. Then she retreated back to her room for the night.

From this moment forward, things were never the same between Niecy and me. During spring semester '94, she hardly returned my phone calls and plain ignored me a few times. I asked her one time in the cafeteria, "Why haven't you been in touch?" She gave a phony excuse, "I've been busy." I said, "Right! You don't need me anymore, especially since you don't have any of the same classes as me." Of course she denied that. However, she continued to ignore me in front of my face two more times. I called her with a low-tone voice bitching how she didn't care about me. She said this wasn't true. Yet, she admitted that her feelings were not nearly as strong as mine. This proved my claim.

Late on another night when I walked back to my dorm frustrated over anger directed towards me at a gym dance, I screamed outside Niecy's window begging for her to come out. Her roommate yelled for me to give her a call the next day, and so I did. We subsequently set up a meeting. I told her, "I love you Niecy." She said in a shocked tone, "I don't know what to say." I responded, "I love you even if you don't feel the same way." Then I walked away.

Niecy still ignored me whenever I passed her by saying hi. So when the semester ended, I gave her an ultimatum. I was preparing for an internship in Memphis, Tennessee with the U.S.D.A. firm, Packers & Stockyard, so I gave her my address and told her, "I love you, but if you don't write me, have a nice life", and walked off. To no surprise, she didn't write me, and I never had another word with Niecy. Our friendship was no more.

Niecy was my first intense heartbreak. Yes, I made a ton of mistakes. I never intended to push her away. I still didn't know how to attract her or any woman towards me in an intimate manner. I thought I treated her like a black queen. Little did I realize during this time that I was only being an obsessive jerk.

Niecy didn't have the hottest of physical attributes. Some even called her "piranha mouth" because of her excessive buck-toothed overbite. Looks, however, had nothing to do with my infatuation. I fell in love with her over sympathy, and sympathy was more of what I would need later when I sought a rebound love affair with an amazingly gorgeous gal.

In summer '94, I worked as a paid intern for Packers & Stockyards. I rented an apartment at the River Trace complex in the Raleigh-Egypt section of Memphis, Tennessee. I didn't have a car, so my co-worker, Ed, provided rides to work for a twenty-dollar gas charge per week.

On the weekends, I was usually stranded at home after walking to the stores. I had cousins, friends, and friends' relatives in Memphis who I often called on for emergencies.

There was one Memphis family who made the biggest impact on me. I met them from contact with my friend Denise, who I knew from a graduate school internship program at the University of Tennessee (UT). She recently graduated from UT in summer '93. Denise stayed home in Memphis in summer '94 while preparing to attend graduate school in South Carolina. After calling her, she had her friend Kat drive her over to my place.

Denise and I recollected on good times while Kat listened. I told Denise I'd be in touch with her while preparing to turn in for the evening. As I started to do my laundry, Denise came back and offered to have me as company with her and Kat. Without hesitation, I accepted.

Kat drove us to the home of her cousins, Dina and Alex Brentwood, who live in a nice two-story home with five children. They made me feel at home while chatting with Kat and Denise. I stayed silent and kept my laughter at bay while Kat giggled and shouted her stories of near accidents. Alex called her, "Kat Kneivel." I told them briefly, "I don't have a car," so Kat offered to drive me to the store on weekends. Dina subsequently invited me over for a barbeque on Memorial Day.

I called the Brentwood's on that holiday, and a young lady answered. I told her I was on my way over. She introduced herself as Titi (pronounced Tee Tee) then offered to pick me up with a vehicle. I said I had no problem walking since the house wasn't far from my apartment.

When I arrived, a young lady answered the door. I asked if she was Titi, but she was only a friend of Titi's. She proceeded to lead me upstairs to the TV room. I introduced myself to Titi with a handshake. She was mild-mannered, wearing a doo-rag and pajamas. I mentioned how I just arrived in town from a quiz bowl tournament in L.A.. She facetiously sighed, "Oh! Kat warned me you were going to talk about the quiz bowl team." Titi proceeded to her room to get dressed. I was already watching TV when suddenly, my nerves rattled as if I was on a rollercoaster when I saw the most beautiful sight of my life. After catching my breath, I realized it was Titi in casual clothes. I remained silent for five minutes in order to digest viewing the finest-looking woman I'd ever seen. This moment was reminiscent of the lyrics in D'Angelo's song "Me and Those Dreamy Eyes of Mine."

As I finally mastered enough courage to speak, Titi and I engaged in a friendly conversation that lasted most of the afternoon. With her eccentric southern belle accent, she said she was taking a few classes at a community college. Then she spilled how she recently quit her job because a male co-worker sexually harassed her. I listened more, then mentioned that I was from Las Vegas. She looked at me with crazed bubbly eyes. No matter how her mood glared, I was happy to be in her presence.

The conversation seemed to die down when Titi started reading a book. I just asked, "So you like reading novels?" She said, "I do, but I also want to read a book called *Stolen Legacy*." When I think of this moment now, I don't think she was talking about the same *Stolen Legacy* book I read by George G.M. James. But I quickly responded, "Really? I've read a bunch of books like that." I went off on a tangent about all the Afrocentric and conspiratorial books I had read. She seemed fascinated. Titi also mentioned how she was afraid of reading Afrocentric books because she didn't want to become hateful of other people. I proceeded to shut my mouth and let her sensitive mind digest my book-worm tone.

Titi looked at my shirt and asked about the symbol of my necklace. I told her it was called, "Thee Ankh," an Egyptian symbol of light and fertility. She appeared more curious about me, but not nearly as much as I was about her.

Kat picked up Titi and took her shopping. I stayed behind observing all the memorabilia in the living room. I noticed Titi's high school diploma from Raleigh-Egypt High School. Her first name read "Nefertiti." I thought, "Whoa! This city is coincidentally divine. I'm into Egyptian culture. Memphis was also the name of a city by the Nile River. Memphis, TN just happens to be next to the Mississippi River, and it also has a pyramid. Titi's birth name is the same as the ancient Egyptian Queen, Nefertiti. Titi's high school has 'Egypt' in its title. And finally, her beautiful black eyes, almondy brown skin, and curvaceous body glow exactly like an Egyptian Queen. Perhaps, Titi is destined to be my Egyptian Queen."

Titi came back. I was starved while waiting for Alex to finish barbequing. Titi offered to drive me to Wendy's. I accepted and further drowned in an illusion of her aroma. Titi and her family were too generous to me.

We arrived back. Alex finally finished cooking. I munched on both Wendy's and Alex's steaks. Titi settled upstairs then her mother, Dina, began words with me. She asked me if I go to church. I told her I had no religion. Dina seemed jolted at first but became amused when our chat switched to relationships. I told her I wanted to get married. With much glee, Dina uttered this to the entire household. Titi walked back to the kitchen sporting the same doo-rag she wore when I met her earlier in the morning. While Dina was preparing to drive me home, Titi barked, "Hey! Why don't you clean some of these dishes you made a mess of?" I walked towards the sink and she laughed. Titi hinted her pleasure of me. I knew I was a little uptight but had no idea that this little joke indicated my willing obsession to do anything for her love.

Two days later, I finally started to feel settled in Memphis.

I was finding the stores with less difficulty, catching rides with seldom problems, and paying my bills without budget worries.

During the first week of June '94, I called Alim and told him I was doing just fine. Surely, I boasted about a "FUUU-OOOO-INE (Fine)" woman I met. Things were so calm after that phone call. Then out of nowhere came a phone call from Titi. My heart raced faster than a speeding bullet. Titi said, "I'm just calling to see how you're doing!" I sat in disbelief, wondering why "the finest-looking woman I'd ever seen" was calling me. I asked her if we could hang out sometime, and she accepted.

We arranged to go see a movie. However, I was in no position to dictate the date since I didn't have a car. Time flew by on the date night, and I sensed Titi wouldn't make it. I called her three times. Twice she said her parents didn't arrive back with the van. On the third call, she said the living room was flooded with silverfish. She hung up the phone in disgust shouting, "OOOO-UH! They're so slimy!" But I was the only one feeling "slimy" and moped in disappointment for the rest of the night.

After this setback, my developing bridge with Titi crumbled.

I called her the following week. That day just happened to be her birthday. I panicked like a damn fool, "I'm sorry for not remembering and buying a gift. I just got paid today and have plenty of money." She giggled, "Don't say that." I asked if she wanted me to come over, and she said she was alright.

I was now a nervous wreck and asked Ed for advice. He recommended I use a more aggressive approach. So I called Titi the following weekend and acted like I was busy in the pool. I invited her and her little brothers over, but she was preparing a birthday party for them. I asked her if she needed help. She said. "Sure. I hope you don't get bored around a bunch of little kids."

Within an hour I was at the house. Dina was chatting with the other kids' mothers in the kitchen. The mothers asked me if I was leaving Memphis soon. Dina joked, "No he's going to stay here, marry Titi, and make us rich." While the ladies laughed, my heart fell to my stomach. I ached for this dream to come true.

I arrived upstairs asking for instructions. Titi directed me to help arrange napkins for the hot dogs. Then she joked with one of her beautiful smiles, "Come on Albert. (Hurry up!)." Watching her act out her motherly big-sister role made me more intoxicated with love potion.

After Titi and friends sang happy birthday to her little brother, I helped her clean up the living room. I told her I had a gift for her birthday, as well. I gave her a stained-glass Ankh necklace purchased from a mall that Kat drove me to. With an emotionless face, Titi thanked me. I said, "I might as well give you a friendship gift. I probably won't see you much after this summer." She responded, "Well! Who knows?" Again, my heart pounded thunderously.

For the rest of this day, I chatted with the adults in the downstairs living room. It was getting dark as the doorbell rang. I answered the door and a young man dressed in all-white casual club clothes asked, "Is Tee here?" Thinking he was looking for one of Titi's cousins, I went upstairs asking for Tee. Titi comes out looking incredibly elegant wearing a white strap-less top along with stylish light blue jeans. I curiously asked, "Why are you looking so nice?" She answered, "Because I have company!"

I sat watching TV for ten minutes before Titi re-entered with the young man I saw at the door. I wailed, "You're Tee?" Titi said, "Some people call me that. Hey! My mom is supposed to drive you home..."

I left with Dina feeling very confused. On one hand I thought I had a grasp on Titi. On the other hand, she was kicking me to the curb.

A few days later, Dina brought her three youngest kids over

to my apartment's pool. None of them knew how to swim so I played with them very carefully. Titi, who also couldn't swim, stopped by briefly. I was hoping to see her in a bathing suit, so I could offer her swimming lessons, but she was wearing plain sweat clothes while babysitting her friend's daughter.

Dina drove us all back to her house for dinner. I brought my camera with wishes to snap a picture of Titi. I asked Titi twice if I could take a picture of her but she rejected me with looks of annoyance. Titi was already upset after giving one of her little brothers a spanking, and I felt even more like a drooling clown.

My attempts at Titi's heart continued to fail. I called her every few days and usually left messages that wouldn't be returned. Titi did return my calls once. She only spoke for a few minutes around four a.m. after leaving her new job. I visited her house again, but she was hardly paying attention. Again, I asked for her picture. She said she would give me one before I left Memphis, but I never got a picture of her.

My frustration over Titi led to desperation. I sought advice from every angle: Ed, Kat, and Denise. Also from my fellow USDA intern friends per phone and e-mail: Roderick, Antonio, and Orelia. After virtually one million conversations about Titi, I conjured up an idea to take Titi out in a limousine. I didn't have a car and never went to the prom. Therefore I figured, "What the hell?! I don't mind spending at least three hundred dollars on her." I was ready to rent a limo, but Ed convinced me to double date with him at a cheaper rate. I asked Titi if she wanted to tag along with me, Ed, and his girlfriend to see a stand-up comedy performance by Jamie Foxx. She refused with the excuse of attending a wedding on the same day.

Now, I was depressed. Every minute, my mind was tormented with thoughts of her coupled with feelings of powerlessness. I remember seeing Titi walk out of a store and kept saying to myself, "I know I shouldn't be thinking about her, *but damn she looks too good, and I still want her.*" So this time, I told all my friends, "I'm ready to tell Titi how I feel." Roderick said, "Go for it." Then Ed told me, "Fuck her. Don't do that. Leave her alone. You'll only set yourself up for a trap. She'll brag to all her friends about how she worked over this guy who was crazy about her, and she didn't feel a thing for you. Protect your pride!" Antonio called me and recommended, "Just leave her alone. The next time you're at her place, ignore her. Hell! A good way to catch her attention is to call her on the phone and ask to speak with her folks."

I heeded Antonio's advice. First, I called her house. Titi answered, "Hello?" I asked for Alex. She said with more volume, "Hell-ooo?" Again I asked for Alex. Titi bit back, "No! He's not here." And she hung up the phone. Even though I got under her skin, I still felt like an asshole. I continued to follow Antonio's advice. The next time I hung out at Dina's, I didn't speak to Titi. She said, "Hi Albert, "I only responded with "Hello." I chilled out in the TV room watching videos by Ashra Kwesi. Then, I saw Titi napping in her pajamas. I couldn't take my eyes off of her sleeping beauty. She awoke briefly and I somberly said, "See you later."

Back at my apartment, I was mooing like a cow. Nothing could get Titi off my mind. Roderick called, poking fun at me all night after I gave him the scoop. He repeatedly ranted comically, "I told you so!" Yet he was still baffled on how I could let this woman work me into a mindless zombie.

My twenty-first birthday arrived. I decided to spill the beans to Titi. I sat in Dina's living room for half of the day feeling like a worn-out train wreck. Suddenly Titi arrives and I told her eagerly, "I gotta talk to you." She said, "I'll be out (from the bathroom) in a minute. As I waited nervously for five minutes, my eyes became overwhelmed with weepy water. I did not let myself shed any tears despite the pending shock I was under.

Titi sat on a table and used the phone. She spoke to a friend for five additional minutes. With a helpless tone, I cracked, "I gotta talk to you." Titi asked angrily, "Can this wait?" I moaned, "No! Can we go somewhere in private?" She spewed, "No! Whatever you have to say, you'll say it in here."

Titi hung up the phone and let me commence to my confession. I said something like, "It's been building for a long time." She screamed, "What?" I finally let it out, "I'm infatuated with you!" She responded unemotionally, "Oh!" I said something else like, "I've felt this way since I first met you." Again she sighed, "Oh!" I paused. Then she spoke in sentences, "Lemme tell ya somethin'. I don't trust guys. I've been through too much already. "I responded, "But you seemed to be interested when we first met." She said, "I was only being friendly. You were a houseguest. I'm a nice person." I almost bit my tongue, "Well. I hope you trust guys again one day." She reacted, "No! That probably won't happen... I had no idea you felt this way..."

I retreated back home giggling with praise over my survival of Titi's blatant diss. At the same time, I perceived my revelation to her as the most humiliating moment of my life. When I told Roderick, he said, "Whoops!" Ed gasped, "How could you sell out like that?" Antonio and Orelia evaded, "Let's not talk about her ..."

To make matters worse, I wrote Titi a sweet goodbye letter. I almost gave it to her before I returned to FSU for my senior year. Ed abruptly intervened, "What in the world did she do to you? Did she kiss you? Did she hug you? I don't understand how a man can be so wooed by a woman without even touching her." I didn't understand either. I never admitted to being in love with Titi. I just called my feelings of that summer '94 "a crazed obsessive crush." I didn't consider it real love since I was still on the rebound from my failure with Niecy. Eventually, I burned my goodbye letter to Titi.

I hung out at Dina's place one last time before taking the bus back to Fayetteville. I took some pictures and made a horde of goodbyes. Titi was on her way to work. I signaled, "Take care of yourself." The only thing she did was walk past me like I didn't exist.

Ed suggested therapy for me. I didn't take this warning seriously until two and a half years later, when my yearning for Titi grew to an alarming near-fatal condition.

My social confidence was very low during fall semester '94. Alim mocked me, "You sound like a hurt ass bitch." Shamefully I was. Stephanie and her husband Damon told me to concentrate on things that only I like doing. This advice inspired me to feel better, and I attracted a genuine love interest at the start of spring semester '95.

In late January '95, I visited Washington D.C. to attend a job fair. I stayed at Stephanie and Damon's house. While they were at work on a Friday afternoon, I took the D.C. Metro train to the hotel lobby location of the fair. I arrived in the lobby waiting for approximately twenty minutes before the conference room doors opened. There were at least fifty other students dressed in their best business attire with resumes and briefcases in their hands. Amazingly, my energy was stabilized. I didn't feel the same pressure to land a job like I did at previous conventions.

Briefly, I spoke with a few students. Then, I saw a short-cut perm-haired black woman with a Georgetown University pin on her nametag. Out of curiosity, I said to her, "So you're a Georgetown student! What's your major?" She responded, "Foreign Relations! And what's yours?'" I said, "Accounting! And by the way I'm Albert. It's nice to meet you." And so she introduced herself, "And I'm Erika. Nice to meet you too!"

From here, Erika and I hit it off quickly. We had a nice conversation for about fifteen minutes before the conference room doors opened. I invited her to have lunch with me after the first fair break and she accepted. We wound up eating at a Greek fast-food restaurant at the downtown mall. Our nice dialogue continued. A light-skinned Howard University (HU) graduate sat at a table directly to my right, even though all the other tables were empty. He listened to our conversation and uninvitedly joined in. Despite my slight annoyance, I stayed cool and proceeded to have a good chat with both Erika and the HU gentleman.

Erika and I finished our lunch. Then we said our fond farewells to the HU man. My energy was harmonized enough to view him as a wonderful challenge. As I walked with Erika back to the hotel, she recommended, "Let's do something tonight." I calmly stated, "Sure! We'll exchange info after the last part of this fair."

After running out of resumes, I waited patiently for Erika to finish her interview. We exchanged numbers and hugged each other goodbye. I left the hotel feeling very upbeat thinking, "I'm gonna have a good time tonight with or without her."

I took the Metro to Stephanie's office. She asked "How was the job fair?" I said, "It was fine. Keep in mind that I may be going out tonight." Stephanie said, "No problem. I don't want anything to interfere with your girlfriend."

My yet-to-be girlfriend called me in the evening. We arranged to meet each other outside a Metro substation near George Washington University. Then we decided to see the John Singleton film *Higher Learning*.

While seated, I placed my left hand over Erika's right hand, which was laid out on her thigh. For at least five minutes, I didn't feel any movement from her. So I started to remove my hand. But then she grabbed my fingers and interlocked them with hers. I sensed, "Mission accomplished." We held hands throughout the movie.

My comfort level with Erika gradually increased into the

night. We stopped at KFC for a late dinner. She briefly explained how she turned away guys who pursued her sexually, even though they were close to her in the bedroom. I only listened. I wasn't hitting on her for just sex.

Next, we stopped by a club in Georgetown. It was crowded, so we kept walking side-by-side with our hands intertwined. Somehow we wound up galloping through an empty closed mall. I was feeling so relaxed that I firmly caressed her face, "No one is around so we can make out now." I leaned in and pecked her cheek. Erika joked, "But someone might be watching us." I proceeded to caress her lips. She shrugged off, "Maybe later!"

We continued our escapade at a fountain area. It was very cold. As I clenched my teeth in frozenness, I said, "My nose is red and frosty." Erika laughed, "You're pale. You need a tan." Little side put-downs were constantly exchanged between us as our chemistry was building. Somehow, we changed subjects. I felt comfortable enough to mention my white grandmother who I never met. She suggested, "You should meet her."

We trotted back to Erika's apartment. Her neighbors were oo-ing and ah-ing at us with gossip. Erika fixed some hot chocolate, and our warmth towards each other increased. I proceeded to kiss her more extending my tongue down her throat. We kissed for several more minutes. Abruptly, Erika tells me to call Stephanie so she can pick me up. I didn't know the street routes, so Erika explained them to Damon. At this point my emotions were rocky. I was having one of the happiest times of my life, but it was ending too soon. Erika laughed at my gloominess, "You can handle it since you're a man!"

We kissed for another half-hour before Stephanie and Damon arrived. They took pictures of us hugging each other in the parking lot. I walked Erika back to her apartment. She asked, "Will you write me?" We exchanged contact info, and I gave her the longest tongue kiss of my life. As I walked to Damon's car, she stood outside of her door and said "bye" three times.

I sat in the backseat feeling flatlined. Damon asked, "Did you score?" I answered, "No! I didn't hit the homerun if that's what you meant!" Stephanie jeered Damon on his "scoring" question. He brushed it off saying he only meant to ask about how much fun I had. I said, "I hit a double." He reached from the driver's seat and shook my hand, "Congratulations!"

Erika and I exchanged letters for the next two months. She mentioned her African boyfriend, whom she met in Japan while studying as a foreign exchange student. She said she loved him but was unsure how to carry on a long distance relationship. Erika was also in the midst of making spring break plans for Montego Bay, Jamaica. FSU's spring break fell during the same week, so Erika asked me to meet her there. I refused due to monetary restrictions. She reacted, "You just don't want to come!"

I decided to lay over at Stephanie and Damon's house that week. Erika arrived back in D.C. from Jamaica on the last Saturday of our breaks, so we met in Georgetown again. This time I didn't feel relaxed. I argued with Stephanie for several reasons. She was happily pregnant, yet she was also extremely moody. Thus she criticized me by calling me socially lazy and philosophically confused. I nearly cut my visit in half before Damon settled us down. Stephanie still chewed me out once more before I got on the Metro and hooked up with Erika.

Erika had fun in Jamaica. This time she had her hair braided. She cooked some food while I looked for an interesting event in the newspaper. We settled on checking out a bizarre adult cartoon movie. Again we held hands. She felt like my girlfriend. However, the same magic from our first date was missing. Erika also seemed exhausted.

After the flick, we hopped through Georgetown and entered a club. Erika appeared looser. She did the tootsie roll dance, and

I finally saw her smile. I stumbled with two left feet, acciden-
tally stepping on hers, so I bought a rose to cheer her up. I tried
to kiss her, but she leaned away.

We eventually skipped back to Erika's for a night cap. Tire-
lessly, we watched TV. Before we got sleepy, I firmly tugged
Erika onto the couch with me. I was intimately kissing her gently. Then I pulled her top off. She helped me untie her bra. Suddenly, I was smooching her nipples. Normally, the next step
would be intercourse. I didn't feel though like our encounter
was committed love. Plus, I didn't want to lose my virginity to
a one night stand. So I interjected, "Do you want me to take
this further?" She looked up at the roof, "Uhhh? I'm fine!", so I
got tired and stopped. As we laid our heads against each other,
I asked "Where do you want me to sleep?" She rattled, "The
couch!" Then she retreated to her bedroom.

The next morning Erika cooked breakfast. I called Damon
and Stephanie telling them I would meet them at their church.
Erika and I said our farewells. I gave her a tongue kiss. She
backed away after ten seconds, "That's enough." I left her place
confused, feeling like nothing was left between us.

Erika and I exchanged a few more letters before we both
graduated from college. I poured out my feelings of frustration.
She responded by saying that our nice time together was only
"fun" away from the loneliness of her long-distance relationship with her African boyfriend.

Even though I was disappointed that Erika and I were not
full-fledged lovers, I forever cherish my time with her. She is still
the best time I ever had with a female, and she remains the closest thing I've ever had resembling a true girlfriend.

Erika and I did see each other one last time. She wrote me
two and a half years later after arriving back in the states from
her extended work in Japan. Again, we consistently communicated from exchanged letters. She and one of her high school

friends visited me in November '98 seeking a warm vacation away from their hometown of Detroit. They ended up dragging me to almost every hot urban dance spot in Atlanta. I tried one last time to get intimate with Erika. This time Erika mumbled, "I don't know. Things are just different. You're in a different location. You have a different career and mindset. You're thinking of changing your name (i.e. Nadir Talib Al-Kareem). You're just ... different." I gave Erika a peck on the lips before watching her and her friend ride off on a plane back to Detroit. Afterwards, I was upset that I didn't make a better attempt to have sex with her despite the way she used her friend as a cock-block excuse. However, things were crystal clear that Erika and I were only a divine time together resulting from our needs for fun. Erika subsequently moved back to Japan. We still keep in touch occasionally by e-mail.

I guess I did try too hard to make my time with Erika into a deep relationship even though it never really had long-term potential. I still think about how different both our lives would be if I met her in Jamaica instead of D.C. during our final college spring break. I also guess that divine intervention is why I decided not take more wild chances with her. My mentality was still clogged from obsession with Titi, which escalated into deeper turmoil (a.k.a. Titi Syndrome) by 1996. And even after my last visit with Erika, my mind was still flawed with desperate futile hope for the Perfect Mythical EGYPTIAN QUEEN!

ANGEL OF DEATH

After college graduation in May '95, I stayed with relatives in Stone Mountain, Georgia. They were near Atlanta, a city noted for having a wide array of successful black professionals. Plus, I didn't like Washington D.C., even though Stephanie lived in that area. I stayed with Aunt Jane's family for my first six weeks in metro ATL. Then, I lived with Grandpa Richard (Pop Pop) and Grandma Philamena for six more weeks before renting my own apartment.

While residing with relatives, I searched recklessly for a job. I passed out resumes everyday and interviewed with temp agencies every week. After almost a month, I finally nailed a temp job at SunTrust Bank's corporate office in downtown Atlanta. I only lasted two weeks.

Uncle Roy constantly stayed on my case about continuing my education. I was offered an assistanceship to Iowa State University's (ISU) Graduate Business School. Almost all of my family wanted me to go. I, on the other hand, was too burned out to fathom more schooling. Yet, I had no immediate job offers and very few leads. ISU looked more like my best choice.

Grandma Philamena allowed me to reside at her house under the sentenced condition, "You're welcome to stay until you go to school."

By mid-July, I was getting rejected for jobs by everyone, including Red Lobster. I was ready to accept ISU's offer. As I arrived at Grandma's after being turned down by another restaurant, Pop Pop told me a guy from AT&T called saying they have a job open for me. I was ecstatic!

I started work at the Atlanta Works factory of AT&T Network Systems (now Lucent Technologies) the following week. I moved into the Peachtree Garden Apartments in Brookhaven one month later. And one month following my move, I earned my drivers' license in time to rent a car for a new hire orientation in New Jersey. Despite my nervousness and the crappy New Jersey traffic, I gained enough confidence from this trip to drive regularly in Atlanta. Thus, I finally bought a Nissan Sentra GXE in late October '95.

Everything seemed upbeat financially. Psychologically though, I was headed for grueling times.

On Thanksgiving '95, I visited Stephanie, Damon, and their newborn two-month old son, Zeke. Stephanie and Damon were very happy with their new family on the surface. However, they were also distraught over other immediate family concerns.

Father lost his Vegas job at E.O.B. in spring '94. Every day, he sank deeper into unemployment, procrastination, and drunkenness. After my college graduation, he decided to search for work in Los Angeles while staying with Grandma Rita. Father, though, whined that he couldn't be without Mother. He convinced Mother to sell their house. Pop Pop and my sisters chastised Mother for this decision saying she should have stayed in Vegas until Father received a guaranteed offer.

Lo and behold, my parents' residency with Grandma Rita and her husband Barney resulted in disaster. While Mother found retail work without a problem, Father had no leads. Barney often complained about Father's drinking and smoking. When I spoke with Father in July '95, he told me he landed a job as news editor. A few days later, this story turned out to be false. Father was overloaded with compulsive lies. Grandma Rita and Barney became fed up and ready to evict Father.

On the day of Father's presumed exit, Grandma Rita received a phone call from a hospital. They said Father attempted suicide by trying to asphyxiate himself in a car. Mother believed Father, so she visited him at the hospital. The rest of the family, including me, thought Father concocted this scenario just to save his own ass from living on the streets. Most of us had to yell sense into Mother to let Father go. He was released from the hospital a week later. Then he relocated temporarily to Uncle Raleigh's place in St. Louis, Missouri.

Meanwhile, the whole family was in disarray figuring out where Mother should live. Pop Pop initially convinced Mother to move to Atlanta. First, she moved all her belongings to Stephanie's. She planned on helping Stephanie work through her first few weeks as a mother before having Pop Pop scoop her up for the drive to Georgia.

These plans worked out in the end but not before there was more impeding drama from Father. Uncle Raleigh wanted his privacy back and called for Father's exit. So Father unexpectedly transferred to D.C.. One day he arrived at Stephanie's job without notice. She called me explaining how his uninformed arrival at her office scared the hell out of her. Stephanie was still projected to be pregnant for three more weeks, but she went into labor two days following Father's surprise visit. She and Damon were very relieved that Zeke was born healthy. They were still very upset about Father's uninvited appearance.

Father landed a job with a D.C. news station one week after Stephanie paid for his hotel stay. This time he wasn't lying. Mother subsequently decided to give Father another chance and stayed in D.C. against everyone's wishes.

During my Thanksgiving '95 visit to D.C., I received even more disturbing family news. Father was worried again over unemployment because his bosses found out about his mental hospital records. Stephanie and Damon didn't believe this. They thought Father revealed this only to save his behind from repeated job errors. Father's manipulative behavior was brought more to the forefront when he revealed how he never actually received a college degree. Stephanie and I were disgruntled since we now figured out another reason why Father ran our household with unrealistic expectations and pressure. I remember him calling Mother "an uneducated bastard" during an argument. Talk about the pot calling the kettle black.

We discussed this with Father. He said, "I wanted out of the South so badly. My summer '63 internship with NBC was my ticket. Back in those days, it was common for news reporters to fake their credentials. So I played along. I have no regrets for pushing you (me and my sisters) very hardly to earn your college degrees... Every man has to make a major sacrifice to do what's best for his family..."

Even though Father was unapologetic for his parental and educational methods, he certainly hated the wrath his lies brought to him professionally. On the day after his revelations, Stephanie scolded Mother for her loyalty towards Father. Then she angrily called Father on the phone. She said he needed to learn how to be "a real man" from Damon. Father left Stephanie's house cussing out Damon the night before. Damon got on the phone attempting to rectify the situation. Father chided, "You're a fucking dummy! You disrespected me in front of my son." Damon responded, "At least I never lied to get a job. Stay away from my family, or I'll rip you apart."

Damon was infuriated. He shouted to Mother, "I can't allow you to come into this house again as long as you're affiliated with Al Johnson." Stephanie vehemently agreed. Mother rebuked this decision at first. I joined Stephanie in her stance and yelled at Mother, "You've got everyone offering you a place to stay and keep jerking them around by staying with Father." Mother responded, "Well you haven't offered me a place to stay." I rebuffed, "I could lose my job next month, and all you're complaining about is me not offering you a place to stay…"

Mother was now more upset and weepy-eyed, yet she listened well to Stephanie and I's pep talk. Stephanie drove us to the Metro station. Father was waiting there to escort Mother from "dangerous elements" on the train. We all remained silent while Stephanie wailed to Father, "Oh you really blew it this time…Cussing out my husband. You probably screwed up at your job too. I suppose a 'Fuck you' is the only way you know how to respond…Now tell Mother how she'll never get a chance to see her grandson again as long as she stays with you. You're screwing up the whole family. And Albert (here) has a mind of his own. We (Damon and Stephanie) are not withholding his communication from you…"

Mother got on the train with Father. I put my arm around Stephanie and told her, "I'm proud of you." Mother returned to Stephanie's house the next day and told us how she criticized Father. Father then left a message a few hours later, "Damon! If you take Mary (Mother) away from me, I'll have you fired from your job." Damon laughed. Stephanie felt threatened, "This is war." She called Fathers' bosses and informed them of his "threatening phone calls." Father was subsequently fired. Mother succumbed, "Okay, I'm going to Atlanta."

Pop Pop scooped Mother up weeks later. Stephanie filed for a restraining order against Father. Pop Pop convinced me to have Mother live in my tiny studio apartment until she got situated in Atlanta.

All my family chaos eventually exhausted my spirit. I couldn't hide my unhappiness regarding my new living arrangement with Mother. I felt Mother needed to get a place of her own.

At the same time, I was also looking to save money with my friend Jakim as a roommate. Jakim and I were ready to move into another apartment. Then our agreement fell apart when we argued over split cable costs. Jakim simply stated, "I don't care for cable." I continued to press how we should split all bills. Jakim summed up our heated chat, "I don't think we should do this." I said, "Fine," and hung up the phone. Our bitter fissure escalated to near physical confrontation. Then Jakim called back," Look! We can handle this like men, or we can handle this like fools!" Thus we exchanged more heated words. Jakim said, "You're acting like an antsy European." I said, "At least I'm responsible by keeping my bills paid!" Jakim said, "Yeah, well you're also two-faced for acting like you trust me when you said you didn't. Being black is about being spiritual from the heart. And not (just about) reading black history just to feel good about being black." I hung up the phone speechless. Jakim rattled a chord in me because I was contemplating going to graduate school to major in Black Studies. Yet my actions displayed character defects of words over deeds.

I met Jakim days later while he roomed with Alim and his girlfriend Bula in Decatur. I apologized, "I'm sorry for not being more honest and admitting I didn't know you well enough to trust you." Jakim was cool, so we reconciled. I also could've been more sympathetic to Jakim, who was still recovering from a suicide attempt after his girlfriend in North Carolina abandoned him. Little did I know how I would soon be engrossed in a similar scenario.

Meanwhile, my Stone Mountain relatives criticized me for not being more supportive of Mother. My sisters and I responded, "We're disappointed in you all for not letting Mother stay in your 'big ole houses.'"

Mother continued to reside at my place for eight more months. I didn't ask her to contribute to my bills until April '96. Stephanie and I were inundated that Mother still didn't rent her own place.

Overall, the whole family was settled with Mother's mess until more ruckus with Father erupted later in spring '96.

On a Sunday night, I received a phone call from Father. He told me of his whereabouts at a bus stop in Stone Mountain. Everyone's worst fears of Father following Mother across the country were coming true. Father sent June a series of letters describing a suffering homeless plight after he was fired. When in reality, he stayed with an ex-girlfriend in New York. Plus, he scrounged up more of Mother's job insurance money. He had no idea where she was after she left him. We knew, though, that he wouldn't stop stalking her.

Father kept pressing me on the phone, "Just let me speak to your mother." I stuck with the lie, "I don't know where she is." I called Aunt Jane, Uncle Roy, and Pop Pop warning them of Father's intrusion. Pop Pop and Aunt Jane told me to stick with the lie saying that he'll eventually leave town. Uncle Roy and Stephanie suggested for Mother to encounter him and discuss a divorce. Mother decided to remain out of dodge in my apartment. She explained, "I even called a battered woman's shelter hotline, and they also recommended that I don't talk to him."

Father left one more message threatening to have the police show up on my job and the house steps of Uncle Roy and Pop Pop. I ignored him. However, Father called my job in a worn out and weepy tone, "I'm tired! Let me stay with you!" I just hung up.

The next day, I prepared to leave work from an overtime shift. Then I received a phone call, "A man who says he's your father is waiting for you in the parking lot." I reacted with disbelief, "What?" The security lady repeated her statement. With shocking rage, I walked to the parking lot and saw Father, smoking his ass off, and now looking frighteningly slim. He tried to shake my hand, but I reached away and began to curse him out. I forget exactly what I said but I remember my words being very nasty and spiteful. Father asked with a shaky voice, "You really mean that?" I spat, "Yes! And no, you're not welcomed to stay at my place. I'm driving you to a homeless shelter." Father said, "Forget it. I'll see myself out." As he walked away, I warmed up my Sentra. Then I attempted to retrieve him for a ride. He flipped me off, "Fuck you," and walked away in disgust. Begrudgingly, I drove by him twice more poking fun at his anger before finally driving home.

I arrived home. Mother unlocked an extra lock she placed on my door as a secondary security measure. She tried to advise me on how to speak to Father again. I threw my newspaper on the floor and cussed her out screaming, "Why the fuck won't you talk to him?"

I received a call from Father the next day. He said, "I'm leaving town now," and hung up the phone. Stephanie reacted arrogantly, "Al Johnson ain't gone. You're all dumber than I thought if you believe he left town." She was right. A few days later, I received another phone call from Father. He was frantic, "Okay Son. I just wanna go home. Someone or anyone just give me a bus ticket to Jackson, TN. I don't want to stay at the homeless shelter. I got raped and may have AIDS. I know you don't believe me. But I promise I won't bother anyone again …" Of course he admitted years later that his shelter story was bullshit, but at least he was offering the family some peace prior to his departure. Pop Pop arranged for Father's bus ticket and gave him food money during the boarding wait. Pop Pop drove me to the bus station. I walked in and saw Father with his head buried in his lap. I said, "You've screwed up your life and received repercussions in return. Now it's time for you to go away and make amends …" Father lifted his head up with a look of confusion and sarcasm. I tried to give him a twenty-dollar bill, but he refused. Pop Pop and I saw him hop on the bus and sit down at a window seat. All we did was stare silently, making sure he tried not to escape. He waved once as we watched the bus drive off.

Father would continue his angry phone calling, letter-writing, and stalking escapades for another year until he landed in a government assisted halfway house program in San Francisco, CA. He only lasted for two months with relatives in Jackson, Tennessee. He got kicked out after they received a recorded message of a threatening phone call he made to me. He also made similar threats to Stephanie and Grandma Rita. He said he would kill us all. Stephanie laughed. Grandma Rita filed a police report, and I submitted Father's picture and psycho phone message to Pop Pop and Lucent security. June stayed close to him while monitoring his whereabouts since she was living in the Bay area.

These days I sparingly contact Father through e-mail. I didn't speak with him on the phone for more than five years. Ever since Mother officially divorced him, he's threatened suicide on several more occasions. He still contemplates a death wish. I pray for Father to get his act together in this lifetime or the next.

Once Father's commotion cleared ATL, I was on a more destructive path.

I was miserable. Unhappiness clogged my Lucent job despite my forty thousand dollars per year earnings at only twenty-three years of age. I was unsure if Accounting was the right career for me. Social time with females was passing me like the wind. And Mother's presence in my home still made me uneasy.

In June '96, I decided to break away from my ATL carnage. I drove to Memphis for a visit. I felt I owed all my friends and relatives there a tremendous amount of gratitude. Plus, I wanted to prove to myself that I could sustain Titi's aura.

After hanging out with Ed and his co-worker friends on my day of arrival, I settled into a hotel. Then, I drove to Dina's house. We chatted for a couple of hours before Kat arrived. I tagged along with Kat and Dina to pick up Titi from work. I promised myself, "I'm not going to fall apart when I see her."

As Kat pulled into the parking lot, I saw Titi dressed in an all white wardrobe (pants, tank-top, and ruble-tinged flip flops), still looking like the most gorgeous almondy goddess on the planet. I said "hi" without making a gesture while she sat next to me in the back seat. Despite my calm demeanor, my heart though ached more.

After Kat dropped us off at Dina's, I hinted to Titi that I needed to talk to her. Seemingly, I was still not over her.

The next day I hung out for an hour at Dina's. Titi arrived back from work. She argued with her brother. Suddenly she gloated a wrath, "Why don't you be a man like Albert, and get an education?" I was too flattered. Titi thought highly of me? I played off her compliment in low-key fashion.

During the last night of my Memphis visit, Titi and her friends prepared to go to someone's pool. My goodness! Titi was fashionably ravishing in her bathing suit and cut-off jeans shorts. They all started posing for pictures. Of course, Titi's seated model pose was the most striking to my vision. Dina intervened, "Why don't you lean your head back so you can make Albert drool!" Titi's friends chuckled. Then Titi introduced me, "This is my friend Albert. He makes a lot of money working as an accountant..." Dina tried to encourage me to tag along with them to the pool. I nervously refused. As I pulled out of Dina's garage, I asked her to tell Titi, "She's an untouchable jewel!" Once again, I was bowled over by Titi's radiant essence. This time it became seriously fatal.

I didn't understand why I was still hooked on Titi. I was exposed to plenty of attractive females in Atlanta. I even dated a few. The most physically gorgeous young lady I dated was only sixteen when I was twenty-two. Danitra blew me away with a monstrous kiss while we viewed *Dead Presidents* at a theatre. Yet I forgot all about her once I saw Titi again.

Titi's Goddess-esque image became my only joyous fantasy as times grew more sour.

I was unhappy working as a cost accountant. I reconsidered accepting the Business School assistanceship offer from ISU, which was still valid until the end of summer '96. I also contemplated studying black history on a graduate level. Neither field though defined what I most enjoyed. Therefore, I decided to give my accounting background a full-throttled attempt at passing the CPA exam.

As fate revealed, the CPA exam was the worst study experience of my life. It felt like my first serious school failure.

I approached this test too seriously. I pressured Mother to move out and find her own apartment, cut off subscriptions for cable and newspaper services, and I let my ticket to a 1996 U.S. Women's Olympic Basketball game go unused.

With little motivation, I had problems concentrating. I remember often passing out asleep for twelve to thirteen hours. Then, I fell into crying spells on several weekends.

Meanwhile, I also had difficulties getting a grasp on my Lucent job. At the end of each month, the Accounting department made closing entries. I was consistently chewed out for failing to justify hundreds of thousands of dollars in inventory differences.

In November '96, the CPA exam date approached. I reserved two weeks off from work for study preparation. My supervisor reprimanded me for leaving my clients with a lackluster perception of my capabilities. Thus, I entered my study break with low confidence. After freaking out from exhausting exam practice, I re-ordered cable television service, rented some videos, and wrote Titi a 5-page letter. Through all this torment, my mind couldn't escape a single thought of Titi. In a nutshell, I poured out to Titi that she was a "GREAT GODDESS ALMIGHTY GORGEOUS ALMOND COCOA MAHOGANY DIVINE JEWEL OF THE MISSISSIPPI MEMPHIS BELLE!" And I said that I was nothing but a "STUMBLING MUMBLING WEAK SQUEAMISH DROOLING FOOLISH LITTLE BOY!"

My mind was so lost that I almost backed out of taking the CPA exam. I went back to work early saying that I was not prepared. My supervisor convinced me to give it a try. Thus I sat through the exam days later. Indeed, I failed with much misery and laughter. After the test day, I was relieved it was over since I already pre-destined myself for the plunge. I told my friends I either needed "a drink, a shrink, or the pink (pussy)!"

I attempted to prep myself to study again for the CPA Exam two months later. Yet, I experienced splitting headaches by just the sight of study review material from the Becker CPA review course.

I also experienced more social failures. I was rejected and/or stood-up by more female dating prospects, several of them who I pursued from my CPA class. Plus, I almost lost five hundred dollars to an African-American social network called Friends Helping Friends, which turned out to be an off-shoot pyramid scheme.

As a result of my low self-esteem in every major functional area, I sought help from a psychologist.

Since most of my sorrows resulted from black females, I had my insurance provider select an African-American woman named Dr. Baskins. Initially, I was glad to finally have a female to express my personal problems to. Dr. Baskins basically listened and asked questions during my first four sessions.

The plight of my appointments took a drastic turn when I revealed the subject of Titi.

About three weeks later after my letter send-off, Titi called me. I didn't recognize the female voice initially. Then, the woman said, "Oh! You're an hour ahead, so I guess you're sleepy." With jubilant disbelief I responded, "I know who this is!" Titi played a guessing game. I said, "It's an Egyptian Queen." She hideously bequeathed, "Oooooah pluh-ease!" My chest thumped so hard that I almost had a heart attack. While catching my breath I said, "I can't believe you called me." She chided, "What else did you expect me to do after that long letter you wrote..." After speaking with her for five more minutes, Titi encouraged me to keep calling her. I tried to be cool, "Of course! You might become interested in me." Titi replied, "We'll see!"

Apparently, I was back on the right track with Titi. Boy was I stupid. I called Titi during the holiday breaks. She brushed me off like she had no time to talk.

Dr. Baskins laughed at this story, "You have a case of TNT – Titi 'N' the Test." I also told Dr. Baskins that I was thinking of sending Titi flowers. Dr. Baskins advised me to wait until my next appointment and listened to more of my ridiculous infatuation tales. Thus she supported my decision to proceed with the floral delivery.

I made sure the flowers arrived on Valentine's Day. While I awaited a response, my friends were mocking me for allowing myself to fall back into a hex — The Titi Syndrome. Ed insulted me, "... She's laughing at you. You're embarrassing all men ... Do you wear the panties? I don't wanna talk about this anymore ..." Roderick made a mock threat, "Let me get the belt!" Alim on the other hand came to my defense, "That bitch! She hasn't responded by now?" And Antonio consoled me in the midst of my sappy whines, "... You're a black man in Atlanta with a job making good money ... Just change your attitude!"

My attitude was steadily sinking into the abyss. I was still a virgin with low self-esteem. Dr. Baskins sensed this and asked, "Do you want to feel depressed?" Surprised, I reacted, "It's not how I want to feel. Maybe it's my destiny. Perhaps I deserve rejection and mockery." Dr. Baskins tried to encourage me to think positively. I wasn't budging.

On February 28, 1997, I woke up with visions of hanging myself with a necktie on my interior roof hanger. I still compiled enough strength to drive to work. On the job, more discouragement poured in. I received a phone call from the florist confirming Titi received the flowers, "She hasn't responded?" I decided I was going to kill myself after work, so I left a phone message with Dr. Baskins, "... I know you said the choice is all mine on how to think and act. So whatever I decide to do, I'll just do it." Dr. Baskins called back an hour later, "You just made a threat. So I'm sending some people to pick you up." I told her that would be too embarrassing. Even though she arranged for my admittance to a mental hospital, I told her I would drive there myself.

Before I left work, my department manager told me how disappointed he was with my performance. I told him I would be away for awhile trying to improve my psychological condition. Apparently, I made my mental problems too public to be respected by co-workers.

As I drove to the hospital, my mind was fluttered with the pre-suicidal visions I woke up with. The OutKast intro song "You May Die" from their *ATLiens* album was playing in my head like a tape recorder. Ironically, this song proved to be a preview of my future encounters as **D-Rock SOUL-Jah** with all the musicians who performed on that track.

Before I was checked into a hospital room, I was interviewed and photographed. The most poignant question asked was, "Do you promise not to hurt yourself." I didn't answer at first. I also refused initial offers to take anti-depressants since I practiced herbal medicinal use.

While I waited for a room assignment in a lounge, I phoned my relatives with news of my illness. Uncle Ka called me back,

"… You're doing the right thing. Let those people help you. I love you, and take care of yourself." I hung up the phone in a frantic weep. Tears overflowed my face, and I buried my head under a pillow.

After resting for an hour, I was called for another interview. This time a husky bearded Caucasian psychiatrist with glasses named Dr. Davis de-briefed me. He started off, "What day is it today?" I looked at him, "Huh?" He explained how he was required to ask basic questions like this to every new patient. He continued his interrogation and recommended that I re-consider my refusal for medication. Then he asked with fury, "Are you going to kill yourself?" I said nothing. He expressed arrogantly, "That's what I thought!"

I proceeded to the lounge. Dr. Davis stopped me, "We need your consent that you won't hurt yourself. Otherwise, we'll have to put you in a straitjacket and assign someone to follow you around. You wouldn't like that unit." Thus, I consented.

I retreated to a room to fall asleep. A red-haired man with a hillbilly accent was in the shower. He was my assigned roommate. He came out of the shower naked before putting a towel on. From an urge to freely speak my mind, I told him, "I'm not gay but I was curious to look at you." He acted shocked. Then he became friendly, "Look if you're gay that's nothing to be ashamed of." I sighed, "I'm not. Don't worry." He shrugged with his deep southern accent, "… Man, it sure took some balls to say what you said without knowing me. The average man wooda sed, 'Get your faggot ass outta hey-er.' But hey, I've had same-sex acts when I was high on cocaine. Somebody asked me, 'Hey are you gay.' I said, 'No, but I've thought about it.'"

Even though I was frightened over my expression of homosexual tendency, I was also relieved that I was finally in a place where people allowed me to speak uncensored.

I later learned that this man was a chicken-wing restaurant

owner and a former pro tennis player. He blew his first million dollar earnings on an expensive cocaine habit. I got along with him just fine after our hazy introduction. I felt like my issues were very miniscule compared to the drug addicts on my assigned floor.

I checked in as a patient for about five days. Constantly, I was hounded with interviews by case workers. I remember a female social intern questioning my family background. I explained how Father abused both Mother and me, verbally and sometimes physically. She said, "He sounds like a monster. You need cognitive adjustments so you won't view yourself anymore as a piece of crap. I recommend *The Feeling Good Handbook* by David Burns."

On my final day of in-patient care, I was visited by Mother, Pop Pop, Alim and his girlfriend Bula. Alim told me to just forgive Father the next time I saw him. I told Mother I was doing fine. Then, I showed them pictures I drew during art therapy classes (I still have these pictures hung up on my home wall). I received goodbye hugs by everyone. The most surprising gesture was from Pop Pop. He rarely hugs anyone.

I was released the following day into an outpatient program. Every day I was involved in group therapy sessions along with check-ups from Dr. Davis. After each session, I felt less tongue-tied by speaking with candid honesty. The most poignant revelation came during a dinner table exercise. I told the group leader that my family hardly ever sat for dinner together. This one tiny detail summarized the poor communication that I was raised with. The assigned counselors of this group recommended my attendance at weekly Al-Anon meetings.

Six weeks following my flirt with death, I returned to work at Lucent. I was prescribed with Zoloft feeling very relaxed. Every time negative feelings approached me, I wrote them down in a journal. Dr. Davis encouraged me to continue my appointments with Dr. Baskins. Even though I was still bummed out about my life, I was feeling more hopeful during my daily pursuits.

There was a wonderful date I ventured on before returning to work. I met Addison at a Friends Helping Friends meeting. She called me once so I invited her to join me at the movies. I had a very positive attitude throughout this outing. I thought, "I'm going to have a good time with or without her." Addison snuggled against me for almost the entire time we watched *Rosewood*. This film overwhelmed her emotionally, so she cried in my arms. After we picked up her daughter from a babysitter, I drove them home. Addison and I embraced in a warm blissful kiss. As I walked down the stairs to my car, she looked out over her balcony waving with a smile similar to a woman from a Crest commercial.

I tried to kick it with Addison again. She on the other hand was still hung-up on some man who asked for her hand in marriage. I guessed it was her "babbydaddy." Nevertheless, I proceeded to date other women without taking them seriously the way I did prior to my hospital trip.

Dr. Baskins was very happy with my progress. My reoccurring sessions with her also helped me realize that I was not happy working as an accountant.

I didn't know exactly which career to pursue until I started exercising more frequently. While still working at Lucent, I participated in several long-distance road races. I wasn't fast, but I kept my legs moving. After jogging consistently for about four months, I was felt in great shape. Late one night, thoughts scrambled through my head while listening to CDs by Groove Theory, Eric Benet, and the *Get on the Bus* soundtrack. "I want to be a DJ. This is what I will enjoy doing regardless of pay. This will give me purpose and a true meaning of success." I ran out of my apartment jogging several miles non-stop until the Sun rose. This was one of the happiest moments of my life.

Part of my happiness resulted from Zoloft medication. After realizing this, I experienced several mood swings. Sure pharmaceuticals work but not without side effects. Therefore, the meds really didn't heal me. This attitude reflected in my outpatient visits with Dr. Davis. Thus, I cut off my communication with him. I also didn't care for the restrictive dialogue of the Al-Anon group I attended. All they said to me was, "You're only supposed to talk about personal stuff with a sponsor ..."

I was full of energy—good and bad. This energy was channeled into another Memphis visit.

Even after all the chaos I experienced from seething Titi, I still had a tremendous desire to express my whole-hearted feelings toward her. Alim supported me on this decision. So on the fourth of July weekend of 1997, I listened to the CD *Are You Gonna Go My Way* by Lenny Kravitz while busting out of Atlanta in my '96 Sentra.

I arrived in Memphis after midnight without notifying friends in advance. Kat and her husband allowed me to spend the night at their house. In the morning, I immediately drove to Dina's house. After I rapped with Alex about the state of black America, Titi arrived with her cousin Nola. Without my normal drooling fear, I lunged into Titi giving her a hug. I told her, "Wow! It took me this long to get a hug out of you." She sighed, "Only because you stayed away too long." As I explained how I was just passing through town, she invited me to tag along to the movies with her cousin, younger sister and her friends. I agreed to drive.

While we rode through the freeway to pick up the young friends of Titi's sister, I told Titi about a business idea I had as my tape deck bumped more of Lenny's tracks. She asked, "Where are you going to open it (a shop) up?" I answered emphatically, "Da SWATS (Southwest Atlanta), East Point, and Collie Park (College Park, GA)." She screamed with mockery, "What da fuck? (In)Those junky projects?" I frowned, "I thought you said you didn't curse." Then she shook her head in denial, "I don't."

Our conversation was amusing until I scooped up the little girls for the final drive to the theatre. I allowed the girls to view my music tapes. Nola suggested that we put on Erykah Badu's *Baduism* album. I wasn't feeling it, "Hell no. I'm driving and we need to make sure the driver is comfortable so we can ride safely." The little girls said, "You're mean." I laughed it off, proceeding to park us at the mall.

We decided to see *Men in Black*. Without hesitation, I paid for Titi's ticket and hot dog. She heckled, "You don't have to treat me." I said, "It's okay! I hardly get your time." She scowled back, "You wouldn't want my time." I sensed she had a lot of ill issues, but I paid no attention.

As we settled into our seats, Titi nearly ran out of the theatre after freaking out over a scene showing an alien mutation. She screamed, "Oh no! I didn't realize the movie would be like this. I thought it was a sequel to *Bad Boys* (also starring Will Smith). I even had trouble watching *Independence Day* (another alien movie with Will Smith)." On one hand I was laughing, but on the other hand I was disturbed by Titi's fragile mind.

Overall, I was still pining over Titi's lack of response to my flower delivery. My anger was misconstrued on the drive back to Dina's house. After dropping off the little girls at their home, Titi pointed to a house she wanted to observe. I resisted and drove on, "No!" Nola screamed, "She just wanted to look for a minute ..." Then Titi joined in for a double-team attack, "Albert, I don't know wut is rawng wit' you. You come across so negative. You're from a different time." This verbal onslaught from a Mid-South dialect didn't faze me initially. But then out of the blue Titi wailed, "You don't even seem like you're down with the Black Community." My heart sunk to my stomach. I was so shocked by the timing of this subtle insult that I remained virtually silent for the rest of the drive. I tried to interject in Titi and Nola's gossip chat, but Nola barked, "I'm through with you," and proceeded to talk like I didn't exist.

I dropped them off at Dina's. They said a quiet "thanks" and drove to another shopping mall. Alex gave me a message from Kat. I called her back. She demanded that I come to her house. Kat and her husband chewed me out for arriving in town without notice. Plus, Kat was seven months pregnant with very little tolerance for disturbances. I only listened with shame while they allowed me to spend one more night at their house.

After their disciplinary attack, I fell back into depression. I took a long walk through their neighborhood later in the night. I decided that this trip to Memphis was a huge mistake. So I drove back to Atlanta the next morning. While pumping more of Lenny Kravitz on my auto tape deck, I searched my SOUL and came to the conclusion, "I love Titi. It was never just an obsession." My depression disappeared again.

I wrote Titi another letter telling her, "I still have love for you despite our differences …" She never responded. She eventually moved to Smyrna, Georgia (an Atlanta suburb) with roommates. I left a few phone messages for her, but I still didn't matter in her world.

Overall, I still wish Titi well. Perhaps she was never suitable for me in this lifetime. Regardless, my experience with her will always be a stain on my SOUL.

After relieving my Spear-it of the Titi Syndrome, I was ready for something wild.

I was very frustrated from still being a virgin. I masturbated often. Then I became more distraught when Alim gave me more information about Tantric Sex and the Tao of Sexology. Basically, these philosophies were designed for humans to conserve sexual energy instead of ejaculating their semen. These practices can be used while masturbating too. Most experts though recommended for this kind of sex to be practiced only with one special mate. I fully complied since Jakim practiced it with four girlfriends simultaneously and literally saw demons. Despite my cooperation with the so-called expert advice, I still attracted no dates.

On a June night, I said, "Fuck it" and proceeded to a strip bar. I had a thrill for a few minutes. Then I became more upset about spending a lot of money while still receiving no pussy.

All this pent-up sexual hunger led me to call on a woman I met in December '96 at a club called Atlanta Live. Vera was married, but this still didn't stop her from expressing a strong desire to jump my bones. For months we had nice conversations. I consistently refused her offers to have an affair. After the Titi Syndrome and strip club visit, I changed my mind. "I'm going to get laid, even it means paying for a prostitute." I told Vera, I needed sexual therapy, so we arranged to meet each other at a Buckhead restaurant.

I waited for about forty-five minutes before she showed up. I told her, "I was ready to rent a hooker if you didn't show up soon." She laughed and proceeded to justify occurrences of extra marital affairs. After we ate and argued for an hour, she followed me in her car back to my apartment. I offered her some Dreyer's mint chip-flavored ice cream. She tweaked this offer because it made her hornier. I proceeded to munch on the ice cream bowl while Vera took off her pantyhose. As she settled on the couch, I was very relaxed sensing, "I'm finally going to get some!" She directed me to loosen her dress zipper. Then she let her blouse flaps down revealing her boobs. She preached, "Sex Therapy is about to begin!" She immediately grabbed my arms and locked her lips on my mouth. One thing led to another. All of a sudden the lights were out with both of us butt-naked. She whispered, "Lemme feel what you have," and commenced to sucking my dick. I gently laid her horizontally on the sofa. First I licked her toes. Then I sucked her breasts. She moaned, "You're good at this!" I penetrated into her vagina wearing a condom. After only five minutes or so, she laid down on the floor spreading out her butt cheeks, pleading for me to poke her in the asshole. I was amazed that she wanted me to hump her in a doggystyle position so quickly. So I entered the booty and ejaculated after only one minute. Feeling unfulfilled, I boasted, "This was too easy for my first time." Vera was shocked, "You've never done it before? You mean you've never had a blowjob? Oh my God!" She stood up, "That's okay. We can work up the mood in the next few minutes." I laid back on the sofa. Vera gave me more head. I moaned as she bitched, "Now this will finally shut you up!" I fucked her in three more different positions for another thirty minutes: me on top of her in the sofa; her on top of me in the bed; and me stroking her ass again on the floor. With a tantric mindset, I didn't let myself ejaculate. But I only became more bored. So I stopped. Vera though was still craving me. So she gave me another blowjob. I was still bored, so I told her to roll my penis more with her hands. My very first intercourse experience just did not feel special like I imagined it would be. She continually sucked my phallus, nearly biting it with her teeth. As I was ready to ejaculate, I warned her, but she kept draining my pipe. Thus, I splurged in her mouth. I couldn't believe she practically swallowed my semen. She rinsed out her mouth in the bathroom sink. A minute later, she laid next to me in my bed for two more minutes. Then she got dressed, saying she had to be home soon. Since she was the wife of a musician who has played guitar and bass for famous bands, I asked her to listen to the song "Tha Payroll" by Spearhead. This song inspired me since I was tired of working jobs strictly for money. When the song finished, we ended up in another argument. Vera said, "You're anti-corporate and wanna be a DJ. I'm a web developer and can tell you that the music business will soon be run by computers. If you hate your (current) job, go ahead and quit." I continued to stress the importance of working a job I liked. After we exhausted our viewpoints, she approached the door and told me that I was the youngest person she ever had an affair with. I gave her a hug goodbye.

I was still interested in continuing my liaisons with Vera. Things however took a downward spiral after I quit my Lucent job. Vera chewed me out. "Oh get an education! How could you let your accounting talent go to waste?"

Vera still seemed into me until I insulted her in an argument. She ranted about how all rappers were raping and murdering our children. I responded, "What's the difference between Lil' Kim "swallowing babies" and you swallowing my cum?" Vera angrily griped, "I gave you a classy caress. UUUUUUGHH! You? You really blew it with me!" Indeed I did ruin my chances with her. We exchanged phone conversations steadily until August, 1998. Each time, we wound up bickering. I was still only interested in sex. She never budged again while always giving me lectures on how to manage business. I became too frustrated. Subsequently, I called her a bitch for refusing to lend me some of her vinyl collections recorded by classic rock and funk artists. After Vera warned me not to ever use the B-word with her again, we argued over a different subject. This time I felt awful. Vera humbly said, "You sound like you truly have nothing to say. You haven't been down my road so you don't have any idea how to achieve my kind of success. And after your use of the B-word with me, this will be our last conversation. Good luck with your radio show (on WRFG)! Thanks for your discerning words with me. It's been real!"

I haven't been in contact with Vera since this ugly exchange. I'm confident that she and her family are still living well in some mansion. If I don't ever reconcile my differences with her in this lifetime, I pray for her progressive evolvement.

No acquaintanceship signified my rough career transition more than my communication with Vera.

On September 2, 1997, I walked out of the Atlanta Works factory of Lucent Technologies without giving notice. I deleted all of the personal files from my work computer and didn't look back. I registered with several accounting agencies. From there I performed multiple temp positions while pursuing a radio broadcast career.

This career change seemed okay on the surface but proved to be a very rough challenge to my spirit.

My depression swung back intensely. This time, I decided to use herbal remedies, St. John's Wort and Valerian Root, instead of prescribed pharmaceuticals.

More challenges followed. My Lucent 401(k) was withdrawn completely. So I used credit cards to pay off bills. Physically, my hair started receding heavily. Now, I was feeling more ugly, especially to be going bald at age twenty-four. With no support groups, no health coverage, and more difficulties, my mind produced sudden death contemplations.

One day while driving to my temp assignment in Dunwoody, I experienced a visual hallucination. I was so miserable that my mind attracted a bizarre vision. A Caucasian red-haired-rock-star-looking witch yelled in my ear, "Choose!" I thought about driving my car into a tree to end my life. Yet, I chose to live.

My struggles with depression lingered on. At this moment, I was filled with much curiosity about death, so I started attending functions by metaphysicians who studied holistic healing and the occult. I purchased a Djembe drum imported from Ghana. At spontaneous healing circles, I played it with harmonious freestyle rhythms.

Discovering my true purpose after inspirational activities,

particularly music sessions, literally saved my life. However, I never would have searched my SOUL for purpose without the blessings and curses provided by the Spiritual Angel of Death.

NADIR TALIB AL-KAREEM

Arabic name meaning "Rare/Precious Student of Allah the Most Generous."

I adopted this name when I first started hanging out with Alim and Jakim at FSU. I last heard that Jakim was in New Jersey working at a bakery. He loves cooking, so I pray he's running his own restaurant these days.

Alim and I enrolled in WRFG's broadcast class. We both served as volunteers for this station as well. Alim though, was planning to move back to North Carolina since his family had farmland for him to nurture.

Late one Friday night in September '97, I hung out at Alim's Stone Mountain apartment discussing ideas for Black Nationalism. As I walked out of his building, I saw two cops sitting around in their patrol car.

The passenger cop asked, "Do you live here?" I shook my head saying "No" in a low volume and proceeded to walk to my car. Before I arrived at my Sentra, the cops pulled their patrol car in front of me. I felt harassed. The driver cop shouted, "Hey! You better answer proper authority when you're being questioned." The two tall and bulky Caucasian cops busted out of their car. The driver said, "Lemme see some I.D.!" I pulled it out of my wallet. The driver snapped it from my hand, while the passenger grabbed me and shoved me against the vehicle.

The passenger pats me down and asked snidely, "You don't have any drugs on you. Do you?"

As I became increasingly irritated, the driver asks, "Where do you live?" I told him, "It's on my I.D.." The driver spat, "I'm warning you!" The driver asked another stupid question, "What's your name?" I begrudgingly sighed, "It's on my I.D.!" The driver didn't like my tone, so he boasted in hillbilly slang, "Alright then, yur going da jail." The passenger immediately put me in handcuffs and pushed me into the backseat. I angrily spewed, "What? I can't believe this. I didn't do anything!"

As the cops drove out of the complex I asked, "What the hell are you taking me to jail for?" The driver answered, "Disorderly conduct! You shouldn't fuck with the police."

I didn't say another word through the rest of the drive to the police station. The passenger taunted, "We were trying to ask you a few questions. There was a robbery suspect in the area. You interfered with my investigation." I immediately thought, "The nerve of these mutha-fuckers to say I 'interfered' with their business when that's exactly what they were doing to me at the moment. At the same time, what else could I expect from petty punk ass peckerwood cops who are racist and deceitful by nature?"

After I was placed in a cell, the driver asked me for more information to continue his booking procedure. I cussed him out and reiterated, "It's on my I.D.!" He said he needed me to tell him for legal purposes. I proceeded to give him the rest of my info.

I sat on a bunk bed for an hour. Then I was re-handcuffed and seated in a different patrol car next to another handcuffed black man. We were transported to the DeKalb County Jail. This facility's conditions made me wish I had remained at the Stone Mountain police station.

The cops patted me down along with a line of twenty other

suspects. Then they directed us into a closet cell packed with fifty men, one toilet, and no air conditioning. I tried to fall asleep but was still too angry. Plus, I spoke with other prisoners who recanted similar accounts of improper police conduct. One sharp-dressed black man was arrested for forgetting to pay a fine over leaving his dog without a leash. Most of us told him, "You're a man who really shouldn't be here." There were two other African-Americans who told me about police encounters similar to mine. They too were jailed for "disorderly conduct."

The cops released us from the "closet" for twenty minutes. They fed us some crappy white-breaded ham sandwiches. Then we were ordered back into the closet with our food bags. As I began to eat, a cellmate defecated on the toilet. This stinky incident exemplified my horrible night. A few hours later, I cursed out the cops more. I was reprimanded, "....Stop cussing and show this young lady (cop) some respect....I don't care if you're guilty or not."

About five more hours later, I was transferred to a smaller cell with a payphone. I called Mother with the scoop. She said, "That's bullshit. Just stay silent, and I'll call Pop Pop."

After sixteen and one-half hours of jail time, Pop Pop bailed me out. I gave him a detailed explanation. He responded, "You know what you did wrong." I screamed, "I just got fucked over, and all you can tell me is how I screwed up." Pop Pop and I argued for the rest of the drive back to the Stone Mountain police station. I retrieved my things, picked up my car from Alim's apartment, drove home, and slept for virtually the whole Saturday. Alim informed me, "You know that Georgia is already under martial law."

Alim and Jakim were stunned about my incident. Jakim said, "You're the last person I thought this would ever happen to." Indeed! How could a shy intellectual high-yellow nigga like me get thwarted like a criminal? This incident only sparked me deeper into studies of metaphysics and sovereignty.

Two weeks later, I acquired a lawyer per the advice of Pop Pop. My attorney was a Muslim and a cousin of my FSU classmate Sonetta. Fortunately, I succumbed to Pop Pop's suggestion. Otherwise I likely would have been convicted by a Stone Mountain judge. The case was waived to a state court. Subsequently, it was thrown out due to lack of evidence.

Later on, I concluded that my attitude was the main attraction for abusive cops as opposed to white racism. I learned to stay calm and view all policemen objectively before presuming that they were already crooked.

My anti-establishment attitude, though, started way before the police incident.

I decided to quit my Lucent job after attending a lecture by Bobby Hemmit in August '97. He recommended for black people to act free of the heart. Bobby is a self-proclaimed protégé of Dr. Josef ben Jochanan and John Henrik Clarke. He's also studied various teachings of Moorish Science, Egyptology, and various other Afrocentric philosophies.

I first attended a presentation by Bobby in September '95 at In My Nature restaurant in Stone Mountain. I was frazzled by Bobby's outlandish claims that 1) 85 percent of all black people are government-engineered clones, 2) Atlanta housed a cloning facility on Holcomb Bridge Road, and 3) The Million Man March was set up to kill black men. Even though I initially perceived his statements as rhetoric, I decided to believe him since I didn't think Afrocentrics and metaphysicians would ever lie.

Bobby's viewpoints were justified by various articles I read on cloning technologies and multiple births resulting from fertility drugs. The mainstream world was eventually introduced to cloning in 1998 by reports of a cloned sheep named Dolly.

After my brush with suicide, I sensed that I lived in a world corrupted by conspiracies. Therefore, I attended Bobby's lectures regularly. He opened me deeper into theoretical plots.

In spring '97, U.S. President Bill Clinton made a formal apology to surviving victims and families of the Tuskegee Experiment. This incident spawned a series of discussions questioning whether or not the U.S. Government should officially apologize and/or repatriate African-Americans for slavery, segregation, hate crimes, and injustice. From Bobby's perspective, the U.S. Government was planning to pay blacks reparations for several reasons: 1) To stimulate the economy; 2) So blacks could spend a lot of money on houses, cars, and other expensive items which would lead to them giving at least ninety percent of their reparations back to the white man; 3) So blacks could shut up for good, no longer complaining about being treated unfairly; 4) To start a race war where white supremacists became furious; and 5) To lay out a plan for totalitarian order in the aftermath of a race war.

I wholeheartedly agreed with Bobby's view. Plus, my right-wing conservative Uncle Roy also told me, "Niggas ain't ready for reparations!!!" Even though I generally don't agree with my Republican Uncle's opinions, much of the information he presents is valid.

Based on information I previously read concerning U.S. Government conspiracies against blacks, I had no reason to disbelieve even more bizarre theories by Bobby, writers of *Frontier* magazine, or any other metaphysican.

For years, Afrocentrics have professed theories that the U.S. Government has waged secret Melanin Wars on people of color. Every year various Afrocentric metaphysicians congregate at Melanin Conferences to discuss methods for using Melanin as holistic healing and defense mechanisms.

Atlanta, a heavily populated black city, has been no stranger to Melanin War theories.

According to a May 5, 2005 editorial of the *Sunday Paper*, Wayne Williams was wrongly convicted of the 1980 Atlanta Child Murders. Most of the victims were young black boys found with holes in their foreheads along with chopped off penis heads. Alim mentioned that both bodily areas are key locations for Melanin production. So he theorized that Wayne Williams was probably a fall guy for a secret government experiment. Bobby added that Melatonin pills were the hottest trend of 1995. Melatonin is a natural hormone made in the brain's pineal gland to produce deep sleep and dreams. Bobby said that pineal glands of black people as well as those of animals were extracted for pharmaceutical companies to manufacture Melatonin pills.

Bobby really cracked me up when he said black people are physically "shit." Basically, he said that black people act best when they express themselves spiritually, thus acting worst when they try to control people in similar ways to European rulers.

With all this talk of conspiracy and Melanin, I was both excited and scared. My spirit was searching for means to immortality, beyond death and fear, so I continued to dig deeper into occult sciences.

As I continually comprehended mystical information from Bobby, I learned how to decode hidden meanings and symbols of several movies. Sci-fi movies often sparked in-depth discussions about realistic events often unreported by mainstream media outlets. For example, there's a study group on the internet who call themselves Gnostics, named after ancient esoteric philosophers, who discuss this information daily. Futuristic movies and comic-book stories like *X-Men, Fifth Element, Spawn, The Matrix, Blade*, and various Anne Rice vampire novels have characters with superpowers comparable to ancient alchemists.

Alim said these movies constantly give "truly conscious" people tips on how to ignite their dormant "Junk DNA."

Bobby frequently decoded mulitiple sci-fi stories. His favorite target was *Star Wars*. He used quotes from these movies and their hardcopy books to validate his claims of secret cloning experiments performed by the Illuminati.

The cloning subjects were intriguing, but they also created an overblown atmosphere of paranoia. My trust level towards most people was at an all-time low. I began to view most humans as "unconscious zombies and deadhead robots."

Bobby also sensed that cloning issues were played out, especially after mass media introduced the world to Dolly. So he flipped on even darker topics that shook the standard beliefs of me and several other audience members.

Black people like me so often get tired of negative connotations affiliated with blackness—blackmail, blackball, black cat is bad luck, bad guys wear black, black magic is evil, and so on. Therefore, it made sense for me to research further into "black" occult science. Alim read the Satanic Bible, but he never thrusted it on me fearing I would go nuts. Bobby, on the other hand, held nothing back. He said it was about time that we (blacks) use any possible means "to get the Cracker off the planet!"

I remember Bobby starting his "Satan" lecture series by tracing the origins of Satan to the Egyptian story of Osiris and Set. Bobby cleverly correlated this story with characters from other ancient myths—Typhon, Cronus, Sut, Seth, Seti, Saturn, and the Titans. Basically, Bobby used these writings to inspire his audience to be like the Titans—rise up against the oppressive Gods and become Gods and Goddesses ourselves.

Bobby's information was indeed golden. Yet, I also think that he tried too hard to make everything "black" sound good. Bobby also studied Hermetics, a philosophy with Egyptian roots pertaining to universal laws. However, I don't believe he applied them to his audience very well.

Nevertheless, I couldn't refute the authenticity of "black" sciences until I read them myself. Thus, I purchased a book called *Pacts with the Devil: Chronicles of Sex, Blasphemy, and Liberation* by S. Jason & Christopher S. Hyatt, Ph.D.. This book gives summarized methods of witchcraft and tantric sex. Plus it provides background history on famous "black" magicians—Afro-Caribbean witchdoctors, Aleister Crowley, H.P. Lovecraft, Robert Anton Wilson, Anton Levay, and Madame Blavatsky. *Pacts* also mentions how members of the rock band Led Zeppelin practiced teachings of Aleister Crowley before and after their guitarist Jimmy Page purchased Crowley's home.

Ironically, *Pacts* along with Bobby's theory on how the Illuminati suppressed creativity of black music, inspired an idea for me to push music by black rock artists.

Bobby said that black music had been corrupted into repetitive undanceable music. For example, Bobby claimed the wildest Black College Spring Break event ever—Freaknik '94—happened in Atlanta at the same time when the Dogon tribe of Mali performed their ritual called the Ziggy dance. According to Alim, the Hopi Native American tribe performed a simultaneous dance. The Dogons perform their dance annually to welcome a powerful surge of energy from the constellation, Sirius, home of ancient Egyptians like Osiris. Bobby emphasized that young melanin-abundant people naturally reacted to this energy surge but lacked sufficient knowledge to apply their reactions responsibly. The preferred music of most of these kids was hip-hop.

Bobby further reiterated that the Illuminati feared blacks would produce another advanced form of dance that would eventually destroy people with calcified pineal glands (mostly so-called melanin-recessive white people). Subsequently, this little idea about rock music became my career objective as *D-Rock SOUL-Jah.*

Meanwhile, my dark science studies became more frightening. Bobby often preached that death was a good thing. This view was justified from primitive African and Native Americans who often say, "Today is a good day to die!" On one hand I understood that no one should be afraid to die because we all eventually pass on. On the other hand, it seemed crazy to encourage interaction with death. Bobby's in-depth analyses into chaos magic, apocalyptic prophecies, melanin wars, the star system Sirius, and black holes (similar to death stars in *Star Wars)* backed up his views that the only true way to immortality was for the flesh to die. He never told anyone to commit suicide, but he often wished for the present day form of existence to disappear. Bobby babbled about times when he practiced rituals in attempts for him to pass on to another realm.

In my waning days of attending Bobby's lectures, I still felt as suicidal as I was during my charter hospital stay. This vibration attracted me to Bobby's ex-girlfriend, Quindoly. She was a very nice woman who taught French at Spelman College. I met her at Bobby's '97 lectures at the A.W.O. (African World Order) store. We both glanced at each other with several promising smiles before ever introducing ourselves. We dated a couple of times before settling into a platonic friendship. I liked Quindoly as a person, but I wasn't attracted to her beyond physical intimacy. She was often depressed like me. So I referred her to a certified holistic healer and clinical psychologist. Eventually, I also sought appointments from the same therapist. I last saw Quindoly in April, 2000 when she was seeking work as a nursing midwife. I pray she's doing well today. As far as I know, she's still on good terms with Bobby. He introduced her at a Melanin Conference before she recited a speech entitled "In Dark Times, We Need a Dark Goddess."

All of Bobby's observations gave me and many others a very potent alternative to monolithic religions like Christianity. I was very happy to hear perspectives of Christ Consciousness expressed from an internal esoteric standpoint instead of a mysterious external view that keeps people waiting on a messiah. Basically, I preferred to look towards God within my SOUL instead of seeking the Creator's spirit from the stars. Bobby summarized his "Satan" lectures by saying that a person must appreciate the darkness in order to find the pathway to their own soul. He mentioned that our brains are comprised by a 3-headed monster – the pineal, pituitary, and hypothalamus glands. Monsters are mantras that call out our thoughts connecting all species as Christ beings of Creation. All this science justifies my belief that no one named Jesus ever existed. Archeologists like Dr. Josef ben Jochanan say that Jesus' original name was Yashua. I also believe that Yashua's character was nothing like the biblical Jesus. Alim goes deeper using scriptural history to say that no biblical characters ever existed.

Today there are more recent stories questioning biblical accuracy. A 2004 ABC News *20/20* special called "Jesus, Mary, and Da Vinci Code" revealed information that contradicts claims that Mary Magdalene was a whore and Jesus was pure of sex. Jesus' character probably had more traits similar to his portrayed character in the film *The Last Temptation of Christ*. In addition to this, a Universalist named Brian Fleming produced a movie in 2006 called *The Beast,* claiming that Jesus never existed.

Overall, Bobby's lectures provided positive inspiration for me to view news beyond the realm of mass media. I soon learned that no life can exist without a balanced concept of Heaven and Hell. Santeria (Voodoo) can be used for evil, but it can also be used for good just like any energy source of creation. Sometimes one must do evil things for "good" nature to survive.

I was so grateful for Bobby's guidance that I later featured his lecture previews on five episodes of my radio show "ALTERNATIVE ROCK SOUL-U-TIONS." His topics ranged from – mind control, housing projects used as concentration camps, "Baby Got Back" themes of white girls with genetically engineered Goddess bodies, and his very cryptic lecture series "Vampires in Heaven" – in which he encourages water consumption instead of blood to enact melanin hydrocarbons.

Bobby has and continues to provide great information. His theories were worthy of research and proved true in many instances.

My main problem with Bobby, though, was that he never applied his speeches to constructive action. His paranoid accusations about government agents eventually drove me away.

Bobby criticized my martial artist friend Amen for bragging about his melanin knowledge to white folks at the Sphinx bookstore. Amen was doing a lecture series with a holistic healer named Anut Khem. Even though the audience was comprised of only a handful of people, Bobby claimed that Khem's house was raided by the Feds. On the next day, Amen refuted this claim saying that Khem had told him differently. No one I knew heard from Khem for many years. Amen recently reported that Khem relocated to North Carolina.

There was even more hearsay spread amongst Bobby's audience as some attendees, including me, starting believing rumors that Dr. L was a government agent and Cultural Communications media store was raided by the Georgia Bureau of Investigations (GBI). Nma, co-owner of this store, warned me, "Listen to Bobby and he'll lead you straight to hell." And so I moved on to other grass-roots groups.

Before Alim moved back to North Carolina, he networked with Dr. L and a Moorish Science member named Prince Ramisis Bey at the First Afrocentric Temple, located near the Atlanta

University Center (AUC). Alim and I attended some of Ramisis' meditation classes. Alim was having a ball while I felt uncomfortable. Alim and I set up lectures at the temple and the Little 5 Points Community Center, which also houses WRFG. Alim was the main attraction with metaphysical interpretations, while I opened with hard copy analyses.

The theme of my presentations was "Money$ vs. Melanin." I provided provocative views about the following: 1) how black people are too focused on material objects; and 2) how they needed to divert their energy towards the greatness of their spirits. I had good information but never developed sufficient confidence to become a regular lecturer.

During a presentation in December '97, Alim referenced information about caustic records in ancient Kemet, while I commented about various conspiracies. The audience was so impressed with him that I had no choice but to let him take over the lecture before I finished speaking. After the speech, I told Alim about my jealousy over his oratory talent. He told me not to worry and stay focused on the hard copy info I knew. This moment signaled to me that I just wasn't fit to be a spokesperson of the so-called Metaphysical Black Conscious Community.

Nevertheless, I continued to follow in Alim's footsteps seeking membership in a constructive black organization. Alim and Ramisis founded the Almorabut Society in January, 1998. This group was modeled on principles of Noble Drew Ali, Moorish Science temples, Prince Hall Masons, and Native American tribes. Alim and Ramisis intended to create a society with master alchemists (similar to those in the Egyptian Mysteries System) that would lead a nation of Moors (people of African and Native American descent) to spiritual sovereignty from the United States of America. They wanted me to be their accountant.

People who claimed Moorish heritage had legal entitlement

to the United States according to a sovereignty-seeking party called the Washitaw Nation—Washitaw de Dugdahmoun-doyah. According to the Washitaws' leader, Empress Verti-ace Golsten El Bey, Moors were entitled to land ranging from Alaska all the way to Florida. The Empress officially disclaimed House Resolution (H.R.) 260 of the 105th Congress cited under the "*Guadalupe-Hidalgo Treaty Land Claims Act of January 7, 1997.*" The Washitaw Nation supposedly had backing from the United Nations to claim this multitude of property. This made much sense to me since leaders of Black Nationalist factions of the NOI and Nuwaubians also sought sovereign land status. I also learned that Morocco was the first nation to recognize the independent status of the USA in 1777[6]. John Hanson, the first president of the U.S. Articles of Confederates, was an African descendant, according to the November 23, 1997 edition of the *Nuwaubian Moors Newsletter*. This contradicts Wikipedia. org's claim that the U.S. John Hanson was easily confused with the Liberian Senator John Hanson who helped African-Americans relocate around this same time period.

Seemingly, the next logical step for me was to be an official member of a Black Nationalist organization, but I never joined after witnessing even more turmoil.

Ramisis set up an Almorabut Society meeting at Cultural Communications in February '98. After an hour, the store own-er Nma proceeded to introduce a speech by an NOI minister, Ridgely Mu'min, based out of Greensboro, North Carolina. I was shocked that a speech was included in the meeting's agen-da. Ridgely basically called blacks "dysfunctional revolutionar-ies," stating that the Million Man March gave white folks a false image of black unity. He reiterated that blacks were still in a state of division and confusion. Ridgley also called for blacks to acquire and manage farmland better. I felt very lost after this

---

6 This is according to http://www.state.gov/r/pa/ei/bgn/5431.htm.

meeting because I wasn't sure that I was up to snuff for Almorabut. My imbalanced emotions were twisted further when Ramisis called me explaining how he cussed out the store's co-owner Emiola for "embarrassing" Almorabut with a speech. I felt more confused about Ramisis' outburst until Alim called me from North Carolina. Alim expressed similar dismay, "I was looking forward to telling peeps up here (North Carolina) about the Almorabut Society, but I don't know what to tell them now. I called you asking about what the meeting agenda was, and all I'm hearing about is a muthafuckin' speech? Now I see why I'm back here and not in Atlanta anymore. From what you're telling me, mugs are still trying to create a (black) nationalist organization. All those efforts have failed. So now it's time to come with something spiritual ..."

I was now feeling unsure of myself more than ever. After one bad day of working at a temp job, I was ready to choke myself. Fortunately, I called Ramisis. He used his crystal-laced wand to cleanse my chakras. He also recommended for me not to take metaphysics so seriously and apply the hard copy info I knew more productively. I thanked him and told him it was best for me not to participate in Almorabut while I sought out more cognitive therapy.

Before I enlisted Dr. L as my psychologist, I attended two more mind-boggling lectures in search of "perfect" spiritual solutions.

Dr. L and Alim both had keen experiences with the Kama Sutra, so they presented a workshop on tantric sex. I was enlightened but also frustrated because sexual opportunities were still nonexistent after I lost my virginity. I told Dr. L, "If I don't attract a mate soon, I'm going to become a monk." Dr. L encouraged me to forget about tantras until I harmonized my spirit better. I obliged. After all, I was trying too hard to attract a mythically perfect woman. I didn't recognize this flaw until a bad relationship erupted years later.

I also attended my final Cultural Communications presentation when I sat for a speech by former Illuminati member, Fritz Springmeier. He provided intriguing stories from his experiences with mind control projects, secret society history, and "Catwoman" experiments testified by his lecture partner, Cisco Wheeler. Everyone in the audience seemed mystified until Springmeier confessed to Jesus Christ as his savior. My thoughts were, "Oh damn! This former Illuminati member is still thrusting the Jesus bullshit on the Black Community with more pacifying propaganda."

I continued my hopeless search for spiritual perfection with the Natural Healers Network. The last drum circle I attended by them was also loaded with commercial propaganda.

Meanwhile, I was filled with fear about Y2K and a potential global display of a holographic Jesus. Thus I sought advice from a survivalist named Seth. Eventually Seth became my nutritional lifestyle consultant known as Dr. Tillman.

In the midst of all my informational torment, I eventually discovered my true calling card to spirituality when I conjured up the idea about black rock artists. Little did I realize during this period, that my affiliations with black alternative culture icons would inspire me to be a rock DJ. I am forever grateful.

As for a few of my inspirational conscious associates, they are still in good spirits.

My big brother Alim and his wife Khadirah now run a Fayetteville, North Carolina store called Cultural Freedom. It's located in the same space which served as headquarters for the Hall of Knowledge and UFP. Alim is also a certified reiki healer and still conducts weekly knowledge classes. He submits occasional freelance articles for *Frontline* magazine.

Prince Ramisis Bey relocated to Fayetteville. He helped Alim manage the store before he passed away from heart failure. I pray his soul is dwelling in a more peaceful realm.

Cultural Communications closed down years later. As a final request, Nma's cousin Kevin dubbed for me the 1984 Brazilian movie *Quilombo*. I told him, "Cultural Communications is forever appreciated. I salute this store by quoting Acotierene from *Quilombo*—'Palmares e eterno! Palamares e eterno!'" In English, this means Palmares (the most famous free-slave refugee camp of Brazil) is eternal.

According to Ramisis and Dr. L, the Washitaw headquarters was raided by the FBI in 2000. Supposedly a ton of legal documents held by the Empress were seized. I don't know officially how true this was outside of mass media, but I never doubted it. This incident sealed my faith in Black Nationalism. Until Black Nationalist organizations have strong leaders, organized armies, and the mutant powers of *X-Men*, they will never have official separation from the United States of America.

Ironically, U.S. President Clinton warned in 1997[7] that global warming would cover "9,000 square miles of Florida and Louisiana." Coincidentally, Hurricane Katrina destroyed many homes of the Gulf Coast in August 2005 covering land occupied by Washitaw members in Louisiana all the way to southern Mississippi, Alabama, and the Florida panhandle.

As one can tell, I still maintain awareness about governmental and occult conspiracies.

Before WRFG granted me a weekly radio show, I read a book by Keidi Obu Awadu—The Conscious Rasta—called *Rap, Hip-Hop, and the New World Order*. This book laid out theories of how the Illuminati conspired to kill Eric "Easy-E" Wright, Tupac Shakur, and Christopher "Notorious B.I.G., Biggie Smalls" Wallace. To this date, these rappers' murder cases still haven't been solved despite a heavy influx of witnesses and lawsuits.

---

7 This is according to an article in *Atlanta Journal-Constitution*, 6/27/97.

Regardless of how true or untrue conspiracies are about these rappers, I strongly believe that urban thug hip-hop was and continues to be a detriment to black people.

Lo and behold, the 1995 James Cameron produced movie *Strange Days* served as a prophecy for Tupac and Biggie's deaths. This movie depicts a rapper named Jeriko One getting murdered by rogue cops of the LAPD. During the investigation, a dispute erupts over a singer named Faith, also the name of Biggie's estranged wife Faith Evans. I also didn't realize when I first watched this movie that it featured performances by two black-female fronted rock bands, Skunk Anansie and Strange Fruit, who I eventually played on ALTERNATIVE ROCK SOUL-U-TIONS!

To sum up this heavy mental informational period, I quote Dr. L when she told me that everyone needs to go through "a school of paranoia and fear." Nadir Talib Al-Kareem was not only my student name, but it will always be remembered as an important journey in my evolution as the *Universal Rock SOU-Lector, D-Rock SOUL-Jah*!!!

ROCK SOUL-U-TIONS

Generally, I grew up attached to the hip-hop music genre. My interest in rap started to fade in '93 when gangsta rap began to dominate the music charts. Tupac Shakur best exemplified the disappearance of socially conscious political rap and the flourishing of urban thug life rap.

When I arrived in Atlanta during summer '95, I listened to various urban radio stations with much displeasure. Initially, V-103 was the only Atlanta urban radio station catering to kids and young adults. They didn't play any rap music and even cut the rap out of TLC's songs. Things changed when Radio One started a hip-hop station called Hot 97.5FM (now 107.9FM). At first, I was glad to finally hear rap on the radio. But after a year, I grew weary of 97.5's overabundance of booty-shaking rowdy 'bout it rap. So I channeled my audio dissatisfaction by opening my ears to other music genres.

One of my favorite movie soundtracks is *Dead Presidents*. This album featured mostly R&B hits from the seventies. Isaac Hayes' rendition of Burt Bacharach's "The Look of Love" is my all-time favorite song. Since this song has been sampled by a multitude of hip-hop and R&B artists, my curiosity of classic soul sounds grew. I started listening to adult-oriented R&B station, KISS 104.1FM. I also listened to various jazz programs like WCLK's S.O.U.L. (Sounds of Universal Love, formerly "Groove Gumbo") hosted by Jamal Ahmad and college alternative stations as well. These classic inspirations led to my purchase of a collective hits CD featuring tracks by John Coltrane. The most notable radio program I habitually tuned into was "Urban Flava" on Georgia State's radio station Album 88. "Flava" was originated by Chocolate Soul Entertainment founder Will G. After he graduated from GSU, a student DJ named Cha Cha Jones helmed as hostess. She described her format as "Atlanta's best in soul and acid jazz." Indeed, I enjoyed this radio show because it displayed mostly R&B artists outside commercial radio norms.

Late one Saturday night in October '97, Cha Cha played a very nice song with a bluesy rock edge. I called her on the request line asking, "Who was that?" She told me the song was called "Sympathy for the Crow" by David Ryan Harris.

A couple of weeks later, I read Sonia Murray's music review of David Ryan Harris' CD in the *Atlanta Journal-Constitution*. She gave this a positive rating and mentioned how Harris used to be part of a band called Follow For Now, named after a Public Enemy song moniker.

In weeks following this review, I purchased Harris' CD at Blockbuster Music. After listening to the whole album for the first time, I was pleasantly surprised with the CD's rock format. I already owned albums by black rockers Jimi Hendrix, Living Colour, Lenny Kravitz, and Prince. Yet, I was still very distant from the rock genre due to its overwhelming white majority. Harris' album however opened me up to a large wave of talented black rockers outside of mass media.

In fall 1997, I ventured into Atlanta's local music scene. This eventually proved therapeutic during my temp job woes. I started by attending Will G's Chocolate Soul concerts, held at several Atlanta venues—The Mill, Variety Playhouse, MJQ, etc.. I remember seeing Sleepy's Theme, formerly Society of Soul, perform. I continuously jumped in the air as their guitarist Billy

Odum roared his strings on the song "Funky Ride," which was featured on OutKast's first album *Southernplayalisticcadillac-musik*.

The next stop on my ATL music journey was A.W.O. Communications. I was familiar with this place from attending Bobby Hemmit lectures. Since I kept a journal of my thoughts, I decided to attend poetry functions a.k.a. open-mic and spoken word.

My most memorable poets' function was hosted by DRES tha Beatnik and 4 Kings Entertainment. I thoroughly enjoyed hearing people openly recite their expressions. I eventually recited some of my own poems on stage as well. The most attractive feature of these sessions turned out to be the band. I was happy to listen to these black male musicians play instrumentals ranging from jazz to metal. From inspiration, I brought my tiny conga drums to 4 Kings' next session at the Cajun Kitchen. The house band was so appreciative of my support that they asked me to join them on stage. The musicians capped off the night with a metallic backing sound for one of the poets. By the reaction of the crowd, I sensed that black folks were starving for some new rock sounds. Later on, I learned that the song was an instrumental of Whild Peach's "It's Just About Over," which was later featured on Goodie Mob's second album *Still Standing*. These same musicians, guitarist Jermaine Rand (Public Enemy, Divinity, Subterranean Sound System, etc.) and bassist Seven (Joi, Esperanza, Jumbo Shrimp, etc.), would also become key characters in my rock pursuits.

The Funk Jazz Kafé, founded by Jason Orr in 1994, proved to be the granddaddy of all underground ATL soul events. This concert series originated at a loft house and became popular enough to attract four-floor level rave-like crowds with thousands of people at the Tabernacle (formerly Atlanta House of Blues). On the second, third, and fourth floors, lounge bands, poets, massage parlors, and vendors were on display. Often, I attended as a WRFG sales associate. During my work breaks, I checked out the house band on the main floor. The name of this band was The Chronicle. This band also featured Billy Odum on guitar along with a saxophonist named Kebbi Williams, who played his instrument with a wah wah pedal blowing similar to John Coltrane. Frequently, The Chronicle played unrehearsed songs and would be joined on stage by vocalists ranging from British soul sensation Omar to mainstream ATLiens, TLC and Joi. In various instances, Billy became soundly erratic and delighted the crowd with metallic riffs. In April '98, I remember seeing for the first time, a rowdy group of young black men break into a mosh pit when Billy ignited a rock fury after a hip-hop song. I was so ecstatic that I joined the pit as a crazy head banger. At another Funk Jazz show, I also saw Billy perform with the all-black rock band Whild Peach. I later learned that Billy's bands The Chronicle and Whild Peach performed regularly at the Ying Yang Café (later changed to Apache Café) and MJQ.

Seeing live soul bands, especially of the rock genre, along with Bobby's Hemmit's lectures, ignited my exploration into rock music. After seeing a black-male fronted hip-hop/rock band called Urban Grind on display at talent shows sponsored by the Atlanta Entertainment Association, I sensed that black rock bands were the next wave of Progressive Music.

As I became more hyped about pumping black rockers, I also became more upset. I constantly recognized blacks' ignorance of music our ancestors created. Rock'n'roll, jazz, funk, and hip-hop were all originally used by blacks as metaphors for sex. In the 1950s a Cleveland DJ was credited for coining the phrase Rock'n'Roll to represent a new style of dance music for racially mixed crowds. The fifties also introduced the world to television. Thus televised mass media help solidify rock as a white man's game.

As I conjured an idea for a special radio show on black rockers, I trained for air shifter certification on nightly Afrocentric/ metaphysical talk shows—"Progressive Spot" hosted by Nma with part-time co-host Dr. L, and "Expressions" by Moorish Science Temple member Ankhnaten. I asked Nma, Ankhnaten, and other programmers if I could host a show about black rockers. They all told me it wasn't their format. One programmer recommended I request a pre-empted program during an afternoon show. I quickly acted on this idea and was approved to air "The Black Rock SOUL-U-TION" on July 17, 1998.

After contacting Organized Noize Productions, I booked an interview with three members of Whild Peach—husband & wife tandem, Dave & Peach Whild, along with Billy Odum. I still had very little knowledge of rock music at this moment. All I knew was that the few black rockers who I heard sounded good.

For further show preparation, I bought CDs by black rockers who I located at the record store (i.e. Rebekah, Imani Coppola, etc.). I wasn't sure I would have enough music to fill up two hours. So I planned the show with mostly music from 4-5pm, the interview with Whild Peach from 5-5:30pm, and caller questions from 5:30-6pm.

Since I had yet to be certified, I acquired Pablo G from WRFG's "World Party" to supervise me on the control board. He also helped me produce a promo with Living Colour's "Funny Vibe." I remember shouting like the man from *Soul Train*, *"Your ear waves are not ready! Your ear waves are not ready ... for the Black Rock SOOOOOOOOOOOOOUL-U-TION!"*

When I finally hit the air, I was spiritually not ready. I was a nervous wreck, often fumbling the control knobs, frantically calling for Pablo's help, and occasionally stymied into a few seconds of dead air broadcasts.

After the first scary hour of broadcasting music, Whild Peach arrived. I finally felt my nerves calm down into a rehearsed interview. Dave, Peach, and Billy summarized their experiences by saying, "Most record labels don't know what to do with a black rock band." I asked what it would take for young black kids to start listening to rock. They simply answered, "Radio play, especially from black stations ..."

Once the show ended, WRFG's broadcast manager Kai grilled me. I apologized for playing a song by Follow For Now without knowledge of its explicit lyrics. Kai barked, "Sorry don't cut it. If the FCC had been listening, we would have been fined and dead. Also, you need to learn not to talk down on people during your interview. Clearly, you're an intellectual and people have trouble understanding your questions. But overall, your show was good. It had substance. And by the way, Greg Tate of the Black Rock Coalition (BRC) called saying how much he admired your efforts ..."

Ironically, I never heard of the BRC until a week prior to "The Black Rock SOUL-U-TION." Through divine intervention, the BRC had a scheduled performance later during the evening of July 17, 1998. They were booked at Variety Playhouse as part of the National Black Arts Festival. Since this venue was just a couple of blocks down the street from WRFG, I grabbed a quick bite to eat before proceeding to the show.

At the entrance, I met a Caucasian couple who were passing out pamphlets about the BRC. Initially, I didn't get their names. Months later, I found out that it was a BRC Newsletter writer named Mark Dyal along with his girlfriend. The pamphlet amazed me with hoards of information about black rockers from all over the USA.

After browsing through the sheets, which included the BRC's

mission statement, I watched the BRC Orchestra perform. I was shocked by the diversity of their performance. It wasn't just a guitar-driven band featuring Vernon Reid (Living Colour) whaling super fast Van Halen-esque riffs. The show also displayed three spoken word artists, two violinists playing with wah wah pedals, three jazz singers, a racially mixed cello section, and a drummer playing different blends of electric jungle rhythms. During the intermission, I networked with several artists. A local cello player with dreadlocks named Okorie Johnson introduced me to a folk rock artist named Doria Roberts. She graciously handed me one of her CDs. Then, I introduced myself to Greg Tate. He left me with an address to send the BRC a payment for subscription.

When the show was over, I met Vernon Reid. He encouraged me to keep the ball rolling for a black rock collective in Atlanta. As the divine day of July 17, 1998 ended, it was clear to me that I needed to steer Atlanta's Black Rock movement into a new cohesive organization.

As I continuously worked toward certification at WRFG, I pondered an idea for an urban alternative mall concert. I attempted to book Whild Peach, Mojo 99 (now known as Heavy Mojo), Edenrage, Basement Jam (now E.X. Vortex), and El Pus at South Dekalb Mall. Meetings at my apartment were attended by Bryan Adams (Edenrage drummer), Baye Osei (E.X. Vortex vocalist), and owners of Neu Planet Entertainment (NPE)—web developer Denise Porter, her husband and El Pus bassist Simon Durham, along with former El Pus drummer Freedom Williams. Initially, everyone was excited about performing at the predominantly black mall, but South Dekalb's mall manager wasn't going to approve our performance unless we guaranteed that people would continue to shop. Since we didn't have a budget and/or radio sponsorship, we postponed this idea. The mall concert never happened, but we continued to communicate regularly per phone, e-mail, house meetings, and Neu Planet concerts. Thus, our grass roots Black Rock clique became known as "The Black Rock SOUL-U-TIÓN Core." I wrote a mission statement modeled after the BRC. We proceeded to build a cooperative movement.

Shortly after the first few Core meetings, I received my certification. This was my green light to host "ALTERNATIVE SOUL-U-TIONS" every late Saturday night into early Sunday morning from 12 midnight-2am. I was able to host this show in the 12-2 slot for one month before being moved to 3-5am at the request of the more experienced house/R&B DJ, Requaya Ward. This upset me at first, but I put it behind me quickly since I felt the music was too important.

At first I advertised "ALTERNATIVE SOUL-U-TIONS" as "an eclectic mixture of Rock and Funk with a SOULFUL twist." Core members convinced Bryan Adams to put this on a three by five cardboard flyer along with a graphic art picture of a black man in cornrows playing a guitar. As I received too many requests for Jamiriquai and D'Angelo, I felt an urgency to clearly state that I was hosting a rock show. So I changed the program name to "ALTERNATIVE ROCK SOUL-U-TIONS (ARS)."

During ARS's first year, I broadcasted several mostly black-oriented rock artists including: black punk legends Bad Brains, Fishbone, and 24-7 Spyz; several BRC artists—Blast Murray, Reggie Ransdell, Val Ghent, Screaming Headless Torsos; multiple ATL rockers – Ondrea, Esperanza, Shock Lobo, Ovid, E.X. Vortex, Sonya Vetra; and featured conversations with esoteric gurus relating to the occult and pre-Y2K fears – Bobby Hemmit along with my friends Alim, Dr. L, and Amen.

The new Black Rock vibe I pumped on the airwaves caused much excitement and anger all the same. On one hand, it was a relief to finally hear black rockers receive their long overdue props. On another hand, it sucked how black rockers were still heavily overlooked by the music industry despite Rock'n'Roll's African-American roots. It seemed so ridiculous to coin the term, "Black Rock," but it was necessary since many people, especially blacks, had become ignorant of these artists. The more Black Rock stories I discovered, past and present, the more my fire was fueled.

The most stand-out Black Rock bands from the eighties all paved the way for the nineties to present day alternative rock genre without receiving much credit. Fishbone masterfully blended punk, funk, and ska sounds. Most hardcore rock fans will tell anyone that Bad Brains was the first band to take punk rock to a worldly level with their dosage of reggae. 24-7 Spyz mixed forays of metal, rap, reggae, and funk. And ATL's Follow For Now daringly amalgamated displays of punk, funk, metal, hip-hop, and Motown. None of these bands ever received much radio play or mainstream success. Living Colour, who skillfully played funked-out Van Halen stylings, fortunately received critical acclaim and platinum-selling success after opening for the Rolling Stones on a concert tour in the late eighties. However, they were eventually phased out of the mass media realm once the industry promoted hoards of grunge rock bands — Nirvana, Sound Garden, Pearl Jam, Alice in Chains, and Stone Temple Pilots.

I became more bitter once I found out that even some of the most popular hard rock bands had pivotal black members. Kirk Hammett (Metallica)[8], Tom Morello (Rage Against the Machine, Audioslave), and Slash (Guns 'n' Roses, Snakepit, Velvet Revolver) are all world-renowned guitarists who are also half-black mulattoes. Yet, I've never heard or read an article about them in any mainstream black publication.

While black (urban) music seemingly digressed into decrepit

---

8 I later learned that Kirk Hammett is actually half-Filipino. I assumed he was half-black because a heavy music fan I spoke with told me how a Rolling Stone magazine interview revealed him as a mulatto.

variations of shit, I sensed the SOUL-U-TION to this problem was predominantly black bands. So it made sense that Stereo Popsicle (later changed to Three5Human) was the first band that I interviewed on ARS. This band's founders, vocalist Trina Meade and guitarist Tomi Martin, have provided session music and tour duties for countless famous artists—Michael Jackson, Madonna, Mick Jagger, B-52's, Fishbone, OutKast, Sean "Diddy" Combs, and the list never ends. On another divine note—Tomi, Trina, Myrna "Peach" Crenshaw, and Joi — were the main producers of OutKast's "You May Die" intro song from *ATLiens*. This song rang repeatedly in my head when I contemplated suicide. Two years later, these artists turned up as my first radio interviews. Overall, one can say that their live band sounds saved my life.

When I interviewed Tomi months later during a tribute radio show dedicated to black bands, he cited, "the dreaded drum machine" as the main reason for the black band demise in the 80s. My continuous research on this topic proved though that there's no shortage of black bands or musicians. Yet, there continues to be an alarming shortage of known black musicians with mainstream success. Session artists like Tomi & Trina are still working to gain recognition for their own original music.

During the same radio show when I aired my first official ARS interview featuring Tomi & Trina, I also spoke with a guitarist named Larry Eaglin. Larry initially heard a promo of ARS and immediately left me several phone messages. Once I called him, he told me about his background in the ATL music scene stemming from 1987. He was so ecstatic about ARS that he invited me to meet him. We first met in person at the Masquerade where we watched performances by local rap-metal act Witches Brew, Athens, Georgia band S.M.O., and SWATL's (Southwest ATL) hip-a-delic funksters Urban Grind. Larry also mentioned how he was part of an organization in the early 90s called United Black Artists, who formed after Living Colour's breakthrough success. They had intentions of collectively promoting black alternative artists, but never got off the ground. After this episode, I invited Larry to Core meetings. His extensive music experience that included a promotion company he co-founded called Common Cause Productions (CCP), and his then current band, Eve of Reality, made him a perfect fit for the Core. Even though he wasn't at the Core's first meeting, I still label him as the Core's "honorary founder in spirit." Larry also conducted much of his WRFG air shifter training on ARS. He went on to serve as my most trusted backup DJ whenever I was absent from the air.

While the Core and I were pumping ARS as one of the few Black Rock radio shows on Earth, larger issues came to our attention.

One of the first BRC recommended artists I interviewed was Blast Murray (now known as Muata 25). He said that he had no involvement with the BRC but was cool with friends of his who were. Blast Murray was also a session guitarist whiz who did work for Lee "Scratch" Perry, Talking Heads, and Terence Trent D'arby amongst countless others. He self-financed and produced his first solo project called *AfroFraktal* after growing weary of performing music for multiple artists in Europe and other places abroad. When I asked him if he felt there was any hope for mainstream music to open its doors to new sounds, he said, "I don't think there is any good music left in the mainstream." Apparently, the struggles of black rockers were bigger than just racial issues.

Meanwhile, the Core attempted to acquire sponsorship and alignments with several musical outlets—BRC (NY & LA chapters), Grenae Baranco (originator of ATL's Rock Lockdown concert series displaying Black Rock artists), ASCAP (ATL chapter), and MusicCares. All these groups gave us spoken praise but had no funding to spare. Therefore, the Core decided to book an event and worry about a budget afterwards.

After I co-hosted several concerts with CCP and NPE, these two companies decided to help out the Core. Larry negotiated with the Somber Reptile's Colombian-American owner, Quique Lopez, to reserve a Core night. CCP & NPE agreed to take twenty-five percent apiece while donating the other fifty percent to the Core. CCP booked Ondrea and Edenrage while NPE booked E.X. Vortex and a comical rap duo called Da Ignants. I booked Mojo 99, who ended up backing out at the last minute due to a sick member. I also created the show's title *Funk-HopMetalFusion*. I proceeded to create the absurd flyers which featured an obnoxiously blended picture of me as the animated Crunky Funk. I listed the bands and venue info along with the slogan "The BLACK ROCK SOUL-U-TION CORE presents *A Tripped out Blend of Funk, Rock, Rap, and Spoken Word— What Da Funk Is This???*" The flyers received mixed reactions. Some people hated the drawing and didn't like that the Core was marketed like another BRC. Others thought the flyers were "Da Bomb."

Nevertheless, *FunkHopMetalFusion* managed to attract a large blend of local musicians and fans alike on October 16, 1999.

After Edenrage finished their opening set, multiple patrons poured in the venue while I changed my clothing into the co-host character, Crunky Funk, a mock degenerate little brother of Digital Underground's Humpty Hump. There was some miscommunication. Larry's CCP Partner O.P. was supposed to escort me into the building, but no one came out. So while I waited frantically, Larry and O.P. broke into a ridiculous freestyle rhyme. At this point, I decided to jump back into the building. By this moment, the crowd was impatient and ready to cuss. I tried to be funny with diaper jokes, candy giveaways, and offbeat dance moves, but no one laughed. Once I finished my neurotic split-personality routine, O.P. grabbed me and ran me into the parking lot. I was feeling like the most stupid jackass on Earth, while O.P. almost died laughing.

The show continued with more absurdities. Da Ignants performed to a barrage of boos, resulting in an exit of twenty customers. After Ondrea performed energetically, a young lady spontaneously recited some whack ass poem while E.X. Vortex was warming up their Thrash-hop sound. BMac , lead vocalist of Ovid, smirked in my face, "What da fuck is this?" I gently let the awful poet finish and escorted her off stage. After E.X. Vortex finished ripping up the stage, the show ended as one preposterous success. Somber Reptile made a ton of money in drinks and The Black Rock SOUL-U-TION Core was introduced to the world by raising more than $300. October 16, 1999 was perhaps the funniest day of my life!

Despite the Core's success, we swirled into controversy. Denise reported that several patrons didn't like the word "Black" in the Core's title. She further explained how the general response was that Atlanta was too diverse to feed into a segregated label. Bryan reported that those who preferred the word "Black" in our title confused the Core as the new Atlanta wing of the BRC. Bryan and Denise further expressed how I made an uncomfortable statement as co-host of *FunkHopMetalFusion* when I told the white folks in the audience, "We're all black tonight!" Denise chuckled to me, "How would you like it if the Rolling Stones said at one of their shows, 'We're all white tonight?'" I was very adamant about not dropping "Black" from the Core's title. I even e-mailed all the Core officers—Bryan, Denise, and Larry—with facetious frustration calling them "a bunch of chickenshit handkerchief head house niggas."

The "Black" issue was still unsettled as it reached ARS. Seven, who was now the bassist of Ovid, called me pleading,

"Could you play just one or two white bands? It's cool that you play black bands, but what about the good white ones and the racially mixed ones (i.e. Johnny Prophet and Sevendust). I'm good friends with Lajon (lead vocalist of Sevendust) and I don't think it's fair that his band should be singled out because they're not all-black." I responded, "Look Seven! If you follow my show closely, you'll find that I play a lot of bands who are racially mixed including Johnny Prophet. It's almost impossible for me to do a radio show with only all-black rock bands. I'm familiar with Sevendust, but I don't have their CD in my collection. I'm still sticking with bands that have blacks at the forefront." Seven kept pressing, "If you expect bands from 2 High Studios (performance studio co-owned by Shay Barnes of Johnny Prophet) to give money to WRFG, then you'd better open up to the white boys. The reality still is that Blacks are less than one percent of Rock's audience. I remember when Pitlock Entertainment (founded by Tony Maury, one of ATL's few black promoters of rock) put on a show at the Masquerade. Some redneck metal band tried to start some racial shit. There were some skinheads in attendance, but even they had our backs because they knew who put in the legwork for these good ass rock shows. So why don't you let me come down to the station with one white band?"

I told Seven again that I was sticking to my format. He lastly broke down, "Weren't you part of the all-black judges that voted an all-white band as the winner of The Bullfight (band competition produced by NPE)?" I answered, "Yes!" Seven boasted, "So what's your problem?"

Seven's conversation bothered me.

Then Bayé pressed me even more, "Tony Maury told me, 'Personally, I love what Talib is doing. But from a business perspective, I can't support him. How can I vouch for him when most of my customers are white?" Bayé also told me how an all-white funk/rock/ska band called Groovestain labeled me a racist for excluding them. I had never even heard of them, but their point was valid. Bayé initially sided with me when I interviewed him on ARS. Two weeks later though, he phoned me, "Hey! It's cool you play the Bad Brains and Fishbone. But if a, let's say, a white owned liquor company like Tanqueray wants to sponsor an E.X. Vortex tour, I'll let them. Living Colour wouldn't have blown up if the Rolling Stones didn't put them on a pedestal. So if Limp Bizkit or Kid Rock want to put E.X. Vortex on a pedestal, I'm going for it. And you'll eventually play Groovestain and Funky Butt Nuggets on your show too! PEACE!"

I was tormented for almost two months by the "Black" issues. While thinking about these topics daily, I allowed my mind to kick back and listen to Rock music by any artist (black or white) period. After watching MTV's special "Return of the Rock," it was finally clear that I needed to release the racial issues. These featured bands were still predominantly white, but their sounds were more diverse than ever. Videos by Sevendust and Rage Against the Machine were also displayed. Sure, white-owned record companies have stolen and continue to steal rock'n'roll from black artists. At the same time, several white bands like Nine Inch Nails and Korn have broadened the genre. Plus, at almost every local music show I attended, I always ended up speaking with white musicians and fans alike who had more knowledge and appreciation of black music and culture than a large amount of blacks I knew. Even Bobby Hemmit often mentioned in his lectures how white folks generally see more things because of their worldwide travels. And right under my nose, Sevendust and Stuck Mojo were two black-fronted rock bands who had legendary followings in metro Atlanta.

I spoke with Seven and Tony Maury again at an E.X. Vortex Ying Yang Café performance. I told them that I was going to release the racial issues on ARS before the end of 1999. Tony was just happy that I was playing Johnny Prophet. Seven said, "I think you should just play one white band per hour. The same way that 96 Rock only plays three black rockers (Lenny Kravitz, Jimi Hendrix, and Living Colour) in their 24-hour format."

On my second to last ARS show before Y2K, a racially mixed rap-metal act Witches Brew, called me to be interviewed. I granted their request since they were the first artist to submit two or more CDs to ARS. My conversation with Walt Cusick and Simon Temple (also of Mojo 99, now Heavy Mojo) was very mellow at first, but as I finished discussing their new CD, I asked a poignant question, "Do you think white artists should be featured on ARS?" Simon angrily sighed, "Look! Play artists for their skill period. If you're good, you're good. If you're whack, you're whack." Walt, the Caucasian founder of Witches Brew, seconded, "Radio is too segregated. When somebody looks at 311, 'OOOOOO? White Boys,' they should recognize that instead they're dope! ..." I was uncomfortable allowing myself to be roasted on my own show, but it proved to be the right thing.

After Walt finished his comments, I opened up the phone lines for the audience. Lo and behold, Seven doesn't answer my question but scoldly asks, "How come young black musicians are never on the cover of guitar magazines. They usually have Jimi Hendrix, who's dead and gone. Or some old blues guy like Bo Diddley. Much props to him but why don't they market the young black guys?" Walt answered, "That's not always true. We did some shows with Sevendust. Lajon Weatherspoon has a very strong presence and the crowd is very receptive to him." Seven continued to shout, "You guys are not telling me anything that I don't already know. It's not an equal market for rock artists of color. Just look at 96 Rock. Anyone who listens to them all day would think that the only black rock artists in existence are Kravitz, Hendrix, and Living Colour. We're up against a big corporate beast." Seven verbally jabbed with Walt & Simon for five more minutes before I interjected, "Look! Seven? Calm down so we can discuss this one at a time." Seven continued his tirade, "You guys (Witches Brew) probably only have black guys rapping in your band." Simon responded, "No. We have a black guitarist and a black drummer. I play keyboard. Sure more promotion of black musicians is needed... Start a Black Rock magazine. Start a Black Rock organization ..." I told Simon, "We've started one already." Simon continued, "Then support Talib and his organization." Walt interjected to Seven, "You're welcome to come to one of our (Witches Brew) shows. I agree we can't vent like this on 96 Rock and 99X, but all of us must make better efforts to prevent radio from becoming more segregated."

To summarize this heated show further, I announced, "ARS will continue to focus on artists of color. However, I'm guilty of one thing in which I won't do again. I will no longer announce the race of each artist by saying this artist is black or this band is Puerto Rican." Simon cheered, "Thank you! There you go!" Walt summarized this topic with more information, "I've worked with plenty of talented black rock artists. As a matter of fact I know at least five local bands that have mostly black membership. Also, there's a band out of Brazil called Sepultura. Their lead vocalist is black. So we can't forget about the Hispanics (Latinos) either.

After the show ended, I was worn out from controversy. Walt graciously praised me for allowing Witches Brew to be a part of this hotly debated show. He also told me, "I know of another good band with a black guy." I told him, "Don't worry! The music is what's most important."

I ran into Seven months later at one of Ovid's Tabernacle performances. I personally thanked him for coming to my defense during this racially contested ARS episode. I am still amazed how Seven vouched for me after being the first person to boldly criticize my radio show's initial narrowness. What Seven did for ARS was truly brilliant!!!

On the weekend following the "race" episode of ARS, I made my monthly trips to the record stores. As usual, my final stop was Tower Records. My typical shopping method was to listen to all types of CDs (rock or otherwise) and then buy those by bands/artists fronted by someone of color.

This time, my music purchase experience was different. I didn't find any new rock CDs by black fronted artists at the store. Yet, I still felt I had to leave the store with at least one CD. After sifting through almost every CD in the rock section, I landed on one with a fascinating cover.

The band was called SOULFLY. I was already aware that their lead vocalist, Max Cavalera, use to be in the Brazilian metal band Sepultura, whose lead vocalist was now an African-American named Derrick Green. The cover of the two-disc CD had Max with balled-up braided hair and a tribal mask sign painted on his face. It looked similar to the masked face of the comic book character *Spawn*. Below Max's face was a photographed image of an African tribe. When I looked at the back cover of the two-disc album, I saw the same tribal sign tattooed on someone's back. I was also mystified by the song titles – "Umbabaraumba," "Tribe," "Karmageddon," "Prejudice," "Quilombo," and various re-mixes of these same songs on disc two including "Quilombo (Zumbi Dub Remix)." I never heard SOULFLY or Sepultura's music at this moment, and I didn't know exactly what Max's racial background was, but neither mattered anymore, so I purchased the CD and gave it a thorough listen.

The results of my initial SOULFLY listening experience were astonishing. The music was some of the heaviest screaming thrash angst I ever heard. After feeling stunned and irritated by the ear-bleeding ferociousness of the first three songs, I became intrigued once I heard primitive tribal rhythms mixed in with roaring metallic riffs. Then, I was more thrilled when I heard tribal chants of, "Zumbi é o senhor das guerras. Zumbi é o senhor das demandas. Quando Zumbi chega. É *Zumbi quem manda.*" I later found out from Brazilian natives at my pay job that the tribal chant (crenca) meant, "Zumbi is the lord of the wars. Zumbi is the lord of demands. When Zumbi arrives, it is Zumbi who orders." My mind was mystified even further after hearing the song "Prejudice" featuring ragga-rock vocalist Benji Webbe (formerly of Dub War, now with Skindred) and excerpts from a Bob Marley interview—"We don't walk upon Black man's side or the White man's side, but upon God's side." Disc 2 enlightened my SOUL as well with spicy jungle and hip-hop mixes intertwined with thrash sounds.

SOULFLY's first album was and still is the baddest most incredible sound I've ever heard. I didn't matter that Max Cavalera just happened to be an angry screaming metalhead white man with long blonde dreadlocks. His praise to Zumbi Alakijade and the Quilombos of Brazil was enough for me to admire him as a SOUL brother. I love how Max yells in the song "Quilombo"—"Zumbi! Zumbi! Blow them away! Zumbi! Zumbi! Got to be free!"

Ironically, the 1984 Brazilian film *Quilombo* is my favorite movie. SOULFLY used excerpts from this movie on one of their songs. The word "Quilombo" was used by runaway slaves in Brazil to describe their freely formed refugee camps with Native Americans and poor white immigrants. Zumbi was raised as a slave named Francisco by a Catholic priest. At age fifteen, he ran away to the Quilombo called Palmares (Palms in the Air). He went on to be known as the Slave King, Zumbi de Palmares, and led successful defenses and raids against the Portuguese army until he was reportedly captured and beheaded in 1694. Brazil now celebrates Black Consciousness Day yearly in honor of Zumbi[9]. My mind was amazed enough from SOULFLY's vibe and loaded with substantial universal joy to enlighten the world.

Before playing SOULFLY on the radio, I had played songs off of Puya's first album. This Puerto Rican metal band also had an awesome sound that pits Sepultura meets Rage Against the Machine and Santana. I coined the spicy rhythmic thrash styles of SOULFLY, Sepultura, and Puya as "Tribal Metal." They all helped me open the doors to several more worldbeat rock bands (known and unknown)— Ill Niño, Ananda Shankar, Ra, Primitive Reason, Asian Dub Foundation, P.O.D., Dub War, and many more. SOULFLY ended up being the most played artist ever on ARS. I still consider Max Cavalera as my Heavy Music Hero.

Even though race was no longer a factor in my music selections, I would still have no problem letting my spirit flow and finding more rock bands that featured African-Americans. Bands played from ATL on ARS included: Blackbeard, Womakk, Da Shiz, Freak the Jones, Kaizer Soze, Empire 44, XL, Kill the Messenger, Brand New Immortals (featuring David Ryan Harris), Kindlespine, Candela, Jill Rock-Jones, Rehab, Minus Driver, Modern Hero (featuring Jeffrey Butts from Shock Lobo), and Baby Jane amongst a huge list.

Despite ARS's refreshing new music focus, I continued to feature Bobby Hemmit and other metaphysical griots on my show. This changed after the Spring 2000 Marathon show. I attempted to get various holistic healers, natural hair stylists, and metaphysical lecturers to donate some money on ARS. Not one of them gave a penny even though I gave them broadcast time to market their products. I felt so used. I can look back now and

---

9 *BBC Report* and *The Dish* newsletter are references for this information.

say I tried too hard to solicit their sponsorship. Nevertheless, this subpar radio show was a divine signal for me to keep ARS's focus strictly on music for good.

To help my strict music focus, I cut off my cable television services so I could channel my senses toward hearing music first before I saw the artists in person.

This breakthrough was official in April, 2000 as I dropped Talib Al-Kareem as my ARS host name for the musically devoted Rock'n'SOUL DJ title, *D-Rock SOUL-Jah*.

Also in April of 2000, I purchased a DJ mixer composed of spinning CD & vinyl players. I was now an official party DJ on and off the airwaves.

"Black" was dropped from the Core's title, and thus we were forever known as the Rock SOUL-U-TION Core (RSC).

The RSC appeared ready for bigger horizons. We came to a standstill though when NPE dissolved. Larry's group, CCP, was willing to produce more shows for the RSC. But since they were busy producing their own concerts at the Somber Reptile and Cajun Kitchen, I decided it would be best to help them out until the RSC got off the ground. CCP hosted shows of diverse genres—acoustic soul, R&B, rock, hip-hop, rap-rock, and hip-hop/reggae. Working these shows reminded me of times when I worked the door for dances at Fayetteville State University. Subconsciously, I was redeeming myself from my college party failures. I also produced recorded compilation tapes and flyers for CCP's Hip-Hop/Rock Extravaganza.

CCP invited me to be a partner in their organization. At first I accepted. Later I rescinded after choosing to focus all my energy on goals for the RSC and my DJ career.

This decision freed up more time for me to practice on my DJ equipment. For about four nights a week, I produced freestyle flows that led to mixed song transitions such as combining Sepultura's "Roots" with Sevendust's "Denial" and blending

Prince with Fishbone. At the end of every practice mix, I jotted down the sequential CD order of my mixes. Then I gave myself praise and constructive criticism for how well I mixed. In addition I wrote each improvement I needed to make. I wouldn't use CD and mini-disc players to record my mixes until 2003.

CCP still kept good relations with me, so they booked my first gig at the Somber Reptile. I spun before, during, and after performances by Ondrea and Hung. I thoroughly enjoyed my first live spin. The crowd was delighted. The sound engineer scolded me for "being too fucking loud" on volume knob adjustments. The criticism was duly noted since I started learning much from my spinning experiences. Nevertheless, Larry called my rock spins "the hottest thing since hip-hop." I would go on to spin at venues all over metro ATL—9 Lives Saloon, The Pointe, Echo Lounge, I.A.G., Atlanta Brewing Company, and several more.

While I gained club DJ experience off the air, I also created a club-like atmosphere on ARS. I hosted/produced several mix-theme shows including – "Thrash 'n' Boogie," "Cinco de Mayo," "Mambo Róck On," "Rap-Metal Fusion 2K1 and beyond," and "Tribal Metal Spear-heads." My angriest mix shows were "Let Da Smoke Blow," "Aggravatingly Tight," and "No Love Songs Allowed," which resulted from my fury over a female's rejection.

Through music-oriented programming, I also blended in more social issues. Topics concerning rock artists of color and racially-mixed bands were frequently discussed. During one show, I chewed out a writer from *Rolling Out* newsletter for making ignorant comments concerning Lenny Kravitz. He said, "Lenny Kravitz is one of the few Black artists to play rock. And he's one of the few artists that does rock well." I responded, "Here on ARS, we not only play a lot of ethnically diverse artists. We play a lot of good artists as well."

Other standout ARS episodes were "Bad Brains Tribute" featuring DJ Don Tonic's CD collections, "Napster Comments," detailing controversy over Zach De La Rocha's (Rage Against the Machine) unauthorized rock-remix release of OutKast's "Bombs Over Baghdad," and an interview with Boston Fielder—producer of the Urban Alternative indie film *Kat, Shaun, and Oz*. I made a cameo appearance in this film as a silent partner lawyer.

To keep up with fashion trends of Urban Alternative artists, I paid some hair stylists to turn my frail, thinning, bushy hair into dreadlocks during October 2000. Initially, I didn't think this style was best suited for me, but as I kept watering my naps, parts of my hair started to lock up naturally. I kept my hair in locks for four years. One RSC artist named Zoser told me during an ARS interview that I looked like the dreadlocked vocalist from Bad Brains, H.R..

As ARS continued to be the unofficial ministry for Urban Rock, the RSC was still seeking another venue for new concerts. After CCP temporarily broke up, Larry had more time to focus as Program Director of the RSC. After I booked an RSC gig in December 2000 at the AHOP (formerly the African House of Peace, now the African Djeli Center) called "The Eve of Rock in Da SWATs," Larry booked a series of weekly gigs at the AHOP called Urban Rock EarAddicts. The "EarAddicts" functions were subsequently held at the I.A.G. (International Artist Guild) in 2001 & 2002 and at the Black Lion Café in 2003.

The RSC was now functional on a consistent basis.

Initially, all RSC meetings were held at my apartment. As our momentum grew, they shifted to a series of venues — 2 High Studios, Auburn Avenue Research Library, the I.A.G., Larry's house, and several restaurants around town.

While I was becoming acquainted with more Urban Rock

bands, I ran into an old college friend. Kurt McManus, who worked for FSU's *Broncos' Voice* while I was a freshman, also played bass in several ATL jazz and rock bands. I asked him how our former editor Barbara Beebe was doing. He told me how she used to be involved in Atlanta's Black Rock Collective before moving back to Fayetteville, North Carolina. I e-mailed Barbara seeking advice on how to make a stronger network. Barbara responded by giving historic details. She told me that Atlanta's loose-knit collective of Black Rock artists formed an organization in 1994 called the Black Alternative Musicians' Movement (BAMM). BAMM's success was followed by a series of ATL Black Rock concerts called Rock Lockdown, founded by Grenae Baranco. Barbara served as a writer for BAMM and Rock Lockdown while running her own magazine called *Real African World (R.A.W.)*.

BAMM produced at least four successful concerts called Black Out. Most of their earnings, though, were eaten by sound equipment costs. This issue combined with insufficient funds and conflicting organizational structure caused BAMM to dissolve in 1995.

Around the summer of '95, Rock Lockdown ran successfully with large audiences composed of predominantly black crowds, well-known corporate conglomerates, and A&R reps from powerhouse labels. According to Barbara, Coca-Cola was unfortunately hailed as the only significant sponsor of this event. So as funding ran out, Grenae stepped down as promoter to raise her new-borns and continued to help her family run Baranco Motors, one of the few black-owned car dealerships in North Georgia.

Barbara's overall advice to me was to utilize personified resources from every profession to nurture a diverse collective of mostly-black musicians. She facetiously said a psychiatrist was most needed. However, this joke proved true in my case.

Nevertheless, I heeded Barbara's advice and went on to organize the RSC in a structure similar to college governments and non-profit cooperatives. I modeled the RSC's constitution after FSU's Student Government, which was modeled from University of North Carolina by-laws. Yet, I gave the officer titles equal powers rather than make any one person the most authoritative leader. The officer positions were Membership Supervisor (Brian Adams), Program Director (Larry Eaglin), Public Relations Manager (originally held by Denise Porter and replaced by Twyla Dudley), and Director of Operations, which was helmed by me. My main functions were to organize/conduct the RSC meetings and serve as RSC spokesperson at all functions we attended and/or produced.

During every meeting, I handed out typed agendas that included event discussions and efforts to solicit sponsorship. We researched methods to acquire official 501©3 non-profit status through SWATs.com (founded by Attorney Marvin Arrington, Jr.), the Southern Entertainment Law Center (SEAL), the I.A.G. (an official non-profit facility), and various I.R.S. websites. This process proved to be too confusing and expensive for the RSC to ever become a certified government -funded co-op.

The RSC continued to build our tiny budget through membership fees. We structured our fees based on the BRC's mission statement. We initially charged $10 per year for individuals and bands alike. But in 2002, we amended that policy to $10/year. for individuals and $30/year for bands.

The RSC tried to get our own business bank account, but we we're denied since we didn't have an official business license. Therefore, we kept the RSC's funds in my personal savings account until we subsequently merged with Larry's resurrected entity, CCP. Most of the RSC's budget was used for promotional expenses (shows, flyers, t-shirts, bumper stickers, buttons, and radio spots). The RSC also produced a compilation CD comprised of RSC member bands. We kept a fun scrap book detailing RSC photos, memorabilia, and comic book highlights.

For RSC shows, we consistently acquired funding from multiple local businesses (restaurants, music shops, independent vendors, etc.).

We went on to be a very productive music showcase in Atlanta for five years. Our shows featured mostly black artists (hardcore and eclectic soul alike) at venues including—2 High Studios, Penrose on Ponce, and several other spots. The RSC's most notably themed parties were EarAddicts, Da True Alternative Feztival, 2003 Spring Outdoor Roar, RSC Thursdays @ Black Lion Café (featuring live bands, DJs, and open mic sessions), and Annual Jimi Hendrix Birthday Tributes (both in concert and on the airwaves of ARS). On the ARS Hendrix Tributes, I learned two interesting facts from Larry while he hosted. Larry mentioned that the term "Heavy Metal" originated from a writer who saw a Hendrix concert and said he was "like watching Heavy Metal fall from the sky." I also read on a Hendrix compilation album that his song "Voodoo Child" referred to his meetings with a Voodoo Priestess from Ghana who tried to give him spiritual guidance. Ironically, I would soon experience a similar meeting with various counselors.

In January of 2000, ARS was finally moved back to 12 midnight – 2 am. Requaya & DJ Omega Black, hosts of WRFG's house music show "Early Morning Moods" agreed that their audience was better suited for the 2-5 am slot.

ARS often served as an inspiration for listeners to pick up and play instruments. I remember a friend of mine from Memphis named Pam e-mailing me with info about how ARS motivated her to buy a bass guitar.

For six years, ARS was the focal point of Urban Rock radio in ATL and throughout most of the United States, especially since there were few radio shows in the world significantly broadcasting ethnically diverse rock artists. ARS constantly attacked issues such as "Alternative R&B vs. Black Rock" and "venue insurance rates for hip-hop vs. those for rock."

Racism never fully died down as an ARS issue.[10] Yet it subdued once I recognized that racism was only a fragment of a larger war in the music industry.

In the late nineties there were several reports of the rock genre's declining record sales. According to an article in the *Las Vegas Review-Journal* called "Coming Unstrung," the future of rock music appeared bleak since its most sought after stars were all at least 40 years of age. Plus, the younger generation seemed to have a grander taste for hip-hop, techno, and electronica. In 2003, more reports surfaced how DJ equipment was now outselling guitars. Two years later, I even read about and observed an invention of a turntable-styled guitar.

Apparently, music's evolution reflected society. Rock music, art, science, and technological professions increasingly improved their inventions and ethnic diversity from the nineties into the new millennium, but the marketability for quality sounds dwindled thus making the industry and society as a whole appear even more segregated. My research and interviews with artists from all ethnic backgrounds proved that mostly mainstream record companies had tendencies to exploit artists hand over fist in their record deals. The bankruptcy case with TLC is very common among mainstream rock artists who often find their finances drained by poor management.

All these grand social issues were thrusted on me during the rough times of my tenure with ARS and the RSC. Indeed, rock music provided long overdue SOUL-U-TIONs to my narrow societal views. It also opened portals to abuse issues from the wounds of my childhood. My personal wars would be waged even more intensely.

10Reference – Bob Davis, Eurweb.com, "Racism in Music Biz," 12/28/05.

All the wonderful artists I played on ARS were missing pieces to my complicated puzzle of atonement.

David "Fuze" Fiuczynski and Witches Brew submitted the most amount of CDs to ARS. "Fuze" was also the most talented world-class guitarist ever on ARS.

E.X. Vortex was the most interviewed band ever on ARS. No band ever made more surprise visits to ARS.

All bands fronted by vocalist BMac (Ovid, XL) were the most talented on ARS. Ovid also featured Jermaine Rand on guitar and Seven on bass. I remember having a ball at Ovid shows. BMac is a tall smoky brown brother who sings like Corey Glover and Sam Cooke. His stage presence reflected Freddy Mercury of Queen, The Clash, and a tribal war chief. Whenever Ovid ripped up the stage, I spiritually felt as if I was grabbed by the throat and thrown to the back of the floor while still shouting "Fuck Yeah!" I am still amazed that they never blew up in the mainstream. Many people including me thought they would surely be "The next big thing." Their soulful goth sound was phenomenally awesome.

Baby Jane was the most requested artist ever on ARS. My most devoted listener, O-train, adored their TLC/Limp Bizkit-esque sound. He requested them every week. O-train became my temporary unofficial rock/soul DJ protégé.

The coolest sex appeal band on ARS was Empire 44. Their synth-pop show often featured two ladies sporting dominatrix wardrobes while holding a flag of the group's mystic yin-yang type emblem. They were referred to by their band mates as "sexy but not submissive." These seasoned death rockers and industrialists often used black female singers for their lead vocals. Johnnie Lee Hooper's voluptuous belly dancing moves along with her sexy R&B voice often put me in a trance.

I also give much more praise to the BRC for their consistent support of me. They were the first outlet to do an article about me and they never hesitated to run ads for ARS and the RSC.

And finally, mad props go to all artists ever played on ARS and/or associated with the RSC!!!

ETERNAL PRINCESS IN THE HEAVENS OF THE SEA

On a cold night, I treated a woman named Jenny to dinner and a movie. We ate at a vegetarian Chinese restaurant called Harmony. Then we saw *Soul Food* at the Lenox Square United Artist Theatre. I tried to hold Jenny's hand, but she shrugged me off, "Why are you stealing my energy?" Jenny specialized in witchcraft, so she sensed body language easily.

As I walked Jenny into her apartment, she introduced me to her roommate who she called her "sista." I forgot her name initially, but I remembered clearly seeing her play some type of board game with chips. I later found out that she was playing with runes, which also had witchcraft roots.

After this night, Jenny cut me off as a potential mate. She left me intact as an occasional conversation. I often ran into her at several health food stores (Return to Eden, Sevananda, Unity Natural Foods) where she worked and shopped. I also saw her sister working and shopping at these stores. Her sister eventually gave me a pound and introduced herself as Amira while she was working at Return to Eden. Even though I didn't have a conversation with her, I sensed that there was something incredibly exotic about Amira. She was a spunky young lady with a very slender petite figure and brown skin that shined like tea. Her presence was reminiscent of a mystical East African or Indian girl wearing a veil over her curly hair.

I would say hi to Amira a few more times at the stores before having my first real conversation with her.

On a cool night at the Funk Jazz Kafé, I was working behind WRFG's promo table on the vendor floor. There was an African garb table to my left. This is where I saw a bright beautiful shiny woman wearing beads in her hair and an outfit of a female East Indian belly dancer. This lovely young lady was Amira. I couldn't stop my onslaught of compliments to her throughout the night, "You're the beautiful princess here tonight…"

Amira though appeared irritated. I asked her what was wrong. She told me that she was tired and needed an early ride home. I told her I would oblige her after checking out the band and finishing my WRFG promo shift.

After watching The Chronicle rip up the stage with rock singer Esperanza and poet Sonya Marie, I returned to the vendor floor. I saw Amira belly dancing in the center of an African drum circle. I told her I was leaving and had to drive two other people home. Amira said, "But now I don't want to leave." I responded, "I got to go now." Amira answered, "Oh well. I'll find another ride." I dropped Sista Efua and Pablo G off at their respective Southwest Atlanta houses. Amira stayed on my mind until sunrise.

I didn't see Amira again until the hour after finishing "The Black Rock SOUL-U-TION" on July 17, 1998. I picked up some food at Sevananda and asked Amira, "Hey. I have an extra ticket to a function by the Black Rock Coalition. Would you like to come?" She flatly rejected me.

After this moment, I didn't think I would ever have any type of association with Amira. The Universe proved me wrong.

In October '98, I acquired an evening job with Phone Georgia. Even though I just got hired fulltime by a major cable company, I still needed extra money to pay off bills. After my first few nights on the job, I spotted Amira working at a computer in a section across from me. We briefly chatted during breaks.

Late one night, our shifts were running late. Amira asked me, "What time do you get off?" I told her, "Ten (pm)." She said, "I could use a ride home."

I had no problem driving her across town. Before I drove her home, we stopped at a Mexican restaurant on Buford Highway. Amira was a very strict vegetarian. She was vegan. She didn't eat meat or any dish that was cooked with meat or dairy products. At this time, I was a semi-vegetarian who occasionally splurged on chicken and fish. Amira chuckled at me, "You're no vegetarian!"

Our conversation started off subtle but grew complex. Amira mentioned how she rode a bus to New York City's Million Youth March. I said, "Be careful! Khalid Muhammad may be a government agent who's leading black people to hell." Amira responded, "I enjoyed the unity spirit of that march. So what if he is dirty?! He provided a positive event." Amira's intellectual strength impressed me. Her wits enlightened me more when she told me, "When I look to God, I look at the Creator as a woman since I'm one myself." Since I was a student of the philosophy "The Black Woman was the first being on Earth," I became more excited to speak with Amira.

As we finished our nighttime meal, I gave the waiter my credit card. Amira smiled, "Huhmm! You're treating me for a date, eh?" I laughed back, "Just consider this a friendship gesture!"

As we pulled out of the parking lot, I put the radio on GSU's Album 88. Omar's song "There's Nothing Like This" was playing. Amira gleefully shouted, "Oh! I love this song. I have to get a copy." I was increasingly more pleased with her company. I eventually dropped her off at her Decatur house. She gave me a hug. I would drive her to dinner and her house on two other work nights. The drives were long and exhausting, but I was willing to pay this price just to receive a smile and a hug from Amira.

During another work night, I asked Amira, "Can we stay in touch on the phone to further our friendship?" She responded, "Well of course! Me and you are already good friends." She was so stimulating while wearing her hair in a curly afro puff. She glanced at me, and I held her hand for a few seconds while kneeling down briefly at her computer station.

We had great hour-long conversations on the phone and stayed in touch after both of us quit Phone Georgia. We laughed about the bullshit charity scripts we were assigned in order to sell magazines. Amira jokingly chided, "I don't give a damn about the Special Olympics." Deep down, we both knew we served higher purposes than working for a corrupt telemarketing firm.

The more I communicated with Amira, the more my attraction for her grew.

On her twentieth birthday, I waited outside her house to present her a gift—Omar's CD *There's Nothing Like This*. A car pulled up in her driveway. Amira stepped out and looked upset until she realized it was me. She spurted, "We we're ready to fight you." Amira was escorted home by a brother with red dreadlocks who worked at Return to Eden. She invited me in and turned on the radio to WRFG's program "Empowerment Zone" hosted by Dr. L. The brother played it cool, but I knew I unintentionally disrupted his mac vibe on Amira. After I gave Amira her gift, I did the gentlemanly thing and left her alone with the redhead.

I called Amira the following week pouring my heart out. "I'm really infatuated with you. I fantasize about you naked, and it doesn't feel dirty." Amira felt uncomfortable listening to this, "I appreciated your interest, but you must know that I'm a free spirit. I'm not able to settle with anyone, especially since my last relationship." I desperately tried to hold her interest, "I swear I won't get jealous." Amira scolded, "If you saw me kickin' it with another guy at the Funk Jazz Kafé, you know you would be mad. Listen, now's not the time for me to be involved. And I don't think you should get in a relationship just to feel whole." I felt very disappointed by Amira's response, yet I still admired her wisdom. She was brighter than most people I knew and amazingly while she was very young.

I spoke to Amira twice more on the phone before meeting her at the Bazaar in Little 5 Points, where she held a table to make and sell jewelry. We initially agreed to see *Beloved* at a discount theatre but when I arrived, she told me she couldn't go because she had to stay for the open mic session. "Don't be mad," she replied, but I was mad. I decided to stick around for awhile until leaving for my radio show.

The vibe on this night was very strange!

First, I ran into Tynesha, a singer/guitarist who I first saw hanging with Larry when I initially met him in person at the Masquerade. Tynesha was preparing to sing during the open mic sessions.

I also crossed paths with another familiar woman. Sefiyah was a then-16-year-old who I dated prior to this night. As I walked with Amira to Sevananda, I saw Sefiyah walking with a man who looked at least my age. I was cool with this brother but was still rattled that Sefiyah didn't return my phone calls. Amira and Sefiyah knew each other and made a friendly chat on the walk across the street to the Bazaar.

I settled in at the open mic sessions for about an hour.

I recognized a couple of musicians in the band—Billy Fields (Follow For Now, Seek) on keys and MC Divnity (DATBU) on bass.

By the end of the hour, I watched Tynesha sing her heart out and apologize for being sick. I told Amira goodbye and shook hands with Sefiyah and her date after watching him attempt to hold her hand. I complimented Tynesha on her performance. Then she asked me for a ride home since she was feeling ill. I left the Bazaar with Tynesha.

I called Amira a couple more times with no response. I was becoming worried so I decided to visit her again at the Bazaar. On this day, I ran into Tynesha again before I spotted Amira. I asked Amira if she was alright. She told me she was busy dealing with some issues. She seemed too preoccupied to consider hanging out with me. I told her I watched *Beloved* on video. She said, "I would like to come over and watch it." I told her that I already took it back to the store. Again, I left Little 5 Points with Tynesha.

Since Amira was no longer a likely mate for me, I hung out with Tynesha more. Amira and I didn't cross paths again until she saw me walking with Tynesha in Little Five Points. I gave Amira a quick hug and proceeded to an E.X. Vortex show with Tynesha.

Ironically, Amira started phoning me regularly two weeks later. Tynesha and I went out together frequently yet our conversations never were intimate like the ones I had with Amira. Amira and I often spoke on the phone for more than hours. Our conversations often lasted past three o'clock in the morning.

The more Amira and I spoke, the more intimate our topics became.

We spontaneously ended up confessing details of our sexual experiences. I mentioned how I didn't lose my virginity until I was well into my twenties. Amira responded, "I wish I would have waited a lot longer for my first time."

The deeper our conversations became, the more I sought advice from Dr. L. She frequently conversed with Amira as if they were sisters. I told Dr. L that I envisioned Amira and me saving each other for a wonderful relationship. Dr. L warned me that

Amira was still healing from her relationship with a "spiritual pimp." Coincidentally, Amira had phoned into Dr. L's show themed "Spiritual Pimps," angrily calling for the exposure of a man who Dr.L and one of her guests called "The Purple People Eater." Amira often sat as a guest on Dr. L's show. I often phoned in along with my friend Amen. As I found out later, the man referred to as "The Purple People Eater" use to own and manage the A-HOP (African House of Peace), where the RSC performed our initial shows named *Urban Rock EarAddicts*. Amira was never comfortable talking about Tantric Sex since "The Purple People Eater" apparently used this practice to exploit her while she worked with him at one of his vendor tables located in the Funk Jazz Kafé.

After my sessions with Dr. L, Amira and I grew constantly more comfortable talking deeper about our backgrounds. I revealed one time that I was admitted to a mental hospital. Amira eventually narrated to me how she ran away from home in Philadelphia at age seventeen, hitchhiking across the country to California.

Amira phoned me one time saying that she wanted to move back to California. She said she felt "free-er" among the people there. I told her, "Whatever you're decision is, the Universe will divinely bless you. I'll always care for you no matter where you're at."

Amira further explained how she used to be a rave kid who was tossed around in mosh pits. She listened to alternative rock groups—Pearl Jam, Nine Inch Nails, Red Hot Chilli Peppers, Soundgarden, and Tori Amos. During her cross country trip, she learned a lot about herself as a universal being. She grew out of her rave kid phase, claiming, "I was cool with those white folks, but they were too destructive." Nevertheless, she made friends with various gypsy white folks in California at the end of her hitchhikes. She told me, "I can still call them up if I ever needed help." Amira mentioned how a former WRFG DJ named Jah-One was going to produce a documentary film about her life. I don't know if he ever made headway on this project since he left Atlanta in the year 2000.

Amira possessed a blissfully divine universal spirit that was loved by people of almost every background. Her shiny youthful energy helped me overcome my racial prejudices as well. She often smeared, "I'm so sick of all these black/white issues." She constantly preached, "I guess all my solutions to the world's problems are in the music." She loved to sing, dance, and express her joy to the world.

Her joyful glee was no more evident than on the night of October 28, 1999.

After several months of playing phone tag, Amira finally hung out with me. I scooped her up from her job at Unity Natural Foods. She looked so happy to see me as her eyes glowed like marbles when she hugged me. I held back my amazement of how beautiful she looked with her perfectly spiraling braided hair to go along with wearing her long-skirted purple dress marked by turtle designs.

We drove back to my apartment and watched my recorded VHS copy of the NBC movie *Y2K*. I was one of those ridiculously scared freaks that stocked up for Y2K fearing massive unrest. Amira watched the film and laughed, "This movie is ridiculous! The only thing I'm going to do to prepare for Y2K is go on a fast." On Dr. L's program she facetiously called Y2K, "Y2C—Year 2 Chill." I was still a nervous wreck.

After finishing the film and a light soup dinner, we drove to the 4 Kings Entertainment benefit show at the Yin Yang Café. There were featured performances by India Arie, The Kebbi & Woody Williams Project, and E.X. Vortex.

Amira moused around the lounge while I sat and spoke with Tony Maury from Pitlock Entertainment about resolving ARS's racial problems. She laughed when Bayé of E.X. Vortex unsuccessfully tried to start a mosh pit. Then the crowd was awed watching the Williams Brothers play the hell out of their instruments (Kebbi on a wah wah saxophone and Woody on drums) in a freestyle jazz set. I will admit myself that this was one of the most incredible instrumental performances I've ever seen. India Arie wrapped up the performances with a solo acoustic set. She made the crowd blush with her song "Brown Skin" as she sung a lyric about caressing a man's "Chocolate Kiss." A DJ wrapped up the night spinning house and classic soul. Amira forayed into a gleeful trance dance. Unintentionally, her magnetism attracted an overly aggressive guy. This man put his hands around Amira's waist and tried to kiss her. She uncomfortably looked at me, hinting for me to get that jerk away from her. As I approached them, he smiled and pushed his contact info into Amira's tote bag before walking away.

Before Amira and I left the Yin Yang Café, she spoke intimately with India Arie. She suggested for both of them to get together one day and sing.

As we drove back to Amira's house, I placed the radio on an alternative rock program. Amira bitched, "Oh! I'm feeling too good to listen to vibes that hard." I brushed it off by talking about various rock bands I played on ARS. I told her about a band named OVID. She said, "That sounds so gothic. The name sounds like VOID."

As I pulled into her driveway, I gave her a hug. I started to back off, but Amira had her eyes closed and still had her arms wrapped around me. I guess she wanted me to kiss her on the mouth. However, my mind was still on Tynesha kissing me two weeks prior. So I gently kissed Amira on the cheek. She sighed, "You're so sweet." And finally, she stepped into her house.

A million thoughts continue to race through my mind today,

wondering if my relationship with Amira would have gone far if I had only caressed her lips that night!

Amira and I continued to bond, mostly through the phone.

On New Year's Eve preceding Y2K, I secured myself like a home hermit. I watched 2000 come in with no reported glitches anywhere in the world. Strangely, I felt depressed about Y2K's compliancy since I wasted thousands of dollars preparing for protection against disorder.

After I drove Tynesha home from a MARTA (Atlanta transit) station, I played back a phone message. It was Amira chuckling, "Well, nothing happened. I LOVE YOU! BE SAFE!" I interpreted her "love" remark as a joke, but I wished for it to have a deeper meaning.

Thus, our conversations would evolve with broader tones.

In January, 2000, I remember calling Amira while I was feeling depressed. She shrugged me off, "I don't have time right now. Why don't you do something creative? Write a poem. Something." I hung up the phone feeling betrayed. I always made time to listen to her sorrows, but she didn't show concern for mine.

I decided I wouldn't call her again, and this changed when she called back the next night. Within the first minute, she sung lyrics from a poem she wrote. I was flattered. No female outside of my family's birthday parties ever sung directly to me. No matter how much I resisted Amira, she always found a way back into my life.

She continued calling me every other day.

One night, I was meditating and took a break when the phone rang. I picked up and told Amira I got in a meditative state. Amira spewed, "Don't you ever do that again. When you meditate you're not suppose to let anyone distract you. Including ME." Once again she was very wise.

In February 2000, she called me to relay her exciting plans to visit Miami for her twenty-first birthday. I just listened while she gloated. She called me back minutes later outlining her travel plans. I thought it was strange. Perhaps she was subconsciously hinting for me to go with her. Regardless, she went there with a female friend and had a ball. I dropped off a birthday card and plastic toy fish tank at her house while she was gone.

Amira returned to town in March 2000 with a rejuvenated spirit. She was very excited about getting her jewelry business and singing career off the ground. Her ambition helped to motivate me out of my distress since I was still contemplating my next DJ career move. Plus, I was melancholy over Tynesha's rejection of my Valentine's Day confession revealing my love for her. Amira said, "Don't worry! I don't think she was right for you." I asked, "Well what about us?" She responded, "You're my big brother. You're attractive in your own way. I have faith you'll find a SOUL mate. You deserve it." I recanted about another woman at work, "I dated Lita a few times but she lacked … Brrrains." Amira laughed, "I was about to slap you." Amira thought I was going to say she lacked breasts. Amira proceeded to thank me for the birthday gift I gave her. She reacted, "When's your birthday? I'm gonna write it down because I'm going to do something for you, whether it's cooking a meal or something." Before we got off the phone, Amira said, "I love you." I responded, "I love you too."

Amira's enthusiasm continued to blossom with the proceeding March, 2000 Meeting of the Masters Conference. I was skeptical of whether any of the booked metaphysicians—Bobby Hemmit, Audrie Williams, Dr. Henry DeBernardo, Reverend Phil Valentine, Llaila Afrika, and Dr. Khalid Muhammad's New Black Panther Party—had progressive strategies in mind. Amira scolded me for being paranoid, "Look. It's good I don't own a TV. There's too much mind control programming and stress from those vibes. Plus, I have a table set up to sell my jewelry.

No new world order conspiracy plan or whatever is going to stop our shining. Me and you are going to look back at these times one day and laugh. There's so much I want to explore in this world, like learning all these new languages. Our progress is just beginning …"

Once again before hanging up the phone, Amira said, "I LOVE YOU!" I wished it meant more than a brother/sister vibe. Perhaps, though, she felt deeper than this, and I was too blind to notice.

I ran into Amira at the Masters' Conference. She looked smashing in a baby blue, African-styled dress and a dashiki hat. I hugged her and then took a seat to listen to the "Masters'" panel discussion. I was not impressed by their resolution calls for Black Unity. After I asked them a question about teaching black kids music with no genre limitations, Amira approached me saying, "Hey. I want to get some dinner. Let me know when you're leaving." I told her, "I didn't bring my car. I'm taking MARTA back home. So I can't help you with a ride." Amira seemed disappointed. I was wondering if she just wanted my time as a mere meal ticket or if she really wanted my company as a whole.

After this conference, my conversations with Amira become sparser since she was now dating a young man. Amira still agreed to catch a movie with me. In late April 2000, I scooped her up from Unity Natural Foods and drove us to a cinema at North DeKalb Mall. Initially, I wanted to stop at a restaurant, but Amira said she was on a tight schedule. After we purchased tickets, Amira was caught trying to sneak in her own organic popcorn. The usher played it cool by telling her to comeback with the popcorn unseen in her bag. The usher then asked me, "Is dat yur girl?" I responded, "No! My little sister."

We watched *The Skulls*. During the coffin initiation scene, Amira commented, "They're trying to copy *The Matrix*." I told her, "This scene is factual. George Bush was initiated like this into the Skull & Bones society." Amira appeared impressed with my intellect. During the film's climax, Amira clapped, "A woman saves the day!"

As I drove her home, Amira joyfully spoke, "We need to do this again. I'm so glad I saw this movie with you. I was supposed to go with this brother I'm kickin' it with, but he wouldn't have been able to explain the movie the way you did." I wrapped my arms around her and gave her a peck on her right facial cheek. She gleamed, "Awww-ah," and walked into her house.

Seemingly, Amira and I grew closer, but she was also close to the young man she was dating.

In early May 2000, we exchanged a few more phone conversations detailing her plans to travel with "the brother" to Costa Rica. Amira was also very excited since she had put in notice to resign from Unity Natural Foods, "Before I arrived, there was no 'Unity' in that store. They don't want me to leave, but it's time for me to move on. After this trip, I'll be ready to put my jewelry business in full gear ..."

I scooped up Amira one last time from the store. The first plan was to drive her to the closest MARTA station. She offered me money to drive her downtown though. I told her I would just take her all the way to her father's house.

As we rode through the freeway, I played a recorded tape of an ARS program. Amira commented on one track, "Those are white boys singing." I said, "My show has been eclectic for awhile." As I drove into her father's driveway, Amira paid me three dollars for gas money and asked what I would spend it on. I told her "Taco Hell (Bell)." She rolled her eyes facetiously, "To each his own!" I walked inside her father's home for a brief visit. Amira greeted her younger half brothers then she walked me outside. I left her with a camera for her to use in Costa Rica. We embraced in what would turn out to be our final hug.

Amira called me later that night telling me how she and her father recorded some music for a DeKalb County politician. We exchanged our very last "I Love You(s)" before she flew off to Costa Rica.

On June 11, 2000, I woke up worried about Amira since I hadn't heard from her after her return flight. When she came back from her Miami birthday trip, she called me about two weeks later. Amira was supposed to be back in Atlanta by May 20. So I sensed something was wrong since more than three weeks had passed without Amira contacting me.

I called Amira's house that very morning. An older man answered the phone. Suddenly, a sick feeling hit my stomach. He told me he was Amira's father. Right then, I knew something was terribly out of place. I asked him if Amira had returned safely. He spoke somberly, "King Neptune took Amira from us during her last night on a beach in Costa Rica." My heart stopped for a few seconds as I frantically thought Amira was murdered. Amira's father continued in his calm melancholy tone, "So you were close to her, eh? Well! Amira left behind many loved ones, including her husband." I responded, "Amira was married?" Her father spoke back, "You have a lot of questions. So come over here (to Amira's house), and I will show you some things ..."

Immediately, I was weepy and short of breath. Without hesitation, I hopped in my Sentra. I drove non-stop on the freeway to Decatur. While pumping Kelis's song "Get Along With You," on my car's tape deck, I boo-hooed like a crybaby. Ironically, this song was produced by artists who call themselves The Neptunes. Perhaps the Universe was sending me some heavy signals in correlation with the "King Neptune" explanation.

As I pulled into Amira's driveway, I saw a short stocky bearded dark brown-complexioned man wearing a T-shirt, denim shorts, glasses, and corn-rowed hair. As I exited my vehicle and placed a CLUB lock on my steering wheel, this man said, "Look. You don't need that here." This was Amira's father. He called himself Ba Ba Rahamm.

Ba Ba led me to the backyard where he and most of his family were lounging. He introduced me to Amira's "husband," Daniel. I was still panicky and dumbfounded with questions about Amira's death. Ba Ba screamed at me, "Look man. Relax. I loved Amira too. I loved her more than you. She was my life, my daughter, my queen, my goddess. You need to have a drink and a smoke." I told him, "I don't do that." Ba Ba screamed back, "Look. You're not calm yet. So while we're generous enough to allow you into our home, you're gonna relax with some wine and corn (weed)."

Since I was an emotional wreck, I figured, "What the hell? I need something to settle my nerves." As I calmly laid myself on a lawn chair, I began an introspective talk with Ba Ba and Daniel. I first asked Ba Ba what he meant by "King Neptune." Ba Ba explained in a vague way similar to Greek mythology that Amira had drowned. King Neptune was a sea god who supposedly spotted Amira and seized an opportunity to add another beautiful young lady to his kingdom. I also asked Ba Ba when Amira's funeral would take place. As Ba Ba briefly explained Amira's body cremation ceremony, he broke down in tears. Ba Ba's story left me confused. He was growing weary of questioning, so he challenged me like a journalist to only ask him and Daniel a combined ten questions for the rest of the day. I agreed, since I didn't want to add any more pain to the tragedy.

For most of this day, I sat with Ba Ba and Daniel absorbing the shock of Amira's death. I let my "journalist" mentality be at ease. So as Ba Ba and Daniel were smoking corn out of African/Native-American styled pipes, I joined in. Ba Ba revealed to me in a relaxed tone that Amira's full name was *Amira Asuñe Lacey Bey*, which he said meant *"First daughter born on a Sunday with the divine energy of the Sun.*" He also told me her mother was of Indian and Irish descent. I wasn't sure if he meant East Indian or Native American. Either way Amira's spicy brown features had a world mixture. Ba Ba also said Amira never liked mentioning her mixed background. Ba Ba proceeded to give me a bottle of wine saying it was for me to use as a light to call Amira like a genie. I didn't believe him. Ba Ba mocked me, "So you doubt?" I drank the remaining wine from this bottle and recited homage to Amira saying something like, "Amira, I know you're in a better place ..." Ba Ba gleefully listened.

Ba Ba went inside the house to cook food while looking after his two little boys. I remained outside smoking corn with Daniel. Daniel gradually became more relaxed with me, "So you were that cool with Amira?" I told Daniel that I was practically Amira's big brother even though my feelings ran deeper. Daniel further revealed, "I just met her at the Meeting of the Masters Conference." From here my journalist questioning began, "How did you two end up married?" Daniel said, "Amira tripped out on one of the days. We were there feeling so happy so she had us get a marriage certificate." I continued interviewing, "How did Amira die?" Daniel summed up her passage, "It was our last day before we were supposed to fly back. We were walking on the beach. Amira was feeling so happy. Then I saw a strange look in Amira's eyes. It seemed she felt her life was already fulfilled. She jumped in the water and told me to join her ... She swam deeper into the ocean, and I told her not to go far. The waves started kicking up strong. Amira was screaming while trying to hold onto my back. If I didn't keep swimming I would have drowned. The next thing I know, Amira was off my back and disappeared with the waves."

Ba Ba had come back outside. He decided to answer my ten questions, but I told him I'd only ask him five since Daniel answered some of the questions. Ba Ba fulfilled my curiosity by telling me how Amira's body was retrieved. After Daniel called Ba Ba and Amira's close friends in the U.S., Ba Ba arrived in Costa Rica within the next three days. As they arrived, Amira's body was found washed up on shore. Ba Ba said Amira's facial expression appeared to be one of joyful sleep. Then Ba Ba and Daniel fixed Amira's hair before preparing her body for cremation. Amira's close family and friends performed a home going service by releasing her ashes into the ocean and placing flowers into the beach's shallow waters.

After Ba Ba, Daniel, and the rest of Amira's family returned to Atlanta, they produced a series of memorials honoring her. Ba Ba sensed that there were still unsettled spirits close to Amira. I was the second to last friend who Ba Ba informed before he put closure on Amira's passage.

Before I left the house that day, I participated in a Yoruba-style rites of passage ceremony for Amira. Ba Ba further revealed that Amira spoke of me with admiration. After I last saw her at Ba Ba's house, he asked her, "Who's that I smell on you? Do you have a new boyfriend?" Amira replied, "He's not my boyfriend, but I love him anyways. And you would love him just the same if you knew him." Ba Ba went on to say that Amira purchased some things in Costa Rica. He pinpointed the items destined for each of Amira's loved ones. He gave me some firecrackers labeled with a picture of a black cat. He told me I was supposed to use them for the passage ceremony. I had no idea what to do.

I kneeled down in a blissful moment and said, "Amira's home." Ba Ba said, "No. She's still on a sailboat to her new realm." I praised Amira with more words, "Amira you meant so much to me ..." Ba Ba pounded a conga drum with two heavily round, padded sticks and intervened, "They're coming. Hurry up." I had no clue what I was involved in. Perhaps Ba Ba was calling some ghosts. I kept ranting on with homage to

Amira. Ba Ba screamed more, "Stop fucking around. Hurry!" I was confused more. Ba Ba grabbed the firecrackers from me, "Fuck it. I'll do it." He lit the firecrackers and I sat in silence for five minutes feeling sour. I guessed that I had to light something for Amira. So I lit the wine bottle on fire. Ba Ba came back outside, "Whoa! That was your light. But it can still be of use to you." I retrieved the burnt bottle and ashy leaves. I still have those items today.

As I exited Amira's house, I asked Ba Ba, "Do I have permission to do a radio show fully dedicated to Amira?" Ba Ba responded, "Sure, I would like to call in, too." Ba Ba also played a recording of one of Amira's songs. My eyes subsequently watered with more sadness.

I woke up the next morning on Monday, June 12, 2000. This turned out to be the saddest day of my life. The shock of Amira's death fully set in. I started crying profusely. I decided not to go to work that day and cried seven more times throughout the day. I played Amira's favorite song by Omar along with some of my instrumental favorites like SOULFLY's ambient cut from their first album. I just let myself mourn for the whole day. I became so sad during the late afternoon that I decided to take a walk. As I trotted on Peachtree Industrial Boulevard, it started to rain. I felt a moment of divine peace with the water dripping on my face. I said, "Amira I know you're forever with me through this water. I will now always say 'Asé Amira Asuñe Lacey Bey' whenever I'm in contact with water." I returned to my apartment and called Tynesha.

On June 17, 2000, I broadcasted ARS and themed the episode, "Asé Amira Asuñe Lacey Bey." This was my prime moment to pay homage to Amira the best way I knew how. It turned out to be the most beautiful radio show I ever produced. It's still the only ARS program where I remember every song I played along with every transitional moment. And it's still the only ARS episode I play consistently on my stereo.

I recorded a copy of this show for Ba Ba. He graciously hugged me several times chanting, "My son! My son!" I visited Amira's family and house twice more to complete the final stages of Amira's passage ceremony.

Ba Ba visited my apartment eight months later during the week before Amira's twenty-second birthday anniversary. He gave me two pictures of Amira and a four-song CD featuring Amira's voice. He asked me to play it on the radio. I did so during a special ARS episode fully dedicated to female musicians. I asked Ba Ba if he was interested in renting or selling Amira's house to me. Ba Ba said the plan all along even while Amira was alive was to turn this house into a studio.

Ba Ba eventually moved his whole family back into that house. He continued his video and music production work for artists like reggae star and lecturer, Mutabaruka. I visited Ba Ba on one last birthday ceremony for Amira. He offered me some weed, but I decided to stay cold turkey. In his own trippy fashion, Ba Ba played some video footage of Amira recorded over some of his music tracks while he smoked out on weed and cigarettes. Since that day, I haven't heard from Ba Ba. I tried calling him, but his number was out of service. I still contemplate driving by Amira's old house to see if he still lives there. I pray that he and Amira's siblings are doing well.

I last saw Daniel in attendance at a WRFG-sponsored hip-hop/reggae show held at the AHOP in November 2000. He was with some cute young lady. Apparently, Daniel moved on from Amira. I hope he's still in good spirits.

Ironically, some of my friends actually believe Amira's death was caused by murder. They all say similar things to the effect that Amira was too good of a swimmer to drown. I concurred that Amira, especially with a Pisces zodiac sign, swam well enough to snorkel one summer in New Jersey. She felt at peace with the dolphins she observed. I don't want to believe that someone would purposely take Amira's life. Yet, I honestly don't have any information about any possible conspiracy plot. If there are any thugs who live on today and had some involvement in her death, then I pray for the Universe to reap the mess they sowed. Perhaps, Almighty Creation will someday reveal to me the full extent of Amira's passing. Regardless of whether her passage was accidental or incidental, my spirit has always felt that Amira is at peace on another realm.

Amira will always be a celebrated spirit. Her mark on this world was even recollected on India Arie's first album. India noted a dedication, "In loving memory of Amira Ajenay(misspelling of Asuñe) Lacey Bey."

Everyday I feel the agony and joy of missing Amira. I still carry guilt for not being strong enough to attract and protect her. At the same time, I feel serene and blessed that Amira was a special part of my life. Her divine spiritual presence helped me grow as a UniverSOUL being! She never blossomed into a fully grown independent Queen. Yet she will always be my *ETERNAL PRINCESS IN THE HEAVENS OF THE SEA!!!*

WORST NIGHTMARE

Rap/metal hybrid band, Witches Brew finished their set at a Masquerade show during February '99. I rapped with their members about my radio show before walking downstairs to see what was going on. That's when I met Larry. I also introduced myself to his then girlfriend—guitarist Tynesha from Bronx, New York.

My first impression of her was, "Wow, a fine looking sista with (dread) locks." She was a gorgeous, petite, honey-beige complexioned woman with sandy brown locks running halfway down her neck. She had eyes like a puppy dog and lips thick like Betty Boop. She was wearing a black-robed outfit laced with a hood reminding me of a witch's wardrobe, a Jedi outfit, and the same gear that Apollonia Kotero wore during her initial scene in the film *Purple Rain*.

While I chatted with Larry in the bar area of Masquerade's upstairs level called Heaven, Tynesha walked around the concert floor smoking a cigarette.

After Larry and I bought some drinks, a racially mixed Athens, Georgia-based band called S.M.O. started performing. I walked over to Tynesha and asked her, "How does this band sound?" She replied, "Interesting!" I enjoyed S.M.O.'s balladry funked-out hard rock display. I wound up acquiring one of their CDs for ARS. I grooved out to Urban Grind for the night's grand finale. Larry and Tynesha left early.

After this night, Larry and I bonded professionally and personally. He became an integral part of the RSC. I treated him and more of his friends to Hawks' basketball games.

While increasing my rapport with Larry, he occasionally rapped about his time with Tynesha. One time, he mentioned how he tried to wake up to listen to ARS, but he was asleep in a bed with Tynesha. She was too relaxed to wake him up. I told Larry, "I admire your ability to attract a woman as fine as that." Larry responded, "Oh it ain't like that man. I'm married. You want her?" I said, "Don't worry! She's hanging with you for now."

Little did I know how impactful Tynesha would become in my life.

I encountered her again at the Bazaar in Little Five Points. This was the same night I was supposed to go to the movies with Amira. Tynesha didn't recognize me at first. This time she was wearing glasses and sported a bohemian look wearing jeans and boots. I told her I met her with Larry. She seemed too preoccupied while practicing on an acoustic guitar with a singer/poet named BaSheba Earth.

After conversing with Amira, I watched a couple of people recite poems during the open mic session. Tynesha did something different by playing her guitar and singing a song called "To Be Free."

She sang very well. Then she apologized to the crowd for muffing a note due to her sickness. After I said goodbye to Amira and ex-girlfriend interest Sefiyah, I complimented Tynesha on her song. Tynesha asked if she could have a ride home. Without hesitation, I escorted her out of Little 5 Points walking her to my car.

While walking, I told her how I had to be back in this area to host ARS. Tynesha mentioned she was an aspiring singer/guitarist who was looking to become a female Jimi Hendrix. She also explained how she got sick because of stage fright.

As I drove her to her Buckhead house suite, our conversation included my insecurity over going bald. Tynesha said, "You still look good." I thought she was just desperately trying to be nice since she had a headache and was grateful for a ride. Yet, her energy felt warm to my heart. Before she stepped out of the car, she firmly hugged me with gratitude. I was totally mystified. I was not used to women with her level of attraction purposely embracing me.

I didn't ask for her number, but I did retrieve it from Larry since I was officially interested.

A few days later I called Tynesha asking if she wanted to join me, Larry, and two more of his friends for a Hawks' basketball game. Tynesha responded, "You really want me to come along? Well, thanks. I'm not sure I can go, but I'll let you know." Tynesha ended up not going to the game. I still spoke with her on the phone more often.

During our next conversation, I told Tynesha I was seeking sponsorship for the RSC. Tynesha asked, "Do you meditate?" I responded, "Sometimes!" She answered back, "Then meditate on that sponsor and you'll draw it to you." I asked another question, "Can you show me how?" Tynesha said, "I can show you many more things, but you have to be ready. I got to go now. Talk to you later."

I hung up the phone feeling both intimidated and intrigued by her confident display of mysticism.

I called her once more before dating her. Tynesha sounded like a blissful yogi master, "I just cry when I think about how many people are going to kill themselves while the Universe is aligning like our chakras and sending us many blessings." I was still afraid of her metaphysical charm, but I was also excited about hanging out with her.

For our first date, we checked out a Neu Planet Entertainment produced concert at the Cajun Kitchen featuring Nadirah

Shakoor and David Ryan Harris. I didn't initially tell Tynesha that I was also hosting the show. After we arrived and ate around 6:30pm, Tynesha appeared pissed that the show wasn't scheduled to start until 9:30pm. However, she remained calm while listening to CDs I played over the sound system. She also wrote a ton of lyrics and poems on paper napkins. I on the other hand was very fatigued because I started a week-long fast. Tynesha asked, "So is the fast good for your spirit?" I told her I was unsure.

The performances finally kicked off by 10:30pm. David Ryan Harris did a stellar solo acoustic set. Nadirah rocked the house with her band and background singers that included Laurnea. Her performance also welcomed other singers and poets on the microphones. I was inspired enough to pound my water bottle like a drum.

While Tynesha was having fun, I felt drained since I ate only one meal that day. I fell in Tynesha's lap and she replied, "Look Talib! You need to eat something!" I drank more water before we exited the show.

As I drove Tynesha home, she raved about what a good time she had. Before she stepped out of my vehicle, she kissed me on the cheek and gave me a hug. From this moment, I sensed that she would potentially be my girlfriend.

On the day before our next date, I injured my back at work. I passed out two days after completing a six-day fast. An ambulance retrieved me from work. I was released about an hour after arriving. The doctor said all I had was a sore lower back and low blood sugar from lack of nutrition. I made a mistake by only drinking water for four days.

Despite my sore back, I was determined to hang with Tynesha the following day. I scooped her up from her house suite. She only wore a head wrap with a t-shirt and sweatpants. I told her that was fine since we had only planned to watch movies after eating.

We ate at a Mexi-Cali styled restaurant called Bajarito's. During our conversation, Tynesha mentioned something disturbing, "Biggie Smalls (Notorious B.I.G.) was a pillager of the community, and I'm glad he's dead." I didn't respond. I was just shocked wondering what she had against Biggie. One year later during a subsequent phone conversation, Tynesha told me she met Biggie and Sean "Puffy" Combs at a club one night. She further explained in vague terms, "They just weren't down with God, and I fucking hate them. Biggie got what he deserved and Puffy's next."

Even though I was slightly creeped out by Tynesha's disgust with Biggie, we proceeded with our date. We rented two movies from Blockbuster, *Junior's Song* and *Future Sport*. Then we bought some snacks at a nearby health food store called Nuts 'n' Berries. Before I got in the driver's seat, Tynesha offered me a piggyback ride. Facetiously, I accepted since I didn't think she could lift me. Lo and behold, she rode me on her back with ease. I screamed, "Whoa! Put me down!" Tynesha asked why I was uncomfortable. I explained that my back was still sore.

We concluded our date at my apartment. I wanted to feel her towards the mood for sex, but I sat motionless since my sore back deterred my confidence. Tynesha enjoyed the movies. As we exited my apartment, she saw a news report on the Bosnian-Serb war and said, "That's in God's hands." Again, I was creeped out because I feared she was a Christian despite her metaphysical aura.

After this night, I thought I screwed up my chances with Tynesha. Nevertheless, we continued to date.

I called her the following Sunday just to see how she was doing. She wanted to see a movie. So we went to the discount theatre on Buford Highway and saw *Virus*. This movie really wasn't scary, but Tynesha continuously tapped my arm seeking comfort. I thought about wrapping my arm around her but decided not to. I sensed more that my time with her was building into a special relationship.

Before I drove her home, we shopped for music at Tower Records. I purchased some blank tapes. Tynesha raved about Nine Inch Nails' musical innovation.

On another night, I invited Tynesha to join me, Larry, O.P., and Ondrea at a Hawks' playoff game. Tynesha replied, "I'd rather be home practicing (on her guitar)." I admired Tynesha's willpower towards her passionate goals. It helped inspire me to lay out realistic goals for my DJ career.

Tynesha hung with me again on a spring '99 night in Little Five Points. This time she brought her acoustic guitar along since I asked her to sing on an acoustic episode of ARS. She frantically replied, "Can we put this in the trunk. I don't want this to get stolen. This is all I have." I told her, "Don't worry! I'll give you my guitar if yours gets stolen, since I hardly use it."

First we checked out performances at 9 Lives Saloon by bands Madfly and Butter. Butter had a decent rhythmic hard sound fronted by a dreadlocked vocalist. Madfly, though, sounded too cheesy pop-like for my taste.

In the middle of these performances, Tynesha was smoking and drinking up a storm. She often repeated she was trying to quit but always ended up indulging. During one moment, she asked me to buy her a beer since she was out of cash. Even though I felt uncomfortable supporting her habit, I engaged in doing so. She gave me a giant kiss on the cheek. Tynesha continued her toxic habits while networking with more musicians before we proceeded to eat at El Myr.

During our meal, all Tynesha talked about was how much she needed to practice on her guitar. She mentioned how sometimes she stayed at home and practiced all day. I was bored and disappointed sensing that Tynesha was not relationship material.

After leaving El Myr, we walked back to my car. Since it was chilly, I wrapped my arms around Tynesha and kept her warm. We chatted for about an hour in the car before entering WRFG for my radio show ARS. At the end of the chat, I sang "If I had a dime" by David Ryan Harris. Tynesha seemed amused.

We settled into WRFG's studio with Larry, O.P., and Kimba. I played acoustic rock tracks, allowed the artists air time for their songs, and interviewed them. Tynesha blew away the sound board by blasting high notes on her song, "To Be Free."

While my guests swirled in joy, I strangely felt depressed. I didn't feel like I had a mission in life while observing all those wonderful artists who genuinely loved their crafts. As my guests were leaving, I told them to take Tynesha home. I had to stick around since the DJ who followed my program didn't show up for his shift. I wanted to kiss Tynesha but only settled for a hug since I didn't feel worthy of her embrace.

After this episode, I was depressed for two weeks. So I sought more psychological help from Dr. L.

Dr. L was practically my big sister from Atlanta's conscious community. She was a fearless feminist who directed an organization called Sisters Helping Sisters. She use to serve as a cop for the Riverdale, Georgia Police Department and proceeded to do a brief stint as Dr. Khalid Muhammad's personal bodyguard. Dr. L eventually earned a masters' degree in psychology, a doctorate and several certifications in naturopathic medicine. She founded an alternative practice entitled Celestial Healing. In the midst of all of Dr. L's accomplishments, she co-hosted "Progressive Spot" with Nma and eventually landed a brief spot hosting "Empowerment Zone." She stands six feet, two inches tall with dreadlocks growing down her ass and is a blackbelt in karate.

Often, I facetiously called Dr. L, "Da Heala (Jila) Monster." This joke though would soon become a scary reality.

In May '99, I visited Dr. L at her L5P office. I felt as though I had no real purpose for living. Dr. L countered with doses of encouragement, "You started a radio show making the community aware of Black Rock artists." I responded, "I didn't start any movement." Dr. L relentlessly thwarted positive darts at me, "You inspired people like me who hardly listen to rock to pay attention. Even if most people hated your show, if just one person liked it, then it was a good show." Dr. L then assigned me to write down my five most important goals. I wrote them down and stated my fears. I most significantly stressed that I felt the goals were worthless because I didn't have a genuine mission in life. Dr. L then demanded I name three things I love, "Tell me in ten seconds, or I'll name some for you!" With humiliated laughter, I told her, "Music, movies, and licking pretty feet." Dr. L repeated my three things with a straight unemotional face. Then she asked, "Well, don't you love rock music?" I hesitantly said in a low tone, "Ye- yea-ah." Dr. L concluded this analysis by saying, "Well that's your purpose. Use your radio show to become the king on your throne!"

I felt slightly better!

Then I forayed into the topic of women. I told Dr. L about a woman (Tynesha) whom I dated that didn't work out. Then I mentioned how I felt Amira and I would end up saving each other. Dr. L replied, "Be careful with Amira. She's still healing from her relationship with 'The Purple People Eater.' That's why I told her not to come on the radio during my 'Spiritual Pimps' episode. If you're going to have a relationship with her, then approach her as just a friend in the beginning and say, 'Let's build with each other one step at a time."

Dr. L wrapped up this session by placing me under hypnosis, playing ambient music, and commanding positive thoughts into my subconscious mind. I left her office with hope. Then I attempted to reach back towards Amira.

Two days later, I recorded a promo with Dr. L in WRFG's production room to advertise an ARS episode centered on "Tantric Sex." After I finished, I walked towards the Bazaar store to see Amira. Before I crossed the street, I saw Tynesha walking forward with a guitar case strapped to her back. She approached me with weepy, puppy dog eyes, "Hey! Long time no hear from. Have you been out with other women?" I said, "No! I've been dealing with some things." Then she asked with a smile, "Can we go back to your place and watch a movie?" Without resistance, I accepted. I proceeded to check on Amira at the Bazaar and left L5P again with Tynesha.

We rented *What Dreams May Come* from a video store. While we sifted through the movie selections, Tynesha gleefully spotted the adult film section, "Porno flicks!" Once again, I was creeped out with suspicion. I thought, "Why did porno films arouse her so much?"

We moved on to pick up orders of Taco Bell from their drive-thru area. While I drove, Tynesha drifted into her metaphysical vibe, "It's so wonderful to be with a spirit." She touched my hand as she said this. I spoke back in resentment, "So you can feel a spirit within me?" Tynesha barked, "Hey? Where did that come from?" We were silent for a minute.

As we waited on drive-thru for a couple more minutes, Tynesha pressed me, "So what have you been dealing with lately?" I said vaguely, "Just some personal things." She persisted, "Then why haven't I heard from you?" I responded, "Because I didn't want to burden you." Tynesha raised a fit and patted my hand again, "Uuggghh! I'll kill you if you don't tell me. I'm not your occasional fuckfest. I'm your friend ..." Tears suddenly filled my eyes, but I didn't let myself cry over her apparent concern for my well-being.

We watched the video and ate Taco Bell at my apartment. Tynesha shed a few tears over the film's exotic heaven-or-hell message. Then she pressed me more, "Talib. Tell me what's going on with you!" I resisted, "Not today. You have to go to the open mic." While I drove her to a downtown club, I played "You're Mine" by The Family Stand. Tynesha replied with much excitement, "Oh my God! That's the song that was playing at the David Ryan Harris show. It was so beautiful. It had me crying." This eventually became our song.

I watched Tynesha sing her trademark songs in the club with a backing house band. She thanked the audience for not throwing rocks and bottles at her. Again, a creepy feeling lurked in me, "Why did she have a constant fear of an audience's rocks and bottles?" She smoked and drank more once she finished her set. I was more uncomfortable paying for her filthy habits despite the fact she paid me back when I dropped her off at her suite.

Two days later, I recorded another promo at WRFG. Again, I spotted Tynesha walking towards me, "I was going to call you." I scooped her in my ride and we made a repeat stop to Taco Bell. They screwed up our order. So I went inside to fix it. Tynesha followed right behind, "Sweety! They forgot to give us some sauce too." She called everyone "Sweety," but she was beginning to feel like my own wife.

We retreated back to my apartment. After she munched down more "Taco Hell," she turned off the television and listened to me rant off my personal sorrows, "You see that picture on the wall. I drew it during an art therapy session while I was admitted into a charter hospital. Two years ago I contemplated suicide. Lately, I've been feeling like I don't serve a purpose on this planet ..." Tynesha listened and then spoke in a low tone, "Killing yourself is not the answer ..." I spoke back, "But no one loves me. "Tynesha replied, "I love you. I can see that your specialty is PR (Public Relations). You have a gift that makes people feel good. You're just afraid to show it." I said, "I don't make anyone feel good." Tynesha continued her motivational assault while smiling, "Yes you do. You have something special. You just hide it too much. You're still hiding it now." I sensed that she truly cared for me. So I leaned my stomach on the couch and asked her, "Can you give me a (back) massage?" Tynesha resisted, "I don't do that Sweety." I was feeling embarrassed. Plus I was sick of her smile. So I gently patted my fingers across her chin twice with a mock bitchslap motion. Tynesha shrugged away, "Hey! Stop that!" I felt like going to sleep afterwards, but Tynesha pushed me to drive her home since she desperately needed to practice on her guitar.

As I released her from the car, Tynesha preached, "We're gonna make a tape for you to play positive thoughts." Before I drove off, Tynesha returned to the car giving me a book she said she didn't need called *How to be a Good Christian*. This moment added to all the creepy ones that left me suspicious. Overall though, I felt more hope after this night. I was not use to an attractive woman showing much of any concern for me.

Tynesha called me the following night. I thanked her for counseling me. Tynesha responded in a weepy tone, "I'm not your therapist. I love you." I asked, "Why?" She said, "We are one." I pressed more, "What makes us one?" She said vaguely, "We're all one in the Universe. We're going to be friends through the hard times as well as the good times ..." I concluded, "I appreciate that. You don't have to do this. I really don't want to hurt you ..."

Somehow, my spirit felt an overabundance of fear that I would end up beating the shit out of Tynesha in a fashion similar to the way Father abused Mother. At this moment, I didn't realize that Tynesha was bringing into my life issues that were unresolved with my parents. The painful lessons that followed into my relationship with her were the consequences of my inability to deal with abuse head-on.

Tynesha and I started hanging out on a weekly basis.

Our next outing took place at Pizza Hut and the Cotton Club.

While munching on our pizza, Tynesha gleamed about her growing meditative powers. She said she could see herself prospering like a mantra (monster). I responded with a nod from while I chewed a slice. Tynesha got angry, "Sometimes I think you don't listen to me." I blew off this tirade with shock. After we settled this brief fissure, Tynesha mentioned how she used to date Missy Elliot. This somewhat explained to me why she was enticed by pornography. I don't think Tynesha was lying about her affair. After all, an attractive woman like her doesn't need to brag about who she's been with, straight or lesbian.

We finished our food and proceeded to see Esperanza at the Cotton Club. She was recently interviewed by me on ARS. I networked with some ARS fans and local bands that included members of the Dungeon Family (artists and producers for OutKast and Goodie Mob). Tynesha smoked several cigarettes at the bar while talking to several guys who approached her.

Overall, Esperanza performed great. I look back at this night with fond memories despite the incident where Sleepy Brown threatened to whip my ass. All I did was tap him on his shoulder while he danced in a mock Carlton Banks fashion. I started dancing like that too, but Sleepy felt homophobic, acting as if I was hitting on him. Nevertheless, I felt closer to Tynesha. My observation, though, of her openly social drinking and smoking still left me puzzled.

On the following Friday, we ate at Olive Garden and saw *The 13th Floor*. Interestingly, Tynesha said she no longer felt the vibe to see *Star Wars I: Phantom Menace* because it seemed like something just for white people. I sympathized but was immediately confused when Tynesha said she didn't want to go to a theatre in Buckhead because she didn't want to be around "ghetto people."

As we rode to the Northlake Mall area, Tynesha mentioned how she was nearly hit by a truck. Her near-death experience was further spoken into her desire to be on another planet with aliens while we ate at the Olive Garden. Tynesha's trippiness was both amusing and scary. She continued to puff away on more cigarettes while repeating that she would quit soon.

On another Friday in June '99, we checked out E.X. Vortex at 9 Lives Saloon in L5P. This time I was very disturbed by Tynesha's habits. Her attractiveness incited a bartender to give her a beer for free. Tynesha was so delighted that she asked me to tip him two bucks since she had no money. Uncomfortably, I laid out about 30 cents in coins. Tynesha refused this. She apologized to the bartender for having no money. As we retreated from the spot, I asked her if she was still upset. She played it off with no worries. Yet, I sensed that something wasn't right in our so-called platonic relationship. One time I asked Tynesha on the phone if she would like to be in a steady relationship with me. She said she just wasn't ready.

On this same June night in our "platonic" relationship, our time together appeared over until Tynesha called me as I arrived back home. She said, "I don't wanna be alone tonight." I told her I had friends in town who were staying over. Tynesha remained persistent, "Well, I'll sleep on the floor. There are too many bugs in my room and I'm on my period."

I immediately picked her up.

As I scooped her up, she joked, "This ain't a booty call. Right Talib?" I told her in a serious tone, "You mean more to me than the flesh."

We arrived back at my place. I introduced her to Alim and his two traveling buddies. Me and the fellas chatted while Tynesha passed out on my bed. I gently placed a blanket over her back, and she briefly winced. After I rapped with my guests for another hour, I told them to keep their volume down so Tynesha could sleep. Then, I retreated to my bedroom floor. Even though I had every right to sleep in my own bed with Tynesha, I chose not to because I didn't want to disturb her and violate our so-called friendship.

Tynesha woke up in the morning and I drove her home. All she could talk about was preparing her guitar skills to rehearse with the musicians at 2 High Studios. She also said she could see herself dating bassist Seven once she made it there.

I returned to my confines to hang out with the fellas. Alim commented, "That woman seems like your wife. You can have pussy eating out of your hand, but you want a relationship." I've never felt like a guy who women would die for, yet Alim was correct in assuming that I had deep desire to be with someone special. Often, I daydreamed about Tynesha being this "special" woman. Time would prove me wrong.

For about a week and a half, Tynesha and I stayed out of touch. She called me to see if I would take her to see Ovid. I told her I was unsure since Larry's CCP group was producing a show. As I pondered her request, Tynesha said, "I miss you." I hung up the phone in disarray. Larry cracked up when I told him about her plea, "Uh-oh, Tynesha's pulling strings." His wisecrack was not further from the truth.

One week later, I picked up Tynesha from her retail job at Aunt Teeks in L5P. Bayé from E.X. Vortex tried too hard in persuading us to come to his show. We were tired, so we promised him that we'd come on another date. As Tynesha and I walked towards my car, a tall dark brown brother with dreadlocks approached Tynesha. He firmly grabbed her arm and she grabbed his arm with equal passion and a smile. Apparently both of them had a fling. As it turned out, this was Hakeem—a guy who

Tynesha mentioned she was also seeing. Hakeem and Tynesha quickly agreed to get together on another night. I was somewhat jealous, but I played it off since Tynesha and I weren't an official item. Tynesha and I retreated back to my place to watch *Black Circle Boys*. She dug this dark occult-esque melancholy drama while I gasped for joy.

The following night, I picked up Tynesha for the Ovid show at the Masquerade. I was in a foul mood all night. I wasn't upset that Hakeem tagged along in my car. I was pissed that he and Tynesha brought their 40-ounce beers into my vehicle. They left their bottles outside as we entered the venue.

Things got worse.

After Tynesha puffed and drank up more toxins, she asked me for more beer money. Despite my angst, I gave her a few bucks like a jackass. My foul mood increased. Tynesha passed by on the floor while I was checking out the bands, "You Leos control your jungle even when you're not involved." I said nothing. Tynesha gave me a shoddy look, "What's your problem with drinking?" I responded, "I don't like it when you drink." She walked away. I continued to enjoy Ovid. Tynesha walked by again, "Can I please have more money for a beer?" I nodded my head "No" with much disgust. I walked downstairs to the restroom. Tynesha ran down the stairs, "Talib? Wait! I still need a ride." I told her I was just chilling out for awhile before leaving.

After watching Ovid rip up the stage and a Limp Bizkit-wannabe band shit on it, Tynesha and I left. Hakeem left thirty minutes prior on his own feet. Tynesha and I laughed for a few minutes, even though I was still pissed. As I drove on Peachtree Road before hitting the freeway, Tynesha asked a driver to her right for a cigarette. I punched on the window button knob and started cussing, "Don't bring that fucking shit in my car. I've had enough of your fucked-up habits ..." Tynesha did not say a word to me for the rest of the ride back to her place. While she exited my car, she mumbled in her drunken tone, "Wanna come inside for some coffee?" I shouted, "No!" and drove away with blazing speed.

I felt depressed for two weeks after this night. What did I do to attract such a gorgeous woman with so many flaws? Adding to the problems, I was nearly fired at my pay job for directing a group of temps to junk heavy loads of tapes, resulting in a dismantled mess on the shipping dock. Man did I need relief. Thank goodness, I was going on vacation to Cancun, Mexico.

I enjoyed Cancun's beaches and a tour of Chichen Itza's step pyramid. I happily walked three times on the pyramid's top, paying homage to the indigenous ancestors who built it.

Despite my cultural joy, I still felt lonely. The only realistic dating opportunity came at my hotel from an older woman, whose two teenage daughters tried to persuade me toward her. A waiter asked me, "Do you like girls?" I was offended and walked on. My flight back to Atlanta was clouded with ill reminders of Tynesha.

About two and half weeks after my foul time with Tynesha, she left a phone message, "Are we still on for the E.X. Vortex show?" I was going to respond two days later, but she called me at work, "I tracked you down. Ha Haaaa!" Still feeling lonely, I agreed to take her to the show. I retrieved her from L5P where I caught her again talking to Hakeem. He was annoyed when I walked away to let Tynesha finish her chat with him.

My jealousy increased more into the night.

Tynesha had me pay her way, claiming Bayé would pay me back. She was right. Bayé also had a thing for her. Tynesha wore the same black-hooded gear I saw when I initially met her. Her witch vibe continued to signal my doom.

The performances at the Tabernacle were nice. Chiedza reminded folks of Prince. E.X. Vortex had a stronger lineup than their previous shows, and Mojo 99 was phenomenal.

After this show, I became more disturbed when Hakeem found another way to my car. First, I thought he just needed a ride home. But Tynesha said I was dropping them both off at her place. I remained silent with much anxiety. Tynesha hugged me as I released them, "Be safe!" I drove away disgusted thinking, "I ain't calling that bitch again!"

Tynesha called me one week later. I said few words. She babbled, "Don't be a stranger. Okay?" I said nothing while she laughed before hanging up. Every time I thought of Tynesha, I would get de-pressed.

Two weeks later on my twenty-sixth birthday, I visited Dr. L. She basically told me to insert ground rules for my "friendship" with Tynesha, "Just make sure you don't let her use you as an entertainment center, a meal ticket, or as a taxi cab." I agreed. Thus, I laid out a strategy for Tynesha to prove her friendship.

Tynesha left a phone message two weeks later, "Hey! Long time no hear from. Call me tonight." I didn't call back since I knew I would see her the following night at a CCP acoustic show I was hosting at the Cajun Kitchen.

As I entered the restaurant, I greeted everyone with hugs. Tynesha had a huge smile, "Hi! Where have you been?" I spoke briefly, "I'll tell you later." I proceeded to arrange tables for the stage floor. Tynesha hyperly ran to my area, "I really would love to hang out again and see bands like Whild Peach. Can you drop me off at the Yin Yang after this show?" I responded, "We'll talk later. I'm busy right now." Thirty seconds later, she ran back whimpering, "Talib? Come on. Talk to me. What? Are we not friends anymore?" I told her, "We'll talk about that later." She walked away and remained silent towards me for the rest of the night. After introducing and watching generally boring string performances, I pounded Tynesha's shoulder, "I'll talk to you later." Once again, Hakeem found his way there and left with her. This time though, I left alone.

The following night, I called Tynesha saying that an imbalance developed in our relationship. I took fault for letting it drag on. She whined, "We we're friends. We were there for each other." I asked, "Then why don't I feel the same way?" Tynesha continued her whimper, "We we're friends and you know it. Your mind's just playing tricks on you." I said I felt drained by her. She responded, "I helped you out that one night." I said, "I appreciate that. Yet your actions have not shown genuine care for me. How do I know that you didn't listen to me that night so you can feel me out as a good taxicab ride?" Tynesha said, "That's messed up." I concluded the phone call by giving her an ultimatum, "If you really are my friend, then you need to come by my place by your own means. I'm not driving you around for awhile. When there's another good show, then we'll meet there." Tynesha agreed but slipped in more bull, "I still love you Talib." I hung up the phone feeling more confused and depressed.

Two more weeks passed. I couldn't get her out of my head. I still thought I did the right thing until she called, "Hey Talib! You've been in my head. Something in the universe signaled that there was an emergency with you ..." All I said was, "Huh?" Tynesha babbled on, "Have you been doing okay?" Somberly I said, "Yeah." Sarcastically, she replied, "Psst. Okay! Well I'm just calling to say that I love you, even though you don't wanna be my friend." I was even more tormented after this chat.

I decided to make a goodwill gesture to Tynesha by giving her tickets to Neu Planet Entertainment's band battle called "The Bullfight: Alternative Rock vs. Hip-Hop." I drove to her place without giving notice. Again, I saw Hakeem with her after she opened her door. I passed her the tickets. Then I suggested for her to stop by my place to talk about my mental problems. Hakeem shook my hand and wrapped an arm around my shoulder. Three minutes later, Tynesha hugged me as I exited.

"The Bullfight" was a fun and disturbing event. I invited a woman named Lita to this show. She just happened to work at my pay job along with one of the show's judges, Gertrude. Tynesha arrived later at the show with Hakeem. While I observed and judged the artists performing on the 9 Lives Saloon's stage, a man was selling flowers. Since I was a generously gullible guy, I purchased two roses. I gave one apiece to Lita & Gertrude and took a picture of them sitting together. I also snapped a photo of Tynesha smiling after she smoked a cigarette with Larry and his current girlfriend. I spotted Hakeem. Then I recommended he give a rose to Tynesha. He said, "Nah man. That ain't my style. You can give her one." I knew Hakeem didn't care for her, yet Tynesha clung to him over me. So I wasn't interfering. I still felt disturbed that Hakeem was able to feel all over Tynesha that night, and I wasn't.

Tynesha called me days later thanking me for the tickets. She and Hakeem sounded stoned, "Who won (The Bullfight)?" I told her that the rock band named S.L.A.M. won. She boasted, "They fucking rock. I hope to hear from you soon. Love you." The more I heard her say, "I love you," the more agonized and confused I felt. I wanted her to "really" love me, but her actions never indicated the type of love I most desired.

I called Tynesha two weeks later encouraging her and friends to make donations for WRFG's annual Fall Marathon fund-raiser. Tynesha repeatedly whimpered, "I told you I don't have any friends." My heart started to worry more for her.

One week later, I took Lita to a Braves' game. It was fun. Yet I wasn't turned on to Lita like I was when I first met her. The bottom line was that I compared her too much to Tynesha.

No matter what I did, I couldn't get Tynesha off my mind. So I decided to drop by her place for an intimate chat. Tynesha immediately poured out her troubles, "I would come over to your place, but I've been dealing with too much. Hakeem didn't want to work. So I let him go. I don't have a job right now. My landlord threatened to kick me out because I couldn't pay rent. And my housemate cooked me some food because I don't have any money to buy my own. So all I got is my music." She said all this while embracing her electric guitar. I asked her, "How do you feel about me?" She said, "I love you for your existence with the Universe." Her vague answer almost confirmed that she would never love me like a soulmate. I told her I feared that she would use me like women from my past. She said, "I'm not one of those women." I stated further that she seemed to only want my time for movies and music. Tynesha said, "That's not it!" I responded, "Then why do you hang out with me?" She boasted, "I like your company. Guys ask me for my number all the time. But I don't want them." I continued, "It seems you don't want to do anything else with me besides check out bands and movies." Tynesha said, "Then we could hang out at a museum sometime." Tynesha switched back to her sad mood, "I really want to check out Chiedza at the Culture Club to-night, but I don't have a ride. I really want to go. I'd ask but you won't drive me around." Like a spineless wussbag, I didn't resist her weepy puppy dog eyes. So I hugged her, "Come on!" She spoke, "You just wanna hug me." I said, "Nuh. Let's go." She hugged me again with joy. We drove to the Culture Club. Tynesha cussed out the parking attendant for trying to jip me for a five dollar fee. She proceeded to enjoy herself while smoking and drinking into her usual frenzy.

While driving her home, she gleefully ranted, "Chiedza was great. It makes me look forward to practice." Her music career-oriented tone hadn't changed. All I said was, "I can't believe I'm hanging out with you again." Tynesha walked to her room, "I'm glad we're friends again." I felt further like a boundary-less jerk. I even journaled on September 12, 1999 that she wasn't the right woman for me. Yet, I let my loneliness overwhelm me into a baseless relationship with the truly "lonely" woman that Tynesha was.

I decided not to desperately seek Tynesha's company even though I was back on good terms with her. All that changed two weeks later on October 16, 1999. She called me that morning sounding upset, wondering why she wasn't listed as one of the workers for the "FunkHopMetalFusion" show. I explained, "Larry told me you didn't want to do it." Tynesha barked, "You know my word is good. I'll call him and straighten this out." Larry called me five minutes later sarcastically laughing, "You ain't shit. Tynesha said, 'I'm working this evening and I'll see you tonight. Bye!' Why didn't you clear it with her?" I told him, "You said she didn't want to work the door!" Larry snapped, "Then you could have spoke with her yourself. I love you man, but remember you ain't shit." I hung up the phone cracking up. This morning signified what a wacky day October 16th turned out to be.

After I arrived at the Somber Reptile to prepare for the show, I saw a gorgeous woman with a dreadlocked ponytail wearing an entirely black outfit of sunglasses, jacket, skirt, and sandals. This beauty was Tynesha. I quickly commented, "I must say you are looking exceptionally stunning tonight." Tynesha just walked away from this compliment acting unaffected.

As Edenrage wrapped up the opening set, I headed out the door. Tynesha was working the door. Then she said, "Come on Talib? Have a beer!" I just walked on. After performing my absurd Crunky Funky act, I changed back into my regular clothes. I thought about doing the routine again. So I grabbed Tynesha from her post escorting her into the parking lot, "Hey. I know everyone hated the Crunky Funk routine. And by the way that was me." Tynesha gloated, "That was you? And no. I never said I hated Crunky Funk." Then I asked her, "Could you help me on stage with part two of my routine. Tynesha let me down easy, "No. I really can't get on that stage. I love you." While my face was glum, Tynesha stood on her tippy toes gently pecking my lips. I stood silent for two minutes in shock. Tynesha immediately walked away since we were seen in this moment by music colleagues, DJ Omega Black and Seven.

Five minutes later, I walked over to Tynesha apologizing for trying to pressure her into a semi-perverted showcase. Tynesha responded, "Nah. It's cool. I just didn't want to be on that stage." I gave her a quick hug. Then I ensued to host the rest of the show. Her stage fright still aroused my suspicion. However, what I couldn't shake was the shock of the show's most gorgeous woman kissing me after saying, "I love you."

Before I left the show to host ARS, I paid Tynesha five dollars for her work. She hugged me, "Thank you." Then we gazed into each other's eyes for about fifteen seconds. I thought about moving closer for a warm embrace, but Woodchuck sneaked behind Tynesha and hugged her – thus killing the moment. While I hosted ARS, DJ Omega Black arrived for his program and asked, "Who was that girl?" I humbly stated, "She's just a friend." He chuckled at me like I was nuts.

October 16th was indeed a wild day. I pursued Tynesha initially for shallow play but wound up falling in love. This funny vibe would ultimately prove disastrous.

Five days later, I stopped by Tynesha's place to talk. She asked me to take her to Home Depot. Without hesitation, I agreed. Tynesha was shocked, "No questions or guidelines?"

We engaged in conversation on the return drive from the store. I apologized again for seeking her out during my Crunky Funk act, "You mean more to me than a mere sex act." Tynesha laughed it off, "Okay. It was no big deal to me, but thanks for apologizing." I wrapped up this chat saying something like, "I may not agree with everything you do, but I care about you."

Tynesha and I started hanging out at least once every two weeks. Often I would show up at her doorstep without calling, especially since her phone disconnected off and on due to her overdue bill payments. She didn't mind as she happily tagged along for nights on the town.

Even though our relationship was only platonic, she often felt like my wife. For example, I fixed her soup prior to a Mother's Finest concert. Then on a cold November '99 night, we saw a band at Smith's Olde Bar. Tynesha nagged me as we exited the car, "Sweety? Hurry up!" I told her, "Say please!"

Frequently, we teased and jawed at each other like a couple. In December '99, we argued about which movie we should see. She eventually saw my point as we watched *The Talented Mr. Ripley*. Tynesha bought a bottle of water for me that night. This was one of the few times she ever bought me anything.

I wanted things between us to become tight, but she always pursued other guys on deeper levels. About a week before X-mas '99, I dropped by. Tynesha, though, was waiting for another "friend." This friend was a young man with dreadlocks. While I sat in her bedroom for a minute, I heard some lips smacking at the front door. Right then, I exited. Tynesha asked me, "Are you gonna grow your hair in locks? It's getting long." I told her that I was considering that route. I left her place feeling jealous not only of Tynesha and her friend's hair but mostly of the fact that I was still second best in her life to all her other priorities.

After this night, my time with Tynesha became more rare.

We went to a movie one night after Christmas vibing like regular buddies.

About two weeks later, I scooped her up to work the door at a Hip-Hop/Rock concert featuring Ovid, Edenrage, Womakk, The Eclectic, Machet T, and E.X. Vortex. She was willing to pay me gas money, but I refused. This time, she curled her growing locks while sporting a sleek black outfit that included black boots elongated above the knees. Once again, she was the most gorgeous female at the show.

Her glitzy looks were both a great attraction and distraction at the door. Tynesha's flamboyant personality would deter business operations. When guitarist Tomi Martin entered, she flew into his arms, "Oh it's my friend." I saw this and said, "Cool now take five dollars from your friend." Tynesha baffled, "No he's my guest so I'll pay." Of course she didn't pay. I was pissed about how she could be such a doormat. So I approached her one minute later, "Look! You're fucking up by letting people in free. I'll pay for your mistakes right now since I trusted you." She hollered, "No! I'll pay for it!" I backed away for a few minutes. Then O.P. yelled at me, "What the fuck is up with Tynesha? She's not strong at the door." I told him, "I know. That's why I'm keeping an eye out on her." I ended up paying CCP five dollars out of guilt for Tynesha's baseless promise.

Tynesha continuously spoke with peers without eyeing the door and the cashbox. I reminded her, "Get back to work." She sarcastically spat, "Yes sir!" The show featured dynamite performances and a mostly black crowd engaging in a mosh pit. While I watched Ovid tear up the stage, Tynesha approached me rubbing my hand, "We're still good friends." I didn't know whether to kiss her or punch her.

After Ovid finished their set, Tynesha left the show with guys from 2 High Studios. I was angrier.

The show's revenue was only $120 despite the huge turnout. There were too many people listed as guests. At least fifteen people walked by the table without paying. Adding more insult to injury, promoters of the Somber Reptile took half of the revenue claiming that not enough money was made at the bar. I drove home in a state of disdain.

Before this night, I thought about making Tynesha my room-mate in order to save money on a larger apartment I sought. After what I saw at the Somber Reptile, I knew I couldn't trust her.

Tynesha called me the following night, "What's going on? Are you mad?" Of course I was. Then she snapped, "I was just being nice to people like a good hostess. I didn't get paid for working. So I deserved some special treatment ... But if you want to judge me as uncaring, go right ahead ..." I felt like a jackass after this call, thus remaining depressed through the weekend.

Ironically, Tynesha called me the next night asking me to take her to the movies since she had free passes. Even though the road conditions were dangerously icy, she persisted, "I was going to hang out with Nate (former Johnny Prophet guitarist), but he lives in Marietta." Begrudgingly, I poured out guilt, "No. I don't want to inconvenience you. I'll only hurt you." Tynesha became frustrated, "Come on Talib. It will make you feel better. Stop trippin'!" I constantly repelled, "I don't wanna bother you. I don't wanna hurt you." Then she flaked out, "Look! I know your judgment of me was fucked up. But I forgive you. You're my friend and I love you..." I moaned on, "I don't want to inconvenience you." She snapped again, "You're inconveniencing me by acting like this." I stuck to my moodiness, "I don't wanna hurt you." Then Tynesha succumbed, "Okay! So how are you going to hurt me?" I had no answer. Finally, she blew off steam, "Look! Do you wanna go or not??? Okay you don't wanna go. OOOO-Ah. I get it. Goodbye!" She hung up sighing as if I ran some game on her. Again, I feared that I would wind up whooping her ass until she looked ugly.

After being depressed for two more days, I decided to go to her suite to chat. Tynesha was practicing on her guitar as usual. I told her, "Sorry I chastised your work. I was disappointed and could have expressed it better. I've decided not to pursue you or anyone as a roommate since I'm still building trust." Tynesha listened with a smirk. I continued, "I don't think CCP will ever allow you to work the door again. But if I ask you for that type of task then I warn you, don't do that shit again." Tynesha arrogantly brushed this off, "They (CCP) know I'm good for the door."

CCP's Larry & O.P. were still cool with Tynesha personally. I was feeling more distraught because I wanted Tynesha to be more than what she really was to me.

Two weeks later, CCP tried to recruit me as a partner. O.P. played a recorded tape of Tynesha's new band – Victory. O.P was originally her drummer. This was the first time I heard Tynesha play her electric guitar, and I became in extreme awe of her.

Initially, I agreed to be a CCP partner, but I was feeling very disturbed after hearing O.P.'s recording. I wasn't sure what I really wanted or what best suited my needs. Plus, I felt overwhelmingly eager to pour my heart out to Tynesha.

A bad omen of my Valentine's Day 2000 anxiety came when my best friend Amen called me. He was enraged. Amen attempted to give flowers to a co-worker whom he desired for companionship. She rejected him, claiming they were only friends, as she also desired a different man. Amen cried his eyes out and then punched a hole in a brick wall before shouting to me on the phone, "All women are bitches! Don't hurt me! Dorothy fucking passed me up for that pretty boy who is gay, when I'm the one who showed the most care. I warn you bro, 'Don't hurt me.' 'Cause I would be your worst enemy." I hardly spoke while listening to his tirade. I was scared of experiencing similar betrayal from Tynesha. Overall, the coming months turned up good results for Amen. He handled this rejection very well. He wore out his punching bag whenever he had the urge to "knee Dorothy in the throat." Unfortunately, I didn't handle my dejected anger this good.

On the night of Valentine's Day 2000, I called Tynesha. I complimented her recording and told her about my indecision in becoming a CCP partner. Tynesha just encouraged me to follow my heart. I took her words too literally. Minutes later, I told her, "I'm in love with you." Tynesha laughed, "Oh Talib! You can't be in love with me." Then I asked, "Do you feel the same way?" She abruptly answered, "No! But I'm flattered, and I love you my friend." I went to sleep that night feeling like the world's biggest jackass.

For about a week, my chest was full of heaving pains. I called Dr. L to sort this out. I told her while in her office, "I feel this anxiety for every woman I'm attracted to. I wish someone would just stab me in the heart and end my suffering." Dr. L summed up this session by saying, "Don't worry about pursuing all those women. From what you're telling me, they're all too flawed. Until you improve your relationship with SELF, you'll never attract the right woman." Dr. L was on point. Yet, my eagerness for companionship would continue ripping through my soul like termites.

From this point forward, I hung out with Tynesha five more times over the course of three months. I felt too much like a taxicab man than an actual friend.

She called me on one cold March 2000 Saturday to drive her to a CCP show. I finally decided by this time not to be a CCP partner since I was focusing my energy on building my DJ career and the RSC. Tynesha said, "I'm working the door at this show." I responded, "I thought CCP banned you from that service." Tynesha snapped back, "Well then I'll go and chill since they said I could get in free! I'll give you two dollars gas money. I insist." I said, "Don't worry. If you're working the door, then

I'll drove you there as a CCP employee." She didn't work the door, but CCP embraced her as "a little sister."

On another March 2000 night, Tynesha paid me gas money to drive her to the I.A.G.. As I pumped gas in my car, she bought a twelve-bottle pack of beer. She was supposed to call me for a ride home, but she didn't remember how she got home the following morning.

Tynesha also revealed to me on this night that she use to be a stripper. She was mentoring a seventeen-year old girl named Evelyn who was also a stripper. This didn't seem like a big deal at first. It answered more of my suspicions about Tynesha's partying and lesbian affairs. Yet, I had no clue that her promiscuous past would play a major role in my forthcoming resentment towards her.

We saw *Pitch Black* a few days later with some of her free movie passes. I was jealous when a white guy with dreadlocks complimented her hairstyle. Tynesha smiled back with much glee. She blew me a kiss goodnight thanking me for escorting her during her "hibernation period" away from people.

I only ran into Tynesha once more before June 2000 at one of Ondrea's performances at the 9 Lives Saloon. Tynesha was slightly bummed out because O.P. left her band. I gave her a number to a Memphis drummer who phoned in during one of my ARS episodes. Tynesha was thankful, but I was pissed that she continually gave other guys in the bar more attention than me.

I practiced on my new DJ gear consistently for two more months until my first gig with CCP in June 2000.

Tynesha, on the other hand, was experiencing drama from a new boyfriend. Her drama coupled with my insecurities led me back to Dr. L.

I gave Dr. L a brief history of my turmoil with Tynesha before telling her about my most recent troubles, "I started hanging out with Tynesha more when I didn't hear back from Amira." Dr. L recommended, "It's time to view Tynesha as your sister." I responded, "I don't need another sista. Plus, my feelings run too deep for her." Dr. L pressed on, "You have a sister (Amira) who recently passed on. So there's always room for another sister. Your view of Tynesha is only perception." I didn't knock Dr. L for her persistence. After all, my attempts to make Tynesha into more than a platonic acquaintance continuously failed.

I proceeded to recall my recent time with Tynesha. First I told Dr. L how Tynesha had been dating a white boy. Dr. L facetiously gasped, " OOOOOOOOOAH!" I laughed back, "I know! Big fucking deal!" I further explained how Tynesha called me frantically one day, "Talib. Thanks for being my friend. I love you so much. Dean (the white boy) and I broke up because he was talking shit about me to his friends. I tried to reconcile with him as a platonic friend, but his friends started feeling on me. I'll call you back later." I concluded this account to Dr. L by telling her how Tynesha contemplated having some- one to beat up Dean, but she wound up safely distancing her- self from that relationship. Dr. L analyzed Tynesha's vibe, "A drunk! A cigarette smoker! A drug addict! A Christian girl! A potential psychopath! This is who you seek out for companion- ship? She's fucked-up!" I couldn't disagree, but I still whaled on detailing why I thought a chance was possible. "On the day after I received news of Amira's passing, I cried my eyes out. I went over Tynesha's seeking comfort. She listened calmly. Then her housemate comes in the room. She heard Amira had died in Costa Rica and goes off into a tangent, 'Oh! I've always wanted to go to Costa Rica on vacation.'" Dr. L snapped, "Nah-Ah!" I summarized how I felt insulted by Tynesha allowing her house- mate to make a mockery of my sadness. Tynesha's housemate apologized to me with a hug. Tynesha only apologized for her roommate's actions instead of her own. Dr. L said, "She still allowed it to happen, so she ain't sorry." I thought, "*Damn! Cut her some slack!*"

I continued narrating to Dr. L my obsession with Tynesha. I told her how I felt bad for not paying for her groceries when she was short on change. As things turned out that day, another customer gave her two dollars. She walked out of the store happy. I told Dr. L it seemed hardly anyone could resist Tynesha's beauty with her locks halfway down her back and growing towards her ass. Dr. L barked, "How do you know that customer wasn't thinking 'Po Nigga!'" I laughed, "Well! Next time I'll encourage her to keep better track of her groceries' cost." Dr. L shouted, "Get that bitch a calculator!"

I concluded my obsessive stories of Tynesha by telling Dr. L about how she used me as a taxicab driver. One late Saturday June 2000 night, Tynesha was on her period. She was ready to call a cab to drive her to a concert at 2 High Studios. Like the usual jackass I was, I volunteered to drive her. Tynesha paid me five dollars in gas money. She was looking like an insanely gorgeous gothic witch dressed in all black with her locks hanging farther down her back. Our drive started out funny. I tried to explain the details of our upcoming CCP gig where her band was debuting and I was deejaying. Tynesha flaked out and yelled at me for no apparent reason. I laughed, "You didn't let me finish what I was saying." Tynesha snapped, "You're perception just represents what's flawed with your mind." I laughed away Tynesha's crappy menstruating mood. But then she shocked me when she asked, "What did you eat today?" She sounded just like Mother. I dropped her off at 2 High Studios and proceeded to drive to WRFG to host another ARS episode. I drove back to 2 High Studios to pick up Tynesha. She was still indulging on a cigarette and some alcoholic beverage. She tried to persuade me to stay. I hung loose for only a minute before telling her, "I'm ready to go now." Tynesha looked at me with irritation while blowing her cigarette smoke, "You can go now!" She walked over to a member of E.X. Vortex asking him for a ride home. I walked over and gave her the five dollars back. She gave me a crazy eye-popping look. I drove off pissed thinking, "*That fucking bitch treated me like nothing but a taxicab ride after I came so far out of my way to pick her up.*"

After Dr. L heard all this, she fired, "I hope that bitch doesn't seek my services (for holistic therapy) because she's fucked-up." I was growing more disturbed with Dr. L's reference of Tynesha as a "bitch." Dr. L still yelled out "Bitch" whenever I said "Tynesha." After three of these exchanges, I succumbed, "Okay, you're right." I was too hurt to admonish that I attracted a "fucked-up bitch" as my sole love interest. Dr. L gave me all the right warnings and suggestions, "You deserve better. You deserve a woman who will offer to pay for your meal and who will receive four dollars in change. She don't have a car, and she makes sistas with locks look bad. Fucked-up sistas like her ought to be cooked up in a pot and trashed. I'm tired of brothas turning out bad because the sistas didn't do their jobs as mothers. That bitch doesn't really want to heal, and you're right here (seeking therapy) which shows she doesn't care to heal. I wouldn't have a friend like her, but treat her as only a sister if you continue to see her. You deserve better!"

I was thankful for Dr. L's bold analysis of my troubles. However, my lack of confidence in attracting a healthy woman sunk me further into a neurotic abyss with Tynesha.

Our Cajun Kitchen gig with CCP went well. It was one of the few times I ever made any money from my DJ services. Tynesha made even more money from her ticket sales. Her band Victory's debut performance impressed most of the crowd. Tynesha still encouraged people not to throw rocks and bottles at her. After the show ended, I gave her a congratulatory hug. Tynesha whispered, "Thanks Talib" and held onto me for a long minute. Even though she seemed happy, her vibration still felt somewhat sad. I wished this overly emotional hug meant that Tynesha wanted me for companionship. Boy was I ever trapped in a fantasy!

Tynesha called me the next day feeling sad, "I feel weird. I still need to improve on the guitar. I'd better practice." I yelled out, "Chill! You worked hard and had a good show. So relax today, and do something fun." Tynesha's nerves calmed down. She reiterated how her music career was the top priority in her life over everything including a man.

The following week, I scooped Tynesha up from work and drove us to the Ozzfest at Lakewood Amphitheatre. Curiously, she questioned why I was willing to wait so long for her to get off work. I kept telling her I had no problem. I was only bullshitting myself just to have her company. The performances started at 2pm. We didn't arrive until 5:30pm. By this time, P.O.D., SOULFLY, and Kittie had already performed on the second stage. My suppressed anger exploded when the ushers didn't allow me to enter with my umbrella. Tynesha sighed, "Come on! We're already here." I succumbed to the ushers leaving my umbrella on a sidewalk. Tynesha and I sat on the lawn watching Godsmack and Pantera perform on the main stage. Tynesha grabbed a cigarette from another concert patron as I drank a couple of water bottles. I thought about sticking around to see Ozzy Osbourne and Black Sabbath, but I was too bummed out from missing the second stage performances. So I gathered Tynesha, and we trotted out of the building. As we exited, I noticed my umbrella was gone. I was so furious that I pushed a large rolling trash can off its wheels. An usher threatened to send me to jail. Tynesha snapped, "Hey! They ain't got your soul, so you're still alright. I can't believe Prince performed at this junky place."

Losing my temper over an umbrella seemed ridiculous. But I

was mostly mad at myself for sacrificing too much of my time, money, and interests solely for Tynesha after she encouraged me not to. I was silent on the drive home. Tynesha muttered, "I had a nice time." This added more insult to the fact that I didn't. After this dreadful day, I distanced myself from Tynesha and all other friends citing a personal need for "hibernation." I told Tynesha I would come out of this stage after my birthday. I had good intentions. Yet, my spirit dwindled farther into instability.

For my twenty-seventh birthday, I drove to Myrtle Beach, South Carolina. I thought that a nice beach resort like this would quell all my sadness from Amira's passing and the rest of my personal problems. Lo and behold, it rained most of that weekend. I wasn't motivated enough to jump in the water even when the sun was out. Most of the time, I stayed in my motel room—watching television, masturbating, and being depressed. For one brief nighttime moment, I sat on the beach's sand playing my djembe drum, chanting, "*Asé Amira Asuñe Lacey Bey*" and "*Zumbi é o senhor das guerras. Zumbi é o senhor das demandas. Quando Zumbi chega. E Zumbi quem manda.*" My eyes were closed. Then a group of stupid little kids poured sand on me. I wasn't fazed as I maintained my meditative pose. Suddenly, it started raining again. The kids ran away. This moment gave me serenity for a brief period. However, I returned to Atlanta feeling even more lost about my life's purpose. So back to Dr. L I went for counseling.

This particular session left me feeling like a car that had just crashed. Dr. L bashed me, "Why didn't you have fun at Myrtle Beach? If that was me, just the sight of that water alone would have brought me joy. Your failure to communicate with new people demonstrates a lack of self love." I tried to explain how I was feeling too lonely, "I know I shouldn't have craved Tynesha. But I love her, even when she treats me like shit." Dr. L bashed me further, "That sounds like what a battered woman says after her man whooped her ass. You know what I told a battered woman who called my office saying, 'My man beats my ass, but I don't wanna leave him because he's my soulmate.' I told her, 'Well if you're soul allows a man in your life who beats your ass, then he is your soulmate.'" After hearing this, I sat silent and ashamed for five minutes. Dr. L gave me a wide-eyed dazed look. Then she asked, "So why do you continuously let yourself be depressed?" I glumly answered, "Because it's safe!" Dr. L snapped on, "Ya See! That's your problem. You're afraid to get out of depression because it's your comfort zone. It's love that you actually fear. Loving a woman who doesn't love you because she really don't love herself won't get you out of your comfort zone of depression." I continued sitting with my forehead buried in my hand. Dr. L pressed forward despite showing obvious fatigue, "Look! I've been in bad relationships too. I broke it off with my fiancée and felt as you feel now. It may take, God knows, months, even years before you find that true soulmate—white, black, whatever she may be. You just need to ask yourself, 'Who are you?' Are you a construction worker? A journalist? A doctor? That's your homework after you leave here and write in your journal. And don't write about your depression because that further feeds more crap into the subconscious mind. You can analyze about your depression until the cows come home, but you'll never get out of depression until you decide how you'll do it. The 'why' in 'why am I depressed' becomes irrelevant ..." I still sat nearly comatose. Dr. L further recommended that I cut off everyone who wasn't down for my empowerment. With frustration, I said, "I already went through a distance period with Tynesha." Dr. L responded, "Just tell her you need more time."

I heeded Dr. L's advice the following day. Since I was still feeling like an emotional wreck who didn't know any way of out of my mess, I decided to do something insane. I drove to Stone

Mountain Park with my percussion bag. Then I proceeded to climb up the steep rocky slopes. From my memory, there was a safe walkway for this mountain, but I was too emotionally erratic to ask for these directions. Despite the incredible danger of the mountain's steepness, I climbed it holding onto my percussion bag along with zero rock climbing skills to assist me. The hills were so rocky and trippy that slipping was unavoidable. Somehow, I managed to control my slips. Thus, I continued to frantically climb up until I reached the gate. One wrong slip and/or misstep, and I wouldn't be alive today writing this book. This crazy adventure along with a subsequent visit to Georgia's Six Flags theme park the next day gave me a brief disconnection from my social anxiety.

After this trip, I also decided not to be called Talib in person anymore. I found new comfort in being plain ole Albert, which also means "The Bearer" in Hebrew, or just being called plain ole Al for short. I answered Dr. L's question of "Who are you?"

I was feeling free of my grueling pain until it returned three days later when Tynesha called.

I told Tynesha I had too much on my mind. Tynesha laughed saying, "Ya know. I've been feeling the same way." Immediately, I interrupted saying I needed more distance. Tynesha boasted, "This (phone calls only) is distance." I explained further, "For now, I don't want you to call me unless it's an emergency." Tynesha was shocked, "Okay." I told her I would call her when I'm out of my funk. She pleaded, "You'd better call me. My number is 404 ..." I interjected before hanging up, "I know your number!"

For the next three weeks, I emotionally starved like a recovering crack addict. No matter how hard I tried, Tynesha couldn't be erased from my mind. I ached so bad that I cried fourteen times.

Despite my severe stress, I resumed meetings with the RSC.

As I prepared for a meeting at my apartment, Tynesha called, "OOOPS. I'm sorry. I meant to leave you a message on your machine. I just wanted to wish you peace, love, and prosperity and let you know that I'm here." I told her, "I'll call you when I'm ready." Tynesha roared a whimper before hanging up, "I didn't ask you to answer the phone."

Tynesha's abrupt display of worry left me more tormented. I was hoping to get a love confession from her. Little did I want to recognize that her phone call was just a desperate plea for company.

After sorting through options of how to talk with Tynesha again, I called her a week later telling her that my hibernation period was over. On that Sunday evening, I drove to her place to discuss how our relationship would continue. She appeared happy to see me, "I'm so glad you're ready to talk again. Did you get enough to eat today?" Again, her vibe was reminiscent of Mother.

Before Tynesha and I settled for a conversation, she had me drive her to some hotel on Peachtree Street in the midtown area. I kept asking, "What is this business meeting about?" Tynesha vaguely answered, "You'll know when you need to know!" My curiosity sensed that it had something to do with the "sponsor-ship proposal" she claimed would free her from her nine-to-five jobs. To this day, I still don't know what her meeting was about. All I know is that she left the hotel after five minutes with con-firmation that her business meeting was taking place soon.

As we drove back, Tynesha constantly asked, "So what do you need to talk about?" I told her that we could talk when I stopped the car. I began my desperate somber-toned love plea after parking in her driveway, "I'm in love with you, and it hurts that you don't feel the same way." Tynesha looked an-noyed with her face turned sideways while I chatted. Then she said, "We're just friends, I got things going for me. I finally got my band together." I asked, "Have you ever thought about us being more than just friends." Without hesitation and her eyes still turned away from me, she muttered. "No." She continued, "You'll find a nice lady. With me and you it's never gonna be like that, and it can never be that way." Despite my dejection I suggested, "I still don't want to lose friendship. Let's say that we hang out once a week. But when we do, you won't drink or smoke." Tynesha responded, "Well I'm gonna give that up on my own anyways." I said our time together would only reassure that. Before Tynesha left the car, I gave her a *Star Wars* figure of Chewbacca as an apology for not talking in awhile. Plus I remembered her saying she wanted to go to the DragonCon festival and dress up like Chewbacca. Tynesha hugged me and blurted her usual empty "Love you."

I was so hurt after this latest futile attempt to win Tynesha's heart that I became even more distant.

I channeled my broken heart into an angry ARS episode themed "Rejection: NO LOVE SONGS Allowed." This show featured only angry thrash songs inspiring people to "create da hate." During one interlude, I sang a mock rendition of Erykah Badu's "See You Next Lifetime." Then I screamed, "Shut da f*ck up and bring da rock ooooooooon." Kurt McManus called and asked me, "Are you alright?" I laughed it off. Yet I really was drowning in pity.

I decided to let Tynesha call me and meet me halfway when we hung out instead of being her chauffeur. Tynesha called me a week later while I was packing my items for an apartment move from Brookhaven to Southwest Atlanta (Ben Hill, Da SWATs, SWATL, etc.). She blurted, "Call me!" I told her I was busy packing. She asked, "Even to go with me to the laundry mat?" I said, "Yeah!" She sighed, "Okay. Be careful! Make sure you bend your knees when lifting the heavy stuff. Love you and be sure to call me!" I hung up the phone feeling more infuriated.

Her "Love you(s)" sounded more like curse words. She still only wanted a ride for her laundry. I still called her a week later leaving a message with my new phone number. She never called back. I assumed I was through with her for good. So for one month, I stayed focused on practicing my DJ spins, writing my journal, and meditating.

My new apartment gave me more space to practice on my DJ equipment and build my career. I also purchased my own personal computer in order to handle my e-mails and files at home instead of at my pay job.

Consistently, I produced several outstanding practice mixes at night. Before I went to sleep, I meditated with crystals placed on my forehead and heart. I envisioned green light healing my heart from the emotional daggers left by Tynesha. Then, I usually woke up on the following mornings taking notes about the dreams I had. All my anxiety seemed under control. But my fears of seeing Tynesha again were unquelled as I practiced for an upcoming gig at 2 High Studios.

On September 30, 2000, I spun before and between Eve of Reality, E.X. Vortex, Womakk, and Johnny Prophet featuring Esperanza. I also had a lot of fun dancing and then greeted some known guests. Tynesha showed up as a party attendant too. I virtually ignored her until she walked by me while I gave my barber a bear hug. She tapped my shoulder, "You still need to give me your number."

As the show finished, I loaded my equipment back and forth on a hand truck to my car. While I was pushing the hand truck on one of my trips, Tynesha jumped in front of me hyperventilating, "I know you don't wanna stay in touch with me. You haven't called me or given me your number." I spit back, "I left you my number on your answering machine weeks ago." Tynesha barked, "You need to leave it again." I wrote it down and pinned it on her shoulder. Tynesha pushed my hand away screaming, "Hey! Stop that!"

After I finished loading my car, I opened my side door to give Ondrea a ride home. Before I took my driver's seat, I waved goodbye to Tynesha while she was boozing with one of E.X. Vortex's guitarists. She spotted me and quickly approached. She snuggled her arms around me murmuring in my ear, "I love you." I didn't know whether I should kiss her or push her off me saying, "*Get away from me you phony bitch!*" Instead all I did was stand silent feeling like an angry lug while Tynesha boasted in a drunken glee, "Thanks again for that Chewbacca figure. I put a spell on it. The cards (Tarot cards) have foretold me that you're going to elevate. We need to discuss this prophecy perhaps over lunch." My blood started boiling sensing she still wanted to use me for cab fare. She continued, "... I told you about this before. But you don't listen. That's what pisses me off about you sometimes. I'm still looking for a new drummer for my band. But on a good note, I'm back to New York for two weeks ..." After she blobbed out all her tribulations, she grabbed my hand, "Me and you are friends forever." I drove Ondrea home and proceeded back to my apartment. My torment over Tynesha's mixed signals would increasingly plague my soul.

While my soul was imploding over increasing distance from Tynesha, I finally had a hair stylist knit my fragile nappy hair into dreadlocks. Never did I imagine that my dreadlocks, which can also be referred to as chords of electricity, would take in charges of stressful energy over Tynesha. At work, I remember my locks feeling like lightning bolts when I thought about her. I guess one can also say that my locks were leftover pieces of my doomed relationship with her.

Tynesha called me two weeks later on ARS with another whimper, "I haven't heard from you in a long time. Are you not my friend anymore?" I said sarcastically, "If I wasn't your friend, I wouldn't have left you my new number." Tynesha reacted, "I lost your number." I sighed with grief. Like a jackass, I left her my number again, "Okay I'll give it to you, but this is the last time ..." Tynesha muttered, "Talib, I'll always be your friend and I'll always be here for you." I angrily spat, "My name is AL. You still don't remember my name. Whatever! Goodbye!!!"

While I made it difficult for Tynesha to catch me, I became more distant and resentful.

Tynesha called me at my apartment one week later. She asked me to drive by 2 High Studios for a concert. I bickered, "Those muthafuckas are having a show and didn't call me for DJ services?" Tynesha still encouraged me to stop by and meet her there despite the fact I had another ARS episode to host and would have been too tired afterwards. She still suggested, "Stay in touch. Will ya?" I sat silent. The she begged, "Pluh-ease!" I still said nothing. She facetiously whined, "I love you!"

Tynesha's continuous nitpicky pleas for my company drove me into madness. So I decided to give her another ultimatum four days later. I called her. She said she just got off work. I told her I wouldn't call her anymore but that she was still welcome to call me. Tynesha said, "Okay. I'll still call and check up on you." Then I asked, "Well don't you wanna know why I won't call you?" Tynesha sarcastically asked, "Okay! Why?" I said, "Our relationship has grown too imbalanced. I'm always driving you around but get nothing in return." Tynesha barked with slow breaths, "Wow!!! I think you bringing up old issues is really fucked-up. If I had a car I would take you out." I interjected, "You haven't shown that you would." Tynesha spat, "Does it make sense for me to meet you at the train station or movies while we hang out." Tynesha repeatedly said. "Oh well. That's your world and your issues." Of course always meeting her at hang-out spots didn't make sense. But I still embarked on a verbal attack after pausing, "You're lack of care not only shows in hanging out with me. You forgot about my birthday, and you only call me just to drive you places. That's why I haven't wanted to hang out." Tynesha muttered, "Well you've made that obvious. You hardly ever call. You never call." I yelled out, "How can I call somebody who loses my number twice?" Tynesha complained more about how I trumped up old issues. While she murmured this, I repeatedly asked, "Can you name one time where you've ever met me halfway? Just one?" After four or five times, she still couldn't answer. Then I yelled, "You can't even name one??? Ya see! That's your problem. Even though we've been only friends. Your actions have never shown real friendship. At least I don't have to say 'I love you' a thousand times just to show that I do." Tynesha responded, "You're throwing my issues in my face." I continuously attacked her for not even remembering my birthday. Tynesha whimpered, "Look! I hardly remember anyone's birthday. I don't even remember my mother's birthday." I spewed, "That just shows how selfish you are." Tynesha whined, "What do you want from me?" I laid down the ultimatum, "Meet me halfway at my doorstep." She bitched, "I'm not at anyone's doorstep." I reacted, "Oh really? You paid me to drive you to the doorstep of Dean's job. And you gave Hakeem a doorstep... So why not try to come to my apartment on your own accord? I know you probably won't because I now live in Da SWATs and you have a problem with the ghetto." Tynesha mumbled, "I don't have a problem with the ghetto. That's just some phase I went through when dealing with the people in Little Five Points. You made all this up. Didn't you? You just started feeling this way?" I said, "No! I've been feeling this way for months. Sure I could have spoke about this sooner. But at least I can admit my flaws. You're not true to your word." Tynesha said, "I'll be over at your place." I spat, "You won't! You're all talk. Until you do, there's nothing more to say." I hung up feeling very irate. It was good for me to finally release my pent-up frustration to Tynesha. But my inability to completely dump her would backfire into more chaos.

Two months flew off the calendar. Tynesha still hadn't contacted me. I assumed she had moved on from me for good. My frustration towards her was growing into passionate hate.

While feeling increasingly bitter, I analyzed all my thoughts into lists entitled "Attributes of the Right Woman," and "Standards of a True Friend." I also got RSC meetings up and running at 2 High Studios before we transferred our agendas to the Auburn Avenue Research Library.

After producing a show at the A-HOP, the RSC met one last time at 2 High Studios. Emotions ran high for most people as we bickered and expressed our musical passions. Brian called me the following day telling me how rude I was for interrupting Bayé. I told him I was keeping the meeting time short as the conductor. This was partly true. Yet, another part of my bad attitude resulted from my bitterness over Tynesha. I remembered O.P. telling me at the A-HOP show, "Yur girl has a message for you." I told him, "She's not my girl." O.P. continued, "She said that you're supposed to tell her about the meetings (of the RSC)." I feared that Tynesha was only interested in me from the start just to boost her music career.

My non-stop neurosis over Tynesha guided me back to Dr. L.

She started off this January 2001 session by telling a courtroom story. Dr. L had a court date because some other holistic business claimed she didn't pay some fees. While she was waiting for her case to be tried, two women (one pregnant) scrapped and stabbed each other in an argument over a jailed convict who served as a boyfriend to both women. This trifling account was funny at first but would come back in our session as a degrading insult.

I gave Dr. L extensive details of all my contact with Tynesha since my last counseling session. Dr. L constantly rolled her eyes with grief on how I let emotions drag on over her. I told Dr. L twice, "I know I should have listened more to your advice." After two hours of babbling chit chatter, Dr. L snapped, "Well? What do you want from her? Either you let the bitch go or pursue her to the fullest. Accept her, and be happy with that." I paused for two minutes and then revealed, "I want her to hate me." Then I recommended that Dr. L use some hypnosis on me so I could practice pushing Tynesha away the next time I saw her. I laid down flat on my back with my eyes closed. Dr. L portrayed Tynesha approaching me at an RSC meeting. I imagined this and told her, "Get the fuck out of my face." Dr. L as Tynesha said, "What's wrong with you?" I responded, "I can't stand you." Dr. L as Tynesha said, "Well. You're the one with a problem. That's your world and your issues." My body started trembling on the floor during this hypnotic state. Dr. L said that I acted like a pussy, "... Even in hypnosis she has power over you ..." Thus she rehearsed another scenario. I spat again, "Get the fuck outta my face." Dr. L as Tynesha again, "What's wrong with you?" I whimpered, "You've never been a real friend." Dr. L as Tynesha said, "I never asked you to be more than I requested. Those are your issues." Now my head was trembling too. Dr. L began a relentless verbal attack, "She got you good. She got you real good. You're too afraid to speak your mind to her and cut her off because you have her on a pedestal. Why don't you cut off her locks? Then she'll really hate you." Dr. L then asked, "Would you go out with a woman with a perm who owned her own business?" I said, "No." Dr. L bit back, "Oh! So you'd rather go out with a fucked-up bitch with locks rather than a woman who owns her own house and makes her own money. You know what? You're no better than that bitch in the courtroom ... You can write all those standard lists of the right woman a thousand times and still act like this ... She's laughing at you knowing she 's blocking you from your true soulmate ..." My whole body was now shaking erratically before I opened my eyes out of hypnosis. Dr. L recommended for me to call Tynesha and tell her off if I was to truly overcome my fear of her. I still asked, "How could she hang out with me for so long and not feel anything for me?" Dr. L answered, "She probably only hung with you because of your powerful Black Rock status. She was looking for contacts and leeway." This made sense to me, and I became more outraged. Dr. L continued her stabbing, "How could you still want her after she lived with a homeless man (Hakeem)? How could you still want her after she dated a white boy (Dean)? And really how could you want her in the first place after she was Larry's leftovers. Sure, Larry got what he wanted from her, and she got played. Then she moved on and got the best of you ... She took a lot of key powers from you. You need to get those powers back in order to move on ... Just call her and face your fears."

I left Dr. L's house in a vengeful state. My frustration was now full-blown hatred.

I despised how I gave too much of my personal power away to Tynesha. There was nothing wrong with my hatred. Yet, I wound up channeling my passionate angst in the wrong direction.

After my tumultuous visit with Dr. L, I called Tynesha later in the evening. She answered in a happy tone, "Talib. Ooops I mean Al. How are you?" I said, "I just called to thank you." Tynesha asked, "For what?" I snapped, "For a fucked-up relationship!" Tynesha frowned, "You were down and out Talib. But now it's a new year." I barked, "I'm fine now that I realize how you fucked me over. Thanks for teaching me a valuable lesson." Tynesha arrogantly shuttered, "Don't worry! I'll come over your place when I get a ride." I said, "No! Our relationship is over." Tynesha continued, "Oh Talib! You'll always be my friend. You, O.P., and Larry will always be my friends." I barked, "You were never my friend. Thanks again for a fucked-up relationship. I'm moving on." Tynesha hung-up on my vengeful verbal attack.

I immediately called Dr. L telling how happy I was to vent some of my anger on Tynesha. Dr. L said that I took a small step towards healing. She was right. I took a "small step," yet I still felt small.

For the next few days, my spirit was even more tormented. I hated every single thought of Tynesha. I hated every reminder of her. So when I spotted the book she gave me entitled *How to be a Good Christian*. I decided I had to do one last ritual to officially end my attachment to her.

While pumping and singing along to "Turn Off the Lights" by Nelly Furtado in my car, I made the long freeway drive from Ben Hill to Buckhead. I was feeling very excited knowing I was going to shove the book back in Tynesha's face. I knocked loudly on her door three times. Tynesha opened the door touching her chest, "You're not going to kill me. Are you?" With burning hate in my eyes, I said, "No. I'm just here to give you something. "I gave her the book, "You can have this bullshit back. I'm not even a Christian. You never gave me anything that helped me anyways." Tynesha sighed, "Oh! I gave you this book? I don't remember it." Suddenly, I was overwhelmed with a combination of embarrassment and rage, "You don't remember?" With little emotion, Tynesha asked, "Are you hungry?" She tried to persuade me back to her room, but I sensed another man was already there. Plus, she only seemed concerned with keeping me on her short leash. Therefore, I busted out of her house and drove back to Da SWATs feeling like the world's biggest sucker.

I felt so used, played, exploited. Whatever word I sensed to describe my shame, I spat. What hurt the worst were not Tynesha's habits— her smoking, doping, ho-ing, drinking, stinking, and overall lack of intimate attraction towards me. What hurt me the worst was that she was never a true friend. She never gave me anything genuine from her heart that had no strings attached. From that moment forward, I couldn't stand the word "Love." It would only remind me of the phony "Love" I felt, gave to, and received from Tynesha.

I called Dr. L the next day telling her how ashamed I felt after giving Tynesha her book back. I told her, "She played me. Hats off to her for being an incredible con artist and taking the best of me. But I still feel like I'm the only one who's suffering." Dr. L replied, "Hey! She was a con artist. She won't feel anything genuine. You have nothing to be embarrassed about. I've fallen for some big cons in my lifetime too." I summarized this chat, "Yeah! I now know better not to pursue a relationship with a woman just because she has locks." Dr. L concurred, "Don't judge a book by its cover!!!"

The aftermath of my separation from Tynesha would only prove more disastrous.

At first, I handled the break-up okay. I artistically channeled my pain into a poem called "Rock Your SOUL Free" and a mock-song called "Trifling Gal." I recited the poem on one of my ARS episodes. Eventually, I drew a picture of a spear ripped through my heart. I referred to this whole stage as the T.G. Syndrome.

For a brief period, I began pursuing other women. On a Friday night during January, 2001, I decided to approach every fine-looking natural-haired sista I saw. I wound up getting three phone numbers. Then, I dated a woman with long beautiful locks named Janetta. We had a few nice conversations and ate dinner at a Chinese vegetarian restaurant called Harmony.

My obsession with acquiring a perfect relationship would hasten my dating progress.

I left a phone message with Janetta three days later, but she didn't respond that weekend. So I felt very lonely and angry. I channeled my dejection into an aggressive ARS episode called, "Aggro-vatingly Tight." Lo and behold, Janetta called the following Wednesday saying she enjoyed the dinner and wondered how I was doing. I immediately told her, "I don't think we're compatible." Janetta replied in shock, "Okay! No offense taken here. I enjoyed talking with you." After I spoke with my best friend, Amen, I thought I did the right thing. Yet, I still felt a deep sense of regret. Years later, I attempted to reconcile with Janetta, but she had moved to a different location.

My regret tore my soul further apart when Larry called me the next day. He told me that Victory was one of the bands scheduled for a March, 2001 gig at the A-HOP's "Urban Rock EarAddicts" showcase. After I hung up the phone, I broke down in tears. My spirit was still too wounded and hung-up on Tynesha to pursue another relationship.

After my teary breakdown, I began attending meetings held by Sex & Love Addicts Anonymous (SLAA). Initially, I felt comfortable. Their literature pinpointed my flaws as a "sexual anorexic—one who has a problem becoming physically and emotionally intimate with his/her partner." My attendance became limited, though, because I was the only person who claimed to have sexual anorexia. Some attendees were frightened when I described my feelings as "rageful" at the conclusion of one meeting. After I sobbed at the next meeting, an attendee told me that Co-Dependents Anonymous (CODA) was more suitable for me. He was right.

I quickly turned to CODA. I was slightly more relieved but still very depressed. I still referred to myself as a vulnerable jerk for allowing myself to depend on poor relationships for security.

Despite my daily moods of dreariness, I continued to prepare for the A-HOP gigs. However, my worst fears would soon be exposed.

On a Sunday morning of March, 2001, I attended a sound-check rehearsal at the A-HOP. I arrived there to make sure the bands were set up properly. While the managers and I chatted in the office, Tynesha walked inside. I calmly told her in a professional manner that we were still waiting for the soundman. My intention was not to start a personal conversation with her since I was anxious to cuss her out. Tynesha though still tried to be friendly, "Talib, I want to thank you for being here." I rolled my eyes and huffed, "(It's) AL!"

As the soundman showed up to set up his system, I briefly confirmed with him that he was okay handling the bands' rehearsals by himself. While Tynesha sat on the stage, she whined, "Albert, I really wanna thank you." I interjected screaming, "Don't try to thank me when you know you don't mean it."

A few minutes later, I gave Brian a handshake and started to exit. Tynesha stared at me with an annoying howdy doody-looking smile. While I was walking out, Tynesha tried to speak, "Hey! So when are you spinning at the show?" I told her the time and then pointed a finger in her face, "Look. We're only going to speak concerning professional matters." Tynesha still smiled, "I was!" I wanted so badly to cuss her out, but I held back fearing I would dent my foot in her ass. I proceeded to walk away in disgust.

Later in this day, I purchased groceries from Life's Essentials health food store. Ironically, I spotted Dr. L. I was angry with her for not returning my phone calls. Dr. L still gave me a bear hug. I pushed her off before shouting, "Where the fuck have you been?" Dr. L shrugged, "What's your problem?" I said,

"I've had to face that bitch during my show preparations." Dr. L said, "Look! You're both in the same genre. It's going to happen more than once. You're gonna have to deal with it. And hey! I've been tied up. I've even been in jail." I stood silent while she walked away smiling, "Have a good day!"

Four days later, the A-HOP show happened. I spun before and between bands. Initially, Tynesha kept a low-key tone only asking me for technical advice. I became infuriated again when she thanked me for turning on her tape recorder prior to her band's performance.

After the show finished, I lifted my equipment back and forth to my car. Tynesha tried to start a personal chat, "That was one kick-ass mix. Do you have a tape of what you do?" I ignored her and kept walking. Once again, I wanted very badly to threaten her by saying, "*If you try to start a personal conversation with me, I will shove my fist down your throat.*" I felt like a pussy for not telling her off. Or worse I felt as a jerk possessed too much by her power.

The following day, Larry called me at work saying Tynesha told him to tell me that she would pay her dues and become an RSC member. I laughed thinking, "*That bitch will never be true to her word.*" Subsequently, I was right. She never officially joined the RSC.

Like a person possessed by a demon, I was continually drowning in self-pity over my social woes. Even though I was still going to CODA meetings once a week, I increasingly felt more hopeless. And so I sought more counseling.

I spoke with Dr. L twice more on the phone. Dr. L said she had a nightmare in which I asked to speak with her after I killed all my co-workers with a machine gun. Then she told me I killed myself after telling her, "Oh well. I fucked up anyways." Dr. L said my condition was worse than she thought. I proceeded to tell her that I really needed a black male counseling perspective on my female problems. Dr. L hung up on me in frustration after my second call to her when I asked her for this type of referral.

While I was searching for a new therapist, I still managed to conduct RSC meetings. During a March, 2001 meeting, the RSC discussed production for a possible gig at the Royal Peacock. Larry mentioned how he had access to a sponsor who chose to remain anonymous.

After the meeting ended, I felt suspicious of Larry's "anonymous" sponsor. Due to my constant grief over Tynesha, I misdirected much of my distrust towards Larry. Larry used to work at an adult entertainment center called Fantasy Fare. Tynesha used to be a stripper. Even though I don't know how Larry first met Tynesha, I felt that Larry had some of Tynesha's same mischievous habits since he introduced me to her.

I called Larry the following day demanding that he tell me who the sponsor was. I persisted, "Is he a drug dealer?" Larry felt very offended, but I pressed on. Larry finally snapped and said, "No! He's not a drug dealer. He's my uncle. He's a blues musician." Larry and I both hung up our phones upset. I felt horrible knowing my unstable emotions were now affecting my work. Larry left a phone message five minutes later apologizing for his emotional outburst. He also pleaded, "D-Rock! You gotta trust me!" I wanted to trust Larry and all my RSC cohorts more. However, I was unable to trust myself.

Later in the night, I tried to admit myself into a psyche unit at a charter hospital. They rejected me and gave me referrals to various psychiatrists. They thought I was too sane to be admitted.

The following day, I located a black male psychologist in Midtown named Dr. Daniels. Fortunately, my job's insurance company paid for ten sessions without charging me a co-payment. Dr. Daniels was stringent in expressing why I should take medication. I didn't like this approach. But I stuck with him because I admired his attempts to counsel me on intimacy. Dr. Daniels said during my first visit, "I see. You're trying not to be affiliated with dick-wielding stereotypes about black males. There are more black males than you think with your same type of social issues. I don't think your problem is lack of sexual intimacy but social intimacy. We'll focus on that." I left his office feeling slightly more hopeful. Yet my lack of social trust would boil into a bigger mess.

After another "EarAddicts" gig at the A-HOP, Larry gave my five dollar earnings to the performing band Sol Factor. He said, "You know D-Rock that me and you are about the love of music first." There wasn't much money made overall at this show, but I still felt shafted. Since I was overboiled with anger about everything in life, I felt it was time to speak my true feelings. I left a phone message for Larry the next morning threatening to dent my foot in his ass if he ever shorted me again.

Later in the day, I visited Dr. Daniels. I told him about my recent squabble. I also told him how I planned to call Tynesha in the evening and threaten to shove my fist down her throat if she tried to speak with me personally at our upcoming I.A.G. show. Dr. Daniels said, "If you do that, she could press charges." I said, "She won't. I know her too well." Then Dr. Daniels interrogated me in a way that haunted me for the rest of the day," How did you feel when you saw your father hit your mother? You felt scared, right? You also felt angry. Angry at your dad for hitting you mom and angry at yourself for not being able to protect her." I sat silent for two minutes. Dr. Daniels practically threw a mirror in my face showing me the monster I was on the verge of becoming. Then Dr. Davis recommended, "I want you to do some research on a battered women's group." I snapped whimpering, "Fuck that. That has nothing to do with my situation. I would only hit her out of self-defense. I don't give a fuck about that information." Dr. Daniels continually recommended I get medication. I went to the bathroom sobbing in angry disgust. Dr. Daniels trailed me. I asked him, "How do I express all this anger?" He said smiling, "You're an artist. Do it through your music!"

When I arrived home, I heard Larry's phone message saying, "Don't ever threaten me again! I will rip you a new asshole. Hey. We're gonna move on to bigger and better things. It was only five bucks. But hey! Learn to throw that shit out the window." I laughed listening to this. Larry appeared to be forgiving. So I called him and apologized. Larry laughed and said, "Think LOVE from now on BRO!"

After this phone call, I felt horrendously bad because I had no real LOVE. I felt too cursed by the word "Love" and still felt snappy with a deep desire to hurt Tynesha. I knew I was out-of-control but I was now too ashamed to face anyone since I appeared headed in the same monstrous path of abuse that plagued my father. I wrote a poem called "A Fucked-up Woman." My anger was still undeterred. I beat on my djembe drum, and I was still reckless. After absorbing all my frustration, I went to sleep mad.

I woke up the next morning still feeling the deepest sense of shame. Now I had a more viable excuse for admittance to a charter hospital. I told the phone operator that I threatened to dent my foot in someone's ass. She said I could call there and be admitted for a couple of days. I wasn't sure of this. So when a social worker interviewed me at the hospital, I told her if I wasn't admitted, I would break the windows. She asked if I owned a handgun. I told her, "Yes." The hospital admitted me for in-patient treatment due to violent tendencies.

Another social worker interviewed me while orderlies ransacked my bags for any substance deemed harmful. She asked me, "How long has it been since you separated from your relationship (with Tynesha)?" I said, "Six months!" Then I shed some tears.

After I was checked into a room, Mother and Pop Pop arrived. Mother quickly gave me a hug. She expressed a positive tone, "You're doing the right thing. You were born with imbalanced brain chemicals. So listen to the doctors. By the way thanks for the tape of your radio show (ARS episode dedicated to female musicians). It made me cry." Immediately, I broke down raining cries of whimper and disgust. I buried my head in my arms.

After this emotional outburst, I calmly told Mother and Pop Pop about my violent tendencies. Pop Pop calmly said, "Never threaten a woman. You'll never win in court." The social worker called for me to go back. She told Mother and Pop Pop, "Don't worry! He's a nice man!"

I became acquainted with other patients who had similar problems. During most of my two-day in-patient stay, I participated in group discussions held in a television lounge. I met and spoke with the following people – a man who was depressed over his wife leaving him; a man who was depressed after losing his job; a wife and mother of two who attempted suicide; a single mother who sat in her house all day watching television; and a flight attendant named Myra who was irate after finding out her husband cheated on her.

Myra was the most surprising and memorable of all my co-patients. She was a very gorgeous and voluptuous 50-year-old African-American. Hardly anyone could believe that a woman with her incredible type of beauty was in a psyche unit. Myra told me how a group of orderlies had to pull her away after she grabbed her husband when he visited her at the hospital. She usually expressed the most vengeful words during the group discussions. Strangely, I felt very much at home during this time because I was surrounded by people like me—ones with deep emotional wounds.

Before my hospital stay, I used St. John's Wort every week to quell my depression. Since I was at a new low, I decided to cooperate with pharmaceutical anti-depressants.

As the first night of my stay drew to a close, I spotted some orderlies wearing gas masks while cleaning up pieces of excrement from a schizophrenic patient who lost control of her bowel and bladder functions. This moment reflected the shit I allowed myself to be caught up in.

The following morning, I woke up calm. I was wearing sweat clothes including my FSU Quiz Bowl Team sweatshirt. I got called into an office by an Arab doctor named Dr. Nassir. He asked me why I stopped using anti-depressants years prior. I told him they had too many side effects. He said, "All pills have side effects. So why are you here?" I told him about my violent tendencies. He said, "I'll also give you some medication for your anger."

The next day, I was released from in-patient care. However, I would be treated in an outpatient program for the next five weeks. I remained off from work on disability. All I told my supervisor was that I was in the hospital due to a personal illness. She wanted to bring me flowers, but I refused.

As I arrived back at my apartment, I noticed my gun box lying on my couch empty. Mother told me on the phone that Pop Pop took my gun after social workers recommended for it to be removed from my home as soon as possible. I never intended on using it on Tynesha. I purchased it prior to Y2K. However, I often had illusions of shooting myself. Thank goodness I never reached for this weapon of mass destruction.

The outpatient program was filled with group chats, exercises, and journaling homework assignments reminiscent of my first mental hospital visit four years prior. This time around the discussions were led by a young-looking clean cut black man. He appeared fashionably dedicated to the church and had a voice sounding similar to a stereotype of flamboyant gay men. I was usually annoyed and embarrassed when he had us do a dance routine while chanting, "Depression ... You Can't Stay ... You gotta go... So Go Go... Go Go ... Go." I did not complain. After all, most of my co-patients were finally smiling. Myra was also in my outpatient group. Almost every day she had a nervous breakdown while rating her depression as "Negative 4" on a scale of 1 to 10. I'm proud of her for venting her anxiety in a way that was surely not secretive. I spotted her months later at an Emotions Anonymous (EA) meeting. She was still looking incredibly gorgeous.

The most memorable discussion I had during my outpatient stay occurred right before my gig themed "Ladies Night Out" at the I.A.G. When I told the group leader that I was going to this gig with the intent to ignore Tynesha, he asked the group a question, "Is that reality?" They answered, "No!" A patient blurted, "That's obsession!" I responded, "I'm going to the gig primarily to handle my business." The patient asked facetiously, "Do you think you can handle her (without snapping)?" I told him, "I know I can!" He smiled, "Good for you!"

Indeed all my mental care was preparing me for a serious emotional test.

On the first Friday of April, 2001, I was slated as the DJ for CCP's "Ladies Night Out" featuring Twyla as the host and a performer, racially mixed all-female funk/metal band – Candela, and Tynesha's band Victory. My tension was high not only out of fear of facing Tynesha, but also because I exchanged more heated words with Larry prior to the show. I was concerned that Larry was putting CCP over RSC interests, especially after he pressed me too hard about retrieving a copy of the ARS episode where I interviewed Twyla. Larry confirmed it when I asked, "If you had to choose between CCP and the RSC, what would it be?" He said, "Common Cause! It is back in effect."

I decided to postpone this issue until the next RSC meeting. As I arrived at the I.A.G. loading my equipment, I gave Larry a handshake. Then I passed him a tape of the ARS episode with Twyla. We didn't say another word to each other for the rest of the night.

Nevertheless, I proceeded to provide good spins and make good chit chatter with several musicians and fans alike. It was funny when I spun "Seed" by Empire 44. One of this band's former dancers approached saying, "I thought I recognized that song."

This night seemed cool until Tynesha arrived with her toxic howdy-doody smile. I kept spinning and tried to pay her no attention. Tynesha still tried to start a chat. She reached her arm out in a handshake pose smiling, "Professional! Right?" I said, "Get away from me!" She persisted, "Okay! Then I'll give you a pound." I looked her dead in her eyes repeating, "Get away from me!" She walked away for a few minutes to partake in her band's setup. But as I kept spinning, she decided to sit on a couch located behind me. She grabbed my pants three times, but I ignored her. She also took my flashlight for a brief minute, but returned it before I could blast her for fucking with me.

After I finished my spinning set that followed Twyla's performance, I went to the floor to observe Candela's performance. Like the rest of the crowd, we enjoyed their sensuously heavy sound. I was talking to Kurt from the band Kill the Messenger. While I did this, I briefly looked back at my equipment to make sure Tynesha didn't mess with it. She smiled and quickly approached me. She bumped her butt against my hips. I quickly thought, "Now this bitch has given me justification to hit her." And so I thwarted my left elbow on her right shoulder. I proceeded to chat with Kurt. Tynesha childishly was speaking in my left ear while I was talking to Kurt and watching Candela. Dark thoughts of punching her raced through my head. I also remembered Father punching Mother. So after I balled up my right fist, I released my fingers into a palm pose. Then I shoved my palm on Tynesha's face and pushed her a few feet away from me. She still walked in front of me two minutes later pouting, "Okay! I'm not gonna touch you."

I proceeded to spin after Candela. I decided to hang out at the I.A.G. and watch Victory despite my disgust over Tynesha. I remember her blasting "fake people," singing rock renditions of songs such as "Sending My Love," and telling her tall white friend Timmy, "I love you." I was thinking, "*She's so full of shit.*"

After Victory finished, I thought I was going to spin out the night, but a group of musicians were setting up for an after-hours jam session. So as I got ready to break down my equipment, I shook hands with Victory's musicians and took a leak in the restroom. I walked back towards my DJ table and suddenly saw Pop Pop. I gave him a hug. Pop Pop said, "I came here because your mother was worried about you. Are you alright?" I smiled, "I'm just fine!" Pop Pop walked out of the I.A.G.. But then Tynesha was suddenly in front of me. I kept walking, but she tapped my shoulder, "Thanks Talib!" I shrugged her hand off me and walked to my table. After I finished loading my equipment back into my car, all the members of Candela and their female manager gave me a group hug thanking me for helping their band with exposure. As I walked towards my car, Tynesha again just happened to walk by me. This time she had a beer bottle in her left hand. And again she tapped me on the shoulder. This time I pushed her arm away. Tynesha whined behind me, "Hey! That's fucking rude. You need to stop that shit right now!" More dark thoughts raced in my head of me punching her and Father punching Mother. But this time, I smiled and turned around to face her without fear. I looked her dead in her goofy eyes jeering, "No! I'm not listening to you. You're fulla shit! You say you love me. You can't back it up. You say you're my friend. You can't back it up. You say you'll be at my doorstep. You can't back it up. You're fulla shit. You can sing about that bullshit in sending your love to everyone else, but don't bring that shit to me. You're fulla shit, and I'm not listening to you anymore." Immediately, I walked away. Tynesha hollered back, "You wanna beer?" I waved my hands down in disgust while she chugged away like a stupid drunk. I loaded the rest of my equipment into my car while Tynesha was lying on the ground wasted talking to some musician. I drove home feeling a slight sense of relief that I survived this emotional challenge.

This "Ladies Night Out" may have been a very small victory for me, but overall I still felt bitterly defeated in my social life. Thank God that my worst fear of beating the shit out of Tynesha never came into fruition. However, all the agony of trying to make her into something she would never be – my true loving SOULmate—would prove to be my life's WORST NIGHTMARE. This horrible relationship experience made me recognize how I still had much forgiveness to express to most people, especially to my parents, for all their mishaps. Tynesha had all the positive and negative aspects of my parents.

My recovery cycle was now in its baby stages, and indeed more emotional challenges were forthcoming!!!

ISOLATION TERROR

On the day following the "Ladies Night Out" gig at the I.A.G., Alim, his girlfriend Khadirah (now his wife), and her son Caesar spent the night at my apartment following a lecture by Alim in Southwest Atlanta. Before they drove out of Atlanta, we rode through town and drank smoothies. During our conversations, I spewed how most women are "fucked-up." Khadirah responded, "Well then you gotta work with them!" I sat silent for a few minutes wondering, "How do I get along with women who lead toxic lifestyles?" I also noticed while listening to their car radio that my hearing pitch was slower than usual. Apparently, this was a side effect of the anti-depressant medication I was taking called Serzone. My anger towards women coupled with pharmaceuticals would lead to further isolation.

Morris, the director from my outpatient program at the charter hospital, always warned me not to isolate from people while overcoming depression.

A few dates later, I attended a drummer display at MARS Music. It featured a performance and panel interview from Cindy Blackmon (drummer for Lenny Kravitz). Before Blackmon started banging on her set, I networked with a few musicians who I had consistently promoted through ARS and the RSC. I sat down next to *dd Dionne*, former lead vocalist of Edith's Wish. She hugged me and gleefully rubbed her fingers through my locks, "I like your hair!" A few seconds later, Tynesha walked up behind *dd* and hugged her. Instantly, I became silent. On one hand, I needed to be quiet and free of Tynesha's drama. On the other hand, I felt like Tynesha deliberately stole *dd's* attention away from me.

I continued to listen in silence. Tynesha told *dd* she was going to Europe the following week. Then she excused herself to smoke a cigarette outside. I ached with jealousy seeing and hearing Tynesha. She was in a happy mood, while carrying her guitar and wearing sandals, jeans, and her locks in girly pony tails.

Blackmon rocked out her drum set. Then she answered questions from everyone in the audience, including Tynesha and I. Tynesha sounded like an asskisser asking, "Does a lot of practice make you sound so good?" I sounded shy when Blackmon asked me to repeat my question since no one could hear me.

I won a prize drawing for a drum cymbal. I shook Blackmon's hand and exited MARS Music. As I arrived at my car, I waved goodbye to *dd* and Pam Wilson, former Edith's Wish bassist. They told me that they formed a new band called American Woman. Tynesha continued to talk with them while paying me no attention. I survived another post-traumatic test from Tynesha. Yet, I still felt like a miserable jackass. My recovery from this catastrophic relationship was still in its baby stages.

A couple of days later, I conducted an RSC meeting in a conference room of the Auburn Avenue Research Library. Before I officially started the meeting, I had a tense discussion with Larry. He enthusiastically boasted, "CCP won't interfere with the RSC's progress. If you want me to resign, I'll be fine. Whuddya say? Still undecided???" I told him we'd wait for Brian to arrive. Twyla rolled her eyes, "This issue can only be settled between you two." Brian entered and listened to my concerns. He quickly denounced them. I said, "Okay Larry. You're still cool with the RSC. But I will be watching your back, making sure you don't put the RSC as secondary bait." Larry shrugged,

"You just need to relax!" Indeed, I was too unrelaxed. I was trying too hard to build the RSC while healing from personal wounds.

At the next RSC meeting, Tynesha unexpectedly walked in the Auburn Library auditorium with a huge grimace. After she hugged Brian, she boasted about how wonderful her trip to Amsterdam was. Then she revealed her plans to move there within the next 6 months. Since the room was empty, I did nothing but stay silent while soaking up Tynesha's glee. Larry and Twyla arrived minutes later. Our meeting turned out to be very short. I quickly packed up all the copies of the meeting agenda. Then I walked out while Larry and Twyla listened to Tynesha's European stories. As I drove home, tears bursted out of my eyes. Tynesha was living out her dreams joyfully, while I was suffering from loneliness.

My neurosis over her still clouded my mind. So I got back in touch with Dr. L.

Even though my job's insurance covered all my appointments with Dr. Daniels, I didn't feel that his standard medicinal approach was strong enough to deal with my problems. I forever appreciate his analysis saying that I needed to focus more on "social intimacy rather than sexual intimacy."

Dr. L, though, pinched my nerves during our next conversation. I told her I was thinking about talking to Tynesha again. Dr. L asked, "What does she have to do with your healing?" I couldn't answer. Yet, I commented on how Dr. L's bold words were too strong. Dr. L responded, "I basically told you to distance yourself from her or accept her flaws and be happy with that. I get tired of people trying to use others like a crutch for their own healing. We'll see if you can get the results you're looking for out of her ..."

After this talk, I decided not to call Tynesha. Thus, I set up more appointments with Dr. L.

A few days prior to my twenty-eighth birthday, I visited Dr. L again. I revealed how I often would stay in my apartment on weekends feeling depressed, while doing nothing but watching television. Dr. L recommended that I go on a "television fast" at least once a month. I further explained how I continuously felt that Tynesha still owed me something when I knew she really owed me nothing. Dr. L said, "There's really no such thing as fair. She had every right to get what she got from you. You just have to stop letting forces like her distract you from your empowerment."

I continued to visit Dr. L almost once a month over the course of a year while taking medication. Her ferocious advice would prove helpful in motivating me out of depression.

Yet there were more situations that proved overwhelming.

Every week I continued to journal and attend EA and CODA meetings. Often I wrote down strategies to attract "The Right Woman." On the surface, journaling kept me sane from continuous mental anxiety over non-stop thoughts about Tynesha. At the same time, my fantasy of an ideal woman lead to an obsession that pushed away wonderful women.

On my 28th birthday, an older Afrocentric woman named Qurdishah rode with me to Six Flags Georgia. She also bought a birthday certificate for me. Overall, we were good platonic friends until I made a plea for a 50/50 friendship. I told Qurdishah that I expected her to take me out in a car or meet me halfway in her car. This offended her, and so our communication was cut off. We spoke on good terms two years later when we ran into each other at a Kroger supermarket. Nevertheless, I still differed from her pro-black views too much.

After my initial cutoff with Qurdishah, I tried to build a relationship with another Afrocentric lady with dreadlocks named Marquisha. Sistas with "natural" hair were still part of my preferences for healthy boundaries. After a few good conversations,

I asked Marquisha out. She chuckled, "Are you asking me on a date?" I responded, "Well we're just friends so we'll pay separately." Marquisha was so irate that she blew off, "How about we not (go out)? Bye!" She hung up, and I felt like I had a dagger in my heart. I immediately called my friend Amen. He told me that women are always turned off by discussions of payment details before dating. I concurred and felt more like an obsessive punk.

My "perfect woman" obsession pushed away one more woman. This time around, I really foiled away perhaps my best opportunity to have a special girlfriend. This short-locked petite sista named Tami had a genuine spark for me. I took her to lunch at El Myr. We had a good conversation about our favorite music and movies. Tami revealed to me that she was high on weed at a weekend party. One of my written "attributes" for "The Right Woman" was that she does not smoke anything at all or do drugs. So on the next day, I confronted Tami at her job, "I don't date smokers." She whimpered, "I thought you said we weren't dating (that we were just friends). I don't like how you approached me. And I don't like what you said to me. Okay you can leave now!" I didn't say another word. I feared too much that another smokin' dopin' Tynesha-type woman would exploit me. Three years later I ran into Tami at a concert. I apologized for dumping her for something as petty as smoking weed. Indeed, marijuana can be a drug too often abused. Yet, Tami's social habits in no way appeared to deter her from showing genuine care for me. My "perfect woman" neurosis continued to cloud my judgment until spring 2003.

Despite my bumbling social life, I still managed to keep ARS and the RSC afloat, but personal health issues eventually put the RSC in jeopardy.

In mid September, 2001 (a few days after the 9/11 events and a few weeks after Aaliyah's plane crash) Brian resigned as the RSC's Membership Supervisor due to complications from a rare kidney condition. The RSC was left with a huge gap. Brian provided exceptional technical skills and unfettered professionalism. He also engineered the RSC's 2001 Compilation CD and started our organization's newsletter.

With Brian gone, I took over all his duties as Membership Supervisor including those of the RSC's newsletter editor. This was supposed to be temporary for me and the RSC. But the RSC was not attracting enough dedicated members to fill in Brian's former position. Therefore, I became more exhausted.

Another side effect of my medication was constant hunger. I had gained almost twenty-five pounds since I started on dosages six months prior. I was also feeling relentless fatigue, so I visited my nutritionist, Dr. Tillman, seeking natural remedies to offset my reactions to pharmaceuticals.

Dr. Tillman sold me one of his herbal detox tonics and referred me to other herbal supplements. He said he had several patients who used both pharmaceuticals and herbs. I told him I didn't like being back on medication. Dr. Tillman responded, "At that time (March, 2001) you were under a lot of stress. If you didn't get immediate care, you could've been one of those hijackers on one of those planes (reported crashed flights of 9/11/01)."

Dr. Tillman had already known firsthand how much I suffered from relationship woes. Before I entered the hospital, I broke down in tears at his office while receiving muscle therapy on his water machine.

After my post 9/11 visit to Dr. Tillman, I remained on both medication and herbs for another year.

My spirit appeared to be on the right track. Yet, more situations challenged my emotional health.

On October 13, 2001, Larry and Twyla called me into a special RSC officers' meeting. They basically criticized my leadership approach as a turnoff. They said I was too stern and business-like noting that people often became bored at the meetings. Overall, they recommended that the RSC offer its members fun incentives. I listened with practically no resistance. Then I wasted little time in inserting their incentive recommendations into the RSC's mission statement. Often times, I gave Larry, Twyla, and several other RSC members ticket certificates to ballgames hosted by the Atlanta Hawks, Thrashers, and Braves.

The RSC continued to produce monthly EarAddicts concerts at the I.A.G. while planning our first annual Jimi Hendrix Birthday Tribute for November 30, 2001.

My heart was just starting to feel relief from anxiety until I ran into Tynesha at an EarAddicts show in late October, 2001.

Initially, I thought I was going to handle this encounter well. Larry told me that Victory was performing. I asked him in shock, "Tynesha is still in town?" I told Dr. L about this. She gave me a look of discontent. Dr. L had also sensed that I was progressing in my recovery, but her expression signaled that I was now in jeopardy. She asked, "Are you sure you can handle seeing her?" I said, "I'm gonna have to face her sooner or later. And who knows? She may still go to Europe." Dr. L asked, "But what if she never leaves?" I responded, "Then I'll deal with it."

As I arrived at I.A.G. for the October EarAddicts, I immediately saw Tynesha practicing on her guitar. She smiled at me, and I waved back sarcastically. After I set up my DJ equipment, I told Tynesha to be quiet for a few minutes so I could test a couple of CDs on the sound system. Tynesha whined, "Okay! I could leave (out the room for a few minutes) right now. I don't wanna bother you." I responded, "You're fine (sitting where she was at). I'm just doing a sound check." My spirit seemed content with her presence. But then she changed clothes. She arrived back in the stage room with her hair down and out of a balled-up ponytail. My heart immediately throbbed into near heart attack-type anxiety. No matter how toxically flawed Tynesha acted, with or without booze and cigarettes, she still had the appearance of the finest-looking and friendliest female in the building. She proceeded to set up her guitar for her performance. While I was spinning, she approached me, "Hey! I would take my guitar with me to the bathroom if I had to, but can you watch it?" I snapped back, "You're guitar is fine!" Of course I didn't watch it knowing nobody would steal it. Tynesha went on to perform three songs. Her usual undertone of God and love seemed like a positive atmosphere for the post 9/11 atmosphere, but for me, it was an irritating deterrent. Despite my vow not to think about Tynesha, my heart's dagger-filled anxiety over her continually tormented me. Tynesha left the I.A.G. with her tall friend Timmy a few minutes after finishing her performance. I spun my set and watched two more bands perform for the rest of the night. However, I left the I.A.G. unable to shake Tynesha away from my thoughts. Therefore, I sought more help from Dr. L and my psychiatrist Dr. Dhonagi.

Dr. L shook her head in disbelief, "You keep viewing her (Tynesha) as this majestic goddess." I kept repeating, "This is something I have no control over. My heart continues to ache over her. Why won't somebody just please stab me in my chest?" Dr. L then asked, "Do you enjoy fantasizing about her and other women like this?" I said, "Shamefully, I do!" Dr. L barked, "Then what are you doing sitting here as one of my patients?" I gave her a look of protest, but she continued, "… There's nothing wrong with you. You enjoy the fantasy. You appreciate the high points. But your spirit has never accepted the lows. And you can't have the best of both worlds." I responded, "Does it really look like I'm enjoying the fantasy now? I can't help the fact that she used to be a stripper!" Dr. L answered, "… Some of my clients are strippers … Big deal! They're just giving you your desired fantasies. You'd better decide whether or not to accept your enjoyment for the fantasy. Because if you didn't feel this way for Tynesha, you'd feel this way for another woman … This (my fantasy) is like a drug …" Again Dr. L nailed an accurate analysis of my dysfunctional obsession. I left her house feeling like a shameful mental case.

My shame grew worse after visiting Dr. Dhonagi for my meds. I explained to him my recent encounter with Tynesha. Dr. Dhonagi said that I only had a panic attack, but he also called my obsessive heart throb a form of "mental stalking." He warned me to be careful saying that mental stalking usually leads to physical stalking. Then he recommended that I call him immediately the next time I had a panic attack so he could adjust my dosage.

The panic attacks continued, but I did not call him. Side effects from the pills combined with counter effects from the herbs already seemed like too much treatment.

I spotted Tynesha again leaving a MARTA station while I was boarding a train towards a Hawks' basketball game. All I did was walk by with a sarcastic "hi." I sat by myself at the game feeling heaving chest pains throughout the night.

My recovery from relationship woes continued to feel like a period of terrifying isolation.

I saw Tynesha for the last time at the RSC's 1st Annual Jimi Hendrix Birthday Tribute. This time my spirit was more mature. I had no intention of saying or doing anything bad to Tynesha. I pretty much avoided her the whole night. But then as I walked back to the stage room for another DJ set, she grabbed my arm bragging, "It's my birthday!" I said literally, "I know," and shrugged away from her.

Despite my personal disenfranchisement from Tynesha, I kept her e-mail address on my RSC distribution list for professional reasons. Lo and behold, I received an e-mail from her after sending out an RSC newsletter in January, 2002. Tynesha briefly wrote, "I have left ATL. I'm on my way back to Europe. Stay in touch and we'll keep exchanging contact information. Luv Tynesha!" Immediately, I felt a bittersweet torment in my soul. On one hand, I was happy she was gone with likelihood that I would never see her again. On the other hand, I was insanely envious seeing how she made her career dreams come true while I was still struggling.

My personal and professional struggles continued in blurs for the next five months. Outside of doctors, support groups, and phone conversations with my best friend Amen, I was pretty much only hanging out with myself. ARS was still broadcasting strong, but I had no vision of how I would take this show to another level. I maintained paychecks from my pay job but still had no promotional aspirations from there either.

Meanwhile, frustration mounted from Larry and Twyla about the RSC's lack of membership. Twyla vented, "Nobody shows up at these meetings. Members only come around when it's time to do a gig, but that's it." I sensed they were ready to quit. I knew the RSC had to undergo some major changes in order to survive, so I decided to make a bold move.

In June, 2002, I wrote Larry and Twyla a resignation letter. I basically told them my personal problems had caught up with me making me an unhealthy leader of the RSC. I also recommended that Larry and Twyla merge the RSC into a network subsidiary of CCP. Larry and Twyla discussed this suggestion amongst themselves. Then, they invited me to dinner at El Myr. They told me how they had decided to move forward with my idea. I thanked them and offered an apology, "It still hurts how I failed as the RSC's leader. Even though I failed, I don't look at myself as a failure." Twyla nearly bit my head off, "That's the most contradictory statement I've ever heard. If you did something, then you didn't fail. Either you try and don't succeed or you just do it." Her whims only reflected the melancholy I felt the rest of the night over my "failures." Nevertheless, I still think I made the best possible move for the RSC.

My grief from this moment forward transcended into more personal challenges.

In late June, 2002 on a Saturday prior to the fourth of July, I started to drive Mother's car up to Largo, Maryland. Mother inherited this car from Pop Pop, who bought this vehicle before he passed away in December, 2001. Ironically, Pop Pop was also born on the fourth of July. Mother never drove on the highway. However, the biggest incentive of this trip was that I needed a break away from my woeful single's life in Atlanta.

This drive was going smoothly until it started raining on a slippery road running through Aiken, South Carolina. Minutes after pumping Empire 44's CD *Crash and Bleed*, I immediately noticed a car was turned sideways and stuck dead in the street approximately one hundred feet in front of me. I tried to turn quickly into the left lane, but another car was already in that lane blocking me. Therefore, I had no choice but to press the brake pedal and prepare for a head-on collision. I screamed at the top of my lungs as I crashed. The front window shattered pieces of glass all over the car, and I felt the wheel's airbag cushion me as my body thrusted backward on the driver's seat.

Immediately following the crash's impact, I yelled "Shit!" I recognized that I forgot to rent a cell phone and couldn't call anyone. Luckily, there was plenty of help around. My arms along with portions of my chest and stomach were bloodied and scraped. After taking about four heavy breaths, I leaned my body out of the wrecked Honda. I looked around and spotted the wreckage of the vehicle I collided with. Then I saw two ladies. One was crying while using her cell phone. I calmly asked, "Why was your car stopped in the street?" She said that her car had slipped out of control during the rain.

The showers were now pouring harder. I was feeling beat

while sitting on a roadside. A carpenter had parked his pick-up four-wheel truck on the curb. He told me how he witnessed the driver in the left lane not letting me over as I tried to avoid the car in front of me. Interstate 85 was now running in one congested mess. While cars were driving around the wreckage, a bearded man wearing an American-flagged bandana walked towards me. He suggested I wipe my wounds so I wouldn't get infected. He also said he would help me more, but he had to get back on the road. Then, the female driver from the car I crashed into gave me an American-flagged beach towel for me to wipe off my wounds.

A South Carolina Highway Patrolman arrived minutes later. The female driver and I both told him what happened. Then he asked if anyone needed an ambulance. I told him I needed one because I wasn't sure whether or not I was bleeding internally. He instructed the driver and the parked witnesses to push the damaged Honda to the roadside. While they did that, I laid down in the backseat of the patrolman's car.

About ten minutes later, the ambulance arrived. They examined me, told me I only had minor cuts and bruises, and said that I was in good enough shape to continue driving.

Then, the tow trucker arrived. He escorted me and the Honda to an auto yard in Aiken, SC before bragging how Aiken is the home of William "The Refrigerator" Perry, former three hundred plus pound lineman who famously ran for a touchdown in the Chicago Bears' 1985 Super Bowl Championship. He also told me how the area of my car accident was one of the most dangerous slippery roads in the whole country.

After I arrived at the auto yard, I was referred to a rental car agent. This agent arranged a vehicle from my credit card. The auto yard confirmed that the Honda was totaled.

A few hours later, I was back driving on the road despite the tremendous amount of anxiety I felt in my chest. After spending the night at Alim's store in Fayetteville, North Carolina, I drove the next day all the way to my sister Stephanie's house in Largo, Maryland. I couldn't get rid of the chest pain, but I was feeling somewhat serene. The accident and the aftermath were signals that no amount of medication could ease my pain. So I decided to stop taking my prescriptions for good. I was now mentally strong enough to face life's challenges without pharmaceuticals.

Larry and Twyla continued to run the RSC by calling monthly meetings, soliciting membership, and booking functions at the I.A.G.. I was hesitant about staying on as an active RSC member. Thankfully though, Twyla kept pushing me, "We need you here (at the meetings)!" As I witnessed Larry and Twyla's successful membership recruitment, I became inspired to write the RSC's newsletters on a monthly basis. Their social savvy compensated for my lackluster rapport with people.

Things appeared slightly brighter with the RSC staying active and my "freedom" from the pills. My social life, however, only became hazier over another woman.

Lana walked in and out of my life in a manner similar to the movie *When Harry Met Sally*.

I first met Lana at a NABA (National Association of Black Accountants) Conference held in Atlanta, Georgia during October '94. Right from our initial introduction, we seemingly couldn't take our eyes off each other. I was dressed in a blue pinstriped suit, and she was wearing a dark blue business dress. My hair was styled in a low clean-cut afro. Her hair was permed with thick bangs over her forehead. Every time we walked past each other, she repeated, "We'll talk (later)!" When we finally talked, our conversation was very brief. All I found out about her was that she was a Senior Accounting major at Tuskegee University in Alabama. I asked her for her phone number. All she gave me was her college address so I could write to her. I took a couple of pictures of her and exchanged a hug before heading back to Fayetteville State University. I wrote her, but she never responded. I thought I would never see her again. The Universe though worked strangely as I ran into her two years later.

During November 1996 while purchasing cafeteria food at Lucent Technologies' Atlanta Works factory, I spotted a caramel-complexioned woman with bright brown eyes. She looked familiar, but I had no idea who she was. I introduced myself to her. She told me we had met before. I asked, "Where?" She said we first met at a NABA Conference. Immediately, I was amused with shock. We exchanged numbers and kept in touch. I was still startled about how both of us ended up working at the same building of the same company. She was working in the Purchasing Department while I was in Accounting. Both of us now had slightly shorter hairstyles. Her perm and bangs were more low-cut, while I sported a shaved head.

We bumped into each other for about two and a half months before finally going out on a lunch date. By this time, I was sinking into depression from job woes and the CPA Exam. I was running a few minutes late for the lunch break. Lana dropped by my office smiling in her raincoat, "You said 12:30pm. Right?" I told her, "I've been busy."

I drove us to a restaurant in Norcross on Jimmy Carter Boulevard. This was a good relief for me since I had few things to smile about. Lana told me how she grew up in Long Island, New York before going through a downward spiral of rural culture shock at Tuskegee. Then she revealed how she changed her major from Psychology to Accounting midway through her college term. I said, "Really? Your conversation could help since I'm seeking a therapist." Lana laughed despite the fact I was being serious. She proceeded to talk about how she was unsure about Lucent being her desired career path. Lana concluded our lunch chat by saying how she enjoyed singing in a church choir.

Despite her Christian faith, she came across as a woman who was open-minded enough for me to talk to. Like me, she also saw Dr. Khalid Abdul Muhammad speak in college. As fate had it, both of us also eventually wound up as patients for the same therapist.

Lana and I exchanged personal numbers after this date. Eventually, we went out again.

We were supposed to go see *Rosewood* together, but one of her friends gave her a ticket to see Kirk Franklin and The Family. Ironically, this was right before my first Atlanta entrance into a charter hospital. Nevertheless, I continued pursuing her.

We saw *Love Jones* in April, 1997. I tried to slip my left arm around her shoulders, but she was quickly disgusted, "I hate it when guys do that!" We still stayed in touch after this night. However, she stood me up on two other occasions. She was supposed to meet me at a bowling alley on a May '97 night. She left me a message saying how sorry she was hoping I enjoyed myself regardless. Indeed I enjoyed bowling with some other friends. Regardless of Lana's ambiguities toward me, I still bought advanced tickets to see Adriana Evans perform at the Atrium. Again, she didn't show up. This time she didn't call back, and once again, I did not think I would ever see her again.

The Universe threw me another strange curve as I bumped into her three years later in May, 2000 at Little Five Points. I was walking with a WRFG crew for the Inman Park Parade. After our walk finished, I headed towards the parking lot. Suddenly, I was patted by a lady with an orange wig. This lady was Lana. She gleefully spoke, "Albert! I heard you on the radio one night. What have you been up to?" We briefly chatted about how we both quit our jobs from Lucent Technologies and ended up suffering severe financial consequences. Lana further explained how she was walking in the parade with a theatre group she performed for. She asked me for my number while leaving hers as I exited the parade.

I honestly didn't feel like communicating with her again, but Lana pressed on as she called me a few days later. I detected some frantic guilt in her voice. I spoke in a low-key tone asking her what was happening in her life. I barely remember exactly what she said. She vaguely said something about finding out what was best for her spirit. She ended our brief chat by wishing me "love and wholeness." She called me twice more telling about her aspirations to be a singer. She also told me she would continue to call me if I didn't call her back.

Lana was trying too hard to reenter my life, and I didn't understand why. I had no intentions of calling her again, yet I had an upcoming CCP gig in late June, 2000 at the Cajun Kitchen. I needed to sell tickets in order to make money for the gig. So I decided to call Lana and make a sale. She agreed to buy two tickets from me as long as I delivered them to her. We agreed to meet at her place one evening. She instructed me to park near the laundry room of her Marietta, GA apartment complex. As I parked my car, I didn't see Lana anywhere. So I called her with my cell phone asking of her whereabouts. She told me I was supposed to meet her at the gazebo. Thus I proceeded to meet her there. My eyes widened after my jaw dropped in shock. Lana was looking organically gorgeous with her hair styled in chin-length dreadlocks while wearing an African-garbed dress. Her bright almondy-eyed smile glared as I shrugged like a goofball, "Wow! My hair fizzled out while yours blossomed!" She laughed, "You still have a good balance." She guided me back to a conference room next to the laundry area and bought two tickets to my gig. Then, she led me back to the gazebo where we sat and chatted for about an hour. She gloated how a brotha told her not to put even more chemicals in her hair after she dyed the ends blonde. She kept spewing, "I can really feel what's going on with my body through my hair." I continued to listen in awe of her newfound "natural" glow as we started to swing on the rocking seat. She revealed more, "I keep calling my parents to help me pay all these bills ..." After further conversation, I finally asked, "Why didn't you go out with me on the night of the Adriana Evans' concert?" Lana vaguely said that she left the phone off the hook that night since she was going through some issues. I didn't dig deeper, but I emphasized how we both were unhappy with our Accounting majors in college and at our Lucent jobs despite the lucrative incomes. Now, we were both aspiring professionals of the music/media industry. I left her complex feeling amazed though nervous about how she ended up back in my life for another period. This confusing vibe remained relentless.

Lana wound up at my gig. She took some pictures from my camera just like I asked her. I instructed her to take too many photos of Tynesha and her band Victory's debut performance. Lana paid it no mind. She still had a good time. Mother and Pop Pop showed up for this gig too. I introduced Lana to them. To this day, Lana is still the only female outside of Keema and Lita I've ever introduced to any of my parents and grandparents.

Lana also showed up and snapped pictures at my October 2000 DJ gig on the stage of 2 High Studios. I kissed her hand, hugged her a couple of times, and thanked her for continually supporting me. Seemingly, Lana and I were headed for more than friendship, but by the time I called her again, she was already involved with someone else.

Her boyfriend, Spirit Fire, whom she met at my Cajun Kitchen gig, was organizing her twenty-eighth birthday party at the I.A.G.. Lana wanted me to be the DJ. I was snotty at first fearing I was being pimped for no money. After settling down, I called Spirit Fire back and told him that I gladly accepted his opportunity for me to spin. Basically, I had dumbfounded fears that another Tynesha was trying to exploit me.

These fears didn't come true at Lana's party. She spewed in shock when I walked into her gathering, "Oh my God! Albert is growing locks!" I went on to have a good spin. The crowd was pleased. Bands performed well. I gathered a list of e-mail addresses as potential customers for my upcoming gigs, and Lana had a ball. She sang her heart out after Spirit Fire serenaded her on a duet rendition of James Brown's "It's a Man's World." Before I left, Lana still wanted me to take a picture with her. It's amazing how both of us were now filmed with baby dreadlocks.

Lana proceeded to make out with Spirit Fire. I thanked him again for having me as the DJ. Spirit Fire eventually submitted multiple CDs to me from his band Fresh Earth along with other bands who were his production protégées. He also allowed me to be the opening DJ at several other Fresh Earth gigs.

Lana dated Spirit Fire for a few months before they officially split. She and I continued our occasional phone conversations on and off for another two plus years. We never talked about dating each other, especially since we were both healing from broken relationships.

My my my! How this all suddenly changed!

At approximately 3am during an early morning of June, 2002, Lana called me. We had a simple conversation, but I hung up the phone feeling curious as to why she would call me in the wee hours of the day. I spoke with Alim about this a couple of nights later. He practically choked with excitement, calling Lana's phone chat a "booty call." He also recommended that I play my cards right by smoothly making her my girlfriend.

A few hours later at approximately 4am, Lana called again. We both told each other how we anticipated speaking to one another. Then, I boldly asked if she ever thought about us being involved together in a relationship. Lana said, "I have envisioned

'Me and Albert would save each other.' But when you told me how you were taking anti-depressants, I thought, 'Albert is still too hurt.'" After chatting for another hour and a half about our life intentions and past relationships, I finally suggested that Lana become more than my friend. Lana responded quirkily, "Your bluntness amazes me ..." In so many words she said that we should remain friends and date other people.

After this conversation, I was more confused. So I called Dr. L for more advice. Dr. L warned me that Lana sounded "dingy." I concurred since Lana was very indecisive about whether she should be an educator, a psychologist, a politician, a singer, or a homeschooler. I also told her I should grab her ass and kiss her. Dr. L said, "You can do that, but you would be forcing the issue by not asking permission." I responded, "A female friend of mine told me that a woman often likes a man to take charge in situations without seeking permission." Dr. L snapped, "That's a woman who does not know her true goddess self. You (men) come from me (the woman). If you expect to enter my womb and give birth to the children of the world, then you must respect me enough to ask." This feminist advice stayed on my mind during my next visit to Lana's apartment.

Again, Lana called me in the wee hours of the morning. Even though I was heading out of town the following day, I had time to visit. Lana led me back to the complex's gazebo area. I showed her pictures from four of my photo albums. I told her that I'm cool with us being friends. She reiterated that she still wasn't ready. She also elaborated how she was now okay with seeing Spirit Fire in person long after their breakup. We spoke for another hour and a half about God knows what. I couldn't help but notice how we both currently had dreadlocks growing down our shoulders. Our hairstyles signified the time periods where we always re-introduced ourselves to each other after drifting apart.

The first part of our chat reached a climax after we discussed guidelines for relationships. Lana said she didn't want a man who already had kids. I said I didn't want a woman who drinks and smokes. Lana said, "Well that rules me out because I drink and I smoke." I sat silent for a minute. Then we started to walk towards my car as I prepared to leave. I told her how often I wished someone would stab me in the chest and eliminate my heartaches. Lana whined, "Oh no! Those are just love pains. Don't you wish any more harm upon yourself!" We didn't make it to my car until another hour and a half later. I hardly said any words while Lana preached healing messages to me. She relentlessly stared me down with her bright almondy eyes. As her words faded, I gave her a hug and kissed her on the cheek. I thought about kissing her lips, but it didn't feel right since we were officially long-remaining friends. Lana still displayed a cuddly reaction.

We continued to call each other on a bi-weekly basis. I didn't expect to see her much since she was now commuting to Atlanta from her newly inherited house on the South Carolina/ Georgia border. The Universe still placed her on my path.

During the first week of September 2002, Lana asked me to allow her a stay at my place for one week while she commuted to a temp assignment. I humbly approved.

During the first night of her stay, we watched my favorite movie *Quilombo* and drove to El Myr for dinner. Lana gave me gas money after offering to pay more for her visit. I facetiously told her she was my guest at the present moment but that I wouldn't rule out taking hotel pay. Lana also told me I had "a calming vibe." Seemingly, her stay would cause no problems. Yet, my physical attraction towards her eventually escalated into a dispute.

I appreciated Lana giving my apartment a cleansing touch-up. Her responsible housekeeping motivated me to do home chores more often. She also cooked me enough cabbage to last for two weeks. I guess this was Lana's way for "paying" for her visit.

Nevertheless, I subconsciously strategized to pursue Lana sexually. I had already ruled her out as meaning nothing more to me than a friend. Lana slept on my sofa bed during her first night. However, she either hung out late or slept at a girlfriend's place for the rest of the week. The only time we hung out together was on a Wednesday night at the Apache Café, where a public television program was recording performances by DRES Tha Beatnik and Three5Human. Lana also hung out on this night into the break of dawn after I drove home.

I grew frustrated with my lack of opportunities to kick it with Lana. So on the following Friday, I decided to honestly express myself to her. Lana arrived at my place asking if I left any veggie pizza around. I told her I ate it all since it was too small. Lana paid it no mind. She ate the rest of her leftover veggie meat sauce-laced green peppers. While she munched, she told me about her rehearsals as a background singer for the neo-soul jazz artist, Jas Tunica-El. Then she rambled off in a tangent about reasons for life occurrences before ending up on the topic of her nails. She flashed her hands, "I haven't had a manicure in a couple of weeks. But this is still a good color." Then she gleefully wiggled her red-polished toes, "My toes are fine too. Even though I have yet to get another pedicure, my feet are still looking very shiny." I had to take a very heavy breath to avoid screaming out over my horny erection. I wanted to fuck Lana so badly, but her friendship was worth more to me. So I said, "You're stay here was pleasant but also frustrating. Let's talk."

I told her how I only had sexual intercourse with one woman in my entire life. I further elaborated how I was tense because I always wanted more than sex. Lana was uncomfortable listening to this. She blurted, "You should call her (my only sexual partner) up!" I was in shock, "What? I have needs too but I wanted more." Lana poignantly eluded, "Look. There are woman who advertise themselves for sex in Creative Loafing. There are women who you meet while deejaying and hosting your show. You can get with one of them. I have a male friend who gets some from his massage parlor. There are plenty of women who offer these services. I'm not one of them. And I won't be one of those to fulfill your desire." I confessed more, "Sure, I've been frustrated, and having an attractive woman like you over only added to it." Lana nodded her head with much grief before growling furiously, "I knew it! That's why I stayed away. I would have slept in the car if I had to. I'm grateful for you allowing me over. But I'm not going to service your filthy, disgusting, despicable energy. As a matter of fact I've never been attracted to you that way and will never be. You don't know me ..." Shamefully I muddled, "I thought we can act out as grown adults." Lana shouted with further rampage,"... You don't know me. We could have sex one night and then argue in the morning. You're imbalanced ..." I ended the conversation, "You're welcome to stay here again. But if you never want to do so again, I completely understand." Lana proceeded to take a shower before leaving my place to work the door at a blues club. She said she was no longer upset, but the way she walked past me showed that she wanted to get away from me quickly. I stayed in my apartment for the rest of this night feeling like a sex-starved jerk.

On the following day, I drearily shopped for food at Kroger and Life's Essential Market before seeing Rob Hardy's *Pandora's Box* at the Magic Johnson Theatre. As I arrived home, Lana parked her car right beside me. She walked into my apartment to scoop up her luggage. Then she returned my key. I turned on my computer preparing material for an episode of ARS. Lana commented, "Wow! I can't believe you actually have food in your place. Why didn't you come to the club?" I said, "I fell asleep." She then asked, "So are you okay now with your issue?" I said I was still uncomfortable. Indeed I was drearier watching Lana glance as an organic natural-haired goddess. I asked her to take pictures from my camera. She obliged me. Right as she opened the front door, I gently grabbed her arm, "Are you still afraid to touch (me)." She turned around flipping off her sandals, "Yes. I am!" I don't want to feed into any more emotional turmoil! How do you feel?" I told her, "I feel like I'm hugging a friend!" She immediately wrapped her arms around my back. I felt slightly relieved that I was still able to embrace her. She then told me how she felt "weird" staying at my place. She said she may need a place to stay the next time she's in town. Then she said goodbye. I said that she served a divine purpose in my life as only a friend. I hosted my radio show later in the night by playing only love songs.

I thought I was settled after my radio show, but I woke up the next morning feeling like a dagger was in my chest. My first frantic thought was, "Oh no! I can't be experiencing another Tynesha vibe—falling for a woman who doesn't care about me." I spoke with Alim and Amen about this. I confirmed that I was suffering from another obsession. They advised me not to pay her any more attention. I also sought advice from Dr. L. She laughed in my face, "It's just the fantasy kicking in!" I told her, "It's killing me!" She giggled more, "It's killing you well!"

By this time, I clearly saw that I was going nowhere with Lana. I started to distance myself from her. She still called me one month later, "I just called to see that you're okay." I somberly responded, "I thought you were still pissed at me." She gleefully spat back, "Nope. I'm over that issue. It means a lot to me that you asked me to be an emergency contact for your family. I just called to see that you're okay. You're still off the medication. Right???" Despite Lana's apparent concern, I didn't trust her. I ran into her at an I.A.G. gig, which coincidentally fell on her thirtieth birthday. November 8, 2002 would be the last time I ever saw Lana. She walked by me, "AL! Give me a birthday hug!" I hugged her. Then I chilled out for the rest of the night.

November of 2002 proved to be a trial on my spirit. First off, things appeared upbeat professionally. I just purchased my own business cards labeled "D-Rock SOUL-Jah." I wrote down a series of goals to progress as a DJ. I had two weeks of vacation reserved before and after the Thanksgiving holiday. For the first week, I headed to Largo, Maryland to see Stephanie and her family. I had a positive outlook heading to the airport until a bad omen occurred.

I spotted a Morehouse University alumnus who'd been a featured actor in a couple of Spike Lee movies. I introduced myself to him before leaving him one of my business cards. Five minutes later, I noticed that the pouch sack of cards I carried in my pocket was gone. Apparently, I lost this sack when I exchanged contact info with the actor. At first it didn't seem like a big deal, but it later reflected the anxiety I felt when I was in Largo.

On my second to last night visiting Stephanie, an overwhelming feeling of sadness unexpectedly swept over me. I told Stephanie I needed to talk. While she was cleaning her kitchen, she listened to me bawl away my sorrows. With my head buried in my hands, I told her I was still weeping over my bad relationship with Tynesha. Stephanie remained calm, "Everyone's been through a bad relationship in their lives. Just move on and let it go..." She proceeded to give her youngest son, Kalen, a bath. I stayed up a few minutes longer. Stephanie's older son, Zeke, called me his "favorite DJ" before he went to bed.

I was unable to explain this sudden sadness until I flew into the San Francisco Bay Area to visit June. By this time, I was far down in the dumps because I wasn't sure I had Tynesha's level of willpower to succeed. On my first day visiting, June came home from work. She spotted me wearing my pajamas as I cried profusely. I told her I tried all day to find a therapist and/or support group but failed. June sympathetically whined, "I don't know what else I can do for you. I'm at work all day. What's wrong?" I moaned with teardrops, "I'm not sure if I have what it takes to succeed as a DJ." June replied, "You love it. Don't you? So why give it up?" I whined, "I'm not sure I have the ruthless willpower to fuck over people and succeed like Tynesha." June sighed, "...All this power your giving her!"

This statement struck my nerves hard. I was not only sobbing from fear but also from the fact that I was close to pursuing pharmaceutical doctors again for help.

June helped me the following day by tracking addresses for EA (Emotions Anonymous) on the web. I rode the BART (Bay Area Rapid Transit) trains to downtown San Francisco. From there I found myself attending an EA meeting at a Catholic church. I was amazed to see and listen to a diverse array of people from multiple racial, religious, and sexually-oriented backgrounds talk about problems similar to mine. Ironically, I feared during one moment that Father would walk in the room any second. At this time, nobody in my family had heard from Father even though his last reported address was somewhere in San Francisco. I left this meeting feeling slightly better.

Despite releasing negative emotions with EA, I still slept with neurotic nightmares portraying Tynesha and Lana as sexual vampires draining my happiness away.

After eating Thanksgiving dinner at Uncle Lewis's house in Davis, California, I flew back to Atlanta. I decided to ponder my life's goals for at least two weeks before further pursuing them. I also used these two weeks to decide whether or not I was going to seek further psychological assistance.

When I arrived at the I.A.G. for the RSC's 2nd Annual Jimi

Hendrix Birthday Tribute, my life's uncertainties became more clouded. Larry explained how Twyla left Atlanta joining her residual North Carolina family to practice missionary work as a Jehovah's Witness. Initially, Larry kept a calm demeanor. But I knew he was hurting since Twyla was both his girlfriend and CCP partner. Since I was still licking my wounds as well, I hinted to Larry that I may be making changes too. We proceeded to have a fun tribute night. However, the fate of the RSC's future was now up in the air.

At the start of my December 2002 trial period, I called Alim. I told him how I was frantic about possibly pursuing another therapist. Alim asked, "Who are you reeling over this time?" I told him, "I'm still not over Tynesha!" Alim giggly sighed, "No! ... Not the same woman!" I replied, "I still can't get her off my mind." Alim snapped, "Everything you still think about is about her. You have 60 thoughts a minute, and 59 of them are about her. Let me ask, 'How long are you going to heal?'" I lingered on, "...I don't know when I'll ever be fully healed. It seems my kundalini chakra keeps bursting with sexual cravings for her even though I consciously know she's not right for me. I'm thinking about taking a Kundalini Yoga class. Alim said, "Yeah! Your kundalini will continue to throw heavy issues at your spirit until you learn how to channel it to your third eye ..." Alim pried deeper, "So why do you keep craving her?" I revealed, "I'm at a turning point in my DJ career right now. I have goals to succeed, but I'm not sure that I have Tynesha's ruthless willpower to fuck over everyone and anyone just to get ahead. In order for me to completely heal from her, some major part of my life must die. I'm not sure if it's my DJ career." Alim advised, "Yes! A major part of you must die! And that part is your emotional imbalances and ill thoughts. Don't give up your passion just to be rid of her. That will only give you more to heal from." I asked him, "But how do I succeed in my career without screwing over others. I can't help but admire Tynesha's willpower. She made it to Europe just as she said she would. She's determined to succeed like Madonna!" Alim fired away, "Her willpower only represents her solar plexus (chakra) opening. That doesn't necessarily mean her spirituality has advanced any further. There are still four higher chakras to reach. Hell! Hollywood movie stars have similar success stories. Like Madonna, they'll fuck and suck whoever it takes to get ahead. Indeed that's strong willpower, but it's not well-rounded progress for the SOUL." I concluded, "Well you're right, but I think I may need to return to a therapist every two weeks for another two years. " Alim recommended, "Well. Give yourself two weeks and maybe just see a therapist only once. But don't allow yourself to recoup forever or you'll never heal!" I thanked Alim for his advice, and I hung up the phone with more hope.

I decided to explore multiple therapeutic options before settling on another recovery program.

First, I tried my initial psychologist Dr. Baskins. However, we played phone tag too much by always leaving messages. Plus, my pay job insurance wouldn't cover my charges well on her out-of –network services.

Then, I tried to set up one last appointment with Dr. L. I left a message, "Hey! I want to have one more intense hypnosis session. If I'm still a wreck, then you don't have to treat me ever again. Thanks for all your bold advice and being my big warrior sister and therapist!" Dr. L never responded. To this day, I still haven't heard from her. In many ways, I felt abandoned. At the same time, I figured this was Dr. L's passive-aggressive way of signaling me to grow up and solve my own problems. Regardless of my resentment towards her, I am grateful for the sessions we had. I wish her well on her life-enhancing endeavors.

While I was still searching for another therapist, I left Larry a phone message saying I needed two more weeks to hibernate before working again with the RSC. Larry called back leaving the following message, "D-Rock! I really need your help running the Rock SOUL-U-TION Core. If you can't do it, then I'll give everyone their money back. Let me know and be well." This message hit home to me. I let my personal problems go too far. So I called Larry back five minutes later saying, "Don't worry Larry! I'll be at the next meeting. I know you're dealing with some stuff too. We're in this together. So we're not going to let the Rock SOUL-U-TION Core die without a fucking fight!" Larry was happy hearing my new-found enthusiasm. Then he set up the next meeting. Coincidentally, he also took a simultaneous two-week hibernation period similar to mine.

I finally decided to undergo a hypnotherapy session from a Jamaican holistic doctor named Sandi. I thought about burning all my pictures of Tynesha, but I decided to keep them and show them to Sandi, so she could conduct her session better.

While I was under hypnosis, she had me visualize my painful relationships with Tynesha and Father. Sandi asked me, "Why are you angry with Tynesha?" I sobbed, "She said we could never be in a relationship ..." Sandi responded, "Tynesha has her own agenda. No need any more to take her rejection as a personal attack. You offered her something great, and she didn't want it. She was rejecting love. Now look into Tynesha's eyes and tell her, 'I forgive you!'" I repeated, "I forgive you!" Then Sandi asked, "... What do you see when you look at your father?" I said, "I see someone angry, hostile, and sad." Sandi churned, "Yes he is sad. Your father is sad about many things. Forgive him too. He is a man that needs much help. He is still trying to reach out to his inner child ... Now, I want you to visualize your inner child. Put your arms around your inner child. Hug him and tell him, 'I will always love you! I will never let you go! I will always be there to protect you from harm and abuse! ..."

I woke up from this state of hypnosis feeling serenely joyous and full of so many tears. I finally made a major step in my life to forgive everyone who hurt me. I carried this vibration into my ARS episode later in the night. I themed this show "Passing of Emotionally (Im)Balanced Spirit." I rectified to my audience that this side of me was now dead. I also decided after my hypnosis session to save the pictures of Tynesha and channel all my painful memories into a future autobiography—this book and a screenplay.

Even though I was filled with an extraordinary sense of hope that I had not felt since I was ten years old (following my preteen suicidal tendencies), I still felt a tremendous amount of fear from upcoming challenges.

Larry left a phone message towards the end of December 2002 saying, "My hibernation period … is officially over! I'm ready to get back to work. Let's hang out for dinner sometime soon." Larry and I met for dinner at The Earl, a band venue/restaurant located in the East Atlanta village. Larry told me that he allowed himself to grieve and be depressed over Twyla's exit. He said he had finally accepted this situation and moved on. I told him how I was still healing from getting played by Tynesha. Larry empathized, "That's how I felt from Twyla. I got played!" I continued releasing my angst, "I finally decided not to let a ho (fuck up my life) …" Larry interjected, "Hey! Let it go!" We ate and chatted for another hour discussing how we would move forward with the RSC and our lives. I told Larry that I would give myself two more years in Atlanta to succeed. If I still didn't accomplish all my DJ goals by the end of 2004, then I would move to another city and succeed. Larry smirked, "You'll (still) be here (in ATL)!" I concluded our chat by telling him that I was going to learn how to face all my pain with the help of a kundalini yoga program. Larry looked at me strangely, with no idea how I would endure any more pain.

I showed up for one more session with Sandi. I thanked her for the therapy. Then I told her that I decided to attend a kundalini yoga class to fix my problems on a regular basis. She humbly accepted my rejection of her qi gong program. Then, she performed an energy healing ritual on me. She placed crystals on various parts of my back while applying some type of telekinetic power. Thus an intense energy vibration rippled on each of my chakras. I was very conscious of these vibrations until she started flicking through a necklace of beads. Suddenly, I felt like a bolt of lightning had struck me. Within a minute, I passed out. When I woke up a few minutes later, I asked Sandi, "What happened?" She said, "You blacked out! That happens often in energy healings. Good luck in future healing classes. Whatever tense emotions you feel for the next couple of weeks, don't fight it! Just go with the flow and know the tension will pass."

Sandi's sessions were a wonderful prerequisite for the yoga classes I subsequently attended. My spirit was finally ready for challenging growth.

As for Lana, we parted permanently.

I called her in January 2003 telling her, "You're not going to like what I have to say … I don't trust you. But I want to build trust with you!" Lana was uncomfortable hearing this at first. But we came to an agreement that we'll be more honest with each other. I promised to let her know when I'm feeling bothered—like when she snapped at my sex-starved issue. She promised to listen better. It appeared that we were on track to become better friends, but my lack of "trust" created too much turmoil.

Lana called me on early Friday morning of January 24, 2003. I told her that I was going back to bed for one more hour before waking up to exercise. Then I told her that I would call back. I called back in the evening suggesting that she meet me at MJQ.

After I got home from MJQ, I checked my messages. The first message played back with Lana snarling, "Hey Albert! After hearing your 'I'm going back to sleep to exercise' crap …, I decided that I need to distance myself from people like you in 2003. I can't be around your type of energy. Don't call me ever again!"

I was shocked but still thought, "Oh well! I guess I need to be distant from certain people to use yoga for aligning my chakras." Then I played back the second message. Lana repeated, "Hey Albert! I can't be around your type of energy. Don't call again!" After this message, I was scared to death. I feared that Lana was ready to drop by my place and shoot me. I wondered, "What did I do to her?" I slept with a nightmare envisioning Lana as some evil witch with orange dreadlocks. I guess her orange hair signified the end of her present stage back in my life, since at the beginning of her last return into my cipher, she wore an orange wig.

Surprisingly, Lana left me a message in November 2003 saying, "Happy Thanksgiving Albert, even though you probably don't celebrate that. I've forgiven you for what you did, and I've been thinking about you. Take care! …" My initial thought was, "What the hell did I do to you in the first place?" After careful consideration, I decided not to return her call. I figured she wasn't worth the risk of trouble anymore.

Perhaps the Universe will strangely have me cross paths with Lana again. And who knows, she may have a short afro while my hair is cut low! Nevertheless, Lana's last appearance in my life signaled how I needed to let go of my isolated behavior. It was time for me to be happy, with or without company. The kundalini yoga would play a major role in filling this void!

SERPENT RISE

Frustration was mounting for me after attending my first kundalini yoga class. Almost 8 years after graduating from college in 1995 and six years after being diagnosed with depression in 1997, I sought guidance from a multitude of gurus: three psychiatrists, two psychologists, three holistic healers, three chiropractors, four 12-step support groups, and over four separate religious temples (Sufiism, African Hebrew Israelites, Buddhism, Moorish Science, etc.). Apparently, there was no settled end to my spiritual imbalances until I got deeply involved in the practice of Kundalini Yoga, a science that I learned about from Tantric Yoga.

Initially, I was intimidated by the complex exercises performed in this class. And so I arranged for the instructor named Ratar, a dark-skinned brother from Arkansas sporting a gray beard and a white turban, to give me a one-on-one session. I wanted him to analyze the best way for me to practice. While I sat on my knees, Ratar started speaking about changes, "... You know that life is all about change. Change happens in everything you do. You can either flow with change or make changes yourself ..." He continued lecturing like a Greek philosopher until I asked him, "But how do I let go of the lies I received from my father?" Ratar replied, "Your father just did what he thought was best at the time. There weren't that many African-Americans on television back then. Sure his actions had negative consequences that came back on him. Yet, the positive ones helped him and his family that included you ..." I was confused by his lecture and continued asking questions about my ill experiences. Ratar responded, "If you're gonna work with me, you have to learn how to listen and follow instructions. You haven't been listening to me. It shows by the way you've been moving while I've been talking." I was shrugging my head and shoulders to prevent further stiffness. I had no intention of offending Ratar, but that's how he perceived it. He proceeded to criticize my attitude towards bad experiences,"... You've had opportunities to be with special women, but you've always sabotaged them." Now, I was offended. Ratar then instructed me to close my eyes and twirl in circles five times. Then he said, "Now open your eyes." I was dizzy. My position was way off from the spot I originally started turning from. Ratar commented, "Your central nervous system is out of whack ... I can tell from your body movements and experiences that you're an addict." I guess I was a drug addict from my pharmaceutical intakes. He ensued, "... There's much work to be done with you. I'll put you on a daily program involving Sat Kriya, cold showers, and waking up at four in the morning ... The question now is not whether you have the desire to do Kundalini Yoga, but if you have the courage ..." He handed me a five-page pamphlet detailing the exercises of Sat Kriya. I left his house feeling very scared!

For one month, I followed the Sat Kriya program. I started each routine by chanting, "*Ong Namo Guru Dev Namo*," which is a Sanskrit saying meaning, "I bow to that creative wisdom that lies within myself." I ended my exercise ritual by singing "*May the long time sun shine upon you. All love surrounds you. And the pure light within you. Guide your way on. Guide your way on. Guide your way on. SAT NAM (*I am the truth, and the truth is my identity.).*" I practiced Sat Kriya three or four days a week and twice during those days (once after waking up and once before I went to sleep.) In the midst of all this, I also attended yoga classes once a week.

Despite this intense regiment, I still felt void of energy, so I called Ratar seeking more help. I told him how I still was engulfed in the throes of depression even after doing Sat Kriya. Ratar was baffled how a person could still feel this way following yoga and meditation. I told him I was almost ready to check myself back into a mental hospital. Ratar responded, "... Thank God you didn't do that." I griped further, "I'm not sure what will work. I've gone through too many doctors and spiritual gurus over the past few years. My energy is still at a rating of 3 or 4 on a scale of 1 to 10." Ratar continued, "All of them gave you programs that weren't effective with very few results. I'm giving you a program that works ..." I bickered, "How are you so sure?" Ratar yelled back, "Look. If you don't ignore certain thoughts and apply this (program) into action, then nothing will work. Just as my daddy told me growing up on a farm in Arkansas, 'You can lead a horse to water, but you can't make him drink.' I can tell you to do something, but I can't make you do it. Do Kundalini Yoga religiously (everyday)! You're welcome to come in for another one-on-one session. I recommend though that you come to a numerology session from my wife. She'll give you good insight on when you'll attract a special woman and the path you'll endure ..."

I was too confused to sign up for the numerology session, but I did get more guidance from Ratar later in the night. I followed Ratar's instructions while he counseled me more about "change." He directed me to do a series of stretches. As I scooted back on my head kicking my legs up into an upside-down stance, Ratar asked me what that position reminded me of. I said, "A stripper!" Ratar boasted, "It looks like that woman (Tynesha) didn't whip your ass enough!" I sighed thinking, "Huh?" One of my last stretches involved lifting my head while curling my legs and arms into a bug position. This was very painful. Ratar noticed my grimace, "You're not loving your movements enough. Did you shower this morning?" I said, "No." He replied, "Do you ever take showers? You need to start taking cold showers. A cold shower every morning! When you wake up, jump right into the cold water and shower every part of your body ... Then rub canola oil all over your body, and shower down again finally with soap ..." I thought this was insane since during February, 2003 we were in the cold season. Yet I had no strong mental capacity to question Ratar's instructions. Ratar then instructed me to kick my legs up for a final jogging exercise. He asked, "What does that remind you of?" I told him, "It reminds me of the last time my body was in great shape." He said, "Do this exercise every time for five minutes when you feel a lack of energy." Ratar sold me a video containing one of his recorded classes. He also gave me an audio tape with a song/chant "Wahé Guru" instructing me to play this every night before I fell asleep.

The next morning I woke up with a tight feeling in my gut. I ignored my obsessive thoughts as I immediately walked into my bathroom. Then I turned on the cold shower water. During the first minute of the water's run, I defecated since I was scared shitless. After flushing the toilet, I slowly stepped into the bathtub. I exhaled about five heavy puffs before finding myself vastly clicking my teeth and rubbing my body quickly under freezing water. I continued to shower with a canola body rub and finished with a soap rub. Seven minutes passed. I got out and buffered my body with a towel. I was relieved to survive my first official cold shower. Every day for the next five months I put myself through this same cold shower process.

A few days after starting my "cold" process, Ratar arranged for me to meet a salesman in DeKalb County. Ratar was a customer and salesperson of the nutritional pills—MSM and Coral

Calcium. He instructed me to purchase more than $200 per month of these products since he felt that my body had become immune to all the herbal supplements I consumed. The salesman boasted, "This stuff really works ... A popular Atlanta morning radio show host took some of this stuff and then gave me praises on his radio show ... So why do you need this stuff?" Ratar answered for me, "He wants his health back." I left the building with my first supply of MSM and Coral Calcium. Ratar smiled, "You're gonna be on fire!"

By late February, 2003 I was busy with multiple activities: waking up with cold showers, yoga, and meditation; taking supplements of MSM, Coral Calcium, and multivitamins while eating breakfast; going to my pay job; coming home, practicing on my DJ equipment, sorting computer files for the RSC and ARS; and doing more yoga, meditation, and supplement intakes before sleeping to the chants of "Wahé Guru!" In the midst of my busy life, my confidence and hunger increased. I was learning better to dodge my relationship obsessions with utter forgiveness. My energy level was gaining much momentum. This was reflected in the bi-weekly RSC Newsletters I wrote and e-mailed to almost 1,000 people. Ironically, I themed my February 11, 2003 RSC Newsletter "Cleansing Celebrations." It detailed how my strict Kundalini Yoga program was cleansing my spirit, especially during the celebratory-filled month of February. Most people I knew responded favorably to my surprising energy surge. Larry was especially thrilled saying, "Damn! Something has inspired you as I've been seeing in your newsletters.

The best example of my newborn fulfillment occurred on February 8, 2003. RSC member, Linora, told me how she owned a CD burner. I told her I was interested in seeing if it would record off my mixer. Thus she allowed me to come over that day to experiment my mixer and an assortment of CDs on the burner. Linora started recording the process while I began an experimental scratch by making scratching loops to SOULFLY's "Fire." I played three more SOULFLY songs in the scratches before engaging in a full-blown 80-minute multi-artist mix CD. After the recording finished, I felt so happy that I envisioned my first recorded mix paving the way for huge amounts of monetary fame and fortune.

After leaving Linora's Decatur home, I stopped to purchase gas. As I drove off heading to the freeway, I remembered how I forgot to screw the cap back on my gas tank. In these types of situations, I usually beat myself up. But since I was still feeling so ecstatic, I moved on to the Pep Boys store and bought a new cap. I drove home still recollecting on one of the most enjoyable "work" days of my life.

Two days later, I told Ratar about this wonderful day. I told him that this day felt unreal. Ratar snapped, "No! That's the reality that we want to see you have every day!" Ratar's persistent coaching kept me humble. Indeed, I was starting to exude a high-spirited behavior that I never knew was possible.

My elated mood continued soaring on the following day after reading an e-mail from someone in the United Kingdom (UK). A DJ named Art Terry explained how Stew (lead vocalist of The Negro Problem) tipped him about ARS. Art then left me details about his radio show in London on 104.1FM, "Is Black Music," which featured sounds by black artists who didn't fit into record company stereotypes. He also welcomed me to network with him. I graciously accepted his dialogue. This e-mail was another divine signal from the Universe that I needed to visit London.

Initially, I didn't plan on going to London until 2004 since I forecasted that my finances would have been more stable then, but I embarked a change of mind after an occurrence at my pay job.

The most pleasant response to my newfound confidence came from a *Creative Loafing (CL)* magazine reporter named Nikhil Swaminathan.

On February 17, 2003, Nikhil emailed asking me to guide him through a possible connection between Cody Chestnutt and a movement of artists he dubbed "a black rock collective." Seemingly, Cody Chestnutt's indie success from his thirty-song album *The Headphone Masterpiece* helped the RSC garner newfound attention. News outlets like *CL* and *The Performer* wrote ads for the RSC in prior publications. However, Nikhil's e-mail marked what would be the RSC's first exposure in a featured article.

With loads of excitement, I e-mailed Nikhil later that night. I copied Larry on this message. Larry called me the next day saying, "... This is a great payoff for all (of) our hard work!" We arranged the interview with Nikhil on the following Saturday. Nikhil interviewed me, Larry, and Linora, who dropped by to help Larry build a pre-production studio.

In the weeks before *CL* released the article, Nikhil exchanged a few more e-mails with me. We also clarified some facts with each other over lunch at my pay job. Initially, he wrote a powerful 3,000-word article in preparation for a front-page display. *CL's* editor, though, decided that our story was not front page news—opting instead to display an indie artist named Cat Power. Therefore, a toned-down piece called "Sound Barriers: In Atlanta, Rock is still a white man's game, so what's a black rocker to do?" was featured in *CL's* March 12, 2003 edition. The RSC was still very pleased.

A few days after the *CL* article was released, I received news that I hadn't won a promotion on my pay job. I wasn't surprised by this since I felt there were better candidates, but when I was told who got the job, I became angered. A temp employee named Brice, who I helped train, won the position over me.

As I entered my yoga class on the following Saturday, I told Ratar how I woke up with leg cramps. He said, "That cramp is probably signaling an unresolved issue ..." I further explained my job snub. Ratar asked, "Is he a white guy?" I said, "Yeah!" Ratar replied, "You may have a lawsuit on your hands..."

On the following Monday, the manager of Brice's job called me in for a meeting. She told me that I was beaten out by Brice because of my body language in the interview. I asked her to explain more. She said that I was sleepy-eyed and did a yoga stretch during the interview which can come across as weird to customers. I laughed off her explanation before barking, "What was really so spectacular about Brice's skills that put him ahead of me?" The manager said, "You'll have to check his skills and match them against yours ..."

After this meeting, I accepted that race was not a factor in Brice's hiring, but I still felt like my snub resulted from bullshit. So I filed a complaint with the Human Resources department. They performed an investigation concluding that the hiring manager needed to be re-coached in some areas but still made the best decision based on her evaluation of both mine and Brice's skills. They also recommended that I never again do a yoga stretch in an interview. This situation was tough for me to put behind.

I was not angry with Brice. As a matter of fact, he and a guy named Rich, who also beat me out for a department promotion, are two of the nicest guys I ever associated with while working at my pay job. They're both progressive musicians who've engaged in great conversations with me despite their Christian beliefs.

However, I was still angry at the department I worked in. So I took this situation as a sign that it was time for me to pursue all my DJ dreams full throttle. I now thought that the Universe told me that my job snub was divine since I didn't have passionate goals there anyways.

I continued to keep my energy upbeat. My yoga exercises were now a daily practice. I maintained and updated my professional and personal schedules on a daily report I called "Personal Expectations for Albert Johnson." After the job snub, I started forecasting daily schedules with imagined work as a full-time DJ. It felt great dreaming about work outside of my "regular" job.

All my DJ planning motivated me to write an outlined business plan to become D-Rock SOUL-Jah full-time. While I was doing this, I received an e-mail from a marketing consultant who asked me to provide her artists for a school fundraiser. Her name was Chimora, self-owner of Rock Net Solutions. She was referred to me by an RSC member named Sfynx. Her company's name struck a chord with me since it was similarly entitled with the network I directed, The Rock SOUL-U-TION Core.

I called Chimora and referenced her request at an RSC meeting. Another RSC member, Taffether, wound up performing at the school fundraiser. Chimora's service sounded top-notch despite my facetious disgruntledness with her overtly Afrocentric views. A week later we ate dinner at Healthful Essence vegetarian restaurant in Southwest Atlanta. I laid out a plan to produce a folder detailing a syndicated radio show proposal. Chimora showed me graphic slides of her past services and I agreed to work with her. She summed up her demands, "I won't start until I get a fifty-percent deposit."

I was making great strides towards becoming D-Rock SOUL-Jah full-time. Chimora was working on my radio show proposal which featured ARS recordings, mix CDS, and new business cards. I was spinning and recording mixes every week at home and on Thursdays at the RSC's open mic sessions at the Black Lion Café.

My life in Atlanta finally seemed stable, but soon more situations would challenge my loyalty to ATL's whole scene.

On the April 10, 2003 edition of RSC Thursday at the Black Lion Café, the featured band didn't show up. I still maintained a positive mood while spinning alternative vibes ranging from laid-back instrumentals to rhythmic hard rock. The attendees though still demanded to hear the booty-shaking norm. A young bubble butt lady with hair extensions ranted, "I wanna dance ..." Immediately following her complaint, the club owner turned off my sound and pumped crunkish hip-hop over the speakers. The vibe was now a second coming of Freaknik. I played along for a few minutes dancing with this lady while the rest of the RSC bounced their shoulders with laughs. Then, I turned off my equipment and packed it in my car feeling disgusted. I channeled my disdain into the April 15, 2003 RSC newsletter entitled "Microphone Fiends." I commented on this night saying that, "If the only way black folks can listen to Rock is Missy Elliot remixing Me'shell Ndegeocello or Ja Rule rapping over Metallica, then D-Rock SOUL-Jah either needs to get paid or split town."

My motivation to "split town" was further incited by the backlash I received at work over my lifestyle changes. I was called into a meeting by Human Resources. They told me several of my co-workers complained about my odor. I laughed this shit off. Sure, the oils I used for cold showers, hair conditioning, and lower back pain relief had strong scents, but I didn't think my co-workers would be too punkish not to talk to me first.

This was the last straw before booking a two-week personal vacation and professional exploration to Europe.

While I was reserving my flight and hotel dates for Europe, I decided to re-open communication with Tynesha. My moods were shinier by this time. I was more willing to forgive everyone and everything. Not to mention, I saw more professional benefits in talking to Tynesha. Ratar summarized this action best to me during a one-on-one session, "She's a success story. And you wanna find out how!"

In May, 2003, I e-mailed Tynesha. I told her in three paragraphs how I've forgiven her and would like to talk to her when I pass through Amsterdam. Tynesha e-mailed back with much glee, "Wow! You're right. That was a surprise. I feel like you're finally growing into the beautiful being I always knew you would become and I'm soooo proud of you ..." She went on to accept my open offer of communication. After this response, I thought, "She's still an arrogant bitch." Nevertheless, I still decided that contacting her would benefit me more-so than shutting her out.

Tynesha and I continued exchanging e-mails while I prepared for the trip. She briefly moved to London but then relocated back to Amsterdam.

My rekindled outlook on personal relationships inspired me to write a metaphysical article in the RSC's May 26, 2003 newsletter entitled, "Christ Children." My words included, "... As a son (sun) of creation, I have experienced Crucifixion from relationships with the two people who I hated most in the world – 1. My "physical" Father who resides somewhere in the Bay Area by the Pacific Ocean; 2. A woman, so-called feminine Holy Spirit (mirror of my Father), who dwells in the Northwestern European Metropolitan Area by the Atlantic Ocean. Even though these entities were my worst enemies, they are also my biggest inspirations for being the Media Guru that I am, and ironically my spirit has called me to explore the music scenes of the areas where they live ..." Indeed my crucified Christ-like spirit was divinely resurrecting!

For five months, I was completely celibate. I didn't even masturbate. All of this changed in the middle of May, 2003. I called Linora one evening and revealed my infatuation for her.

She spoke in a flattered tone but really sounded agitated. She said that she was not ready to be in a relationship since she was focused on building her finance business and reclaiming her spirituality through kundalini yoga. She was taking some of the same classes as me after I gave her a reference.

A couple nights following this call, I jacked off thus ending my five months of celibacy. I was feeling relieved since I decided to release the weight of a "perfect woman" mentality.

My spirit was so free that I also relieved myself from Ratar's class. At the end of what resulted in being my last session with Ratar, he consistently hounded me about attending his wife's numerology session. I snapped at him, "Look! I'm tired of hearing about that ... I'll take it when I'm feeling it." Ratar snapped back, "Now Albert I'm only doing what's best for you ..." I interjected, "Nobody can decide what's best for me except me ..." Ratar bickered, "Well then. I'll keep mentioning it until you do come." I said, "Then I won't listen to you..." Ratar pointed his finger at me, "I'm going to tell you what you're going to do." I spat, "No you're not! I'm leaving." I stormed out of his house into the parking lot. Ratar ran behind me, "Hey! You're lucky my wife was inside (another part of the house) otherwise I would have cussed you out for talking to me like that ... You've begun to feel a little better, but you haven't fully coped with your pain, and it's only going to get worse ..." I retorted angrily, "I know you still want me to take your wife's class. I'm not scared like you say I am. I'm just not feeling it. But since you're challenging me, I'll probably take it soon ..." Ratar preached, "When you first came into this program, your energy level was as you said a 3 or 4 (on a scale of 1 to 10) sometimes dipping to 2. I sensed that you were ready to heal. I could feel your progress ... You're still trying to understand why your father and that girl (Tynesha) didn't live up to your expectations ..." I snapped back, "Hey! I'm a nice guy. Fuck 'em!" Ratar sighed,

"Being nice has nothing to do with it." I ended our squabble saying, "Look! You don't live for me! You don't breathe for me! You don't pay bills for me! You don't shit for me! Therefore you have no say-so in what I decide. So I'll take your wife's class when I decide!" Ratar finally started moving away, "I know nobody can live for you or poop for you. But how come no one else could put you on a program like mine that worked?" I replied, "Thanks. But remember I'm the one who decided to apply it." I started my car. Ratar retreated inside his house after slamming his back door.

While I drove home, I felt the strangest sense of joy. I felt proud of myself for finally having the courage to stand up to Ratar like a man instead of following his instructions like I always did. I also thought, "Pay $50 for a numerology class? Man I'd rather fuck a cheap ass ho." Lo and behold, I immediately spun through the pages of *CL*. I called an escort service requesting one of their girls. I told the madam I wanted the female to wear a black shirt with blue jeans and shoes showing her pretty toes. The madam asked facetiously, "What (nail) color do you want her toes to be?" I told her, "Preferably red or silver, but I'm cool regardless." The madam told me to have two hundred dollars in cash ready and that a girl would arrive in a few hours.

While waiting for my "ho," I made necessary preparations. I drove to an ATM machine and withdrew $200. After arriving back home, I placed a steak knife and the money in a secret location in case the ho attempted to rob me. Next I called my best friend Amen with the scoop, "You're gonna think I'm crazy for doing this, but I ... um ... I've made arrangements to have sex with a prostitute ..." Amen was silent for ten seconds before replying, "There's nothing wrong with that! What led you to finally make this decision?" I told him, "My yoga instructor kept hounding me to take his wife's numerology class. Plus, he constantly fed me bullshit about waiting for the perfect woman. I decided, 'Fuck a date.' On a date, you have to pay for the woman's attention, and you're still not guaranteed pussy ... Therefore, I'd rather fuck a ho." Amen agreed, "Yeah! I can see what you're saying. I don't think a numerology class is worth all that either ... Do you have a gun?" I told him, "No. It was taken from me after my last (mental) hospital visit. But I do have a knife stored in a safe place. Plus, I called you to see if you got my back just in case this ho tries to jack me with a whole slew of crooked muthafuckas." Amen supported me, "Go ahead Bro! Get your freak on! Call me in case shit gets out of hand."

After I hung up with Amen, I gathered my condoms from my bathroom and played a couple of soft CD tracks on my boombox. The ho finally arrived an hour later than I reserved. A shiny black Mercedes stopped in my apartment's parking lot. It stayed there while a cute, petitely-shaped, beige-complexioned honey with a curly ponytail entered my place wearing everything I requested.

I pulled off her sports jacket and settled her onto my couch while pumping the soft music on my stereo. Briefly, I relaxed and chatted with her, "So tell me a little about yourself!" She spoke, "My name is Trisha ... I'm a student at Georgia Perimeter College ... I have a boyfriend ..." I asked, "Does he know you're doing this?" She said, "No!" I further asked, "So how did he charm you, and what does it take for a woman like you to finally feel attraction?" Trisha said, "He slipped me notes under my desk in class. He's proof that if you come strong with your game, then a woman will reward you." I asked one more question, "So why is a nice young lady like you about to have sex with me?" She explained, "I need the money! I'm relocating from New York down here." The New York logo on her black t-shirt showed her roots. I finally shut up and commenced to lick her toes. I asked her to release her ponytail. She obliged further to get me in the mood. I started to kiss her lips. She briefly shrugged off laughing, "You like kissing a lot!" I licked her toes for five more minutes before leading her into the bedroom. She was enjoying the music. She even grinded her hips a little. I kicked off my shorts joking, "You don't want to get pregnant. Right?" She laughed in a shy tone with her cute smile while I slipped on a condom. She gently squeezed my scrotum to further excite me. I turned off the lights. And then I penetrated her vagina, "Hmmmn? You're tight! Let's see what I can do to loosen you up." I licked her breasts, kissed her cheeks, and poked and stroked her for twenty minutes. I was becoming bored with only penetrating her vagina. She seemed to enjoy it as she continuously pulled my penis back into her cunt every time I slipped out. After I ejaculated, I asked her for a blowjob. She nervously said, "I gotta go!" I pouted, "Well. Can we do it one more time?" She refused again, "I gotta go. But you are a very nice person!" She got dressed. I gave her coat back along with $200. I felt so unfulfilled that I masturbated after she left. Amen called me hours later just to make sure I was still safe.

Despite my emptiness over this meaningless sex act, I still felt a newfound freedom like I had never known. I was now compelled to act and speak without worries of consequences. I continued to channel my awakened serpent on and off the airwaves.

Subsequently, I canceled my subscription for Coral Calcium and MSM. I found cheaper brands at health food stores.

I decided after all to call Ratar's wife to set up a numerology session. However, she refused to give me service, "I don't want you taking this feeling you've been coerced to do so. I spoke with Ratar about how he tried to push you into a session before you blew up at him. He swore he would never do that again … I think you should stick with the kundalini yoga …" I thought, "Coerced? Man, forget both of them!"

I went on to take yoga classes at other locations before settling at home, deciding that I should practice yoga in a mostly private environment.

I was feeling so free that I flowed happily with whatever urge I had. I remember feeling so high on a Saturday night that I walked and drove anywhere without worries of any type of schedule and finances (i.e. job, deejaying, yoga, etc.). I ended up retreating home by renting the stupidest movie I could find—*The Friday After Next*.

In the midst of my free-spirited vibe, my wild sexual ride was coming fully into fruition like never before. At an RSC Thursday function, I took pictures of pretty feet from three women. One of these women, RSC member Nedrah, wound up bitch-slapping me when she angrily reacted to my rant "I'm going to fuck some more hoes."

I heavily anticipated my trip to London and Amsterdam. There were now about six weeks remaining before I traveled there. I still couldn't wait to get freakier. I despised Atlanta for not being receptive enough to the RSC and the whole Urban Rock movement. I channeled all this pent-up energy into ARS episodes and RSC newsletters.

On the weekend following my fornicating escapade, I happily announced on ARS, "I got busy with a prostitute." The audience seemed to enjoy the anticipation I gave them leading up to the announcement when I said, "Me and Bill Clinton have more in common than you think." Larry reacted with joyous surprise, "I knew you eventually had to get just a little dirty in order to loosen up."

The following ARS episode though was my worst and most forgettable. After lashing out at the organizers of the SOUL Sista's Juke Joint function for not providing enough of a Heavy Music vibe during their June 6, 2003 show at the Apache, I realized an epiphany, "I hate Black Women." Even though my mind perceived this feeling as bad, I didn't feel bad since I accepted this as truth. So I went on ARS telling the world that I had experienced a phase of hating black women. I even considered playing Body Count's "Mama's Gotta Die Tonight." Thankfully though, I decided at the last moment to nix this song since WRFG literally could have been killed by the FCC. After this episode, I felt an awful feeling. I had better ways to constructively express my frustration, so I themed the June 18, 2003 RSC Newsletter "Ho Nest." I had a ton of fun expressing my plea for legalized prostitution. Lots of people on my e-mail list were amused. But far more people were generally offended by the review I wrote about the SOUL Sista show. Ironically, the only e-mail of concern I received was from one of the SOUL Sista organizers who only asked why I felt so angry. Most of the backlash was expressed to me by Larry at an RSC meeting. He told me, "I've been getting a lot of bad feedback about your last newsletter. I guess you can say it was controversial, especially when you said, 'This aura (lack of rock vibes) sent me into a tailspin of temporary hatred for Black Women.' Dayum ... Coupled with the Ho Nest vibe, people didn't like what you said. They felt you disrespected the Sistas." I responded, "I stand by what I said. It was healthy and a true expression of anger." The RSC concurred. However, they decided that I must use a disclaimer on all future newsletters. I obliged. I still didn't think that my "Ho Nest" expressions would have a long-term negative impact on me and the RSC. Boy was I wrong!

My hatred phase of black women was also channeled negatively towards Chimora. She called me one day advising me not to use the *CL* article in my portfolio because "The European will throw it in the trash" out of fear they (radio executives) can't control me. She also said with a little anxiety, "You hear that guy on morning talk radio. He raises much hell. Just sign the contract first. Then you'll eventually be able to say what you want." I lashed out at her calling this advice "paranoid Afrocentric garbage." I further expressed how this was part of the reason I hated black women. Chimora was hurt, "No, no, no. You said a curse word and yelled at me. I'm going to cry." I felt absolutely horrible after this conversation. I ended up in the bathroom releasing my own healthy dose of tears.

Later in the evening, I met Chimora for dinner to discuss more of my portfolio. I apologized for my outburst and paid for her meal. From this point forward, Chimora only communicated with me from a professional standpoint. She finished my "UniverSOUL Rock" radio show proposal—which was comprised of nineteen pages, mix CDs, ARS tape recordings, business cards, an RSC newsletter, and the *CL* article. I ordered nineteen copies of this portfolio.

Chimora gave me good advice about trying to copyright the "UniverSOUL Rock" radio show title in case radio stations tried to copy my idea. Unfortunately, I researched some information revealing how radio shows can't be copyrighted. I was still excited about sending this portfolio to prospective radio stations to let that faze me. I was still feeling wild and in the best shape of my life while channeling all the energy I acquired from kundalini yoga.

My "wildness" was directed more constructively on ARS!

On the June 25, 2003 edition of ARS, I invited my best friend Amen to join me for a discussion themed "Domestic Abuse SOUL-U-TIONS." Despite the serious nature of this subject, we had a ball. We shared many laughs revealing how we almost threw our fists at women who were our worst relationship experiences.

Off the air, my wild tirade continued. I wound up paying over three hundred dollars for a foot fetish service at an adult entertainment venue called Fantasy Fare. Despite my joy over licking a pretty mocha-beige woman's feet, I felt drained after this night since I didn't get any pussy. Amen confirmed to me afterwards that this place was "a rip-off."

Overall, my mood was still unquelled until my association with Linora fell apart. Linora left the RSC in April, 2003 claiming Larry made uncomfortable advances toward her. She told me this in strict confidence. This caused some minor friction between me and Larry. I only told him that three anonymous women labeled him a sleaze. He bitterly refuted this claim pledging, "I love women." Larry and I settled this dispute peacefully.

I continued to reach out to Linora for friendship. I didn't think there would be any issues by giving her a present for her fourth of July birthday. All I wanted to do was show her how much I appreciated her assistance with RSC and ARS by giving her a few copies of ARS episodes. So I left her a phone message requesting her address. I also mentioned how I would drop off the gift by her house if I didn't hear back from her. Linora responded by phone and e-mail, but her tone caught me off guard. First her bitter e-mail said, "I've made myself very clear to you DRock that I have no romantic interest in you ... Nor am I attracted to you in any way. Do not drop by my place because that would be completely unacceptable ... And take me off your RSC list ..." The subject line to her e-mail was a response to my "Ho Nest" newsletter. Apparently, she was disgusted with what I wrote and now wanted to disassociate from me. I was disappointed but remained calm. Then I played back my phone messages. I heard her say the same thing in a bitter yet affectionate tone. She soothed, "... I appreciate your offer for a gift but I don't want to send you the wrong message. You can call me back perhaps in a month. I'll send you an e-mail relaying this message as well ..." Once I heard all this, I felt an utter sense of betrayal. I understood how she wasn't attracted to me, but I still thought I meant enough to her as a friend to give her a gift. I commenced to drive to her place without fear of her disapproval. I decided I was going to leave her alone after dropping off the gift. When I arrived, Linora's roommate answered the door. She told me Linora wasn't around. I told her to leave the package with Linora and that it was nice knowing both of them. I also left Linora a note on the package saying that it was her choice whether or not to enjoy it. I didn't think I'd even hear from her again. To my surprise, Linora boldly instilled a deep array of fear in me the next day. She left me a phone message at WRFG and filed a police report threatening to have me arrested if I ever dropped by her place again. Suddenly, I was shaken with disbelief. I couldn't believe that so much drama was heaped upon me over a gift.

Immediately, I called Larry seeking more clarification behind Linora's warped personality. Larry mentioned how Linora and him had a nice time hanging out together. Linora apparently liked hugging Larry and enjoyed getting high with him. Larry couldn't explain her sudden departure either except to say that she may have not wanted to get high anymore. I also sensed that Linora's proclaimed sexuality as "a qualifiable bisexual" also contributed to her fickleness.

I was now humbled by sudden social outbursts against me. Even Amen e-mailed me expressing his disdain towards me for rejecting his request for an interview about his Jeet Kun Doo martial arts class. I explained to him how ARS had strictly been focused on music with the exception of prior episodes due to personal issues. Amen and I got back on good terms. However, it was now clear that I was in dire need of a break from Atlanta. My vibe was too overbearing for this metro area as I started to push away even my closest allies. I thought about continuing my personal escapades on ARS. I even considered calling out Linora as Miss "Mute" Heifer from my greatest "DISS-MISS-AL" and "DIS-MISS-BITCH" lists. Yet after my squabbles with

Amen, it was time to get ARS back to strictly music programming while preparing for my birthday party and European trip.

With help from the RSC, I arranged my pre-thirtieth B-Day bash at a loft owned by Urban Mediamakers founder, Cheryle Reynolds. While I enjoyed promoting this event with newsletter and flyers, I also received a bad omen.

My last loctician (dreadlock stylist) remained unresponsive to me when I told her about my "Black Women Hate Phase." And so I found a new stylist. During my first session with Maasili, I communicated to her that I wanted part of my locks cut. I pointed my hand to a various location of my head. Maasili asked, "Are you sure?" I said, "Yeah!" Minutes later I saw my locks were cut in half, and I freaked out. After going through depression that weekend, I positively stated that the haircut was divine since I needed to release the angry vibes of past locticians. It also may have been karma similar to the Samson & Delilah bible story, where a man loses his hair over a woman. My hate phase over black women coupled with my recent ho explorations likely signaled the sudden change for my hair.

Regardless of this shock, I was still excited about my birthday celebrations. The flyer was themed "D-Rock is turning 30 - 'Bout F*ckin' Time!!!" The RSC party didn't have a good turnout since the location was difficult for attendants to find. Nevertheless, I deejayed the night and was thankful for the support from the RSC and the few party guests. They sang "Happy Birthday" to me after I did my spinning Carlton Banks/Bruce Springsteen "Dancin' in the Dark" type-moves to Linkin Park's "Somewhere I Belong."

My disappointment with the RSC's money loss over my birthday party didn't last long. Hours after the party ended, I was on a plane to London.

Once I was cleared through customs at London's Gatwick Airport, I hopped on train towards a transit station as instructed by Art Terry. About an hour after I arrived at the station, I spotted a swarthy brown skin brother with a smooth bald head and clean-shaven face. I knew immediately this was Art since we gave detailed descriptions of our physical appearances during one of our phone conversations. We smiled and hugged each other like brothers.

Art walked me through his neighborhood. He gave me brief historical accounts of how a few of the buildings were rebuilt after World War II. Once we unloaded my luggage in his 3-bedroom high-rise apartment near the Tate Museum, I laid out flat to sleep for the whole day. I woke up around 4:30pm.

Art commenced further as my unofficial tour guide showing me more streets of his neighborhood where artists and musicians thrived. Then we ate at an Indian restaurant. Art told me that I was one of his heroes on the radio. He admired journalists like me and Nelson George for keeping the progressive music fight alive in the United States. Art further explained how he arrived in Europe from Los Angeles in his mid-twenties, landing multiple gigs through his singing and keyboard skills. I asked him why he settled in London. Art told me that he would have stayed in Amsterdam if he hadn't gotten involved with a British woman who subsequently birthed two of his three children. Art concluded his introductory story by telling me how he makes his living as a piano teacher to support his work as a songwriter/musician/journalist. I proceeded to tell him how I purposely came to London and Amsterdam to submit my radio portfolios, business cards, and mix CDs to several radio outlets and club circuits. I also told him about my frustration with the U.S.'s responses to my DJ vibes and how I intended to put closure on a woman (Tynesha) in Amsterdam. Art interrupted, "Whoa! You sound like a completely different person when you talk about her! And it's scary....Perhaps, Europe is what you need for awhile."

After we walked back to Art's place, he gave me a magazine that listed all the venues for London's music scene. I wasted no time hopping a train to a different part of town. There was an interesting heavy music band that had I read about. By the time I arrived at the bar, they finished their performance. I didn't let this letdown deter me before moving on to another club that was blocks away. This spot played mostly house music, which I hate. Regardless, I swayed along with the crowd for about two hours and took pictures with some cute women. After I left, I suddenly realized that the Tube (London's rail system) had shut down for the night. I was bewildered. Next, I boarded a bus destined for the Westminster section. After I was dropped off, I kept walking, thinking I was closer to Art's place. Yet in actuality, I became more lost and called Art from a pay phone. He graciously met me near a bridge at approximately 4am. I was very lucky to make it through my first London night.

The next day, Art and I rode a bus and walked towards downtown London. We crossed a street leading out of his neighborhood. As I began to take a step, Art pushed my belly back before I spotted a car driving towards me in the blink of an eye. Amazingly this near death experience proved to be a divine warning for me to act responsibly on my gleeful European exploration.

Art continued to guide me downtown. We walked through Trafalgar Square. Art pointed to a building which housed the South African Embassy and said, "This is how we remember Britain's involvement with South African apartheid." We walked to an artsy district loaded with shops and record stores. I was elated seeing such a wonderful amalgamation of people whose racial backgrounds I couldn't identify. I introduced myself to about three people. Art was baffled, "You have this catch vibe that people cling to. It amazes me!"

After we returned to Art's and reflected on a nice hangout

day, I returned to London's night scene. This time, I made sure I was in close proximity to the open operations of the Tube. As I walked towards the Metro Club, a young man walked towards me asking, "Do you have any weed?" I laughed and walked onto the Metro Club.

At this place, I stood around and watched a hard rock band dressed in motorcycle-clad leather called The GA GAs. Their members were a mixture of Brazilian and Japanese immigrants. Their manager gave me a CD after I told him about my DJ credentials. I also took pictures of some cute young ladies—a Sri Lankan woman who already had a boyfriend and the only black female I saw in the place.

After this set, I was still in the mood to groove, so I walked to another club located in an alleyway. This club's interior had a luxury setting despite the fact that it catered to mostly kids 18 and up. The DJ was playing mostly mod/Brit-pop music. I wasn't feeling it. However, I continued to take pictures with more cute young ladies. Suddenly, I was asked by another white male if I had any weed. I retreated back to Art's place on the Tube without trouble from the bearings.

On Tuesday, July 29 (the eve of my thirtieth birthday), Art walked me to his show's radio headquarters, Resonance 104.1FM. While we walked over a bridge, I snapped distant pictures of an erected Egyptian obelisk.

As Art and I set up for an episode of "Is Black Music," he introduced me to several radio staff members including his co-host Amber Don along with her husband Elan Pulushko. Amber then passed me some headphones. From this moment right onto the beginning of Art's broadcast, I felt like a pampered Lion King in the country often referred to as Mother England (i.e. Mother Lion while U.S. is often referred to as Baby Lion or Babylon).

Art launched into the show broadcasting a recorded radio promo featuring Public Enemy's Flavor Flav. Then he played an acoustic instrumental while introducing me. With much excitement, I quickly championed myself as "D-Rock SOUL-Jah" representing WRFG Atlanta, 89.3FM and the "Dirty South." Art proceeded to play two songs off the RSC Compilation CD— "My Ghetto" by Edenrage and "On my Way" by Twyla. Then, we launched into an interview. Art asked, "What brings you to London?" I said that London contained artists with the coolest amalgamated sound out of all the songs I featured on ARS from artists all over the world. I mentioned how I was inspired by several multicultural London bands: Dub War, Morcheeba, Skunk Anansie, Primal Scream, and Asian Dub Foundation. Next, Art asked me to give him a brief history of my involvement with Atlanta's Black Rock scene. I gave a brief explanation of how ARS got started and evolved into an outlet for "UniverSOUL" rock artists. Art proceeded to play a cut by Kelsy Davis and The Radical SOULs, another RSC member. While this song was playing, I spoke briefly with Amber off the air. Our conversation about Sean "P.Diddy" Combs' acting portrayal of blues legend Robert Johnson spilled over onto the airwaves. I didn't intend to talk about this, but the topic reflected my passionate angst against Mass Media pop images. This conversation virtually concluded my interview.

For the rest of the episode, Art played other black alternative tracks. Then he introduced me to a couple of editors of a black alternative lifestyle magazine called *DRUM*. Paul and Mbeti repeatedly spoke the magazine's motto, "Live Life to a Different Beat." Their conversation was very friendly. Even though I was slightly annoyed by having my interview time shared with them, I had fun vibing as an in-house guest. I cracked up when Mbeti said I looked like Osama Bin Laden.

The July 29, 2003 episode of "Is Black Music" concluded with Paul and Mbeti saying how *DRUM* is a free publication distributed to the Black Diaspora all over the world, especially

Gambia, West Africa, where they sold out five thousand copies. Paul himself is a mixture of Ghanaian and Jamaican parents who raised him in London. I gave my final radio shot-outs to Larry, RSC artists, and yelled out the call letters for WRFG's website.

After the show, I hung out in the studio for a few minutes. I spoke with Amber and Elan about my guest residency. Since Art needed to make room for his kids, I asked Amber if I could stay over at her place. Amber and Elan said it was cool.

Art continued to introduce me to more staff members of Resonance 104.1FM. I told them how I was visiting London to market my DJ services. As Art and I exited the building, Art chastised me, "Whoa! Cats in there weren't feelin' you. They expected you to be Mr. Underground, but you flipped it with them talking 'bout how you're interested in commercial syndication." I responded by telling Art how I'm tired of being an unpaid DJ. Art said, "Most DJs here (London) would kill to have a radio show ..." Art and I continued our discussion before he ventured to his piano teaching. I told him, "Man. How times have changed! I thought I would visit Africa before Europe. But deeper exploration into my DJ career brought me here first." Art smiled, "Times ain't changed BRO. You've changed ..."

Art walked away, and I trotted into a nearby café. Ironically, I spotted the *DRUM* editors being interviewed by an Afrikaner who worked at Resonance. I sat by them and gave a deeper account of my experience as a Rock DJ. After I finished my chat and saluted them farewell, a gray-haired Englishman interjected, "Teach black kids about jazz! It's classier!" I told this bloke that young kids, especially black kids will always vibe more towards heavier music. He said, "Yeah, but for Texas rednecks that come through here (London) and say that blacks invented nothing, I tell them about jazz ... I have a grandson and he's black. I'm going to teach him about jazz." This conversation was very enlightening. It symbolized to me how London was the only city in the world I ever visited where racially mixed couples were no big deal.

After eating at two more sandwich shops and briefly returning to Art's place, I ventured back to London's club scene. Again, I landed at the Metro Club. And for the third time, a resident (this time a young man of Middle Eastern or South Asian descent) asked me for me some weed. Despite this petty array of racism, I was still excited more about the current night.

Two bands were scheduled to play followed by spins from a group of Rock DJs.

The first band to play called Freedom was dressed in American-flagged garb. Their lead vocalist/guitarist had a painted American-flagged clown face. There were also at least three female dancers shaking their booties while hyping up the crowd. Even though I wasn't feeling this band's sound, I was very amused by their silly display of angry political antics. I also noticed that one of their roadies wore a black T-shirt entitled, "Fuck George Bush." After their performance, I shook hands with the bass player telling him, "I'm from America, and I agree with your roadie's T-shirt." He smiled back, "You can have Tony Blair too!"

The second band that followed was called Carnival of SOULs. Their sound reminded me of early U2 spliced with some of The Police. I was digging it so much that I started hopping like Bob Marley. Their performance served as a wonderful pre-requisite for the Rock DJs. After they finished, I immediately shook their hands, praised their show, and grabbed a CD after revealing my DJ qualifications.

And then, the ultimate nightclub experience started!!!

A DJ immediately began the set with a song from Nirvana's first album. The people on the floor scattered to make room for the dancers and moshers. Carnival of SOULs pulled their last amplifier off the stage. A few people began dancing on the stage. I joined in, twirling in a Bruce Springsteen/Carlton Banks/Bob

Marley-esque fashion. The DJs played a couple more songs before flipping on Linkin Parks's "Fade." After this cut, the floor and the stage were completely full. The crowd energy was so hot that I took my shirt off. The DJs launched into a ferocious alternative hard rock mix. I wanted to dance with a cute young lady wearing a red tank-top, black sweatpants, and two ponytails. She shrugged me off twice while dancing in a hip-hop fashion. I paid it no mind. I was feeling so jubilant that I just kept dancing, taking pictures, and giving high fives to all the young men on stage (including a young black brother sporting a Slipknot shirt). I put my wallet to the side of a speaker along with my WRFG shirt. I was feeling so wonderful that I didn't even worry at all throughout the night if it would be stolen and how I would get back to Art's home. I continued to do a hip-hop-esque dance on stage, swaying my hands over the black clothes-clad crowd of heavy music fans. They moshed and crowd-surfed in circular pits to songs like "Aerial" by System of a Down and "Jumpdafucup" by SOULFLY featuring Slipknot's Corey Taylor. Then, the DJs suddenly flipped on a track by Dr. Dre featuring Snoop Dogg. A lady to my left, who wore a plaid miniskirt under a leather tank-top, was grinding her butt, hinting for me to dance with her. I quickly grinded behind her and slithered my hands from her hips all the way up to her chin. I grinded with her twice more that night while she puffed away on cigarettes.

The DJs proceeded to pound away other styles of rock mixes: punk, ska, hard rockin' mod, speed metal, industrialized alternative, etc.. A lot of their selections didn't match my DJ style, but I was still ecstatic about finally arriving in an environment displaying DJs very similar to me. The most surprising cut they played was a rock remake of Adina Howard's "Freak Like Me." I was so jolly that I stood on a rack holding the lights. Then I started grinding like a stripper. While I did this, I saw a male metalhead with long hair break-dancing and pop-locking. This was the coolest thing I ever saw. Three more young blokes dressed in casual buttoned-tops and blue jeans swayed their arms to my rhythm. I smiled back and kept partying like there was no tomorrow.

I danced more, took pictures of some more cute girls (especially the rarely seen black ones), graciously praised the DJs, and splashed a ton of water on my body. This night, the eve into the early morning of my thirtieth birthday, proved to be the greatest vibrant night of my entire life. I roared out of my twenties and into my thirties with an incredible bang. The Metro Club died down at 3am. I was finally ready to cool off. As I exited, the hot grinding Brit girl who smoked a lot tapped on my shoulder. All I gave her was a head nod. My attitude was that I was in London focusing solely on advancing my persona as D-Rock SOUL-Jah. So I let her go. When I walked outside, the rain was pouring hard. I wasted no time catching a cab back to Art's place. I arrived back and dove into a deep fantasy sleep reflecting on this monumental time of sheer joy. I finally found the throne for my kingdom. YEEEEE-AAAY-AH!!!

I didn't wake up until about 3pm in the afternoon of my thirtieth birthday. Art arrived home from his job. Then we hopped on the Tube to Amber & Elan's house in Willesden Green. While we sat on their front porch drinking tea, the conversation erupted on the topic of race relations. I was intrigued hearing Elan, the son of Jewish immigrants who escaped Nazi Germany, say that African-Americans should receive reparations. I threw my two cents into the chat saying how the U.S. government was too bankrupt to give blacks anything and how the majority of blacks would spend it up in less than two years if they were compensated. I then suggested that a separate sovereign country may be the only hope for all progressive Americans. Amber jumped in, "America is our (blacks and progressive people) country, we shouldn't have to separate." Even though this discussion was heated, I felt very amused to have an open dialogue like this with a racially mixed couple. I also remember facetiously mentioning how George W. Bush was so ignorant that he didn't even know that black people lived in Brazil.

After this delightful exchange of opinions, Elan drove us all to a neighborhood hub. Art purchased my drink as a birthday gift. Then we toasted, took pictures, and watched a couple of bands perform. One band featured an acoustic musician with two Afro-Caribbean conga players. The other band was a multicultural R&B act who also recited poetry. Their guitarist/keyboardist was a nineteen-year old with dreadlocks named Verbona. She said to me with her eccentric British accent, "You look like you're in a heavy metal band." I chuckled and then told her about my Rock DJ credentials. As this band wrapped up their set, they sang happy birthday to their bass player and also gave me a birthday shot-out. I took a picture with Verbona before giving her a business card. Elan and Amber drove home while I walked with Art and his friend back to her place.

While we walked, I noticed how London neighborhoods are very reminiscent of New York high rise buildings. Art told me that London's neighborhoods are just like any other urban area in the world except that one doesn't feel fearful of guns in London like everywhere else. Art mentioned that England has restrictions so tight that most of their police also don't pack guns. Art then warned me how London has a high rate of illegal prostitution imports of children from all over the world, especially Africa and the Middle East. Coincidentally, I would later learn about more of these sex slaves in Amsterdam.

We hung out at his friend's place for about two hours. I asked the young lady, "Who's this in the picture (that of a young black girl)?" She said, "That's my niece!" I was really curious since Art's friend was a white woman. I began to ask if she had a sibling that was married to someone black. She told me, "She (her niece) is adopted!" This just gave me another positive view of London as a multicultural paradise (if ever such a city existed).

Art and I left, walking back to his place. He gave me more insight about Amber & Elan since I was checking into their place the following day. He told me how Amber was like his little sister since she grew up near him in his L.A. neighborhood. It didn't cease to amaze me how Europe was presented to me as a safe haven for world music artists, especially those of black African descent.

The next day I relocated to Amber & Elan's. Art came over later in the afternoon with his kids. He had Elan help him edit an interview he did with Public Enemy's Chuck D. Amber fixed some snacks and hosted two more of her friends, a racially mixed couple (a white man and his black wife of Nigerian descent) who were both aspiring musicians. Again, I was involved in another heated dialogue about race relations. This time the conversation shifted to talk about how every person must work towards a healthy relationship. Amber responded to my frustrated expression over bad relationships by saying, "... After my bad relationship, I had to look deep inside myself to find out what was wrong. Soon as I got that straight, I was open to new and healthy relationships." We all commenced to eating catered snacks along with fish and chips.

Amber and her friends puffed away on cigarettes. This was another example pinpointed to me how residents of London smoke, drink, and eat crappy foods more regularly than Americans. Yet, they also seem to dwell more peacefully amongst each other than Americans.

Later in the evening, I ventured to another club. This place had murky scenery with gothic industrial sounds. I was digging the vibe until a group of keyboard players started performing. This slowed the vibration. So I channeled my energy elsewhere and took a picture of a mulatto woman with dreadlocks kissing her blonde boyfriend after she got drunk off Tequila. Then I exited the club.

I boarded a bus and hopped off about three exits sooner than I was supposed to. I ended up walking a far distance before calling Elan, telling him that I was lost. While I waited, I figured out the correct bearings. Thus I made it back to Amber & Elan's house. Elan arrived back later. I apologized for having him leave the house. Elan was cool and nonchalant about this mess.

I woke up the next morning as Elan fixed toast and tea. He also showed me some of the artifacts hanging in his house. Some of the items included primitive African string and percussion instruments. Elan told me how he acquired those instruments while visiting Africa. I listened closely while he preached how the oldest strings, horns, and drums were invented in Africa. Elan also said, "There have been black kings and queens in Europe ... We need to teach the kids more about other cultures." I added my knowledge into his lecture by saying how all humans originated from dark-skinned Africans. Elan interjected, "But there have been people of every complexion since the beginning of time ..." I responded, "Sure humans come in every shade, but it wasn't always like that. I think that we need to correct miseducation about human origin by teaching how white people came onto this planet from both adaptation and albinism." Elan listened very closely, but our conversation was cut short once Amber woke up. I was still very relieved about having constructive dialogue that dove deep into human skin origins. Years prior, I was too angry and narrow-minded to talk with a white person like this without using racial slurs.

For my last three days in London, I continued to enjoy the city's wonderful display of liberal multiculturalism.

I visited one more rock music club located in an alleyway of downtown London. The same rock DJs from the Metro Club spun mostly punk/ska and Brit-pop on a huge dance floor filled with mostly British teenagers. I passed the DJs a copy of my first recorded mix CD, and I wound up dancing mostly on the second floor. It contained a lounge area with DJs spinning mostly American pop and hip-hop as well as a bar area where DJs were spinning metal. I took loads of pictures in this area before dancing in a circular pit when the DJ spun "Roots" by Sepultura. This night's vibe was okay. Yet, I was a little disappointed that none of these DJs spun any of my favorites like SOULFLY, P.O.D., Sevendust, etc..

On Friday, I learned about some of London's history at the London Museum. The most interesting fact was how the Romans originally called the city London based on its loads of metal called Londinium.

On the next day, a Saturday, I toured another museum as recommended by Elan and Amber. The British Museum was full of ancient Egyptian artifacts that I originally saw on a videotape called *The African Origins of Civilization* by Ashra Kwesi. I had some tourists take pictures of me in front of the mummies and walked on to a theatre and watched an American independent movie called *Buffalo Soldiers*.

Later in the day, I traveled through the predominantly black section of London called Brixton. An RSC member who use to live in London recommended, this section, which was vastly becoming more integrated. Some blacks were unhappy about that. I was just happy to visit this area. I finally ate some authentic spicy Nigerian food outside of the British norm of crappy sandwich shops coupled with greasy fish & chips. I also bought some plantains just as Amber requested.

While I rode the bus back to Willesden Green, I had a nice chat with a young lady from New Zealand. I told her that I was flying to Amsterdam the next day. She boasted, "Cool! Anyone who goes to Amsterdam is cool with me. They got mad weed." She went on to tell me that she lived with six roommates and traveled to several European cities experiencing life like a drifting gypsy. I started thinking, "If I was ten years younger, faster, and hyper; I would live here in London with five or six roommates pursuing my DJ career." Indeed London proved to be a very fast moving, expensive, and exhausting city for working class artists. I enjoyed all my eight days in this metropolis. I accomplished a lot professionally by dropping off my portfolios to radio stations and clubs. Personally, I felt a ton of relief by hanging with people whose vibes were similar to mine. Now it was time for me to go to Amsterdam, kick back in more of a resort vibe, and settle my ills with Tynesha.

On the following Monday, I flew into Amsterdam and settled at a hotel. My anxiety over not knowing Dutch was quickly squashed when I picked up a map at the city's Grand Central Station. It didn't take long for me to discover that practically every Dutch person (from 10-80 years old) speaks fluent English. The more I spoke with Dutch residents the more embarrassed I became as a spoiled one-language speaking American. Regardless of disdain over my American ignorance, I proceeded to enjoy the city's surroundings.

On my first night, I wasted no time exploring the famous Red Light District. Earlier, I tried contacting Tynesha by phone. The number was out of service. Nevertheless, I came to Amsterdam with the attitude, "If things don't work out with Tynesha, then I'm going to have fun and get some!" So I walked through downtown Amsterdam witnessing firsthand their "legal" displays of gambling, marijuana distribution, pornography, and prostitution. I didn't care for the casinos, pot-smoking coffee bars, and porn shops. But I was still destitute on purchasing poontang.

As the evening grew into night, loads of scantily-clad hookers were on display posing like models through red light windows. These prostitutes were from almost every persuasion and ethnicity around the world. The predominantly male on-lookers and soon-to-be customers had origins from the whole Earth as well. I soon learned that Amsterdam has a large population of multicultural residents. London and Amsterdam were my observed foundations of the multicultural Europe I sought.

The on-lookers continued to scatter and multiply. Subsequently, I became one of these on-lookers and customers too. While I roamed the district, I spotted a blonde prostitute standing outside her quarters puffing away on a cigarette. She told me, "None of you have been paying all day. You want some?" I peeked into her room and spotted an auburn-haired prostitute. She spoke with her British accent, "You'll have quite a good time!" I didn't feel a good vibe from these two, so I walked off. The blonde hooker barked back at me with her Slavic (possibly Dutch or German) accent, "Fuck you!"

I walked on to another section of the district exploring the sights. I was delighted by a window sight of a luscious Latina woman wearing curled-up hair, a black tank top, and red sweatpants. She alone had the most interested customers. I decided to be bold by poking my nose on her window for a close-up view. The woman immediately put her right hand in a chop pose threatening to cut me. I walked away laughing.

I continued touring the district and stopped once I noticed a whole section of scantily clad bikini thong-dressed black women. I settled in the section for the night. The "sistas" per se presented the friendliest invitations to my libido. They waived their fingers to me, "Come on!" Perhaps they figured that a dreadlocked brother like me would be the most likely to give them business. On this night, they sensed correctly.

First, I asked one brown sugar-complexioned "sista" if she would put on jeans and a shirt before I fucked her. With a Caribbean accent, she refused. So I peeked at the room next to hers and noticed a voluptuous dark chocolate sista with brown hair extensions on display. She immediately asked in her Jamaican dialect, "Do you want a fuck or a suck?" I asked, "How much do you charge for both?" She told me they cost fifty euros apiece. Then I requested, "How about two (fucks and blowjobs)?" This woman wasted no time dressing in sweatpants. She directed me to an ATM making sure I withdrew two-hundred euros (equivalent of two hundred fifty U.S. dollars).

We arrived in her red-lighted bedroom. I immediately started licking her silver polished toes pointing out of her black leather sandals. She squinted at me several times with looks of shocking amazement while licking her lips. I commenced to strip all her clothes off. Then I licked her breasts. She quickly fussed that I was moving too fast. I shrugged off her feisty mouth with a grin. She was just fronting so she could seem like a challenge. She proceeded to put a condom and Vaseline on my penis before she sucked it. I commented, "Wow! I admire the way you're protecting me and yourself." She continued to give me oral sex for five more minutes. Then I penetrated her vagina. Fifteen minutes later, I became bored. So I asked her to get on top of me. My attempt to effectively fornicate in the position failed since my back was hurting. Thus I backed off asking her to proceed with the next blowjob. She asked, "Wanna lick my coochie?" I spurted, "Hell No! I don't know you that well." Plus her coochie stank. I had no idea who else tapped it. She commenced to give me another "safe" blowjob. And I again, I entered her pussy. This time though, she was grunting at the top of her lungs, "You fuck too hard!" I guess I damn near raped her, but I still shrugged off her feistiness with a grin. I calmed her down by asking, "Do you enjoy your job?" She responded, "Sometimes I do. Sometimes I hate it, too."

I grew bored again and tried to place her in a 69 position. Next, I placed my foot on her face. She winced it off. So I placed my foot on her vagina. She moaned, "Ooooh! Stop! You're making me cum!" I didn't want to risk having her potentially diseased fluid splat on me. Thus I stopped. I laid down for the rest of the session. She tried to squeeze an orgasm out of my dick, but I wasn't feeling turned on. She even barked, "Cum on or I'll chop it!" I facetiously told her, "Whoa! You're quite psycho!" She blurted, "You have a nice dick! You know that!" She kept rubbing my genitalia, but I was too bored. A decision was implemented in my mind to think about a different woman with pretty feet. Lo and I behold, I ejaculated.

I laid down for fifteen more minutes. She gave me a wash cloth, "Wash your dick!" As I got dressed, She boasted, "I'm in love with you boy! I said, "(Bitch) Please!" After I put on my pants, another Jamaican woman wearing a cap and jacket came in the room preparing to solicit herself. Then I noticed pictures of little boys. I asked them, "Are those your sons?" They nodded their chins down. I told them, "I'm glad I helped in raising them." Suddenly, I felt a tremendous amount of humbled anger. The prostitute I fucked puckered her lips at me while I walked out of the room. She may have given me her body for one night, but I was still the only ho giving up hard-earned cash. I still prayed that one day they would raise their sons in a healthier environment.

Strangely, as I silently walked away from the Red Light District, I envisioned Tynesha working as a prostitute in Amsterdam. This city was not all that she cracked it up to be. Plus, I had an epiphany, "No matter how many hoes I fucked, they all would never be able to take away the pain I endured pursuing love from Tynesha.

On the next day, I stopped at an internet café. I e-mailed Tynesha. I never received a response from her. This was another sign that Amsterdam had nothing of substance for me. I proceeded to tour the city's sites: parks, rivers, restaurants, diamond factory, and a post-apartheid South African-era museum.

This city had beautiful boat & water scenery similar to Venice, Italy. Yet, the scenes could not save me perceiving Amsterdam as "an international tampon (duchebag) city."

My best highlight of Amsterdam was chatting with a Spanish woman named Gisela, who sat next to me on a city bus tour. I took a picture with her. Then I asked her to hang out with me one night. She left me an e-mail address as she decided to ride through the city on a bicycle. I guess it was too late to seek out romance in Europe after placing my energy towards wasteful sex.

Gisela e-mailed me a year later saying how she gave up her career as a doctor in Madrid, Spain and moved to New York to pursue acting. I hope to see her in the movies soon.

I continually stay in touch with Art, Amber, and Elan. Art still plays several gigs in London while Amber & Elan eventually landed a distribution deal for their dance sounds. I am forever indebted to their hospitality and friendship.

After four days in Amsterdam and twelve overall days in Europe, I flew back to the states with a recharged DJ spirit. At the same time, I was personally sidetracked.

I offered to send Tynesha one final personal package with an angry release letter. She responded by e-mail, "How was your trip?" She went on to say how she would love the package but she didn't have a postal code while she was in the process of moving back to New York.

All the hard work I did to awaken my serpent (kundalini) and balance my spine was quickly diminished from frivolous pursuits. Drastic chakra changes soon followed!!!

BURN OUT

Prior to my European trip, Larry and I often bickered intensely about everything. One of our main disputes centered on the vibe of RSC Thursdays at the Black Lion Café. The Café was a small laid-back lounge whose customers were primarily into R&B and jazz. I often accommodated the customers by spinning ambient instrumentals. Yet, I was growing tired. I felt the urge to breakout with heavier sounds.

On a Thursday afternoon in June, I told Larry that I was not spinning unless I could play mostly hard rock tracks. Larry initially refuted my request by saying that all live musicians pretty much do rock and don't always have to play loud guitars to express themselves. Then he changed his mind by accepting my proposal after I clarified to him that he was in charge of the program format.

Even though Larry and I settled our musical differences, the crowds at RSC Thursdays were grew sparse. Bands of all genres were booked every week. Most of these bands were not RSC members. They did little to promote their performances. To add to the problems, the fallout over my RSC Newsletter, "Ho Nest," still resonated in people's minds.

July and August of 2003, turned out to be very unproductive months for the RSC. Despite our energized meetings, which included discussions about sponsoring out-of-town funk rock bands and screenings of the recently released documentary *Af-*

roPunk: A Rock'n'Roll Nigger Experience, the momentum was dying down.

Larry sensed the overall dismay and called an emergency RSC meeting. On September 9, 2003, most of the RSC members met at Larry's house, which still serves as headquarters for the band rehearsal space called Anger Management Music Services. We primarily discussed restructuring our cooperative into a non-profit corporation along with making much needed improvements at our concerts. Another WRFG DJ, Sage, attended our meeting laying out grant proposals pending establishment of official 501©3 status. Overall, this meeting had positive intentions. However, bad vibes surfaced when we voted on a various issues. A few members were angry with the unstructured voting procedure. I told everyone, "We used to have an organized voting procedure when we were initially striving for non-profit status." Another RSC member, bassist Tami, interjected, "Used to???" As I called on everyone to vote on a concert policy, RSC member Taffether (soul-pop songstress) screamed out, "That's it ... This could be the end of the Rock SOUL-U-TION Core. I want an organization. We can't expect to accomplish anything until we have our stuff together ..." Larry conceded, "Taffether's right! We'd better hold off on all these issues until we get ourselves established ..." Everyone still left the meeting with hope, hugging each other, and saying, "We gonna be alright!" I facetiously tapped Nedrah on her tooth telling her to shut up. She laughed, "Hey you slapped me!" I giggled, "Consider that retaliation for that slap you gave me at the Black Lion Café."

Little did I know that Taffether's outburst would serve as a prophecy similar to one of a witchdoctor.

Larry called two more RSC meetings. Only Sage and I showed up. By the second meeting, Larry was so frustrated that he proposed ending the RSC and splitting the remaining funds with me. I told him, "Let's give ourselves some time to think about this ... I still want us to run the organization for at least one more year." Larry accepted my plea. We remained upbeat for a few more weeks.

In late October, 2003, I met Larry at an I.A.G. Halloween party that I spun for. I told him that the RSC needed at least three more strong leaders outside of me and him. I further elaborated, "... If no one else from our current crop of RSC members steps up (as a leader), then let's end the organization. Larry was shocked, "Damn! I got a call from Tomi Martin (Three5Human guitarist) encouraging us to help sponsor the *AfroPunk* film. What changed your mind?" I told him that both of us had sacrificed enough of our personal goals for the RSC. Larry understood my view and was cool with my ultimatum.

I proceeded to write an e-mail directed to all RSC members entitled, "RSC Leadership Challenge." It contained five paragraphs explaining the RSC's need for three effective leaders. The last paragraph was worded: "LARRY AND I ARE GIVING EVERYONE IN THE RSC ONE WEEK FROM TODAY 11/4/03 BY 11:59PM 11/11/03 FOR 3 PEOPLE IN OR OUT OF THE RSC TO STEP UP AS LEADERS AND HELP US RE-STRUCTURE THE RSC! It's your choice and your organization. Either Step Yo 'AfroPunk' Asses up and lead the RSC to the Promise Land, or Bow Down and let this Organization lay to rest. We know there is a WAR going on to get 'Progressive' music as the norm in Urban/Multicultural Areas and it will eventually be won. Now we must decide whether the Rock SOUL-U-TION Core is going to be a full-throttled leader in this victory or just another casualty!"

The only response I received was an e-mail from an RSC member telling me that he wasn't active because I didn't listen to his CD. So on November 11, 2003, the RSC dissolved. On November 18, 2003, the RSC's burial was officially announced in a newsletter entitled, "Rest In Peace." *CL* did a write up called "Rock SOUL Surrender" by using my quote, "... *hopefully there will soon be a forthcoming group of younger, fresher, more charismatic music lovers to step their 'AfroPunk' asses up and lead a stronger collective of artists to longer-lasting success.*" Indeed, the RSC served its purpose well!

Larry moved on. He continues today with the following: running Common Cause Productions as a promotional entity, soliciting his basement as band rehearsal space, hosting "Good Morning Blues" Part 2 Wednesday editions on WRFG, and playing guitar for several ATL bands. He continues to acknowledge my quote from an November 2003 ARS episode featuring the band XL in which I said, "We all must learn to work smarter as opposed to harder."

For seven months after the RSC's departure, I continued to solicit my DJ services to radio/club circuits in Atlanta, San Francisco, and London with more burning desire to be the UniverSOUL Rock SOULector full-time.

During the 2003 Thanksgiving holiday break, I visited my sister June in the San Francisco Bay Area. I also used this time to distribute my portfolio to several local radio stations. After calling LIVE 105FM, their program director Shane invited me to speak with him at his office. It never occurred to me until after I arrived at this radio station that I was being led directly to an interview. Needless to say, I was still excited.

Without hesitation, I gave Shane a detailed yet poignant summary of my DJ history and credentials. Shane then told me how he used to be a manager for Atlanta's alternative rock station, 99X. Then I summarized the info in my portfolio by explaining how I was looking for a station like his to sponsor a syndicated radio show entitled "UniverSOUL Rock." Shane skimmed through my booklet before asking how I would guarantee high ratings. I told him that consistent club and radio exposure would create new rock fans. Shane then referred to some artists I had on a playlist. He said that all were either un-known, produced a low market share, or were old news. I told him that I was willing to play well-known popular acts as long as I can mix in relatively unknown artists too. Shane appeared interested in this idea. Yet, he also gave me more challenging comments, "... Your proposal sounds wonderful, but it's going to take a lot more results to show 'idiots' like me that this will work ..." I told him to make sure he listens to my radio tape recordings and mix CDs. Then I told Shane how I planned to check out one of San Francisco's clubs which featured a vibe called "Butt Rock." Shane told me that "Butt Rock" was inclu-sive of heavy sounds like Sevendust, Evanescence, and Slipknot. I commented, "This is exactly the type of Rock vibe that young people are craving." Shane interjected, "... Radio programmers have forecasted that in five years Rock music is gonna be dead ... DJ equipment is now outselling guitars...My young daughter just bought some of her own turntables ... Linkin Park might be due for one more good album and after that people will be looking for the next new thing ..." I still preached, "I believe that one day all of humanity will have to come together for a higher cause and progressive rock sounds will lead the way for inspiration." Shane added, "You're looking for Utopia ... People don't settle their differences easily. San Francisco has a heavy population of people from all over Asia. Most of their countries have bitter blood feuds that span back over centu-ries. Those tensions are still present in the way those people act toward each other today....Once again, your proposal sounds great, but it's going to take a lot more work to prove to 'idiots' like me that this is the next wave ... I think you should just do a regular radio show that's focused on rhythmic rock as opposed to ethnic rock ..." I responded, "Just listen to my recordings and you'll see that my focus is rhythmic rock. I constantly let my spirit flow with the music, and it automatically attracts artists of all ethnicities from all over the world ..."

Shane concluded our interview by giving me a tour of the radio station. He introduced me to several staff members. I walked out of the building feeling confident that I was going to be D-Rock SOUL-Jah full-time soon enough.

I didn't get a chance to check out the "Butt Rock" club scene. June and I visited Mother in Las Vegas. I became sick when I arrived back in the Bay Area. Even though I enjoy San Francisco whenever I visit, I always get caught up in family matters.

Numerously I left phone and e-mail messages for Shane and representatives for London's Capital Radio over the next few months. I also phoned several Atlanta stations and received very little response. Shane never responded back to me. Capital Radio eventually rejected my proposal saying that they couldn't find a station to place a vibe like mine that was "so heavy and focused solely on the music." Despite these disappointments, I continuously applied nonstop to radio stations across the country. At the same time, I kept applying for positions at my pay job's corporation in and out of Atlanta. I was dead set on making a major career change that would leave me happy for the rest of my life.

2003 proved to be a wonderful year of releasing baggage. Yet, I still had unresolved feelings towards Tynesha. She consistently responded to my newsletters with brief greetings, "Tell everyone I said hello and love." By December, 2003, my tolerance toward her had dwindled.

On December 20, 2003, I e-mailed Tynesha with a subject entitled "Dialogue Challenge!" It reads as follows:

This has been a great year for me in regards to releasing "Baggage." Yet, you are still the only thing from the "Past" that still plagues my SOUL. Even though I practice "For-

giveness" of you every day, I still perceive you as ABSOU-
LUTELY THE PHONIEST BITCH ALIVE! You are still the
WORST RELATIONSHIP EXPERIENCE of my life! After
my trip to Europe this past summer, I had no desire to stay in
touch with you on a "Personal" basis. I tried calling your Cell
Phone # when I was in Amsterdam from Aug. 4-8th, but it
kept coming up invalid even when I checked with operators.
I e-mailed you twice from an Internet Café and left my hotel
contact information for you several times, and I still heard
nothing from you. Perhaps with good reason, you were either
too busy for me with your career (as usual) or you were seriously afraid that I was coming there to "KILL YOU!" Even
though I still felt a deep bitterness towards you, what I wanted most of all was a "Personal" closure resolution with you
along with a good networking conversation. But once again,
your actions toward me showed no "Genuine Concern." So I
decided to keep you in the loop on my Professional e-mail list
with no expectations from you on a personal level. You have
consistently responded with friendly greetings and "LOVE"
talk. Yet I have once again grown a huge intolerance for your
language of "I LOVE YOU" as it bares no merit or authentic
value of any kind. Until I witness or experience actions from
you that demonstrate REAL LOVE, my ill feelings toward
you will likely linger on indefinitely. But from the heart, I really don't want to take this shit to the grave. Therefore, I now
offer you another opportunity for DIALOGUE. You have
a choice! You can call me here at my home number, XXX-
XXX-XXXX (which will soon be dissolved), and both of us
will give/receive explanations for our estranged association.
If you decide not to contact me, then I really do not care if
I ever hear from you on a "Personal" basis again (even with
your address on my e-mail list), and it won't matter to me if
your FAKE BUBBLY LOVING ASS goes to hell! Regardless
of your choice, you will eventually learn about my detailed

story on the Mass Media Realm since you are forever an integral part of my Personal Pain!

Goodbye for NOW, and May the Universe give you what you "Truly" Deserve!!!

AL, D-Rock SOUL-Jah

Tynesha e-mailed me back three days later saying:

Hello! Believe me, the Universe, or shall we say, God, will give me exactly what I deserve. No doubt. As for your hateful feelings towards me, how can U call your issues resolved, and still harbor deep hatred for someone, and really expect that person to want to see you on a personal basis? That, I find truly interesting, those are your issues, not mines, U should deal with yourself and not put the blame of whatever emotional anxiety you have on others. I was dealing with some situations when U happened to be there, like finding a new home and such. I will call U with the # U've given me. Have a safe and happy holiday!! TYNESHA!!

Apparently, she was not living as comfortably as I anticipated in Europe.

For the next week, I heard my phone ring several times without anyone leaving a message. I was thinking that Tynesha was too scared to leave a recording. Honestly, I also wasn't courageous enough to pick up the phone, but I still felt that she would have a least left a message if she really wanted to talk.

On December 30, 2003, lo and behold, Tynesha e-mailed the following message:

Hi. I had to think twice about this. Why would I call someone, who hates my guts? Does that make sense? Not to me. And if someone hates someone, why would he or she want that person to call them? It doesn't even matter. There's a verse in the bible that states."The battle is not mines, it be-

longs to the Lord." That means, any one who wars against a child of God, is warring with God. He'll fight the battle for his children. I'm not the same Tynesha I was that long ago, when we were acquaintances. I'm not even the same Tynesha I was a year ago. Life is about growing, and learning. I don't drink, smoke, party, or ingage in fools play anymore. I thank God for changing my life, and blessing me with wisdom. I pray you find Peace within, Luv, and many wonderful Blessings in your life, always. If I want to contact anyone else, I'll find a way to do so, without having to bother you anymore. Peace, Luv, & Blessings! LUV TYNESHA!

I was a little surprised by her "changed" revelation but was not a believer, so I responded with the following message:

Hola Señora,
I will believe you are a "CHANGED" woman when I "witness or experience" it. If I don't see it this lifetime, then maybe I'll catch you in a better light the next go around. From the heart, I really do hope that you "CHANGE" into a "Genuinely" Loving woman if you are not already. Perhaps one day, you will understand the seeds of my story which you became a viable part of for whatever reason the Universe destined. In the meantime, I will let the Most High Forces at Hand judge you on your character. My overall "Perception" of you from past and present situations carries little weight in this system's evolution.
Bye and Bye FOREVER!!! AL, D-Rock SOUL-Jah

Despite the fact that Tynesha and I are permanently estranged, I truly do forgive her. I pray that she's evolved into a genuine spirit with healthy boundaries. I figured from our final bitter exchange, "If she can move on to a more peacefully productive existence, then so can I." I moved on but still faced intense situations challenging my peace and productivity.

I continued to market my DJ services by providing spins for "Feed the Hungry" programs in honor of the late civil rights leader, Hosea Williams. During the Thanksgiving show, I brought my DJ equipment and chanted the Zumbi crenca over the microphone. I invited people to join me in this chant. A little girl with locks stepped towards my djembe drum. I asked, "What's your name young lady?" She softly spoke, "Amira!" I gleefully said, "That's the same name as my little SOUL Sister in Heaven, Amira Asuñe Lacy Bey, Asé Asé..." I proceeded to spin three songs by SOULFLY before breaking out into my own floor dance. Some adults played on my percussion instruments. The kids seemed a little irritated by the heavy guitar-laden sounds. After I finished, a woman praised me, "You alright, brother. You're trying to teach something cultural ..."

While I sought out radio and club circuits on a permanent basis, resistance towards me grew on my pay job. Several of my co-workers privately complained about my job performance. When my managers approached me about this, I cussed them out. After the meeting, I was furious thinking that practically the whole world was against me. Then I read an e-mail link forwarded to me by one of my managers. The web link contained a shocking story about an eighteen-year-old named Marcus Dixon. This teenager was serving a ten-year sentence for aggravated child molestation. After reading this, I strangely felt relieved. Sure I have problems, but they don't compare to those of this young man and billions of other people around the world who are battling grave injustices. I went on to sign the petition for Marcus' release. Then I posted the web link on an ARS Newsletter dated January 12, 2004 entitled "Justice Bandwagon!" I also thanked my manager for informing me of this story before apologizing for my swearing outburst. My co-workers eventually reconciled their frustration with me. I decided that I was going to make a good attempt to have productive relationships with them since the job was still my "best leverage." Plus, I thought that making promotional strides on the job would be a good back-up plan in case I didn't succeed full-time as D-Rock SOUL-Jah. This perception immensely changed the following year.

At the next Hosea "Feed the Hungry" show, which took place on the 2004 MLK birthday celebration, I only brought a CD, an acoustic guitar, and a picture of Marcus Dixon. I stressed that people needed to pay attention to issues like Marcus Dixon and "Wake up!" When I sat down with the guitar, I got booed once I revealed that I didn't know how to play it. I explained that I brought it as a showcase to encourage people to play instruments. Then, I took off my head wrap and jacket—letting my locks, t-shirt, and spirit freely flow to a SOULFLY track— "One" featuring Christian Machado of Ill Niño. Three young boys got excited. They pounded the drums. As the song faded out with me screaming over the track, "*Come around. Come around. Predatory Jungle Law,*" the boys kept banging over the mic. The crowd had a good laugh, but I still felt like a bumbling idiot. I tried too hard to get people to listen to rock vibes. I thought, "Next time I'll just book a band." One of the organizers I spoke with concurred, "That's a good idea. I'm tired of (booking) hip-hop. That's all these kids wanna do. I'm talking with the Hispanic Community to see if they can provide some artists ..." This program was indeed a learning experience, but it also revealed my first sign of burnout.

Immediately after the RSC ended, I met with singer/songwriter/dancer Misty. Misty's most notable experience stemmed from her background vocals with Atlanta's hipadelic funk rock band Urban Grind. Occasionally, she dropped by WRFG to co-host some of my ARS episodes. During a phone conversation, she told me, "... If you want people to start dancing to your tracks, then you need to have two ladies on stage with you shaking their asses, encouraging others to do the same." This sparked an idea for a rock dance troupe.

Misty and I met regularly. We decided to implement dance rehearsals for our newly named troupe, Tribal Metal Spear-its (TMS). Misty came on ARS with two friends, left her e-mail address, and announced that TMS would soon hold auditions.

TMS appeared ready to get off the ground until I sent out an ARS December newsletter themed "2K4Insurrection Dance." I said in this e-mail that TMS was forming and would inspire people to dance to heavy music. Misty immediately phoned her displeasure to me, "... Don't hype us up too soon. Biters will come in and feed off of us. We need to keep it on the down-low until we meet and establish ourselves ... And stop referring me on the radio as you're 'co-host in training.' You're setting me up for failure ..." Misty was also training under me to be an airshifter at WRFG. Yet, she was unsure whether she wanted to pursue this and TMS full throttle. I repeatedly asked her to submit a WRFG volunteer application. She recanted, "It's just a piece of paper. Big deal!" Eventually she turned in an application, but she never consistently trained under me. She also told me, "I'll be involved with WRFG and the dance troupe until I change my mind ..."

In January 2004, I called a TMS meeting with Misty and former RSC member, singer Niesha. Two of Misty's friends showed up early. They told me that Misty was meditating earlier in the day because she was involved in too many activities. I was also furious with her. I had cussed her out in a previous phone message expressing my disdain over her lack of responses to my phone calls. Later in the evening, Misty and Niesha showed up at my apartment for the meeting.

Misty laughed, "You take things too seriously, Al. The old me would have cussed back at the way you spoke to me over the phone. But life is too beautiful. I'm moving on to better things ..." We proceeded with our agenda and emphasized that I was ready to start the troupe, "We should fuck around no more." Niesha said that we should take our time and make TMS a community effort. Misty agreed stating how we should take our time since biters could copy us in a way similar to how Goodie Mob copied Urban Grind's antics of a stage entourage. Misty and Niesha toppled my plea to start TMS immediately. Then somehow we ended up in a conversation about personal relationships. Niesha told me, "... When I first met you, I was digging your interests in Kundalini Yoga. I sensed that there was a beautiful person inside just waiting to be released ... I've been through bad relationships too, but I've learned to let them go...Often times one tends to think that the mate they were involved with was the reason for the bad relationship when most of the time, it was something wrong with yourself..." Misty seconded, "Yeah ... Like that woman (Tynesha) who you think screwed you over, when in reality you took her affection for you the wrong way." I was silently in disbelief as it now seemed like I was being sandwiched. Niesha continued the assault, "You really need to stop being the D-Rock SOUL-Jah personality all the time ... Try being a little more down to earth starting at your job ... Being D-Rock all the time turns off women. Misty joined in on the attack, "I've heard women say that you're overbearing..." Niesha agreed before Misty added, "You need to change people's negative perception of you ... People often sigh, 'Ewwww! D-Rock!'"

I took their constructive criticism in perspective. Sure I could tone down my D-Rock personality off the air. Yet, I disagreed with the "overbearing" comments. I figured that most of the heifers who said that probably ain't into the Rock vibe anyways.

Misty then recommended, "Why don't you get two dancers, and let us know how it goes?" I said that I still wanted to have an organization started beforehand. Niesha then forecasted my actions, "Don't worry. Let's take our time ... I work with schoolchildren ... You notice how a lot of adults still act like kids ...They're still living out their childhoods through co-dependencies ... I'm working on overcoming my addictions through CODA and learning to quit smoking ... You and Larry are still living out your childhoods." This comment stemmed after my revelation about fucking hoes. Niesha continued her sermon, "Both of you were the shit (for the RSC). There were just too many bands playing who weren't members....I don't think the dreads fit you as well (agreeing with Misty). I can see you cutting them off this year...." Niesha's prophecy proved to be correct later in the year when I cut off my locks. Meanwhile, Misty spewed at me as she and Niesha exited, "You still act like a child. The way you cussed me out on the phone—it's just like a child saying, 'Mine! Mine!'"

After this night, I still planned to start TMS dance practices with Misty and Niesha at the Bunker. I wanted badly to get TMS off the ground, but I didn't trust Misty and Niesha enough. I didn't hear from them again regarding our fantasized dance troupe. Our visions for TMS just differed too much.

Misty attempted to have a Prince tribute show on ARS and at a club. She stayed home while I rolled on with an ARS episode owed to the Purple Rocker. She claimed that the "Beats & Lyrics" DJs screwed her out of air time that was supposed to run directly into my program. Indeed some miscommunication transpired between Misty and another WRFG air shifter. Yet I wasn't mad. I perceived that Misty was trying to exploit me and everyone at WRFG in order to make herself look like the number one groupie of Prince's fan club. I don't know if her Prince tribute club party took place. This proved to be the last time I spoke with Misty until I ran into her two years later. I wish her, Niesha, and their families' good fortune.

Meanwhile, I was spinning at the Bunker every weekend along with WRFG DJ Reality and several Rave DJs affiliated with Q.T. Promotions. A band I played frequently on ARS called Blackbeard was also performing there every weekend too.

For three months, the Bunker appeared to be a promising spot until its owner, NYC native filmmaker Anthony, drove the rental prices up. As a result, Q.T. Promotions ended their services at the Bunker. I still had a lot of fun spinning with the mixing equipment of mine and other DJs. Apparently, a strong network was building along with a growing audience. Despite the distance from the Bunker, I felt a surge of confidence. However, my relationship with Q.T. Promotions escalated into a sour grape over a glitch that transpired at one of the Bunker parties.

To sum up my dispute with Q.T. Promotions, I wrote my Muslim lawyer the following letter on February 19, 2004:

Greetings Attorney,

Thanks for listening to my civil issue and lending an offer to write a letter on my behalf. Here is a summary of the issue and what I need done to resolve it.

During the early morning hours of Saturday, January 10th, 2004, I was performing DJ spins at a place called The Bunker located on 420 Donald Lee Hallowell Dr. (formerly Bankhead Hwy). I was one of the featured DJs at a party sponsored by Q.T. Promotions. I used my own mixer and CD players to make the spins. After my set was finished, I was asked to lend my mixer to other featured DJs for their set since the mixer provided by Q.T. Promotions was out-of-service. I verbally agreed to let them use my American DJ mixer (purchased in April of 2000 for approximately $550) as long as they took care of it long enough for me to retrieve during the evening of January 10th, 2004. As I retrieved my mixer for usage that evening, I found that the headphone outlet was missing. My mixer was still able to function, but with limited *ability since I had no way of hearing the sounds from the CD players with the headphone outlet being indisposed. After I noticed this damage, I approached T.R. (one of the organizers of Q.T. Promotions) and asked him if he knew anything about the damaged headphone outlet on my mixer. He said the damage resulted from DJ Quan plugging his headphones into the mixer with an accidental result of the headphone outlet breaking off from the surface of the mixer. T.R. promised that he would get it fixed on his own and had DJ Mat provide me with his old-style mixer as a back-up to me while I wait to have my own American DJ Mixer repaired.*

In the midst of my wait I have called T.R. several times with no results. During the first weeks since the incident, I called T.R. at least twice a week and left messages. When I finally reached him he said the mixer was still in repair and he would get it back to me at The Bunker parties sponsored by Q.T. Promotions. Then I called T.R. on 1/29/04 to inquire again about my mixer. T.R. claimed he was very sick at the time and informed me that Q.T. parties at The Bunker were cancelled. Again, T.R. stated he would call me soon to let me know when I can pick up the mixer. T.R. stated at the time that the mixer was fixed. So over the next two weeks I called T.R. once or twice every day asking him when I can meet him and get my mixer back. I left several messages and did not receive a phone call from him until Thursday, February 12th, 2004. He stated again that the mixer was done and he would drop it off at my home in Southwest Atlanta. I gave T.R. directions to my apartment as well and told him that I tried to contact DJ Mat to give him his mixer back. T.R. told me he would take DJ Mat's mixer on his behalf because DJ Mat was wasted during the phone call and lives by him regardless. T.R. did not call back or arrive that night. Similar scenarios have taken place over the past week in which T.R. promised to drop off my mixer and never did. He even stated earlier this week that my mixer just got fixed this past weekend, which contradicts earlier statements of my mixer already being in full repair. I offered to meet him at his last location and exchange my mixer but once again he promised to call me and drop off my mixer but never did.

Now, I have no patience left and am completely irate. I've begun to think that my mixer is either not fixed at all, even more damaged, or has been fixed and used continuously by other DJs affiliated with Q.T. Promotions for their own personal/professional benefit. T.R. even stated that my mixer was with a couple of DJs who were driving his car. Because I have been given a very annoying run-around scenario on this issue, I now feel it's time for me to take legal action in order to acquire my American DJ mixer back in the same quality condition before it was negligently used by DJs from Q.T. Promotions. I would like a letter written to T.R. of Q.T. Promotions requesting that he get my mixer back to me within 7 days and warn him that if he doesn't I will subpoena him to Small Claims Court and sue him for even more of a dollar amount than the value of my American DJ mixer. T.R. can be reached at XXX-XXX-XXXX and lives at XXXX Springs Trail located in the Springs neighborhood of Roswell, GA. He also associates with Rigo Pelini, another organizer of Q.T. Promotions, who can be reached at XXX-XXX-XXXX.

Again, I appreciate your assistance on this matter, and hope to get it resolved as soon as possible with very limited involvement from those in the legal system.

Sincerely,
Albert Johnson

A few days later, my attorney sent letters to T.R. and Rigo Pelini demanding that they safely return my DJ mixer to prevent further legal action.

I didn't hear from anyone affiliated with Q.T. Promotions. So on March 12, 2004, I filed a tort claim with the Magistrate

Court of Fulton County suing Q.T. Promotions for monetary damages, negligence, and a safe return of my DJ mixer.

After waiting patiently for more than two weeks, I received a barrage of angry phone calls from Rigo Pelini on March 29, 2004. He frantically screamed, "I have nothing to do with those guys (T.R. and Q.T. Promotions) ... If I had known you were having this problem I would have gotten you back the mixer personally ... If I was in your shoes I would have done the same thing ... but don't include me in your suit ..." I responded, "I'll get back to you. I have to talk to my lawyer first ..." I immediately called my attorney. While I was questioning him, Rigo left two more frantic messages on my cell phone, "The police have come by my house and are threatening to come by my job ... I have nothing to do with this ... I'll get your mixer back from those DJs that T.R. hangs with ... If I lose my job over this, I'll have my lawyer sue you for everything you got based on malicious prosecution ..."

After my eardrums nearly bled from these screams, I called my attorney again. He said, "This is escalating (too much) ... (Just) take the offer and get your mixer back ... Once you get your mixer back, then you can talk to T.R. and state your terms before threatening to take him to court ..."

Once I finished chatting with my attorney, I called Amen with an explanation of this mess. At this moment, I didn't trust Rigo and T.R. enough to meet them in a secluded location. T.R.'s father was a wealthy club owner in New York and Miami. Plus there were customers at The Bunker rave parties who induced substantial amounts of drugs. So I was curious about whether they had any ties to organized crime. Amen recommended, "Have him meet you at a public neutral location like a gas station. I won't make myself visible unless they try something funny ..." I responded, "You sure you wanna do this? This is my mess, and I don't want you to help clean it if it inconveniences you ..." Amen had my back, "Don't worry! I'm not going to do anything that I don't want to do ..." He asked, "What's his (Rigo's DJ moniker) name?" I told him, "DJ Uncle Polo!" Amen barked, "What type of bitch ass name is that???" I laughed.

This situation still didn't cease to be tense. Rigo called me later that evening telling me that he acquired my mixer from one of the Q.T. DJs. He asked me to meet him at his job, a restaurant in Duluth. Since this was a public place, I didn't sense any possibility of trouble. As a precaution, I still called Amen and told him to be on stand-by in case the situation went astray. Amen's martial arts and weapons training was great security for me. I was prepared for some *gangsta shit* while keeping faith that this meeting would go peacefully.

The restaurant meeting on April 1, 2004 took place without trouble. Rigo and I communicated like professional gentlemen. He handed over my mixer in exchange for my signature on a note releasing him from any liability. We shook hands and chatted briefly. Rigo said, "I'm sorry this happened ... I'm not talking to those guys (Q.T. Promotions) anymore ... I would still like to include you at future parties ..." I said, "I'm glad I finally got my mixer back ... Now I still have to get those DJs to pay for it ..." We shook hands one last time. Rigo walked back to the kitchen to continue his cooking job.

I called T.R. later in the evening. I told that I'd received the mixer back in the same condition as it was when it was initially damaged. Clearly I stated, "Either you pay for the repairs, or my suit against you still stands ..." T.R. whined, "I'm not paying for it ... I didn't break it." I said, "Oh well ... Just give me your whole name so I can file this case in full." He told me, "Terry Ross."

The next day I amended the tort. I dismissed Rigo and added even more monetary value to the negligence inflicted from

Terry's crew. As more weeks flew by, I received calls from the Fulton County Court telling me that they couldn't find a valid address for anyone named Terry Ross. I called his number at least three more times. Initially, a woman answered saying no one named Terry lived there. Then I asked, "Do you know anyone named Terry Ross?" She responded, "If you hear from him, tell him to fuck off!"

For all I knew, Terry split town. He weaseled his way out of my lawsuit. I thought about having the police track him down, but I decided I'd endured enough stress over this situation. It was time for me to move on. I never officially closed the case, but Fulton County Courts have their statutes of limitations. After all, I did receive a mixer from one of the Q.T. DJs as collateral before I started the court proceedings. I eventually paid seventy-three dollars to fix the headphone jack.

Thank goodness this situation didn't escalate further. Regardless, it still proved to be another sign of my exhaustion from the music business.

Even though fatigue had set in deeper, I was still promoting my DJ services with heightened optimism. I paid Amelia of Acres Entertainment for her wonderful business card designs that displayed front and back images of my DJ performances. I distributed these business cards all over town. I was so pleased with these flyer-like cards that I pasted the filed images onto my ARS Newsletters and on the ARS Summary link of WRFG's website.

My marketing was constantly improving, but I still received an onslaught of overwhelming challenges.

In early 2004, I sent my sister June a copy of my DJ business plan. I purposely did this to give her a hypothetical example of how I would function pending her approval. Upon her permission I would suddenly leave everything behind in Atlanta and move into her place in the Bay Area. June was impressed with my strategy but still rejected the idea of me living with her. I wasn't mad at her. After all, the San Francisco Bay Area is one of the world's most expensive metro areas. June further reiterated, "It makes no sense for you to leave a job you hate, possibly max out your credit here, and potentially have to work another job you hate ..."

I even made an attempt at making WRFG my full-time job. I applied for some of their paid positions and was declined. I also spoke with management about the possibility of syndicating ARS through WRFG but was repeatedly told that WRFG will always operate as a volunteer-run radio station. Thereby most of its funds would go towards operating costs not including air shifters. I respected WRFG's policies and proceeded to apply to several other stations. However, I grew intolerant toward WRFG's intermingling with my DJ services. On February 4, 2004 I received an e-mail from WRFG's Operations Committee requesting that I refrain my ARS Newsletter from using expletives, even though the words written like "F#@k" were already censored. I responded by saying that I would start using disclaimers separating my opinions from WRFG, but I wouldn't censor my expletives anymore. I know WRFG's staff didn't intend to upset me. Yet my anger over lack of pay from my DJ services couldn't be restrained.

On the March 7, 2004 ARS episode, I yelled off the air, "I hate WFRG!" after my tape-recorded interview with Mike Shinoda and Phoenix of Linkin Park got jammed in the cassette player. Fortunately, I had my own recorder on site. So I used it to play the interview over the air. Linkin Park ended up being the last famous band I interviewed on the radio.

Before I played this interview on the air, I felt like a star reporter at Philips Arena. I walked into Linkin Park's dressing area with help from Warner Brothers Records representatives. This was the most special treatment I ever felt as a journalist. I also said hi to some people with familiar faces and voices from other radio stations. Once I was shown into the area that featured massage tables for Linkin Park's members, I envisioned that I would be working this type of lifestyle full-time very soon.

I continued seeking open DJ outlets from conferences as well only to be met with more roadblocks. Organizers for the 2004 Florida Music Festival told me that my DJ style was hot and unique, but they also said they had no place where I could fit it. They still welcomed me to attend the seminars. I graciously refused their offer. Instead, I drove to Maryland and North Carolina to visit family and friends.

When I arrived back from this break, I attended the 2004 Million Dollar Radio and Music Conference in College Park, Georgia. The radio personalities who lectured only re-emphasized what I already knew about how to market my services. After listening to a speech by V103 FM's morning talk show host, Frank Ski, I was compelled to question him, "Hello. My name is Albert Johnson. I've hosted a radio show on (WRFG) Community Radio for the past five years and made no money as a DJ. What do you think it will take for Urban Audiences to finally open up to Alternative forms of music like Rock?" Frank Ski responded, "Unless there's a whole slew of Black Rock artists that breakthrough, then urban audiences won't listen....Can anyone answer me why hip-hop broke through and not rock in the Black Community?... Number one, you didn't have enough artists playing rock ... Number two, there was no marketing of these artists ... and Number three, you didn't have any venues for these artists to play ... Do you think "Hey Ya" by OutKast would have gotten any radio play if they hadn't already established themselves as breakthrough urban artists? ..." I boasted to him what I already told many people in my lifetime, "Not all of that is true ... There are venues for these bands to play at but urban audiences don't check them out enough ... I know musicians from at least six rock bands that have played on all of OutKast's and Goodie Mob's albums ..." After this seminar portion of the conference finished, I shook hands with Frank Ski and acquired his e-mail address. Even though we didn't see eye-to-eye, I left the hotel with a tremendous amount of respect for the path that Frank Ski traveled to for success. He was a protégé of Urban Radio's creator of the "Quiet Storm" format, Melvin Lindsey. The next day more conference attendants came up to me, "I admire what you're doing ... I love rock!" Despite their praise, I still saw the big picture of the conference. It was designed to push the standard display of "Black Radio," hip-hop and R&B. This conference was just another glitch in my momentum to be a full-time rock DJ.

I was now more pessimistic and lost than ever. I sought motivation from Reggie Hicks, creator and executive producer of the WCLK-based syndicated radio show "Power Point." Reggie recommended that I send radio tapes to a select quality of public broadcasting companies who are seeking new ideas. Then he told me to offer them recorded broadcasts free-of-charge until I acquire sponsorship. I told him that was the direction I needed even though it's still a lot of hard work. I also offered to buy him dinner as a consultation fee. Reggie said, "Don't worry about the fee. Just don't give up. You're persistent and that's what it takes to get innovative programs like yours heard."

I left Reggie's office with renewed hope. I decided to implement a more fun approach to broadcasting, so I brought my DJ equipment on several ARS episodes. I performed some fun hyperactive mixes and sensed that 2004 would somehow be my last year on WRFG. Thus I decided to make my remaining time there as enjoyable as possible. This premonition proved to be so true!

I ventured further into full-time DJ explorations by networking with several more club DJs. I learned that most of these cats were either familiar with rock or spun it in some form. DJ Cozy Shawn often included Fishbone, Lenny Kravitz, and Jimi Hendrix in his funk mixes. DJ Wildlife spun popular songs from all genres and time periods. Jamal, Preston Craig, and Brian Paris spun Brit-pop, classic punk, and elements of indie rock at weekly parties they call "Trashed Rock." And Don Tonic along with DJ Kemit are good friends with several rock musicians. Despite my requests to join all of these DJs on gigs, I never received responses from them. Indeed I was disappointed. At the same time I awakened. My rhythmic Heavy Music style differed from all of these DJs. Plus, their avoidance of my communication signaled that I needed to stop pleading for exposure and establish my own club audience. I was trying too hard to get booked at any and every possible club while also exhausting too much energy into becoming a full-time radio DJ by 2005.

Today, Don Tonic remains my club DJ mentor.

All my failed career pursuits also diminished my social life. I was good at acquiring contact information, especially from attractive women. Most of the women, though, never responded to my dating offers. And the few females I did date either didn't spark enough attraction for me or vice versa.

In the midst of my social seclusion, my eyes opened to more horrifying signs. I received an e-mail from Amen warning that AIDS can still spread while using a condom. The virus is microscopic in size compared to a rubber. Condoms prevent pregnancy but are still very vulnerable to disease. I immediately feared that I'd contracted AIDS from the sex I had with two prostitutes despite the fact I wore condoms both times.

Also during spring 2004, I noticed while masturbating that my right scrotal area was larger than the left area. Without hesitation, I consulted first with my natural pathologist, Dr. Tillman. He recommended that I buy more of his men's health brand tonic. Then he told me to get a thumb examination for my genitals.

I listened well and proceeded to have both an AIDS test and an examination for testicular cancer. Fortunately, the AIDS test revealed that all of my immune functions were normal with the exception of high cholesterol. The testicular tests didn't show any benign activity either, but the doctor referred me to a urologist for treatment of a scrotal condition called hydrocil. I had an overabundance of liquid in my scrotum, but it wasn't serious enough for surgery.

I was so relieved by all of this news that I announced on an ARS episode, "No more pro hoes for D-Rock SOUL-Jah! I'm fortunate to be HIV negative. I will take an AIDS test in a few more years. In the meantime, I will do my best to stay in perfect health. And I recommend you do the same ..."

On May 4, 2004, more good news came. Marcus Dixon was released from prison after the Georgia Supreme Court voted four to three to reverse the "aggravated child molestation" charge against him. Suddenly, I was optimistic again. I highlighted this story in the May 5, 2004 ARS Newsletter themed "Youth Empowerment." I also advertised the upcoming Sweet Auburn Avenue Festival, at which I was scheduled to spin during a Saturday evening at the Calhoun Park Stage.

My optimism didn't last long!

The following letter details the last straw of my frustration with the music business:

> Hello "Friends" of Auburn Avenue,
> I'm writing this e-mail to express my dismay over this past weekend's festivities. My name is Albert Johnson. I was selected to spin as a DJ named **D-Rock SOUL-Jah** on the Calhoun Park Stage for Saturday, May 8th at 9:45 pm. I paid the required $35 application fee when I auditioned. When I arrived at 10:30 am on Saturday to set up my table as Che-

rone Louis requested, the soundperson told me that the best he could do was to have me give him 2 CDs to spin because the stage "was not designed for DJs." He also warned me that too many acts arrive "late" between 7 and 9pm and that the stage would likely get cut off early. I called Cherone about this and she told me not to listen to him because everything would run on schedule. So I came back to the stage and set up the rest of my DJ equipment at 7:30 pm. After I waited patiently for 2 hours to spin, the soundman announced that the last 3 acts were going to perform and gave an order from the police to shut down at 10 pm. He did not mention my name even though I was scheduled as the last act to perform at 9:45 pm. After a few more acts performed, the soundman cut off the stage at 9:40 pm. Therefore, I was not able to spin as promised. A lot of other acts complained as well that they had been waiting by the stage all day to perform and never got their chance as they were scheduled. I was also promised that I would be able to spin for an hour. So with the combination of disorganization on the schedule, late-arriving acts performing, police pulling the plug early, and "scheduled" acts like myself who arrived on time for their performances but got shunned – the overall Festival experience was a bust. Therefore, I request that you refund my $35 Application Fee. I left the festival with a wide array of disgust that festival organizers did not allow me and many others to do what we were promised. I am now almost sure that I will never support another Atlanta Music Festival again. There is no excuse for performers like me to get shut-out the way we did! If you do live up to my refund request, then please send me a $35.00 check…..

   Sincerely,
   Albert Johnson

   The following day I received an e-mail from Cherone Louis. She referred me to Conrad Jacobs to seek a refund. To add more injury to insult, I also lost my sixty-dollar table that I used to set up my equipment. Larry was supposed to pick it up the next day since he gave me the initial ride to the Festival with all my gear. He didn't spot it. I should have trusted my feelings more when the soundperson facetiously warned me, "Brother, I love you. I'm not lying. There won't be enough time for you." After thinking about all this, I decided that seeking a refund was too much hassle for me. Sure I lost one hundred dollars worth of services during the Festival mishap, but worst of all, I lost complete motivation to pursue a full-throttled DJ career.

Coincidentally, I wrote a pros & cons list of "Life Without WRFG" two weeks earlier on April 24, 2004. I wrote in this analysis, "Unless someone from the community steps up with sufficient desire to join me as a fellow DJ on the air, it's better for me to release myself from ARS (WRFG)!" Some WRFG volunteers expressed interest, but never enough dedication to train under me. Originally, I was going to wait until the end of 2005 to leave WRFG. After the Festival bust, though, it was almost clear that I needed to move on. Plus, the Marcus Dixon case and my own dangerous crossroads with human diseases appeared to be more significant issues where my services could render help. That's when I became ecstatic deciding to write this book—MY AUTOBIOGRAPHY!

Since this wasn't going to be an easy decision, I decided to make the rest of May 2004 my grace period before making my radio departure official.

Again, I sought guidance from Reggie Hicks. This time he allowed me to pay for his lunch. He tried to encourage me to stay on the radio, "You don't want to lose your audience ... In a few years you may be regretful hearing about someone doing a similar radio show with much success ..." I told Reggie, "It's likely I won't be in Atlanta by the end of this year, so I'll be giving up WRFG sooner or later..." Reggie responded, "That makes sense ..."

During my "grace period," I also attended a screening of *Waiting In Wings*, a documentary about African-Americans in country music. This was produced by an independent media production company out of Nashville, Tennessee, which includes one of Oprah Winfrey's female cousins. They subsequently sold the rights of this film to Viacom, who aired it on Country Music Television (CMT). This film further inspired me to retire. I told Rissi Palmer, who performed at the screening, that I have a lot in common with Cleve Francis. He was a Black Country artist and promoter who retired as a doctor to pursue a music career. Francis wound up returning to medicine. It was time for me to return to more significant life-preserving tasks too.

As May 2004 was closing, I still pursued job openings with other companies like WEA (Warner Entertainment Association). Their doors slammed shut as well. On May 20, 2004, an announcement was made in the Media that WEA's newly formed company Warner Music Group was cutting some of their artists in addition to their prior layoffs of half their staff.

The doors of the music industry were clearly shut in my eyes. However, I now saw new existing opportunities in other media projects and service ventures.

On the ARS show of May 30, 2004, I announced that June was going to be my final month at WRFG.

The following Tuesday, June 2, 2004, I dropped off a resignation letter at WRFG. The office manager, Joanie Baptiste, hugged me with grief.

Later that same evening, I e-mailed my final ARS Newsletter entitled, "RETIREMENT PARTY!!!" I included four bright pictures of me along with the following written speech:

Hello Progressive Music Inquirers,

The speculation is over!!! I am officially retiring from "AL-TERNATIVE ROCK SOUL-U-TIONS (ARS)" and WRFG Atlanta, 89.3FM on Sunday, June 27th, 2004 after I broadcast my final episode! Doing ARS has been a bless-ed honor, and I've enjoyed almost every moment of it. However, I am just one source of energy. Therefore, I was due to reach the ultimate peak of burnout. I am gratefully proud to have provided years of dedicated service as the only proclaimed Rock DJ at an eclectic, Multicultural, ground-breaking volunteer-based radio station. I knew coming into this year that I would have to decide upon major changes if those did not already come my way for the sake of Spiritual Growth. So many of you may now wonder – "Will D-Rock SOUL-Jah ever be on the radio again?" Only the Spear-it of Almighty Creation within me can answer this! I will still be a spinning/dancing DJ off the air whenever called upon for fun no matter how long the duration of my residence in ATL continues. I still dream of witnessing a room full of diverse people, especially those who are Melanin-Abundant, dancing to Rock tracks spun by me and other DJs alike. And when my momentum recharges, perhaps the Universe will call upon me to broadcast over the airwaves on a full-time basis. In the meantime, there are more significant life-enhancing projects that I will pursue. They include learning new languages; writing/producing a book, screenplay, and soundtrack; and eventually providing community service at shelters for battered women. The world will soon learn the detailed story about how Music, especially that of the Rock Genre, saved my life and served as the most potent tool in overcoming (internally/externally) abusive relationships & racism. It may take me 5-10 years to accomplish all these tasks and finally distribute this story, but this is divine because it may also take 5-10 years before we eventually see the following: Rock/Alternative Sounds as the Norm in Urban/Multicultural Areas; DJs very similar to me all over the radio and club circuit; and Atlanta being fully established as an International haven for people, music, and culture. And as for the fate of ARS, including the music of all the wonderful artists that created this program, I have asked WRFG to keep a program like this somewhere in their format. I can only hope and pray that there will be DJ(s) with passion at least equaling mine to continuously pump Univer-SOUL Rock sounds on WRFG and beyond. But remember, without the vibes of all the wonderful artists I've displayed from around the world and the support of everyone who listened to ARS, there would be no D-Rock SOUL-Jah. So it's up to everyone in the community to demand that WRFG does not let progressive Rock sounds run astray. Be sure to consistently contact the World of Radio Free Georgia....I will glad give any artist a referral to WRFG's staff and provide this station with musical references whenever asked! So now let's release the sadness and begin the Party! With only "The Final 4" episodes left of yours truly hosting ARS, I cordially invite all of you to listen and hang out with me during these closing celebrations. Therefore, I will be accepting guest appearances from artists/bands/community members (no more than 4 per episode) on all shows. FIRST REPLIES TO D-Rock SOUL-Jah, FIRST SERVED from June 27th going backwards!!! REJOICE EVERYONE – D-Rock SOUL-Jah is not giving up, he's GROWING UP!!! BEST WISHES TO EVERYONE ON ALL YOUR ENDEAVORS TO PRESERVE LIFE AND MUCH THANKS TO ALL FOR ALLOWING ME TO SERVE YOU WITH 'FUNKY METALLIC SOUL-FUSION'!!! OGUN, OGUN-IE!!!!!!!!!!!

The shockwaves reverberated throughout cyberspace and metro ATL for the next two weeks. Most people disbelieved that I'd retired! The overall response though was one of praise and good luck. The BRC gave me mad props for one who "al-

most single-handedly bigged up Hotlanta's Black Rock scene."
And Boston Fielder gave me the warmest response of all:

> *Alafia, D-Rock*
>
> *Hey, brother, you've done your time. Congrats on not growing up but GROWING OUT! I've always had much respect for your dedication to the ATL music scene but I'm happy to see you moving on to focus your energy into your life/film story that you've mentioned to me on a couple of occasions. You are obviously a determined brother and that is what it takes to make film projects work. Take a minute to truly appreciate what you have accomplished. Whether some of the selfish music business personnel in Atlanta realize it or not they are losing a major source of exposure, team building and inspiration from their airwaves. Keep moving and don't look back. You did your thing and you did it well....*
>
> *Congratulations again, brother!*
> *All the best,*
> *Boston*

After this greeting, I rushed outside to the parking lot of my pay job showering and crying tears of joy inside my car.

Larry invited me to dinner with his girlfriend a couple of days later. We ate at the Cajun Kitchen, the same place where I spun my first DJ gig. Larry told me, "Sage and I discussed taking over ARS since a lot of artists will be impacted. Then again I thought, 'Let them go without hearing their music on the air so they can see how important the radio really is ...'"

Larry was my brother-in-arms during my six-year tenure as Atlanta's unofficial Urban Rock Minister.

On June 27, 2004, I broadcasted my final episode of ARS. My in-house guest was O-Train and his girlfriend Denise. O-Train was the most ardent listener of ARS. He alone made Baby Jane the most requested artist ever on ARS. Larry phoned in at the top of my last hour. He demanded to speak on the air, and I gladly obliged. After he chastised Atlanta for being "too cliquish," He requested, "Will you play somethin' funky for me, BRO?" I chuckled, "It's all funky if you feel it!" After the final promo break at approximately 1:50 am, I let everyone know that I was teary-eyed, but now ready to go. I screamed my final, "Alternative Rock SOOOOOOOOOO-U-TIONS (SHUNs)" with help from O-Train. Then I played a couple of songs by SOULFLY with vibrations as if I was riding off into a peaceful forest (just like Acotierene did in the movie *Quilombo)*. The same song portion of "Tribe" that I used to start ARS episodes was now the song I ended with on my final night. Requaya didn't show up for her program, so I left messages for the operations manager, Wanique. I officially shut down the airwaves around 2:30 am. Finally, I headed home feeling a tremendous amount of bittersweet relief.

O-Train continued to stay in touch with me while making his own DJ pursuits. I told him often, "We need a thousand more dedicated fans like you." Unfortunately, business venture differences eventually dented our relationship.

I was now ready for new joys and battles in the realm of retirement!

RETIREMENT WARRIOR

A couple of weeks after announcing my retirement, I received an e-mail from Stace Jareti, editor of Volume Entertainment Magazine. She offered me an interview for their July, 2004 Atlantis Music Conference edition. I accepted her offer but asked, "Are you sure you still want to interview me even though I retired?" Stace responded, "I can understand the burnout. But according to Ike (lead vocalist of Augusta, GA rip-hop band Jemani) you've done a ton (of work for the music industry) …" I was greatly flattered by Stace's generosity, so I proceeded to answer all the written questions e-mailed to me. A write-up about me was featured in the section highlighting disc jockeys who frequently supported unsigned artists.

One month later at the 2004 Atlantis Music Conference, I met Stace at 10 High while checking out a performance by Atlanta-based Jád (now known as State of Man). I hugged her, promptly thanked her, and grabbed multiple magazine copies that would later be displayed to family and friends.

The Conference turned out to be my fond farewell to Atlanta bands. I thanked them for all their support during my radio stint. On the first of the Conference's three nights, I saw a Women-in-Rock display at the Apache Café featuring Girlparts, Divinity, Baby Jane, K-Noir, and Milka. After watching Jád on Friday, I vibed at the Masquerade to tunes by E.X. Vortex, El Pus, Crazy Anglos, Heavy Mojo, and Jemani. During all of these shows, I danced without care and enjoyed speaking with many familiar faces. Almost every concert since this Conference has felt like a family reunion.

I contemplated continuing the application process for full-time radio. Instead, I took a break for one month before moving on to new ventures.

In September 2004, I enrolled in a Spanish class. Initially I didn't have goals for fluency. All I knew was that it was time for me to expand beyond the status of a "spoiled-rotten American."

While I was studying Spanish, I ran into more challenges.

My social life remained stagnant. Another woman who I dated proved to be a disastrous prospect. She ended up making my "greatest dis-miss bitch list." After my infatuation with this "bitch" faded, my heart fell for a female co-worker with an incredible smile. Unfortunately, things with her never got off the ground. She told me that she wasn't ready to date since she recently ended a five-year relationship. From this point forward, I started thinking that I wouldn't find a soulmate in America.

As my romance prospects continued to be stale, my attempts at landing a new pay job stalled too. I was rejected left and right by every other department and company I interviewed for. Suddenly, I was unsure whether living in America was still my best option.

As the 2004 Election inched closer, I often exchanged info links and commentary e-mails with friends in cyberspace. After Amen wrote a piece calling the Election a "signover to the New World Order," I wrote the following rebuttal:

> Hello Amen and Conscious E-chain Gang,
> First off, thanks Amen for your insightful words about this "upcoming election." Now I must give my feedback. I agree that there is definitely a corrupt Elitist plan in effect to put us all deeper under 'martial law.' For all I know, were

*headed for futuristic National ID days similar to what I saw displayed in **Minority Report** last night. Yet, I still plan to vote. Sure, there are a lot of ill-minded forces who may be manipulating the outcome of the process. But as long as your intentions and your selections on the ballot are to vote for better changes, then I see no reason why you shouldn't vote. I respect all those who don't plan to vote for whatever reason you chose. After all, I didn't vote for a period of 8 years. For so long, I felt that this system will never get better and therefore sought "improved" outlets from organizations seeking governmental and/or spiritual sovereignty: Moorish Science, Nuwaubian Ansaarallah, Washitaws, Nation of Islam, African Hebrew Israelites, Yahweh ben Yahweh, Sufis, Buddhists, Almorabut Society, various militia groups, occult/metaphysical practitioners, health conscious cliques, 12-step programs, Rock SOUL-U-TION Core, and the list never ends. Despite their philosophical differences, all these "programs" commonly have great intentions but still have too many flaws that consistently fail to provide viable SOUL-U-TIONS to the "New World Order." So my point in saying all this is that there is no single perfect method to survive and overcome ill-fated Conspiracies. Yet there is constructive action we all can do by observing all options and deciding which is best. So if you don't vote, fine. But at least come real with action that will display more progressive change than not voting at all. Our ancestors fought and died for the right to vote. If any of us just sit back, do nothing, and let powers-that-be carry on, then we're no better (than) those assholes who are implementing the same mess. Plus, we'll be dishonoring our ancestors' efforts. No one person can totally prevent apocalyptic shit that may already be "pre-destined" by karma, yet every entity as a source of energy has the power to choose and act out what it feels is best to preserve life. So if you vote like me, best wishes to you all in determining the best outcome for this country. In the meantime, I am always open in listening to*

and observing "better" ideas for creating a more "peaceful"
society in or out of this land. And as long as I'm a "resident"
of the U.S., I will continually hope, pray, and strive for better
living methods in this country........
     Peace & Salutations,
     *AL – still known to many as **D-Rock SOUL-Jah***

Today, I still exchange e-mails like this with even more friends.

While I acted like a "progressive American" by voting, I also planned my trip to Brazil (Brasil). It seemed twisted that I was studying Spanish, despite the fact that most of my cultural interests (i.e. *Quilombo* —film, SOULFLY —Tribal Metal music, and Capoeira—dance/martial arts) represented Brasil, a Portuguese-speaking country. My Spanish teacher was delighted by my Spanish-spoken presentation about Brasil, which featured Spanish and Portuguese renditions of the tribal crenca praising Zumbi and the Quilombos. Yet, she was also unsure about whether Spanish was the right second language for me to explore. My bilingual ambiguity became more obvious. Since I was also unsure about settling in the U.S., where Spanish is the most important second language, I decided that I needed to experience Brasil first before pursuing any more language classes. I always wanted to visit Brasil to check out their music scene. Now, Brasil was clearly a spiritual journey as opposed to only a vacation.

After I reserved my Brasilian exploration, I encountered more anxiety.

In January 2005, I was rejected for a job promotion despite being told I did well in the interview. This was the final sign foretelling my undecided career objectives. My supervisor said, "You just need to improve your social savvy here (at work)." I thought, "My social savvy will only matter for a job or a company that I have passionate goals for ..." After this latest disappointment, I researched several language schools on the internet. My mind was stressed out over contemplating multiple living scenarios in or out of America, Brasil, and Costa Rica (where Amira's ashes lay).

One week before the date of my reserved Brasilian flight, I called Amen expressing my dismay. I was so depressed that I asked him, "What if I decide to cancel my trip to Brasil? ..." At this point I was so rattled by my unsettled life in Atlanta that I wasn't sure if investing lots of time and money towards a foreign land was the right thing. Amen listened. Then he spoke out my options before facetiously saying, "If I were you, I'd rather get some pussy ..." Need I say more about Brasil's reputation for gorgeous women! Nevertheless, Amen's poignant display of friendly advice sparked me to proceed with my reservations. Thank God I decided not to cancel. Brasil proved to be a blessed covenant for my soul.

While the U.S. was preparing to re-inaugurate George W. Bush, I was on a plane to Salvador da Bahia, Brasil.

I decided to make Bahia my first stop since it was a city known as both a cultural and tropical resort. Initially, I intended to only explore Sao Paulo's club scene. However, some Brasilian co-workers grimaced, "Ewwww! Sao Paulo is just like New York but worse. You should go to Bahia and check out the Black Culture ..." First I resisted, "I'm not going to Brasil for just 'black' culture. I'm going there to experience myself as a UniverSOUL being." But then I asked another Brasilian native, "Where is the Quilombo of Palmares located?" She said, "Near Bahia!" After this conversation, it was clear that I must go to Bahia to praise Zumbi and all the ancestors who dwelled in the Quilombos.

As my flight inched closer to landing, anticipation about this trip was now becoming excitement. The lovely vibes of bilingual female flight attendants were a great preview to this journey.

Once I cleared customs, my heart started racing erratically as I observed a few voluptuous Brasilian women. It didn't take long for me to recognize that Brasil contained the most incredible quality of gorgeous women on the planet. Regardless of my awe, I came to Brasil for a purpose far more significant than chasing females.

As a cabbie drove me to my hotel, I notice dilapidated houses with dark-skinned people sitting in them. These homes looked very similar to the favelas I saw in the Brasilian film *City of God*. Some info I read on Brasil explained that a significant number of their low income residents live in third world poverty conditions. According to Wikipedia.com Brasil is one of the ten richest countries on the planet, but it's also one of the worst countries to distribute wealth evenly amongst their residents.

As I arrived at my hotel in downtown Bahia, I anticipated receiving treatment like a tourist who was seeking African-rooted culture. The hotel attendants, most of whom spoke perfect English, suggested I inform them well in advance of my check out date. They were trying to book all possible rooms for the Carnival occurring the following week.

I tried to reserve a hotel and flight for the Carnival, but they were all sold out. A travel agent recommended that I should immediately reserve my Carnival visit for the next year. Despite this minor letdown, I chose to come to Brasil before the Carnival. I was more motivated to explore culture rather than parties.

The hotel attendants also recommended that I check out a music festival that was occurring at a park on this night. Since this was my first night in Bahia, along with the fact I was tired from a long flight, I chose instead to walk around downtown Salvador. Just like my first night in London, I became lost and confused. This time, though, I settled at a music bar and ate.

After finding out that the music was going to be mellow, I left and walked back to the hotel with a better sense of the city's bearings.

Without friends and reserved travel agents to guide me, Brasil quickly proved challenging. Once I woke up on the following morning, though, I was ready to make this journey a memorable treasure.

While I was eating a continental breakfast, a waiter asked me a question in Portuguese, and I didn't understand. Then a blonde-haired Brasilian woman spoke for me. We wound up having a nice conversation. She told me that Afro-Brasilians have no problems calling themselves black while blacks in the states demand to be referred to in the politically correct term —African-American. After I revealed to her that Sepultura was one of my favorite bands, she told me that Sepultura only gets play in the clubs. I wanted to talk with her further, but she said that this day was her last stay in Bahia. I asked her for contact info since I was still considering a visit to Sao Paulo. She left me a phone number. Then I had the waiter take a picture of us.

After breakfast, I swam and sunbathed at the hotel pool. The scenery of Bahia's sunny ocean coastline and fish lakes were astonishingly beautiful. While I sunbathed, I met a voluptuously dark-skinned curly-haired Afro-American woman. She migrated to Bahia from Washington D.C. after forming a youth outreach program. I wanted to take her picture too, but she was too shy as she continued reading some American book.

I trotted back to my hotel room, took a shower, and donned in a blue bandana, black sneakers, long striped shorts, and a green SOULFLY T-shirt with the rear reciting lyrics to "Tree of Pain." Next, I took the elevator to the downstairs hotel lobby and reserved a seat on the Private Túr historical drive through downtown Salvador. While I was waiting for the bus, I flirted with the lovely Private Túr agent named Chantussia, who possessed the curvaceous vibration of a beauty queen. She also told me she had a boyfriend who lives in Portugal. I asked her if I could be her boyfriend for a day. She chuckled with her Brasilian accent, "You so crazy!" She still allowed me to take pictures of her and another cute travel worker.

The Private Túr bus arrived. My spiritual exploration of Brasil was now in full swing.

Initially, I sat alone on the right side of the bus, but it became packed very quickly, so I moved to a seat near the front left side of the bus. Sitting to my left was a lady geared in a white summer hat and dress. I asked if she spoke English. She said, "A little!" It turned out that she, like half of the Brasilians I eventually conversed with, spoke near-fluent English. She introduced herself as Gabriela. Then she mentioned how she was working on her Master's Degree in Finance while maintaining an analyst job in Sao Paulo.

The bus briefly stopped at a nautical museum. The guides allowed us a few minutes to take pictures. When I arrived back on the bus, a new tour guide had introduced himself as Jefferson in Portuguese, Spanish, and English. He was a medium-height, brown-skinned Afro-Brasilian pretty boy with long dreadlocks and a mustache. As I walked to the back of the bus, Jefferson looked at the wording on the back of my SOULFLY shirt, and hummed "In this Tree of Pain." I didn't know whether or not he had heard of SOULFLY. It wasn't impossible. After all, SOULFLY's fanclub from their first album was based in Salvador. Jefferson then gave everyone a detailed historical account about the city of Salvador while the bus was driving.

The bus stopped at another museum. This building was tall with at least four floors. As I walked off the bus, I asked Jefferson, "Are you going to give a history of the Quilombos?" Jefferson chuckled, "Ahhh! We don't talk about the Quilombos. People's feelings get hurt." Then he squinted, "Ya see. This is a private tour. But me and you will talk later ..." I sensed that Jefferson was being protective of his job. At the same time, I perceived that he was still willing to help me gather more insight on my journey.

Jefferson continued to guide us through the museum. Ironically, his storytelling explored alliances of runaway slaves with Native Americans (Indian tribes). The only reason I could explain his reluctance to talk about the Quilombos was that I was the only person of color on the tour. Regardless of my unsettled inquiries, I proceeded to walk with the group into Pelourinho Square (downtown Salvador). Wilson told us that this section was named after a tool called a pelourinho, which was used for punishing slaves.

Salvador's rich history from slavery couldn't go unnoticed.

Salvador was perhaps the first major port city of the western hemisphere where the slave and spice trades flourished in the early 1500s. This is a major reason why Salvador is a city rich in African-rooted culture. A significant portion of Salvador's black residents practice a religion called Candomblé, which combines Yoruba with European Catholicism.

As the group arrived at a fountain in Pelourinho Square, I took some pictures. A few black men were giving us multi-colored wristbands inscribed with the words "Salvador da Bahia." They pleaded for money as well. I took a picture of Gabriela sitting by the fountain, and then she took a picture of me.

Suddenly, I noticed a sign worded, "Reparacao Agora." In Portuguese, it means "Reparations Now." Afro-Brasilians have pretty much the same struggles as Afro-Americans. Yet, their struggles appeared more challenging to me since their culture was more closely connected with their African ancestry. Blacks intermingled very freely with whites in Brasil after slavery ended in 1888. Nearly half of Brasil's population consists of residents who call themselves brown (mulatto – a mixture of black and white). But black and brown residents also make up at least eighty percent of Brasil's poor population. The poverty conditions of American ghettoes seem like day-care centers compared to the favelas of Brasil. I wished I had an abundance of money to give the beggars. Since I didn't, I was very resistant. However, I still gave five dollars to one of the Afro-Brasilian ladies dressed in a wide-skirted, white-colored cook dresses. She laughed. Perhaps she didn't ask for a donation, but I didn't understand enough Portuguese. I thought, "Oh well. What the hell!"

Jefferson led us into a Catholic Church. He demanded that nobody take pictures since it could damage the gold. Tourists snapped shots regardless. Jefferson said that the gold used to construct the church was provided by Chinese settlers in the 1500s. This church had scheduled evening services for Bahia's residents. Jefferson encouraged us to give some coins to the patrons waiting outside. Then he directed us to a vendor area featuring more Afro-Brasilian women dressed in wide-skirted white-colored cook dresses. This time they served us some very deliciously spicy fish cakes for five reais (approximately two U.S. dollars at the time).

After this brief munch, we ventured further into Pelourinho Square. Jefferson mentioned how slaves were tortured and punished during weekly public displays in the heart of downtown Pelourinho. He remained silent for a few minutes while we approached our next stop. I stepped to him asking about when slavery ended in Brasil. He told me "1888!" Then I asked, "Did a civil war break out just like the one in the U.S?" He nodded a yes. Suddenly, I pleaded for Jefferson to entice me about the Quilombos, "Look. I came a long distance. I am very inspired by the Quilombo of Palmares. I have my (dread) locks in this bag (white plastic bag hung on my belt). I want to release them in the forest (of Palmares) and give praise to the ancestors. Will you show me the way? ..." Jefferson paused for ten seconds while intensely staring me down. Then he said, "I see the truth in your eyes. Stick with me. I will take you to a place ..."

Now, I anticipated the specialty of this tour. Jefferson led us into a stable at the trip's end. This area also had a cathedral, but this house of worship was more significantly tied to Bahia's brutal slave history. This time we were allowed to take pictures. In the back of the church, I noticed a statue of a black male religious figure. I snapped a shot, but my disposable camera wasn't strong enough to get a clear picture from the gloomy background.

Jefferson gave a detailed account of the church's angelic designs. He said that slaves were not allowed to attend the church's services. They were still forced to build and structure the interior. Jefferson also indicated why the genitalia of the angels were noticeably missing. They were cut off because the slaves designed the angels according to the larger than normal size of their own anatomy. Since they didn't feel comfortable designing beings that didn't have their same skin color, they rebelled, thus making the body parts in their image. Slaves were often punished over this at Pelourinho Square.

Jefferson's storytelling was very compelling. I now sensed that he was open to tell more disturbing tales, so I seized the moment by asking, "Which church was Zumbi raised as a slave named Francisco?" Jefferson blurted out, "This is the church!" Suddenly, I was engulfed in amazement. I could feel the spirit of Zumbi around me. Jefferson explained to the rest of the group, "Normally I don't talk about this due to racism and fear. But he asked if this was the church where Zumbi was raised. Zumbi was raised as a slave named Francisco at this very church before escaping to the Quilombo de Palmares and leading runaway slaves in battle against the Portuguese army ..."

We exited the stables area. Jefferson encouraged us to give more coins to the church guides. Jefferson then gave us thirty plus minutes to shop around the bricked streets of Pelourinho. I walked in and out of a few Afro-Brasilian clothing stores. Some of the items included dreadlocked wigs and Bob Marley T-shirts. I didn't see any black people working at these shops. So I sensed that these stores may have unintentionally exploited black culture. No materials were purchased before I found Jefferson puffing away another cigarette in an internet shop. I checked some of my e-mails before telling Jefferson that I was not affiliated with any religion. Lingering on I said that I'd still rather have young people worship Zumbi than Jesus since Zumbi's story has more authentic value. Jefferson concurred, "Even the Bible says that God is too big for one religion ..."

Jefferson guided us further into another brick street area. This alleyway was home of Olodum headquarters. Again, Jefferson suggested we provide donations to this center to keep the youth active.

Jefferson gathered all the tourists onto the bus and then brushed me aside, "Come with me, my friend." I was uncertain and excited at the same time. I shook Gabriela's hand telling her it was nice meeting her. I also told her that I was staying at a different hotel. Then I had a patron take a picture of me and mi amigo, Jefferson.

The bus drove off as Jefferson led me to a secluded alleyway. I asked him if it was a favela. He said it wasn't one of those but rather a house of extraordinary significance. Before we walked in, a Bahia resident smiled while asking if I had any pot. I thought he was stereotyping me as a smoker because of my beard and bandana, but I quickly discovered his real reason for requesting weed. Jefferson led me through the dark alleyway. He told me that this was a sacred site of the Quilombolas (descendants of free slave refugee camps). Next he pointed me towards a tree. I forgot what type of tree Jefferson told me it was. There were three young men sitting in front of the tree smoking pot—one with beige skin and straight hair, one dark-skinned with a low cut, and a brown-skinned brother with dreadlocks running halfway down his back and chest. The tree was located down a small yet steep dirt hill. On top of the hill lay a white farmhouse with chickens. Jefferson told me that this exclusive tree area was where Zumbi met with fellow slaves to plot escapes and revolts before they become known as the Olodum. He said they also gathered around here and smoked pot. Jefferson continued saying that young black men guard this tree daily and smoke pot. No white people are allowed in this area unless they say they're black. Jefferson moved us further down the small yet steep dirt hill. I felt a surge of forceful air surrounding my body. I was now in the process of praising Zumbi and the Quilombos. I passed Jefferson my camera instructing him to take multiple pictures. Jefferson told me Pernambuco, the location of the Quilombo de Palmares, was a long four-hour drive, but he suggested that I pay some homage at this tree.

Without hesitation, I opened the aluminum foil with my cut-off locks. Jefferson boasted, "Wow! You have beautiful locks." I passed him the bag before taking the three locks out with seashell ends. I galloped into a prayer pose with the locks, "All praise is due to Almighty Creation. Thank you for this moment I have to praise Zumbi and all the ancestors eternally dwelling in the Quilombos. In honor of their spirits, I dedicate these strands (locks) of my spirit as D-Rock SOUL-Jah to this sacred tree ..." I kneeled down reciting (singing) the crenca four times with my hands in a prayer pose, eyes closed, and the three locks now placed in the middle crevice of the sacred tree, "*Zumbi e ó senhor das guerras. Zumbi e ó senhor das demandas. Quando Zumbi chega. É Zumbi quem manda ...*" Jefferson flashed multiple pictures. The birds and chickens were silent. The tree guardians were talking loud. After I finished the crenca, I bent down and kissed the ground. Jefferson yelled, "Whoa! I have never seen an American give praise to this culture the way you just did. The residents here could feel you. It's a shame how most tourists only come to Bahia for parties and sex ..." It also seemed divine that I was wearing the SOULFLY shirt inscribed "Tree of Pain" during this special passage ceremony. This song's opening lyrics, which correlated so beautifully with the moment, were sung by Asha Rabouin as follows:

My pain is as deep as my roots.
The yearning the hurting. What am I to do?
Indeed I plant seeds for the path I walk. And my voice
helps them grow like water when I talk. But I'm hurting yall.
You didn't die in vain. Your thought with me remains. And
your soul gives me strength to face another day. Without you.
In this tree of pain. In this tree of pain. In this tree of pain.
In this tree of pain. In this tree of pain. In this tree of pain.
Till the day I see you again.

Jefferson and I walked away from this tree. I shook the hands of the three young guardians thanking them, "Obrigado Amigo!" Jefferson led me out of this sacred place. He asked, "Was that Yoruba you spoke?" I said, "No. It was Portuguese! Zumbi e ó senhor das guerras..." He nodded, "Oh (now I get it)!" He went on to lead me out of this sacred place. He pointed to an Afro-Brasilian museum which was only worded in Portuguese. He suggested that I get directions from them for a ride to Pernambuco.

Years later, information was revealed to me that contradicted what I learned during this ritual. According to Cobra Mansa, a Master (Mestre) of Capoeira Angola, Zumbi was actually raised in Recifé and not Bahia. He also told me that the sacred tree site I visited is operated by a Black Secret Society. As for the Olodum, it's a word that originates from the Nigerian Yoruba deity, Olodumaré. According to *The Little Capoiera*

Book, Yoruba was intermingled with several other African cultures into the martial arts now known as Capoeira. There's no proof to credit or discredit the claim that Zumbi's army of revolting slaves were ever called the Olodum. Bahia though was known as the most rebellious anti-slavery state and home for Quilombos in Brasil. It remains today the urban capital of Afro-Brasilian culture. This is a significant reason why they often take credit for the history of the most famous Quilombo leader, Zumbi dos Palmares.

Even though I was naively caught up in hysteria over history, I continued to walk with Jefferson through downtown Salvador feeling elated from the proudest moment of my life.

Jefferson led me to a snack shop. I gladly paid for his food. Then he puffed on another cigarette, "I need to quit this shit." Jefferson and I continued walking through Salvador. I told him I was considering going to a language school in Brazil. Jefferson replied with amazement, "You wanna move here? If you do, you can stay with me and my family ..." Jefferson revealed more about his offspring. I learned that he was the father of four kids in three different countries (two with his wife in Bahia, one in France, and one in San Francisco). Jefferson earned a Masters' Degree in History at a school in Portugal and learned to speak six different languages —Spanish, English, French, Italian, Japanese, and Yoruba. Jefferson's international status intrigued me. And here I was—a single privileged American who spoke only one language without children to claim anywhere.

Jefferson led us onto a tour bus. We rode to a hotel where Jefferson was assigned to guide for the dinner program "Bahia A Noite (Bahia at Night)." As we rode, Jefferson told me, "This (Bahia) is our (Blacks) city!" I responded, "America has similar issues with Black cities." Jefferson quickly flipped the subject, "So why does Bush continue to impose his policies on the rest of world?" I said, "I don't agree with Bush's policies. But he's part of the elitist plan to corrupt the world. America is not the only problem. My grandmother warned me about Nazis here in Brasil ..." I further reiterated to Jefferson that the Bush family did fund Nazi bank accounts in World War II, and then many of those same fascists from Germany, Italy, and Japan escaped to Brasil after World War II to avoid persecution. This is the main reason why Brasil has the largest amount of Germans, Italians, and Japanese outside their respective countries.

After the bus dropped Jefferson and me off at the hotel, he arranged my seat on a van driving the hotel group to a restaurant called Solar Do Unhoa.

"Bahia A Noite" was a sensational display of Afro-Brasilian dance, Capoeira, Maculélé, and theatre. A rhythm section of mostly men played percussion, acoustic guitars, and berimbaus. The dancers, both male and female, wore multiple wardrobes —ranging from tribal gear honoring the Native Americans who housed runaway slaves, to wide-skirted pants, to ancient gear of the Yoruba deities called Orishas. During the showcase, I conversed briefly with fellow tourists. Most of them were from Hispanic countries such as Chile, Spain, and Argentina. I tried to speak in Spanish, but their English was far better.

As "Bahia A Noite" drew near its climax, I had a man from Chile take some pictures of my dance under the Samba stick. Unfortunately, those pictures didn't produce since the flash wasn't on. Despite this faux pas, I enjoyed the nightly praise to the Quilombolas. The food was superb. I wrapped up this night by taking a plated picture with Jefferson and a lovely Afro-Brasilian restaurant hostess.

I left Jefferson my e-mail address. He wrote his as well, but his e-mail didn't work. Regardless of the bad luck from losing communication with Jefferson, his guidance is forever treasured. The Universe served my purpose well by divinely blessing me with Jefferson's presence. Therefore, I don't complain about our lost contact. I pray that Brother Jefferson and all his family throughout the world are doing well. Axé!!!

The next morning I woke up full of excitement. I sensed this day was going to be relaxing. I didn't have any worries about time.

I reserved my spot on a boat around the island beaches of Bahia— Baia do Todos os Santos (Bay of All the Saints). As I boarded the bus with the tour group, I spotted Gabriela with some friends. It seemed the Universe destined me to hang with her.

The boat drove off the shore as I began my silent view of Bahia's beautiful sea. A rhythmic acoustic banda started jamming. I joined in by grabbing a shaker, singing along to "Guantanamera" Then I snapped a picture of Gabriela in her bathing suit.

The boat made its first beach landing. I followed Gabriela and her friends to a table. Gabriela wasted no time jumping in the water. One of her friends noticed the sunburning redness of my skin. She sprayed more Neutrogena sunblock on me. I swiftly retreated under the table's visor. Even though Gabriela's friends spoke very little English, I had good communication with them. I used my Portuguese dictionary to convey some messages. They asked if I was going to the Carnival. I said that I was in Brasil just for the culture. Gabriela's friends still knew enough English to facetiously tell me, "Go in the water and give her (Gabriela) a kiss!"

I proceeded into the shallow beach waves. Gabriela was twirled around by me faking as if music were playing. Our eyes interlocked for about five seconds, but then I heard real music playing behind us. A trio of young Afro-Brasilian girls was leading the touring patrons into a rhythmic dance called the Axé (pronounced Ah-shé). Since it looked like so much fun, and it wasn't the played out Electric Slide, I gradually left the water. I encouraged Gabriela to tag long, but she retreated back to the table, looking on with envy while I galloped along to the drum beats of Axé. I knew I let an opportunity for a romantic moment slip through the cracks. Yet, my desire to fully experience Brasil and weigh my residual options proved more important.

The tour group was solicited to exotic jewelry vendors before retreating back to the ships. These vessels sailed us to another remote tropical island. Here, we ate lunch and were treated to a Capoeira display by a group of mostly teenage Afro-Brasilian males. Their spectacular tumbles and kicks enlightened the crowd. Hardly anyone could resist giving them money while snapping pictures with them. Gabriela continued to use her English language skills to help me speak to more patrons.

As we boarded back on the ships, a few more teenage Afro-Brasilian boys tried to sell me some T-shirts. One of them asked, "(Are you)French?" I responded, "American!" He gave me a thumbs-up saying, "Michael Jordan! ...Mike Tyson! ..." I thumbed-up back, "Zumbi! ... Max Cavalera!" He responded in Portuguese, "Rock?!" He still tried to sell me a T-shirt, but I refused. I really wish I had more money to offer the fabulous culture of Bahia.

The last boat ride back to shore was pleasantly long. Despite the sunburnt redness of my ears and nose, I was overjoyed in a state of euphoric calm. I told Gabriela, "I hope I've represented my country well. I'm not here to be just another spoiled-rotten American." She continued to take a nap despite my offer for a dance.

We exited the ship. I took pictures with Gabriela and her friends. She left a phone number to her friend's place and kissed me on the cheek as I hugged her goodbye. I rode the bus back to my hotel feeling, "This has been the best day of my life." The beauty of the water along with the African-rooted exhibitions of Axé, Maculélé stick fighting, and Capoeira was the most incredibly inspiring cultural observation to my spirit. It also didn't hurt that I had a friendly woman tagging along on my journey.

I called Gabriela later in the evening. I asked her to join me for dinner and Samba dancing. She said she was too tired. Then she asked me to call her the next day. She outlined her plans for swimming at other Bahia beaches. Gabriela said goodbye twice saying, "Jesus to you." I felt awkward trying to get with a religious Brasilian woman. Nevertheless, I still wanted more treasurable moments with her. I ate dinner at the hotel restaurant before retreating to bed with blissful dreams.

Initially, I planned to go back to downtown Salvador for the next day. I wanted to get a t-shirt of Zumbi, a possible tattoo, and information about Pernambuco. Yet, I thought there would be a chance to link up with Gabriela. So I booked a tour to another beach area. This time though, Gabriela was nowhere to be found.

Despite my disappointment, I enjoyed this tour. I snapped plenty of pictures at a turtle museum before taking a nice swim at the beach. While I washed off the sand in a shower area, I had a good conversation with a Hispanic-American lawyer from Miami. He told me that Americans need to start seeing ourselves first as members of the world before members of just America. I agreed that Bahia was a wonderful tourist area where residents from around the world can feel like they're becoming a part of a culture. The lawyer told me San Jose, Costa Rica has the same feel. I warned him, "That's where my sister (Amira) passed on. I'm not sure I should go there." He said, "If you do, it will help you cope better." Ideas started popping in my head. He concluded by saying that America better learn how to improve its receptiveness to the world before it falls behind. He explained, "The American monetary exchange rate with Brasil use to be five to one, but now it's less than two point five to one." This talk was great insight. However, I was more confused about whether or not I should attend a language school in Brasil.

When I arrived back at the hotel, I called the number of Gabriela's friend. Her friend answered. I tried to ask questions in Portuguese. She said something to the effect that Gabriela was in Sao Paulo. I didn't think this had anything to do with the island of Bahia called Ba'ia do Sao Paulo. So I assumed Gabriela had flown back to the city. Without hesitation, I made several attempts to call her house number with my phone card. I tried to use the card on my hotel phone. Then I tried a pay phone in downtown Salvador. Neither was successful.

My time with Gabriela was a blessing. I decided though that this area would be a great resort for me to live when I'm ready to be more settled during retirement. Even though my trip was fulfilling, I sensed it was time to leave, so I checked out of the hotel and caught a cab to the airport.

First I tried to rearrange my round trip ticket. Unfortunately, all flights to Miami out of Sao Paulo were overbooked on this airline.

Next I asked a different airline to book me a flight. They had an available seat, but it was selling for more than 3,700 reais (approximately $1,480). This had me pondering whether or not I should stay in Bahia for the remainder of my reserved airline ticket time.

After sipping on some coffee, I decided, "To hell with it! This trip (in Brasil) is a once-in-a-lifetime journey that may make positive changes to my life forever!" Therefore, I was on a flight to Sao Paulo.

I was continually amazed with how many Brasilians (tourists, professionals, and residents alike) spoke fluent English.

When I arrived at the Sao Paulo airport, I immediately left a phone message for Gabriela. Then I sought guidance from a tour guide. A young lady of Japanese descent reserved a hotel for me in downtown Sao Paulo. She didn't look a day older than fourteen years of age and still spoke perfect English.

I caught a cab to the hotel. The young man driving hardly spoke English, so I tried to converse with what little Portuguese I knew. He understood me enough to comprehend that I flew in from Bahia. Then he blurted, "Bahia's cursed!" The witchcraft practices of Bahia's residents frequently spark mixed emotions amongst Brasilians. The cabbie continued speeding through the heavy traffic. I quickly noticed a Wal-Mart and McDonald's. Sao Paulo's metropolis culture seemed like an extension of America.

After the cabbie dropped me off, some English-speaking hotel workers checked me in. This hotel room was very small, containing bunk beds and a window view over the skyscraping billboards of Sao Paulo. I unpacked before walking to the hallway's pay phone. I called the blonde lady who I met in Bahia. Her number turned out to be a dud. A guy answered asking, "Do you speak English or Spanish?" I said, "English!" He told me his number was for an office of American Express. No one by the lady's name worked there. Then he asked where I was from. I told him, "Atlanta in the U.S.." He said, "Oh, I visited there. That city was nice... So you came to Sao Paulo just to find a girl and she gave you the wrong number?" My jaw suddenly sunk to my heart. Sure, the blonde lady's interest was a hoax, but I was more flabbergasted when I realized that Gabriela was likely still in Bahia at the island Ba'ia do Sao Paulo instead of back in the city. I was now depressed about letting my hyper emotions coerce me out of Bahia over some females; and the $1,480 I paid for the plane ticket only added more injury to insult. Regardless, I still decided to make the most of my time in Sao Paulo since I wanted to explore the city's club scene and living conditions.

I sent some e-mails on the computers located in the hotel

lobby. One of those e-mails was a letter to Gabriela in case she was miraculously in the city. I left the hotel and walked through much of downtown Sao Paulo. This city was cold, cloudy, damp, and full of smog despite the fact it was summertime in Brasil. The longer I walked, the more I saw homeless people on the streets. I became very tired and lost. So I caught a cab to the venue I sought. When I arrived, I quickly sensed that it was merely a large band performance-oriented bar instead of a diverse dance club. A thick-bodied Brasilian woman dressed in all black leather with a velvety ponytail used her English to help me out. The band sounded like an average jam cover group. I became bored too soon. I hit on the black-clad lady, but she wasn't feeling me. So I caught a cab back to the hotel and re-treated to bed feeling guilt-ridden. Just less than a day into my Sao Paulo visit, I already felt like this was the absolute worst travel mistake of my life.

I woke up the next morning bummed out. Thus I handled this mood the best way I knew how. I watched television for the first part of the day. I was dissatisfied with MTV-Brasil. Even though Brasil's quality of music was better than the U.S., their marketing was very poor. MTV-Brasil's overwhelming display of non-music programming was even worse than MTV-America.

I also flicked through some telenovelas. They appeared to be more horrible than American soap operas. One novela was staged with a time period in the midst of slavery. From the little I saw of Brasil's programming, black characters had limited exposure with representation lacking more than the U.S..

Watching TV was making me more lethargic, so I ventured out to a movie theatre. I saw *Tainá 2: A Adventura Continua*. I never even knew about *Tainá 1*. Yet this film left me delighted with watery eyes. The positive environmental message of this film signaled that I must go back to the U.S. and get my shit together before I can expect to come to another country to prosper.

My wonderful experience at the movies motivated me to pursue another club.

Later in the evening, I took a long walk in search of a Samba Rock club. Unfortunately, it was closed. It seemed that clubs were preparing for the upcoming week's Carnival. While I searched for another club, I heard a lot of sounds from a street area. I decided to walk over and check it out. Immediately, I saw a concert bus in front of a neighborhood of high-rise buildings packed with residents on the streets. I decided to stick around and flow with this event.

The concert bus featured a band. As they warmed up, a large portly bald-headed black man with glasses introduced three gorgeous beauty contest winners. I pounded my right hand against my mouth making tribal "Wah Wah" sounds. The rest of the guys were whistling. I also banged my water bottles against the street poles several times. I stayed jubilant while the band took too much time warming up.

As the band continued with their slow sound checks, I observed the crowd and police. I noticed some guys improperly fondling some gorgeous females. The young ladies continuously pushed their faces away. Other guys became more drunk and obnoxious. Ten military policemen quickly swarmed one guy beating him down like Rodney King. This scene told me that Brasilian police don't play around.

The band finally started playing. My first impression was, "This isn't London, but I'll have as much fun as possible." I flowed with the Samba rhythms by continually pounding drum beats on the poles. Two policemen suddenly approached me bickering with serious sneers. I didn't understand any of their Portuguese, but I was in no position to dispute. So I stopped drumming and started dancing. Then I saw Samba lines forming. At least this dance was something different than the Electric Slide. I became so warm that I took off my shirt. More pictures of gorgeous women snapped from my camera. Two of these women then took a picture of me bare-chested. Next, I spotted a woman with breasts similar to Dolly Parton's measurements. A janitor smiled at me indicating the vibe, "Damn this woman has incredible knockers!" About three bare-chested males on the concert bus stage danced and displayed some martial arts. They got flipped off by several of the crowds' males. I agreed with their sentiment, "We're here to dance not watch male strippers."

Dancing, hopping, and chanting "Wah Wah," my soul was flying free like a bird. A young black lady with a long braided weave who also wore a sweatshirt labeled "Star" then tapped me to follow her dance steps. I swirled in more circles. Then this young sista threw mock punches at a brotha as they displayed Capoeira dance moves. The police quickly dispersed this.

The people of Sao Paulo appeared very free-spirited, but they struggle daily with a controlling government represented by their police.

As the concert wrapped up, I stuck around a while longer communicating with some of the residents despite my lack of Portuguese. First, I shook the hand of a cute honey with long curly hair, wearing a pink tank top. She told me her name before saying "Ciao" while puffing a cigarette. I then sat on the sidewalk. A teenage boy started complimenting me. Even though I didn't understand any of his words, his body language and facial expressions were full of praise. He couldn't believe that I wasn't a Brasilian native by the way I danced and blended with the crowd.

As I started walking away, I noticed a cute friendly young lady with a thick figure posing with some guys. She liked my approach so much that she took a picture with me too. One guy shouted out, "She's just a friend." They knew enough English to encourage me to hit on her. I tried using body language to tell her to call my hotel number. She gave me a hug, a cheek kiss, and left with her girlfriends saying, "Nice to meet you!"

I hung around for a few minutes longer conversing with some young men. I understood enough of their speech to receive an invitation to play soccer at a park. I shook their hands and commenced back to the hotel. I went to sleep feeling like Sao Paulo may be a good possibility for a language school.

On my final day in Sao Paulo, I used their transit system to travel to the park. Unfortunately, I didn't see any of the festival residents there. Regardless, I took great pictures of soccer players, pond ducks, and an obelisk. Even Sao Paulo has an Egyptian monument.

On a bus back to the train station, I nearly got lost. I was afraid of these residents misdirecting me like a lost New Yorker. Sao Paulo came across to me as a third rate crappier version of New York. Just as Brasilian natives in Atlanta had warned me, "It's just a big city, but there's nothing there."

After I got off the train, I walked through more of Sao Paulo's malls. I noticed multiple couples kissing each other publicly. This is not something I'm used to seeing regularly in America.

I ventured back to the hotel to change my clothes. Once again, I was on the town to check out the night scene. Since the club I sought didn't open until later, I entered another movie theatre. This time I saw *Closer* with Portuguese subtitles. The couple sitting next to me featured a black man wearing an M.I.T. sweater. He spoke fluent English.

As I exited the mall, I started a conversation with a group of teenagers who were dressed in heavy metal garb. After they heard a couple of my warped Portuguese sentences, a man said, "You can speak English now." The shame of my language skills hit me further listening to him say, "Americans are very closed-minded …" I agreed since I played good Brasilian rock bands like Sepultura and SOULFLY, who rarely received radio play. This theatre experience told me, "No wonder it's so easy for other countries to learn English. American programming is propagated all over the world every day."

Another club area was pursued. There weren't any rock sounds blazing. I walked back to the hotel thinking, "Sao Paulo had nothing for me. I've made too many worldly travels looking for the perfect DJ spot. There is no such thing. It's time to head back to the states."

As I checked out of the hotel, I spoke with an Afro-American R&B singer from Chicago. He chastised Brasil's race relations, "In Sao Paulo, there are actually more black people than white people … Have you ever been to one of their jazz clubs? Whites aren't comfortable with blacks unless they're servants or entertainers or both!" The U.S. has similar problems, but at least our distribution of wealth isn't bad compared to Brasil.

A cabbie dropped me off at Sao Paulo's airport. Disparagingly, I had to wait twelve hours for my flight. Sao Paulo's airport was small and dirty compared to any major U.S. airport. Despite the wait, I was kept awake for most of the day looking at the barrage of gorgeous women. Plus, I had a good political discussion with a German who was returning home to his Brasilian wife. He worked for Siemens and spoke four languages including English. According to his studies as a financial analyst, South American economies including Brasil, were run by corrupt governments. He went on to say that the U.S. and European Union still had the most stable means of living. I told him the U.S. standard of living won't last long if we stay spoiled and ignorant about the rest of the world. We shook hands. Following my trip, I e-mailed him.

This conversation further reiterated that I needed to return home. It was time to make myself into a less naïve American and a stronger resident of the world!

On February 25, 2005 (the twenty-sixth anniversary of Amira's birth), the closing process began for my purchase of a one-bedroom condo in Sandy Springs, Georgia. After a rocky weekend, I officially became a mortgaged home owner on February 28, 2005. Even though my home's appearance didn't matter much to me, the Foxcroft homes were designed with a British style. Its pool was reminiscent of the beautiful Atlantic water I swam on in Bahia. This was divine intervention from the Universe for me to keep building a lifestyle similar to the best day of my life in Bahia, Brasil and the best night of my life in London.

I applied for one more position at my pay job. Again, I ran into turmoil. I was unexpectedly given a pre-screened interview. The human resources representative picked up an unpleasant vibe from me calling me "bitter and cynical." I left her office wondering if my angry words on my yearly evaluation triggered this surprise session. I called the company a bunch of "two-faced bureaucrats." After sorting through my emotions the following weekend, I decided that my anger resulted not from any possible character bias by my job's reps, but actually from my own lack of passion for the job. I had career goals of ideal jobs that differed from the company's purpose. Plus, I remained untrustworthy of my job's parent company from a pending copyright infringement lawsuit citing them for a disputable history of corruption.

On the following Monday, I rescinded my application for a job promotion. I promptly started writing the rough draft of this book.

Over the next three months, I sought part-time work to pay for my huge credit-card debt (half of which came from my trip to Brasil). I quickly landed a gig at a mall coffee shop before being released after a week. I couldn't fill the time slot that the manager wanted. This was cool with me since I wasn't happy with the work. Plus, I nearly cussed out an assistant manager for sounding like a gay ass house husband after he arrogantly chastised my job, "… That's all you do?! That sounds challenging and exciting!"

My part-time woes signaled that it was time to pursue more projects that I possessed a passion for, so in July 2005, I became a volunteer for a battered women's shelter.

Initially, I did not intend on volunteering for a battered women's shelter until after I finished writing this book. Yet circumstances from part-time woes made me more passionate about community service. I decided to use my time at the shelter as a motivational factor while working on this autobiography. After all, domestic violence impacted my life more so than any other form of human abuse.

I also had no intention at first of writing about my working experience at the shelter. I wanted to encourage everyone to support the cause instead of bragging about how I do it. But as one reads further, it will become clearer why I couldn't stay silent about this part of my life.

On July 18, 2005, I attended a volunteer orientation in Gwinnett County. I was one of only two males in attendance. Everyone was asked to introduce themselves and tell why we wanted to volunteer. When my turn came, there wasn't a single eye ignoring me as I said, "… I grew up in a household with domestic violence. It's affected every relationship I've been involved in. So I'm hoping this experience will help me learn how to function better in more positive relationships …" The ladies' reactions appeared mixed. As we took a food break, an Afro-American lady tapped my shoulder, "I commend you for doing this. We need to see more men do the same thing." The orientation continued with presentations about situations and statistics concerning domestic violence. I left this program perceiving that this cause was exactly the best way for me to combat abuse.

One week later, I made my first ever entrance into a battered women's shelter. My spirit was overcome with both nervousness and relief. It was about time that I confronted my demons of domestic violence. I was ready to denounce them with productive tasks. Since I was the only grown man in the building, women and children glanced at me with combined suspicion and shocking joy. I told the ladies in the administrative office that I was there to work on facility functions. They quickly assigned me to scrub an air conditioning vent. I proceeded to change a couple of light bulbs before helping to replace a mattress for a bedroom.

After two hours of service, I signed a volunteer form documenting my time. A coordinator told me, "Don't worry. We'll have more work for you next week."

For the next month and a half, I performed a multitude of house assignments: replaced several curtains; cleansed more vents; screwed in more light bulbs; lifted ladies' luggage to their rooms and the attic; helped move heavy desks and beds up the stairs; patched back together game floors for the kids; and spent one whole evening mowing the lawn.

These house choirs were not fun, but I still felt a proud sense of accomplishment, knowing I was contributing something positive to the fight against domestic violence.

My dedicated facility work drew criticism from a volunteer coordinator. She told me that several ladies complained that they didn't find enough work for me. I told her that I wanted to start out as a facilities assistant in order to get used to the environment. Plus, I had no experience as a childcare coordinator, the only other field where men were allowed to work. She told me that the shelter's organization was still deciding whether or not to allow men to work in other fields such as legal advocacy and support counseling. She also said that my service was becoming a distraction. I responded, "The least I want to do is get in the way of the ladies." She interjected, "No! You're doing a good job. We would just like to see you do other things." I told her, "I plan on doing childcare soon. Right now, I'm still getting adjusted to this environment. Regardless of what I'm doing, I feel it serves a higher purpose. I had never used an electrical lawnmower before. Even though I was sweaty and dirty, I felt good about doing that job too ..."

After this conversation, I volunteered to do childcare for the month of September. I still had two more evenings of facilities' work. During this time, I mostly copied and arranged paperwork.

As I wrapped up this day, the coordinator directed me to take a set of suitcases to the attic. This luggage belonged to a young lady who I couldn't take my eyes off of. For confidentiality issues, I won't describe her physical appearance in detail. Yet I will say that her wardrobe and vibration was quite organic. For safe keepings, I'll refer to her as Lily. Her eyes gazed at me with so much strength and curiosity. Indeed, I was perplexed.

On the second to last week before switching to childcare, I completed some paperwork. Lily walked in to receive medicine. I didn't say a word while she spoke with the coordinator, but then she extended her hand toward me for a handshake. I shook her soft yet jittery hand while she smiled and thanked me for placing her luggage in the attic. She went on to say, "You used to have dreads! Right?" I nodded my head. Lily said, "I knew that I've seen you before at the Apache." Our ensuing conversation revealed that she was an aspiring artist. As she walked out of the office, I wrote a note with information about Larry and Common Cause Productions. I asked the coordinator to leave this with her. Lily's spirit touched my heart and fanned my flames.

Around this time, Hurricane Katrina swarmed the news and spirits of almost everyone during my last day as a facilities' assistant. A volunteer coordinator with dreadlocks was working in the office and said to me, "I should give something to help the victims of Hurricane Katrina. After all, I didn't give anything to the victims of 9/11." I told her, "Chill! You're already giving enough of your time and service to humanity by helping out victims of domestic violence." She boasted, "Well everybody should be helping somebody!" This conversation signified even further that I was serving the most appropriate anti-abuse cause for my spirit. Every individual, even Superman, cannot save everyone on this planet. But we can all do something we most desire to save multitudes of beings.

While most people I knew donated several items to Hurricane Katrina survivors, I donated some t-shirts, towels, and toys to the shelter for residential use. I also gave away pre-paid tickets to various sporting events. There was hardly anything I wouldn't do to support the fight against domestic violence.

In the midst of my dedicated service, I noticed that at least 95 percent of the women and children residing at the shelter were Afro-American. At the same time, at least 80 percent of the volunteers were white females. Even though domestic violence is a problem amongst people from all socioeconomic backgrounds, I couldn't help but be the slightest bit disturbed by the disproportionate amount of Afro-American families I witnessed with this issue. Nevertheless, I proceeded to do my duty without referring to any racial disparity. My perception was still, "The best way to fight any form of human abuse—racism, sexism, poverty, domestic violence, drug addiction, etc.—was to work passionately on the one issue I felt strongest about."

Childcare assistance was abruptly the challenge I needed to evolve in my anti-abuse mission.

On my first day of childcare, I followed instructions by two other volunteers. One of them told me how happy she was to have a male help out with the children.

As the children finished dinner, they increased their presence in the backyard. A couple of them sat on a volunteer's lap. She said, "We have a new friend with us. Say hi to him! "I introduced myself as "Mr. Albert." From this point forward, almost every child called me this.

It was fun watching the kids play around. They swung on the swings and tossed balls all over the yard. Challenges came on me quickly to discipline their behavior. During this first day, I observed some of the children's initiation contact. Then I politely told them to stop being mean to each other. As childcare wrapped up on this day, I recommended to one mother that her daughter needed her diaper changed. She gave me a cold stare as if I didn't know what I was talking about. Indeed, I was learning how to babysit spontaneously.

Lily picked up her kids and thanked me. Then I signed out before grabbing a cup of water. As I headed towards the exit door, Lily was walking with her kids in the hallway. She boasted loudly to me in front of a few women, "You a good brother ... (Being) Here helping out women ..." I stood silent for thirty seconds. I was touched by her compliment. I didn't think this comment was necessary. After all, I was only doing the appropriate duty to redeem my past mistakes. If everyone else in the world thought of me as some monster, at least I can take comfort knowing that this one person saw me as someone praiseworthy.

During the next week, childcare was tougher. The boys started wrestling and pounding each other. They were having fun on my supervision, but then another volunteer screamed at them to stop. I asked her why she stopped the boys' rough game. She reminded me that no one including the mothers was allowed to use violence at the shelter. I respected that policy. I learned a lot about discipline this day when I witnessed a resident place a girl in a timeout corner after she punched a boy.

As I walked into the kitchen to grab some water before working on my next session, a couple of kids walked towards me. They quickly swarmed their arms around me in a warm embrace. Then I glanced at Lily holding one of her kids. She was also wearing a wig to protect her identity. She glistened to me, "Well! Well! It's a new you!" I had cut my hair and shaved my beard a few days earlier. She seemed amazed despite the smugness of her voice. So I responded, "And I can say the same for you!"

After this session, Lily picked her kids up. I asked again if she received my note referring her to Larry. She laughed sarcastically, "Yeah! I got it!" This turned out to be the last time I ever saw her. She certainly aroused my interest. The shelter however was no place to seek out romance and intimacy, especially amongst the residents who were repairing their damaged life pieces. I pray that Lily and her children are dwelling safely today. I forever cherish her graciously strong spirit.

Over the next three months, I continued to look after the kids with improving supervision. I blended in well with them by: playing board games; participating in duck-duck-goose; passing and kicking around sports balls; helping them with toy blocks and artwork; and watching children-oriented movies with them. Ironically, I also watched a few episodes of ABC's *Supernanny* to gain better insight on childcare.

There were three moments that stuck out in my mind as fond memories of my dedication.

First, I remember starting a duck-duck-goose circle with the kids. A volunteer coordinator stayed late that night to suffice for the shortage of volunteer workers. Her enthusiasm inspired me. She was encouraging a couple of girls to dance. I followed suit by telling a couple of boys, "Go ahead and dance with the pretty lady!" The coordinator blushed, "Are you saying I'm pretty?" I coughed, "If you think so." Then some of the boys got tired of the game. They immediately became rowdy. I separated two boys from one another, grabbed one, and placed him in a timeout corner. While I sat and instructed the young man to count to 100, the coordinator smiled at me. I wasn't trying to impress her, but I was glad she witnessed my joy of childcare. She initially perceived that I was uninterested. The boy finished his count. I told him to shake hands with the boy he got in a fight with. Then I instructed them both to say to each other, "I'm sorry." After this session ended, I apologized to the coordinator for calling her out as a "pretty girl" in front of the kids. She paid it no mind. I tried to hide the fact that I unofficially made a flirting gesture toward her. Indeed I was fascinated by this young lady's combination of leadership and inspiration, but I gave her no more hints of attraction. It would've only deterred from our priorities to the shelter. Plus she already had a live-in boyfriend.

The next memorable moment took place in the cafeteria. Another volunteer and I supervised the kids while they were finger painting on table paper. As they finished, they quickly became bored and started smearing paint on each other. Honestly, I was also a little fed up with the limited activities the kids were given. So I stepped in and led them on a chant. First I mistakenly said, "All the naughty kids be quiet." They weren't fooled. So they screamed out more noise. I laughed and then said, "Okay. All the naughty kids make noise." They silenced immediately. I repeated this maneuver three times. Then I told them the story behind my "Quilombo" tattoo. I explained how it was a place of refuge away from abuse. I went on to emphasize that the shelter was their "Quilombo." I also gave props to the white female volunteer who wore an Angela Davis t-shirt. She said, "Make sure you give props to Angela Davis." Subsequently,

I had the kids clapping their hands to the same rhythm I was beating while I sung the crenca, "*Zumbi e o senhor das guerras. Zumbi e o senhor das demandas. Quando Zumbi chega. É Zumbi quem manda...*" I tried to get them to sing along, but the oldest girl of thirteen years spoke out, "Can you sing it in English?" I sung in English, but they were too far gone in the drum clap. They dispersed as their mothers retrieved them. The other volunteer praised me, "That (sing along) was wonderful. It was universal. Even the Hispanic boy was able to participate." Other volunteers made fun of me – just a sarcastic way of expressing their appreciation. I commended the thirteen-year old on her painting. Then I helped her post it on an office wall. She was very courteous and strong. She continuously helped volunteers and staff members take care of the kids.

My third memorable moment came from a playroom. Since the weather was colder in November, the kids were squeezed tightly together in a small space. They sorted through blocks, stuffed animals, and several other toys before eventually picking on each other. During one night, a few of the girls screamed loudly and moved fast. Neither I nor the two other volunteers could control them despite our constant pleas for them to calm down. This energy trickled contagiously as a new girl would start crying every five minutes. We eventually got them settled down slightly by turning on a cartoon video. However, they only sat still for three minutes before their rants resurfaced. A toddler girl who wore diapers started crying profusely in her toy baby seat while another girl was whimpering the whole night. I scooped the baby outside the room. Another volunteer picked up the other teary girl. The toddler had hair wrapped in cornrows and was wearing a baby blue overall-styled dress with straps. I raised her above my head gently shaking her, "Shhhh. It's okay. You're a good girl!" I did this for fifteen more minutes. I suspected that she may have needed a diaper change, but that wasn't the problem. Thank God because I've never changed a diaper. As she calmed down, I held her in my lap for the rest of the video while she sucked on her thumb. I continued to tell the rest of the kids to be quiet. The toddler's mommy was the first to retrieve her child. I passed her back and said, "She's a good girl." I think this girl only missed her mommy. This was the last time I saw her. I pray that she and her mommy are in a safe place.

Overall, there were many wonderful moments I endured with the kids from this shelter. Yet, I was growing tired of the repetitiveness of my limited duties. So I e-mailed the following message to the volunteer directors:

> *First off, I already mentioned that I won't be available this week since I'm heading out of town tomorrow night. So I'll be back for Childcare Service on 11/30!*
>
> *Next, I request to be moved to a different function in December. I enjoy childcare. However, I feel that I need to do something new so that my organizational contributions don't become stagnant. I know that my maleness already places limitations on duties I can perform. I still voice no opposition to the current policy. Another director mentioned that I may be able to contribute services to some kind of Parental Counseling group. If this is possible, please pass me more information on this task.*
>
> *Finally, I plan on continuing my Volunteer Service at the shelter until either the end of January, 2006 or until the rough draft of my book is finished (probably around May 2006). I understand more why males are not allowed to facilitate in the Support Groups. I have no intention to ever facilitate one of these meetings. Yet, I'm interested in sitting in and watching the doors for two meetings before my Volunteer Service ends. And don't worry, all details of my shelter time are excluded from my book. When my book is published, it will include a message encouraging people to donate to the*

shelter and all Anti-Domestic Abuse organizations. I feel that my shelter service provides inspiration to tell the world my survival stories from abuse and racism.

I look forward to reading your responses, and have a great holiday!

Albert Johnson

They responded favorably with the following messages:

Hi Albert,

I did not realize you are writing a book. What is it specifically about? Is it an auto-biography? I am interested to hear more about the book.

We took you off the schedule for Wed. Have a great trip!

As far as assisting with support groups, the final decision would be up the Staff Director. Previously, male volunteers have not been allowed to help facilitate. I will talk to my Supervisor more about this.

Thanks Albert!! I'm sure the kids will be disappointed. I hear that they love having you around.

Hi Albert,

I was not aware of your book either, but it sounds terrific. We have a new children's advocate coming on board in December. She was previously facilitating the children's support group which I think you would be great at and she is a great teacher. Let me know if you are interested in this position. As far as watching the doors for support groups, you can certainly do this; however, I think we can find better uses for your time that you may enjoy more. We value your volunteer work so much, and so do our children! I am going to hate seeing you leave us, but I know you are going to do great things!

It will be fine if you take the 13th off!! Our (Atlanta) Thrashers need you!

Despite their approval of my time off to see the hockey games, I gave away those tickets to help out at the shelter. Even a fun sporting event couldn't deter me away from the significance of my anti-abuse mission.

In December, I started working with the advocate in the children's support group. She told me from the start, "I've heard great things about you."

For the first two sessions, I trained by observation. I watched and learned how material from a psychological children's game book were used to encourage the youngsters to report and dodge any bad behavior by their parents. For example, the kids were assigned to color the pictures of people in their assistance community—cops, neighbors, friends, etc.. We also rewarded them with extra chips in games where they answered questions like, "What do you do when you hear your parents arguing?"

During the last two sessions, some of the older kids were upset. The advocate and I often had to discipline them into a timeout corner or what ABC's *Supernanny* called "the naughty chair." This wasn't enough to deter two children. So I spent most of one session holding onto a five-year old boy to prevent him from running amuck. The advocate thanked me, "I appreciate your help. If you weren't around, I would've cried."

My training to become a children's support group facilitator was going well. Perhaps my service though was too good to be fathomed by the women. Lo and behold, a couple of conversations made them uneasy.

First, the advocate and I had a nice conversation prior to a child support group function. She asked me what inspired me to become a volunteer. I said, "I grew up in a household with domestic violence… And I was in a bad relationship … I don't wanna talk about it …" She responded with a curious look, "So what? Is doing this therapeutic for you?" I said, "Yes! It is!" We proceeded to our session. The women's support session was getting under way. I had to help escort the kids through their chat. This was the closest I ever came to witnessing one of their female counseling programs. The advocate delegated me to read a couple of lines from a motivational children's book. One cute young girl, whose mother had dreadlocks, asked for a hug. I scooped her on my arms.

This affection was so contagious that a three-year old boy with cornrows also asked for hug. I told him to walk towards me. Then I hugged him. Little did I know this would be my last time appearing with these incredible kids.

A couple of days later, I received an e-mail requesting volunteer help at an upcoming February seminar conference entitled "Hearts for Hope." I poignantly refused, "I humbly reject this offer. As I mentioned before, I prefer not to be publicly affiliated with this organization until my book is finished. However, if you need help at the shelter that day, I'll be glad to assist." The coordinator quickly wrote back, "Albert we really need your manpower that day. I know you want your service to be confidential. So could you help out in the morning before it starts? There won't be anybody from the general public there at that time." I gladly accepted this proposal.

Unfortunately, things took a turn for the worst at the shelter after this e-mail exchange.

A volunteer director asked to meet with me and other coordinators. I said, "Okay. May I ask what this meeting is about?" She responded, "We want to talk about other volunteer opportunities and your book." I couldn't meet with them that week. Thus they postponed the meeting until the following week.

Before the meeting, I received an attached survey on e-mail. I didn't think this was a big deal. But then I saw the words "Active/Inactive" before "Survey." I immediately suspected that I was being targeted for elimination from the organization. I completed and forwarded the survey back to the director regardless. Yet, I was now fearful of being dumped.

The next children's support session was canceled, which further heightened my suspicions.

The following week I arrived at the shelter during my work lunch hour. Two of the coordinators led me upstairs while the director settled some business downstairs. They immediately asked questions about my book. I reassured them that my experiences at the shelter would not be mentioned. They seemed relieved but still expressed concern about using the organization's name in the book.

Minutes later, the director entered the room. She joined the current conversation about the book. Suddenly, she threw me into a funk, "Hello Albert. Thanks for meeting with us. I have to say that I am very adamant about the men who volunteer at this organization. So of course, I did another criminal background check on you. And I didn't find anything." I nodded my head while listening. Then I sarcastically smiled, "You won't find anything. Nothing major! If you want to know more about me, just go to Google and type in my DJ name, *D-Rock SOUL-Jah*, to locate past articles about me. I'm not that hard to research. Only a few of my professional colleagues know I'm doing this. This cause serves a higher purpose than bragging to the world about my service. I'm not ashamed of it. I'm very proud. I just prefer that no one knows until they can make sense of it in the book."

The director continued her interrogation, "I am still concerned. You were the first male allowed in any support group. Ever!" I said with surprise, "Really?!" She continued, "So why were you reluctant to volunteer with 'Hearts for Hope?'" I said somberly, "I used to be in the public eye. I hosted a radio show. So I know how people can misconstrue things that they know little about." Then one of the coordinators snapped, "When I volunteer at a function and some friends see me, they just say I'm helping out. They don't assume anything else." The director interjected, "Hmmmmn? I would think that someone would want to be anonymous about writing a book. Not a volunteer service!" I was in shock for a few seconds. My fear of being condemned by this organization was now coming into fruition. It was now obvious that all three of them had deliberately met me to give me the boot.

The director continued her persecution, "I've told other volunteers (mostly women) before that this is not a place to heal. If you still have issues to heal from, then working here won't help... So tell me if I'm wrong. I don't know. You just have this vibe..." I paused humbly with my head down for fifteen seconds before looking her in the eye, "Well. You're fifty percent correct. First working here serves a higher cause than me, and it can help others. And yes ... it does help me cope with issues from domestic relationships in the past." The director wasted no breath, "Then I ask that you not return!" My head sunk while I breathed out a huge sigh of disgust. Then I looked up at the director. She frantically swayed her hands, "Oh and Albert we hope you're not mad at us!" I shrugged, "I'm not angry. But I am disappointed." The director tried but failed to give me some real sympathy, "Well. You can say it worked out for the best. You only had so much to do in facilities. You didn't like childcare..." I quickly blew a sneered breath while looking at one of the coordinators thinking, "Bullshit!" I proceeded to ask, "Well. Can I still find out whether I can use the organization as a positive cause referral in my book?" The director left me a name of their marketing coordinator. She glanced at me, "You've done a wonderful job!" As I stood up to be escorted (thrown) out by the director, I shook the hands of both of the coordinators saying, "Nice working with you!" As I exited the room, I couldn't help but notice both of their heads turned away from me with cold stoic expressions. I sensed that they were in disbelief. They probably had misconstrued thoughts of me as some batterer who sneaked his way into their protective domain. The director led me to the building's exit. I said in a low tone, "Well. I didn't want to leave like this, but I kind of knew I would eventually receive a similar reaction." The director shook my hand. I walked away into the parking lot. She shouted out, "Albert! I'm sorry!"

I drove away from the shelter fearing they would call the cops on me. Even though I would never break the law and reveal their confidential location, I was afraid the ladies would go further and seek misguided "legal proceedings" of revenge against me.

Minutes later, I parked my car back at my job. I stayed in the vehicle for ten minutes releasing the sad tears from my betrayed spirit. I never asked for anything in return from my six months of dedicated volunteer service at the shelter. Neither did I imagine that I'd be disgraced from that organization like some kind of disease.

My struggles in writing this book didn't begin and certainly won't end with the battered women's shelter.

Roadrunner Records rejected my offer to make and include an interview with SOULFLY's Max Cavalera for this book. I was so upset that I wrote them a three-page letter of disgust. At the end of that piece, I vowed to boycott all of their artists. After a few months, I forgave them and attended an Ill Niño concert. Months following that show, I attended a SOULFLY concert. My admiration for Max as my Heavy Music Hero and all the wonderful bands as my Tribal Metal icons is more important than my anger at their label. I still dream of meeting and interviewing Max someday.

I was also scorned by my sister Stephanie for considering the revelation of all the characters' true names in this book. She scolded, "You're selfish! You don't care about anybody! ... And you can write that in your book!" She proceeded to threaten me, "If you say anything to hurt my family, I'll sue you!" Stephanie and I are now estranged enemies.

The worst effect of my work came after applying over a course of one year for positions at multiple humanitarian relief organizations. I asked the battered women's shelter for a letter of recommendation in order for me to explain to other organizations why I was released. They told me that it's their policy not to recommend anyone who they've released. I further requested a letter of explanation. After all, they even told me personally that I did a good job. They still refused citing that all they're allowed to say is that I worked for them and eventually got fired for being a detriment.

This dagger to my heart and career hurts only slightly less than my nightmarish relationship fallout with Tynesha!!!

Despite the painful aftermath of my anti-abuse mission, I still found refuge in another arena. It's no fairytale ending, but it's sufficient enough for me to push on.

Before my Brasilian trip, I took one Capoeira class at the Afrikan Djeli Center in the West End area of Southwest ATL. Unfortunately, I strained my back after this class while outlining the chapters of this book on my couch. Subsequently, I received four months of chiropractic therapy.

Initially, I didn't plan to return to Capoeira classes until after this book was published, but the fallout from the battered women's shelter changed my mind.

In March 2006, two months after resting from my ill-fated volunteer departure, I started taking two Capoeira classes per week at the Djeli Center. Of course I was extremely intimidated by the complexity of the movements—tumbling, hand stands, head stands, wide leg stretches, etc..

Despite my barrage of near paralyzing fear, I continually

improved in class. What kept me going was my fascination with Zumbi and the Quilombos. Capoeira has origins in an Angolan tribal dance called the *N'goloo*, which translates to "The Dance of the Zebras." It made its way to Brasil through the Trans-Atlantic slave trade. Multitudes of runaway African slaves dwelled in the forests (Capoeira) and combined all their cultures to make this a self-defense art form. It was regularly disguised as a game and dance amongst slave masters.

In 1930, Capoeira became legal in Brasil. Master (Mestre) Bimba established the first school of Regional Capoeira, a style that became synonymous with international martial arts sporting competition. Around the same time Mestre Pastinha formed the first school of Capoeira Angola, a style dedicated more to African cultural preservation.

My first view of Capoeira was a scene from the movie *Quilombo*. Since this story is my favorite inspiration, I decided that the best way to honor Zumbi and the Quilombolas was to practice Capoeira. The classes at the Djeli Center were Angoleiro style. Even though I was first disappointed that the movements didn't involve many fast or aggressive punches and kicks, I continued to immerse myself as an Angoleiro. It made more sense since my body is virtually too old to endure the constant rigors of Regional. Plus, Angoleiro style dedicates half of the class time to learning the songs and instruments of Capoeira – berimbau, pandeiro, atibaki, ago-go, reco-reco.

In the middle of March 2006, my fragile body amazingly survived a two-day conference conducted by an instructor form Philadelphia. My lower back was straining, but I persevered.

Overall, I developed good chemistry with the instructors and fellow Capoeiristas at the Djeli Center. This experience proved that Portuguese had the most priority as my developing second language. I eventually stopped my Spanish tutorials. I still want to learn Spanish, but my commitment to Capoeira was stronger.

The Universe, though, signaled to me that I got involved in the organizational structure of Capoeira sooner than my spirit was ready. I disagreed with some of the policies of the newly-formed fellowship based at the Djeli Center. Even though I had already helped conduct their business meetings, I decided it was best for me to distance myself from their organization. I would still cooperate with them at upcoming Capoeira rodas (live games) and conferences. This fallout was the final reminder of why I moved out of Da SWATs.

I moved on to classes at the Little Five Points (L5P) Community Center. They were conducted by the Atlanta chapter of the International Capoeira Angola Foundation (referred to in Portuguese as FICA). It's ironic how I ended up back at the same building where I began my plight as *D-Rock SOUL-Jah*. L5P has been my home away from home for most of my residency in metro ATL.

After two more months of practicing Capoeira three times per week with FICA-ATL, I suffered another near-crippling lower back injury. This was a stronger sign that I got involved too soon with the organizational core of Capoeira Angola.

Even though I am still virtually paralyzed from doing the physical movements, I still participated in the music portion of class. I attended all the monthly rodas and played in the bataria (band section) when needed.

Capoeira Angola was the Spiritual Church I searched for my whole life. Every morning when I wake up, I still recite the crenca, "*Zumbi e o senhor das guerras. Zumbo e o senhor das demandas. Quando Zumbo chega. É Zumbi quem manda.*" Sure Zumbi will never return in person to save me or anyone else in this world, but at least I and every other Capoeirista had the will and capability to be just as great if not greater than Zumbi and every Quilombola that came before us. Together, we have inspired everyone around us to live and thrive in their own Quilombo – a protective and prosperous shield against all forms of abuse.

I also continued to practice Yoga every week striving for a healthy spine that will someday soon be fit enough to play (joga) Capoeira again. I've often called my "religious" practice everyday— CAPO-YOGA!!!

I have taught some of the music portion classes of Capoeira Angola to various students. During one of these classes, one of Lily's kids ran towards me and hugged my shoulders as I kneeled down. Then I spotted Lily smiling. *IS THIS SCENARIO FACT OR JUST INSPIRATIONAL FANTASY???*

In the meantime (realtime), I communicated with Father per e-mail. He still dwells in San Francisco. He also has a Spiritual Church as refuge from his own inner and outer demons. He is now a devout Catholic. A Nun looks after him. He calls her his Godmother. Father receives government assistance program checks every week.

I still don't believe that we can solely rely on Jesus or any other so-called savior to physically retrieve us from our sins. I do believe, however, that we can always look to heroes as inspirations to improve our spirits.

As for my DJ career, I still strive towards an elusive club audience. I hosted a day concert during a two-day Black Rock Conference at the Atlanta University Center. This event was practically a family reunion as it featured many artists who I've worked with over the years. I returned to my CD mixer months later. I now host occasional DJ gatherings exposing friends and music lovers to sounds provided by yours truly – Thee *UniverSOUL Rock SOULector*. My favorite job will always be that of a Rock DJ. Yet, I always maintain other passions as back-up plans.

To sum up this autobiography on a positive note, I reveal what Albert the person is about. Albert still applies for work on progressive media and anti-abuse missions. He also is working on improving his socially challenged skills so he can one day soon attract and protect one special strong woman to live out the rest of his existence with. Albert still remembers talking to a lady who was riding home on MARTA after suffering blows from an abusive boyfriend. He often envisions slamming a string instrument against that purveyor of harm.

So who again is Albert? I am Albert. And who am I? I am *D-Rock SOUL-Jah* – a Spiritual Warrior – one who continues to help SOULs toward divine existence. I am just one Univer-SOUL being of energy. Sure all sources of energy eventually conflict, but they can also balance that out with cooperation. I don't have SOUL-U-TIONS to every problem. I am no Super-hero, Savior, Messiah, or Conqueror. And I may not be a Saint according to Society's definition, since I have been tainted by abuse. However, I am a Spear-it of Almighty Creation who will always do what he senses is best for Cultural Enlightenment.

Ironically while working on publication for this book and exploring more culture, my big brotha Dr. Alim Bey established the Mu'urish Holy Science Temple of the World in Fayetteville, North Carolina and became a Chief of the Unity Washitaw de Dugdamoundyah Naga Mu'ur Nation. This proved to be the best route for me to venture during the U.S.'s "Great Recession," and so now I am a resident helping to build and reclaim a nation.

Thanks to everyone who has read and shared in my life's story! I pray my experiences inspire you to do what's best for your overall empowerment. Axé! OGUN, OGUN-IE!!!

AL Bey is an accomplished Inventory Journalist. For more than 16 years he has worked in television, radio, & telecommunications as the following positions: Disc Jockey, Operations Director, News Editor, Writer, Media Coordinator, Sales Representative, Accountant, and Library Services Specialist. AL Bey currently lives in Sandy Springs, GA. To learn more about AL Bey, log on to: www.taintedsaint-drocksj.com.

E-mail: DRockSOULJah@aol.com

CPSIA information can be obtained at www.ICGtesting.com
Printed in the USA
LVOW080721050412

276222LV00001B/4/P